KT-455-518

Hospitality and Tourism Law

Mark Poustie, Jenifer Ross, Norman Geddes and William Stewart

UNIVERSITY OF PLYMOUTH
SEALE HAYNE
LIBRARY

INTERNATIONAL THOMSON BUSINESS PRESS
I(T)P® An International Thomson Publishing Company

London ● Bonn ● Johannesburg ● Madrid ● Melbourne ● Mexico City ● New York ● Paris
Singapore ● Tokyo ● Toronto ● Albany, NY ● Belmont, CA ● Cincinnati, OH ● Detroit, MI

Hospitality and Tourism Law

Copyright © 1999 Mark Poustie, Jenifer Ross, Norman Geddes and William Stewart

I(T)P ® A division of International Thomson Publishing Inc.
The ITP logo is a trademark under licence

All rights reserved. No part of this work which is copyright may be reproduced or used in any form or by any means – graphic, electronic, or mechanical, including photocopying, recording, taping or information storage and retrieval systems – without the written permission of the Publisher, except in accordance with the provisions of the Copyright Designs and Patents Act 1988.

Whilst the Publisher has taken all reasonable care in the preparation of this book the Publisher makes no representation, express or implied, with regard to the accuracy of the information contained in this book and cannot accept any legal responsibility or liability for any errors or omissions from the book or the consequences thereof.

Products and services that are referred to in this book may be either trademarks and/or registered trademarks of their respective owners. The Publisher/s and Author/s make no claim to these trademarks.

British Library Cataloguing-in-Publication Data
A catalogue record for this book is available from the British Library

First edition published 1999

Typeset by Laserscript Limited, Mitcham, Surrey
Printed in the UK by Antony Rowe Ltd, Chippenham, Wiltshire.

ISBN 1-86152-181-2

International Thomson Business Press
Berkshire House
168–173 High Holborn
London WC1V 7AA
UK

http://www.itbp.com

Contents

WITHDRAWN
FROM
UNIVERSITY OF PLYMOUTH
LIBRARY SERVICES

Series editors' foreword

The International Thomson Business Press series in Tourism and Hospitality Management is dedicated to the publication of high quality textbooks and other volumes that will be of benefit to those engaged in tourism, hotel and hospitality education, especially at degree and postgraduate level. The series is based on core textbooks on key areas of the curriculum and is complimented by highly focused and shorter texts on particular themes and issues. All the authors in the series are experts in their own fields, actively engaged in teaching, research and consultancy in tourism and hospitality. Each book comprises an authoritative blend of subject-relevant theoretical considerations and practical applications. Furthermore, a unique quality of the series is that it is student oriented, offering accessible texts that take account of the realities of administration, management and operations in tourism and hospitality contexts, being constructively critical without losing sight of the overall goal of providing clear accounts of essential concepts, issues and techniques.

The series is committed to quality, accessibility, relevance and originality in its approach. Quality is ensured as a result of a vigorous referencing process, unusual in the publication of textbooks. Accessibility is achieved through the use of innovative textual design techniques, and the use of discussion points, case studies and exercises within books, all geared to encouraging a comprehensive understanding of the material contained therein. Relevance and originality together result from the experience of authors as key authorities in their fields.

The tourism and hospitality industries are diverse and dynamic industries and it is the intention of the editors to reflect this diversity and dynamism by publishing quality texts that enhance topical subjects without losing sight of enduring themes. The Series Editors and Consultant are grateful to Steven Reed of International Thomson Business Press for his commitment, expertise and support of this philosophy.

Series Editors

Dr Stephen J. Page
Massey University – Albany
Auckland
New Zealand

Professor Roy C. Wood
The Scottish Hotel School
University of Strathclyde
United Kingdom

Series Consultant

Professor C.L. Jenkins
The Scottish Hotel School
University of Strathclyde
United Kingdom

Preface

The idea of this book was conceived some time ago as a result of the fact that there is no single textbook covering all the principal aspects of hospitality and tourism law and moreover no such textbook which deals with the position both north and south of the border. Good works exist on aspects of each of these areas, mainly in relation to the law in England and Wales. The aim of this book is to fill that gap by providing an accessible introduction to the principal areas of law which are relevant to the tourism and hospitality industries in both England and Wales and Scotland.

The book is designed to be suitable for students at universities and colleges studying a range of courses which might include aspects of hospitality and tourism law including hotel management, food safety, package holidays and travel agency. Since many of these students may have little knowledge of law the book provides considerable introductory material on the English and Scottish legal systems in Chapter One. It covers several important general areas of law which are relevant to the hospitality and tourism industries including contract, agency and tort (Chapter Two), business organisations (Chapter Three), product liability law (Chapter Four), criminal liability (Chapter Five), employment (Chapter Six), discrimination (Chapter Seven) and planning and environmental law (Chapter Eight). It also provides coverage of more specialised legal topics which are particularly relevant for the tourism and hospitality industries including innkeepers' duties, liabilities and rights (Chapter Nine), food safety (Chapter Ten), licensing (Chapter Eleven) and holidays (Chapter Twelve). For reasons of space certain areas of law including property have been excluded from the ambit of the work although some further reading on that topic is suggested. It is also hoped that the book may be of some use to those who work in the tourism and hospitality industries.

The book is designed to be suitable as a textbook both north and south of the border and the differences between English and Scots law are highlighted throughout the work. However, it has been an interesting experience for the authors, all of whom are Scots academic or practising lawyers, to write a book which deals to such a large extent with English law. The book endeavours to provide examples of general legal principles in such areas as contract, tort, employment and planning law which are drawn from the hospitality and tourism industries wherever this is possible. For those who are interested in pursuing particular topics in more detail suggestions on further reading are provided for each chapter in a select bibliography at the end of the work.

The law is stated as at 31 December 1997. Readers should however note that there are considerable constitutional developments occurring in the United Kingdom at present which may have an impact on hospitality and tourism law in a variety of ways. These developments include devolution legislation for Scotland and Wales together with legislation incorporating the European Convention on Human Rights into domestic law. The book does deal with these fundamental legislative developments in so far as they impact on the hospitality and tourism industries and in so far as it has been possible to do since these Bills had not finished their Parliamentary passage at the time of writing. Legislation on freedom of information is also to be introduced in the near future and this may also impact on the hospitality and tourism industries, for example in the area of information on food safety held by Government.

Although the law in the text is as stated as at 31 December 1997 the following paragraphs are designed to highlight a number of significant developments since the text was written.

As regards EC law, the Treaty of Amsterdam agreed in 1997 has still to be ratified by the United Kingdom, but once this has occurred and all the other member states of the EC have ratified the treaty, it will make considerable changes to the current EC Treaty (p. 7).

In Chapter Three (pp. 75–76) we consider the issue of business names. The use of certain names is completely prohibited and certain other names may only be used after the appropriate permission has been obtained. An interesting example involving the hospitality industry was reported in *The Times* on 9 July 1998. The owners of a well-known London restaurant called Pharmacy are being taken to court by the Royal Pharmaceutical Society for unauthorised use of the word 'Pharmacy' which can only be displayed by authorised chemists under the Medicines Act 1968. The owners are facing a fine of up to £1,000 for using the name.

In relation to employment law, the UK Government has brought forward a number of measures which will affect the material contained in Chapter Six and which are likely to become law by the end of 1998. These are the National Minimum Wage Bill which will provide for a minimum wage for employees and self-employed workers; the Public Interest Disclosure Bill which will give protection to employees who 'blow the whistle' (see pp. 127–128); and the Working Time Regulations which will implement the EC Working Time Directive (93/104/EEC) (see pp. 135–136). In addition the Government in 'Fairness at Work' has indicated that it intends to amend the law so that the qualification period for unfair dismissal will be reduced to one year (see pp. 136–137); employment protection rights will apply to self-employed workers as well as employees (see p. 118); those dismissed while involved in official strike action will be able to raise an action of unfair dismissal even where the dismissal is not selective (see pp. 145–146); and the ceiling on unfair dismissal compensation is to be removed (see pp. 146–147).

There have also been a number of recent developments affecting discrimination law which we discuss in Chapter Seven. The Court of Appeal in *Smith* v *Gardner Merchant* (see p. 155) has referred the case back to the tribunal to compare the treatment of homosexual man with that which a lesbian woman would have received. In *Marschall* v *Land Nordrhein-Westfalen* [1998] IRLR 39, the European Court of Justice has upheld the legality of a provision that female candidates be preferred to male candidates, so long as there is a savings clause allowing it to operate in favour of a better qualified male. There has also been some case law interpreting the Disability Discrimination Act 1995. For a review of those cases, see *Equal Opportunities Review* Nos 79 and 80.

Since the completion of Chapter Ten, interest and controversy surrounding food safety regulation has continued unabated. A Food Safety Minister has been appointed and a draft Bill on the proposed new Food Safety Agency has been promised by the Labour Government, which has generally endorsed the proposals put forward in the James Report (see pp. 255–256). In the interim, a Joint Food Safety and Standards Group has been established which, reflecting the concerns of the time, includes representation from the Department of Health as well as the Ministry of Agriculture, Fisheries and Food. The Government has stated that the key aims of the proposed Agency will be to 'create a clear separation between the responsibilities for regulating food safety and for promoting the interests of food-related industries' and to 'promote food safety from plough to plate'.

Activity in the courts has continued to highlight the difficulty encountered in enforcing the law in relation to particular incidents, no matter how high-profile the cases. The major outbreak of E-coli in Scotland, which caused 20 deaths, resulted in two criminal cases. In the first of these, the prosecution of the butcher, John Barr, collapsed when the Sheriff ruled that there was no case to answer (i.e. that there was not enough evidence to found a case against him) and found him not guilty. In the second case, charges against Mr Barr and two members of his family were withdrawn although his firm was fined £2,250 for food hygiene and food safety offences. There was widespread concern at the low level of the fine. At the time of writing a Fatal Accident Inquiry is in progress. This will endeavour to establish the cause of the outbreak leading to the 20 deaths and will consider the effectiveness of the investigation process which ensued.

The new Beef Bones Regulations 1997 resulting from the BSE crisis have also given rise to controversy in the courts. Scottish hotelier Jim Sutherland deliberately served bone-in roast beef at a dinner arranged in defiance of the Regulations and was subsequently charged with contravention of the Regulations. At his trial the Sheriff found the Regulations to be defective and dismissed the charges. However, the Crown appealed the case to the High Court of Justiciary, where the Sheriff's decision was overturned and the case referred back to the Sheriff for further consideration. At the time of writing the case had not returned to the Sheriff Court.

The record of prosecution in high-profile food safety cases continues to be dismal and it is to be hoped that the establishment and empowerment of the new Food Standards Agency will lead to improvements in this record and restore public confidence in food safety.

We have also provided readers with tables of cases, statutes, statutory instruments, EC provisions and international treaties. These are designed to enable the reader to find a reference to a case or statutory provision on a particular page. So, for example, if a reader wanted to know whether we discussed certain sections of the Food Safety Act 1990, he/she should consult the Table of Statutes to find out if we refer to those sections and, if so, on which page(s). We hope that readers find these useful. A list of abbreviations and an index are also provided.

Thanks are due to a large number of people in connection with the preparation of this book. A particular debt of gratitude is owed to the publishers, International Thomson Publishing for their patience and forbearance as a number of deadlines for submission of the text were missed or only partially met. Particular thanks must go to Jenny Clapham for all her patience and support. A number of people from the University of Strathclyde must also be thanked for their assistance including Arlene

Carruthers, Peter Demick and Emma Steeds and Professor Roy Wood of the Scottish Hotel School for all his encouragement and support. Deborah Henderson of Frazer Coogans Solicitors also deserves thanks. I would also like to thank Jacqueline Williamson for all her patience and support during the preparation of this book.

Finally and above all I would like to express my sincere gratitude to my co-authors, Jenifer Ross of the University of Strathclyde, Norman Geddes of Frazer Coogans Solicitors and Bill Stewart of MacMillans Solicitors. Without their sterling efforts this book would not have been written.

Mark Poustie
Glasgow, July 1998

Table of statutes

This table is designed to enable you to find references to statutes and provisions within statutes. If you know the name of the statute you are interested in, consult the left-hand column to find out if we refer to it and the right-hand column to find the page(s) on which we refer to it. We also list each part and section of each statute referred to and the page(s) on which we refer to them. Statutes are listed in alphabetical order. We also provide the chapter number of each statute e.g. the Airports Act 1986 (c.31). The chapter number, c.31, indicates that the Act was the thirty-first to receive the Royal Assent in 1986.

Table of statutory instruments

This table is designed to enable you to find references to statutory instruments and provisions within statutory instruments. If you know the name of the statutory instrument you are interested in, consult the left-hand column to find out if we refer to it and the right-hand column to find the page(s) on which we refer to it. We also list each regulation or other provision of each statutory instrument referred to and the page(s) on which we refer to them. Statutory instruments are listed in alphabetical order.

Table of EC provisions

This table is designed to enable you to find references to EC treaties and other legislative provisions. The table is divided into three sections: Treaties, Regulations and Directives. Treaties are listed by the year in which they were made. Regulations and Directives are listed by the year in which they were made and by their particular number for that year e.g. Regulation 1612/68/EEC is the 1612th regulation made in 1968 and Directive 90/314/EEC is the 314th directive made in 1990. If you know the year in which the measure you are interested in was adopted, consult the left-hand column to find out if we refer to it and the right-hand column to find the page(s) on which we refer to it. We also list each specific article of each treaty, regulation and directive referred to and the page(s) on which we refer to them. The names of the various provisions are also given to assist you.

TREATIES

REGULATIONS

DIRECTIVES

Table of international treaties (other than EC provisions)

This table is designed to enable you to find references to international treaties (except for treaties relating to the EC, for which see Table of EC Provisions). Treaties are listed by year in which they were made. If you know the year in which the treaty was made, consult the left-hand column to find out if we refer to it and the right-hand column to find the page(s) on which we refer to it. The names of the various treaties are also given to assist you.

Table of cases

This table is designed to enable you to find references to cases. If you know the name of the case you are interested in, consult the left-hand column to find out if we refer to it and the right-hand column to find the page(s) on which we refer to it. Cases are listed in alphabetical order.

Table of abbreviations: series of case reports and law journals

AC	Law Reports, Appeal Cases (1890–present)
All ER	All England Law Reports (1936–present)
All ER (EC)	All England Law Reports, European Cases (1995–present)
B & Ald	Barnewall and Alderson's Reports, King's Bench (5 vols., 1817–1822)
B & S	Best and Smith's Reports, Queen's Bench (10 vols., 1861–1870)
BCLC	Butterworths Company Law Cases
BTRLR	Brewer's Trade Review Law Reports (22 vols, 1913–1937)
Beav	Beavan's Reports, Rolls Court (1838–1866)
Bing NC	Bingham's New Cases, Common Pleas (6 vols, 1834–1840)
C& P	Carrington and Payne's Reports, Nisi Prius (9 vols, 1823–1841)
CBNS	Common Bench Reports, New Series (20 vols, 1856–1865)
CLY	Current Law Yearbook (1947–present)
CMLR	Common Market Law Reports (1962–present)
Cal 3d	Californian Reports (Third Series) (USA)
Ch	Law Reports, Chancery Division (1890–present)
Ch D	Law Reports, Chancery Division (45 vols, 1875–1890)
Co Rep	Coke's Reports (13 parts, 1572–1616)
Cox Eq Cas	S C Cox's Equity Cases (2 vols, 1745–1797)
Crim LR	Criminal Law Review (1954–present)
D	Dunlop's Series of the Court of Session Reports (The Second Series) (Scotland) (24 vols, 1838–1862)
Digest (Repl)	English and Empire Digest Replacement volumes
E & B	Ellis and Blackburn's Reports, Queen's Bench (8 vols, 1852–1858)
ECR	European Case Reports
EGLR	Estates Gazette Law Reports (1985–present)
ELM	Environmental Law and Management
ENDS Report	Environmental Data Services Report
Env LR	Environmental Law Reports
Ex	Welsby, Hurlstone and Gordon's Exchequer Reports (11 vols, 1847–1856)
Ex D	Law Reports, Exchequer Division (5 vols, 1875–1880)
F	Fraser's Series of Court of Session Reports (The Fifth Series)(Scotland) (8 vols, 1898–1906)
F 2d.	Federal Reporter, Second Series (USA) (1924–present)
FTLR	Financial Times Law Reports
GWD	Greens Weekly Digest
H & C	Hurlstone and Coltman's Reports, Exchequer (4 vols, 1862–1866)

H & N	Hurlstone and Norman's Reports, Exchequer (7 vols, 1856–1862)
HL Cas	Clark's Reports, House of Lords (11 vols, 1847–1866)
ICR	Industrial Cases Reports (1975–present)
ILM	International Legal Materials
IR	Irish Reports (1893–present)
IRLR	Industrial Relations Law Reports
JC	Justiciary Cases (Scotland) (found within Session Cases (SC))
JLSS	Journal of the Law Society of Scotland
JP	Justice of the Peace (1837–present)
JPL	Journal of Planning and Environmental Law
KB	Law Reports, King's Bench Division (53 vols, 1901–1952)
L Ed 2d	Lawyer's Edition, US Supreme Court Reports, Second Series
LGR	Local Government Reports (1902–present)
LJCP	Law Journal, Common Pleas (1831–1875)
LJQB	Law Journal, Queen's Bench (1831–1946)
LMELR	Land Management and Environmental Law Reports (now ELM)
LR Ch App	Law Reports, Chancery Appeals (10 vols, 1865–1875)
LR Exch	Law Reports, Exchequer (10 vols, 1865–1875)
LT	Law Times Reports (177 vols, 1859–1947)
Lloyd's Rep	Lloyd's List Law Reports (1951–present)
M & W	Meeson and Welsby's Reports, Exchequer (16 vols, 1836–1847)
Mod Rep	Modern Reports (12 vols, 1669–1775)
Mor	Morison's Dictionary of Decisions of the Court of Session (Scotland) (43 vols, 1532–1808)
OJ	Official Journal of the European Community
PAD	Planning Appeal Decisions
P & CR	Planning (Property) & Compensation Reports (1950–present)
PD	Law Reports, Probate, Divorce and Admiralty Division (15 vols, 1875–1890)
QB	Law Reports, Queen's Bench Division (1891–1900 and 1952–present)
R	Rettie's Series of the Court of Session Reports (The Fourth Series) (Scotland) (16 vols, 1873–1898)
RDLR	Race Discrimination Law Reports
RTR	Road Traffic Reports (1970–present)
S	Shaw's Series of the Court of Session Reports (the First Series) (Scotland) (16 vols, 1822–1838)
SC	Session Cases (Scotland) (1906–present)
SC (HL)	Session Cases (House of Lords) (Scotland) (1906–present)
SCCR	Scottish Criminal Case Reports (1981–present)
SCLR	Scottish Civil Law Reports (1987–present)
S Ct	US Supreme Court Reporter
SJ	Solicitors Journal
SLR	Scottish Law Reporter (1860–1924)
SLT	Scots Law Times (1893–present)
SLT (Sh Ct)	Scots Law Times (Sheriff Court) (1893–present)
Salk	Salkeld's Reports, King's Bench (3 vols, 1689–1712)
Stra	Strange's Reports (2 vols, 1716–1747)
TLR	Times Law Reports (71 vols, 1884–1950 and 1951–2)

UKTS   UK Treaty Series
Water Law   Water Law
WLR   Weekly Law Reports (1953–present)

Table of abbreviations: general

ABTA	Association of British Travel Agents
ACAS	Advisory Conciliation and Arbitration Service
ADR	Alternative Dispute Resolution
AITO	Association of Independent Tour Operators
ATOL	Air Travel Organisers Licence
art.	Article
BA	British Airways
BCC	Bus and Coach Council
BNA	Business Names Act 1985
BSE	Bovine Spongiform Encephalopathy
CA	Court of Appeal
CA 1985	Companies Act 1985
CAA	Civil Aviation Authority
CCP	Critical Control Point
CJD	Creuzfeld Jacob Disease
Cm, Cmd, Cmnd	UK Government Command Paper
Co	Company
COPA	Control of Pollution Act 1974
CPA	Consumer Protection Act 1987
CPS	Crown Prosecution Service
CRE	Commission for Racial Equality
DC	Divisional Court
DDA	Disability Discrimination Act 1995
DPP	Director of Public Prosecution
DTI	Department of Trade and Industry
EA	Environmental Assessment
EA 1995	Environment Act 1995
EAT	Employment Appeals Tribunal
EC	European Community
ECHR	European Convention on Human Rights
ECJ	European Court of Justice
EEC	European Economic Community
EMAS	Eco Management and Audit Scheme
EOC	Equal Opportunities Commission
EPA 1970	Equal Pay Act 1970
EPA 1990	Environmental Protection Act 1990

ERA	Employment Rights Act 1996
ETOR	Economic, Technical or Organisational Reason
EWC	Expected Week of Confinement
ex p.	ex parte
Exrs	Executors
FEPA	Food and Environment Protection Act 1985
FSA	Food Safety Act 1990
FTO	Federation of Tour Operators
GCHQ	Government Communications Headquarters
GOQ	Genuine Occupational Qualification
GPDO	Town and Country Planning (General Permitted Development) Order 1995 (SI 1995/418)
HACCP	Hazard Analysis and Critical Control Point
HASAW	Health and Safety at Work etc. Act 1974
HL	House of Lords
HM	Her Majesty's
HMA	Her Majesty's Advocate
HMIP	Her Majesty's Inspectorate of Pollution
HMIPI	Her Majesty's Industrial Pollution Inspectorate
HPA	Hotel Proprietors Act 1956
IPC	Integrated Pollution Control
IPPC	Integrated Pollution Prevention and Control
JJ	Justices
LA 1964	Licensing Act 1964 (as amended)
LAPC	Local Air Pollution Control
LSA	Licensing (Scotland) Act 1976 (as amended)
Ltd	Limited (company)
MMC	Monopolies and Mergers Commission
MS	Member State(s) of the EC
NPPG	National Planning Policy Guideline
NRA	National Rivers Authority
OLA 1957	Occupiers' Liability Act 1957
OLA 1984	Occupiers' Liability Act 1984
OLSA 1960	Occupiers' Liability (Scotland) Act 1960
PA	Partnership Act 1890
PC	Privy Council
PF	Procurator Fiscal
plc	Public Limited Company
PPG	Planning Policy Guidance Note
PSA	Passenger Shipping Association
para.	Paragraph
Pt	Part (of an Act of Parliament)
QBD	Queen's Bench Division
R	Regina
RRA	Race Relations Act 1976
reg.	Regulation
s., ss	Section(s) (of an Act of Parliament)
SDA 1975	Sex Discrimination Act 1975

SDA 1986	Sex Discrimination Act 1986
SEPA	Scottish Environment Protection Agency
SI	Statutory Instrument
Sch.	Schedule (to an Act of Parliament)
t/a	trading as
TCPA	Town and Country Planning Act 1990
TCPSA	Town and Country Planning (Scotland) Act 1997
TSO	Trading Standards Officer
TULRCA	Trade Union and Labour Relations (Consolidation) Act 1992
TUPE81	Transfer of Undertakings (Protection of Employment) Regulations 1981 (SI 1981/1794)
UCO	Use Classes Order
UCTA	Unfair Contract Terms Act 1977
UK	United Kingdom
UKIAS	UK Immigration Advisory Service
WIA 1991	Water Industry Act 1991
WML	Waste Management Licence
WRA 1991	Water Resources Act 1991

The legal system

1

INTRODUCTION

In this chapter we examine the nuts and bolts of law and the legal system:

- the sources of law;
- the classification of law into civil and criminal law and public and private law;
- going to law in the courts and alternatives to court action;
- the system of precedent applied in the courts;
- some of the important rules of interpretation used by judges;
- the role of judicial review.

SOURCES OF LAW

Introduction

There are several distinct sources of law. We will examine the following sources: statutes, delegated legislation, international law, European Community (EC) law, case law, equity, soft law and new forms of legislation which will result from establishment of a Scottish Parliament and a Welsh Assembly.

There are other sources such as Roman law and custom. These are not unimportant in certain areas of hospitality and tourism law as, for example, the reader will note in our discussion of the law relating to innkeepers in Chapter Nine (see pp. 227 and 233). The special legal position of innkeepers derives in England and Wales from custom and, in Scotland, from Roman law.

Statutes

Status of statutes

The primary sources of law are statutes which are more properly known as Acts of Parliament. With the exception of EC legislation which we discuss below, statutes are the most authoritative source of law in the United Kingdom. The courts must give effect to statutes and cannot override them unless they conflict with EC law (see p. 6).

Enactment of statutes

Statutes begin life as Bills and pass through various stages in both Houses of Parliament, the Commons and the Lords where they are debated and often amended. In each House this involves a first reading, second reading, committee stage, report stage and third reading. The first reading is a mere formality and there is no debate. The merits of the Bill are debated in the second reading while detailed consideration is given to the Bill's specific provisions in committee stage with further general debate taking place at the report stage and third reading. If the Government has a working majority it is very difficult for the opposition to amend the Bill or to prevent its passage through Parliament.

The House of Lords cannot prevent the passage of legislation but may delay it for up to a year although in certain circumstances if the House of Lords does not back down the House of Commons may force the Bill through without the consent of the House of Lords. This rarely occurs, the last occasion being in the case of the War Crimes Act 1991.

Following a successful passage through Parliament the Bill receives the Royal Assent and becomes an Act of Parliament.

Extent of statute

Acts which apply only to Scotland contain the word Scotland in brackets in their title, for example, the Licensing (Scotland) Act 1976. A statute which does not contain the word Scotland in the title may apply to England and Wales only or to the whole of Great Britain (i.e. England, Wales and Scotland) or indeed the whole of the United Kingdom (i.e. Great Britain and Northern Ireland). There is a section of each Act, normally found near the end of the Act, which indicates what its 'extent' is, that is the country or countries within the UK to which it extends. If an Act extends to Northern Ireland this will be mentioned in the 'extent' section.

Commencement of statutes

Acts do not always come into force on the date on which they receive the Royal Assent. The coming into force of an Act, known as its 'commencement', may be postponed for some time or may be carried out in stages. A section of the Act, once again usually found near the end of the Act, will provide details of when it is to come into force. Ministers are often given the power to bring particular parts or sections of Acts into force at any time following the Royal Assent. This is done by means of pieces of delegated legislation known as commencement orders. Where an Act requires considerable changes to a section of the economy or to a regulatory regime, for example, environmental protection measures, the staged introduction of an Act may be used to give business and other sectors of the community time to prepare for the new regime. However, this practice often makes it difficult to ascertain what parts of an Act are actually in force.

Structure of statutes

For our purposes the principal structural features of statutes of which you should be aware are their division into sections (abbreviated to ss or s. for a section, e.g. Food

Safety Act 1990, s.1), and subsections (abbreviated to subss or subs. for a subsection) within a section. Larger Acts which deal with various topics are often divided into Parts which are designated by Roman numerals (abbreviated to Pts. or Pt. for a Part, e.g. Environmental Protection Act 1990, Pt. IIA).

Statutes and the hospitality and tourism industries

There are many statutes which affect the hospitality and tourism industries directly or indirectly. Examples of such statutes include the Hotel Proprietors Act 1956, the Trade Descriptions Act 1968; the Race Discrimination Act 1976; the Food Safety Act 1990; and the Environmental Protection Act 1990.

Delegated legislation

Need for delegated legislation

Because of the shortage of parliamentary time and given the complexity of certain areas of law it is often impossible to set out detailed rules or standards in Acts of Parliament. Acts are often designed as 'framework' statutes which only set out the general principles applying to a particular subject while delegating the power to make the necessary detailed rules to government ministers or other bodies such as local authorities. The resulting laws are known as delegated legislation. Huge amounts of legislation are made in this way although we would point out that this form of legislation is not very satisfactory since there is hardly any consideration of delegated legislation in Parliament.

Making of delegated legislation

Where powers to make delegated legislation have been given to ministers, the Act will specify the manner in which the delegated legislation may be made by the minister. The most common method is the 'negative resolution' procedure whereby the minister lays the draft delegated legislation before Parliament and, if Parliament does not reject the legislation within a stipulated period, normally 40 days, the legislation comes into effect. In the case of powers given to local authorities to make byelaws, any byelaws made by a local authority will normally require the approval of the Secretary of State before they come into effect.

Forms of delegated legislation

Most delegated legislation comes in the form of statutory instruments (SIs). These may be called Regulations (which should not be confused with EC Regulations: see p. 7) or Orders but will still have a statutory instrument (SI) number for the year in which they were made as, for example, the Disability Discrimination (Employment) Regulations 1996 (SI 1996/1458) and the Restriction on Agreements and Conduct (Tour Operators) Order 1987 (SI 1987/1131). For simplicity, we do not give SI numbers in the following text, but they are listed in the Table of statutory instruments (p. xxxi).

In addition, local authorities have powers to make byelaws for purposes including the regulation of conduct in public parks or bodies of water: for example, the Loch Lomond Registration and Navigation Byelaws 1995. These are not called statutory instruments and do not carry SI numbers.

Status of delegated legislation

Such legislation does not have the same status as an Act of Parliament and for this reason is also known as secondary legislation. Its validity may be questioned in the courts if the minister exceeds the powers he/she has been given in making the delegated legislation or follows the incorrect procedure in making it. An example of a minister exceeding his/her powers is provided in *DPP* v *Hutchison* [1990] AC 783, in which byelaws made by the Secretary of State for Defence to restrict access to Greenham Common, which at that time was a base for nuclear cruise missiles, were struck down since the byelaw making power in the Military Lands Act 1892 provided that byelaws must not take away or prejudicially affect the rights of commoners.

Delegated legislation and EC law

You should also note that by virtue of the European Communities Act 1972, ministers may also make the necessary delegated legislation to implement EC law. The Package Travel, Package Holidays and Package Tours Regulations 1992 which implement the EC Directive on package travel, package holidays and package tours (90/314/EEC) provide a good example of this (see Chapter Twelve). EC law is considered in more detail on pp. 6–9.

Delegated legislation and the hospitality and tourism industries

Examples of delegated legislation which are relevant to the hospitality and tourist industries include the Transfer of Undertaking (Protection of Employment) Regulations 1981 (see Chapter Six), the Town and Country Planning (Assessment of Environmental Effects) Regulations 1988 (see Chapter Eight) and the Civil Aviation (Air Travel Organizers' Licensing) Regulations 1995 (see Chapter Twelve).

International law

Introduction

International law is also an important source of law in the context of the hospitality and tourism industries. There are various sources of international law including international custom, treaties, general principles recognized by civilized states, judicial decisions and writings of jurists.

Treaties

Our discussion will focus particularly on treaties since they are the most important source of international law for our purposes. A treaty is an agreement between two or more states and may be called a 'treaty' or 'convention'. A 'protocol' is usually a subsequent agreement made to modify part of an earlier treaty or to make more detailed provisions following on an earlier agreement in principle. For example, the Montreal Protocol 26 ILM 1550 (1987) to the Vienna Convention for the Protection of the Ozone Layer 1985 26 ILM 1529 (1987) introduced specific targets for phasing out substances harmful to the ozone layer, to make concrete the Vienna Convention's provision that such targets should be set.

Treaties and domestic law in the UK

If the UK signs a treaty, the provisions of that treaty do not automatically become part of English or Scots law (*Blackburn* v *Attorney General* [1971] 2 All ER 1380). For that to occur, implementing legislation is required. Hence it is not possible for a person to seek to enforce a treaty provision in a court in the UK in circumstances where the UK is a signatory to the treaty but that treaty has not been implemented by domestic legislation enacted by Parliament. At most, the courts may be prepared to try to interpret the existing UK legislation in a manner which is not inconsistent with the treaty provisions. The court, however, will not hold an Act of Parliament to be invalid because it conflicts with a treaty (*Cheney* v *Conn* [1968] 1 All ER 779) except in the case of the EC Treaties (see pp. 6–9). Where Parliament does enact a treaty into domestic law, the courts are only required to give effect to the provisions of the Act not to the treaty (*Blackburn* v *Attorney General*), although once again different considerations apply in the case of the EC (see pp. 6–9).

Treaties and the tourism and hospitality industries

This area of law is known as public international law, the principal function of which is to regulate the relations of states. Matters covered by public international law which impact directly or indirectly on the hospitality and tourism industries include freedom of navigation on the high seas (United Nations Convention on the Law of the Sea 21 ILM 1261 (1982)), rights of aircraft to overfly the airspace of other states (Chicago Convention on International Civil Aviation 1944; Chicago International Air Services Transit Agreement 1944 UKTS 8 (1953), Cmd. 8742), environmental protection measures designed to preserve or enhance water quality (e.g. London Dumping Convention 1972 11 ILM 1294 (1972); International Convention for the Prevention of Pollution by Ships 1973 (MARPOL) 12 ILM 1319 (1973) and reverse ozone depletion which is a cause of skin cancer (Vienna Convention for the Protection of the Ozone Layer 26 ILM 1529 (1987) and especially its 1987 Montreal Protocol 26 ILM 1550 (1987)). These measures have all been implemented by the UK. For example, the London Dumping Convention 1972 which seeks to prevent the dumping of waste at sea is principally implemented by the Food and Environment Protection Act 1985. These treaties do not give rise to individual or private rights, they simply regulate conduct by states.

Treaties on the international carriage of passengers

Treaties agreed between states may give rise to rights which are privately enforceable in domestic courts. For our purposes, the most relevant treaties are those covering the rights of passengers being conveyed by sea, air, rail or road on international journeys and those covering compensation for personal injury or damage to or loss of luggage.

For example, the Warsaw Convention for the Unification of Certain Rules regarding Air Transport (1929) (as amended) makes air carriers strictly liable for damage caused to passengers and luggage in return for limitations on the levels of compensation payable. Certain defences are available to the carrier. Claims may be brought by passengers in their domestic courts if they are citizens of a state which is a signatory of the Convention. The Carriage by Air Act 1961 is the UK statute which implements this Convention. The House of Lords recently held that the Convention provides an exclusive remedy for those passengers seeking damages and that where the type of damage suffered is not covered by the Convention, (as, for example, in the case of psychological problems as a result of imprisonment during the Gulf War where passengers were captured by the Iraqis when their aircraft landed at Kuwait to refuel shortly after the start of the Iraqi invasion) the passenger is left without any other legal remedy: *Sidhu* v *British Airways plc; Abnett (known as Sykes)* v *British Airways (Scotland) plc* [1997] 1 All ER 193, HL.

EC law: a special case

European Community (EC) law is also a form of international law but it is of special significance and we consider it in detail below.

European Community law

Introduction

You should not underestimate the importance of the EC for the hospitality and tourism industries. For example, employment, product liability, package holiday, and environmental laws in the UK have been introduced to implement EC legislation.

The EC is governed by the Treaty of Rome 1957 (as amended by the Single European Act 1986 and the Treaty on European Union 1992) which is now known as the EC Treaty and has established its own legal system which binds member states.

Before we consider the various sources of EC law in more detail you should note two important principles of EC law which are of cardinal importance. First, the principle of supremacy of EC law which was developed by the European Court of Justice (ECJ). The doctrine is simple: EC law takes precedence over national law and, where the two conflict, EC law always prevails (e.g. *Costa* v *ENEL*, 6/64 [1964] ECR 585; [1964] CMLR 425). This has been recognized in the UK in the important case *R* v *Secretary of State for Transport, ex parte Factortame*, C-213/89 [1990] ECR I-2433; [1990] 3 CMLR 1. Therefore EC law in effect overrides conflicting UK statutory provisions as was the case in *Factortame*.

Secondly, the doctrine of direct effect was also developed by the ECJ. It provides that certain EC Treaty provisions or legislative acts may confer enforceable rights on individuals (*Van Gend en Loos* v *Nederlandse Administratie der Belastingen*, C-26/62 [1963] ECR 1. The person who benefits from these rights may seek to uphold them in their national courts. The rights must be respected regardless of what national law provides and thus direct effect is an inherent part of the doctrine of supremacy of EC law. For an EC Treaty provision or legislative act to be directly effective it must be clear, concise, unconditional and allow no discretion to member states in its implementation.

If, however, the provision in question is not directly effective but nonetheless confers rights on an individual and that individual can demonstrate that they have suffered loss by reason of the failure of a member state to implement the provision in question, they may be entitled to compensation for the loss from the member state concerned (e.g. *Francovich and Others* v *Italian Republic*, C-6 & 9/90, [1991] ECR I-5357; [1993] 2 CMLR 66). We discuss this further at p. 9. The various sources of EC law are discussed below.

Treaties

The principal treaty is the EC Treaty as amended by the Single European Act 1986 and the Treaty on European Union 1992; but the European Coal and Steel Community Treaty 1951 and the Euratom Treaty 1957 are also important sources of law. The Treaties are prefaced by preambles setting out the purposes for which the EC and the other communities exist and their individual provisions are known as Articles.

The Treaties create rights and obligations which often require no implementing measures in the UK. Some of these rights may be directly effective. For example, Article 119 of the EC Treaty, which provides for equal pay for equal work for men and women, was held to be directly effective in *Defrenne* v *Sabena* C-43/75 [1976] ECR 455 (see also Chapter Seven, pp. 176–179).

Regulations

These are legislative acts of the EC which are of general application and you should not confuse them with the UK delegated legislation known as Regulations (see pp. 3–4). The purpose of the Regulation is set out in a preamble and the individual provisions of the Regulation are known as Articles.

Regulations are binding in their entirety unlike a Directive which simply sets out the aim to be achieved. They are directly applicable which means that they do not generally require implementing legislation in a member state. They may also have direct effect. An example of a Regulation which has directly effective provisions is Regulation 1612/68 on freedom of movement for workers within the Community which deals with access to and conditions of employment for workers moving to other member states in the EC.

Directives

These are legislative acts of the EC which require member states to achieve a certain result within a specified time. This achieves the EC goal while respecting national differences. However, it is not sufficient for a member state to make best endeavours to comply with the objectives set out in a Directive: the objectives are binding and must be achieved by the member state within the time frame stipulated (e.g. *EC Commission* v *UK*, C-337/89, [1992] ECR I-6103). Enforcement proceedings may be commenced in the ECJ by the EC Commission against a member state under Article 169 of the EC Treaty where the member state has failed to implement a Directive or has failed to implement it correctly. Where the ECJ finds against the member state, the member state must comply with the Directive as soon as possible.

Like a Regulation, the text of a Directive is prefaced by a preamble which explains its purpose. The individual provisions of a Directive are known as Articles.

Directives are not directly applicable but they may have direct effect although this must be ascertained taking each case on its merits. A Directive may be directly effective if, at the expiry of the deadline for its implementation by a member state, it has not been implemented at all by a member state or has been implemented incorrectly, and the conditions mentioned above for direct effect arising are satisfied. An example of a Directive's provisions which have been held to be directly effective is Directive 76/207 on the implementation of the principle of equal treatment for men and women as regards access to employment, vocational training and promotion and working conditions (see e.g. *Marshall* v *Southampton and South-West Hampshire Area Health Authority*, 152/84, [1986] ECR 723, [1986] 1 CMLR 688).

However, you should note that Directives can only produce what is known as **vertical direct effect**, not **horizontal direct effect** (*Marshall* v *Southampton and South-West Hampshire Area Health Authority*, 152/84, (above)). The former is where a private party is seeking to enforce rights against a branch of the state. The question of which bodies are a branch of the state has been answered very broadly and has been held by the courts to include not only public authorities but also private sector utilities which are subject to close regulation by the state: *Foster* v *British Gas plc*, C-188/89, [1990] ECR I-3313, [1990] 2 CMLR 833; *Griffin and Others* v *South West Water Services Ltd* [1995] IRLR 15.

The latter is where a private party is seeking to enforce rights against another private party. The reason for Directives not being capable of horizontal direct effect is that the obligation to implement a Directive falls upon the state not upon private parties. This should be contrasted with both EC Treaty provisions and Regulations which are not addressed to a member state but to everyone. This therefore means that where the appropriate conditions are met, they may be horizontally directly effective as well as vertically directly effective.

Since there is injustice in being able to enforce rights in a Directive against any branch of the state but not against another private party, the ECJ has developed two methods by which individuals can assert their rights under Directives against private parties. First, the ECJ has developed a principle (known as the **Von Colson principle** after the case *Von Colson* v *Land Nordrhein-Westfalen* C-14/83, [1984] ECR 1891; [1986] 2 CMLR 430 and also known as the principle of indirect effect) which is based upon Article 5 of the EC Treaty, which requires member states to 'take all appropriate measures' to ensure fulfilment of their EC obligations. As the courts are a branch of the state, they are also under the obligation imposed by Article 5 of the EC Treaty, and must therefore interpret national law in such a way as to ensure that the objectives of a directive are achieved. You can see this principle in operation in the Scottish case *Litster* v *Forth Dry Dock and Engineering Company Ltd* [1990] 1 AC 546; [1989] SLT 540 in which the House of Lords held that the relevant Directive lacked direct effect because the defender was a private party but the pursuer nonetheless benefited from the Directive since the court went on to hold that the UK Regulations which implemented the Directive had to conform with the Directive. In effect this meant that the court read into the UK Regulations the words which were necessary to enable them to conform with the Directive even though this meant construing the UK Regulations in a manner contrary to their apparent meaning! The Von Colson principle was developed further in *Marleasing SA* v *La Comercial*

Internacional de Alimentacion SA, C-106/89, [1990] I ECR 4135; [1992] 1 CMLR 305 where the ECJ held that a national court is bound to interpret national legislation (whether it pre- or post-dates the Directive) in the light of the text and aim of the Directive in order to achieve the results envisaged by it.

The second approach to the problem of conflict between EC and national legislation has been to hold member states liable to persons in certain circumstances for losses suffered because of total non-implementation or incorrect implementation of EC law. We can identify two tests. The first applies in cases where there is a total failure to implement a Directive and is more stringent since Directives impose obligations on member states to achieve a particular result which reduce their margin of discretion. In *Francovich* v *Italian Republic*, C-6 & 9/90, [1991] ECR I-5357; [1993] 2 CMLR 66 the provisions of a Directive had not been implemented by Italy. While (as a result of a lack of precision in its terms) the Directive was held not to be directly effective, the ECJ took the view that as the member state had failed in its responsibility to enact implementing legislation, the member state was to be liable for damages to individuals prejudiced by its failure to implement the Directive, provided:

1. the Directive conferred rights on individuals;
2. the contents of those rights could be identified from the Directive; and
3. there was a causal link between the failure by the member state to implement the Directive and the damage suffered by the affected individual.

Thus article 7 of the Directive on package travel, package holidays and package tours (90/314/EEC) requires tour organizers to provide sufficient evidence of financial security for the refunding of money paid by consumers and for their repatriation in the event of an organizer's insolvency. Germany failed to implement the Directive and, as a result of this failure, various holidaymakers were either left without a refund, or had to come home at their own expense, when two tour organizers became insolvent. The ECJ held that article 7 did confer identifiable rights on individuals, who accordingly had a right of action for compensation against Germany. (*Dillenkofer and others* v *Germany*, Joined cases C-178, 179, 189 and 190//94 [1996] All ER (EC) 917; see also Chapter 12, pp. 299–302).

The second test applies where member states have enacted implementing legislation but that legislation does not adequately implement the EC Directive or other measure or is actually directly contrary to the EC law in question. In joined cases *Brasserie du Pecheur SA* v *Federal Republic of Germany*, C-46/93, *R* v *Secretary of State for Transport, ex p. Factortame Ltd*, C-48/93 [1996] All ER (EC) 301, ECJ, both of which involved the enactment of subsequent national legislation which conflicted with earlier EC law, the ECJ held that member states may be liable for a loss suffered by an individual where (1) the rule of EC law that had been infringed confers rights on individuals; (2) the breach of the rule is sufficiently serious; and (3) there is a direct causal link between the breach of EC law and the individual's loss. In *R* v *HM Treasury, ex p. British Telecommunications plc*, C-392/93 [1996] All ER (EC) 411 the ECJ confirmed that the test from *Brasserie du Pecheur* (above) also applied to cases where a member state had incorrectly transposed an EC Directive into national law.

Principles developed by the ECJ and other sources of EC law

The principles of supremacy of EC law and direct effect (discussed on p. 6) are the best examples of this important source of EC law. There are also other sources of EC law, including Decisions (which are binding measures but only upon the persons to whom the Decision is addressed) and Recommendations (which are non-binding) but it is not necessary for us to consider these further.

Case law

Case law is a very important source of law. There are some areas of law which largely consist of case law, that is, law made by judges in individual cases, rather than statutes enacted by Parliament. This is known as common law. The area of tort (in Scotland, delict) still largely depends on case law. For example, a nuisance may arise as a result of smells from a restaurant as in *Adams* v *Ursell* [1913] 1 Ch 269 and an action in negligence may arise where a person becomes ill after eating a meal in a restaurant which was bought for him by someone else (e.g. *Buckley* v *La Reserve* [1959] CLY 1330; *McInulty* v *Alam* 1996 SLT (Sh.Ct.) 71) (see Chapter Two). Many cases in contract are also based on the common law rules as, for example, *Jarvis* v *Swans Tours Ltd* [1973] 1 All ER 71 concerning breach of an express term of the contract to provide an entertaining and enjoyable holiday (see Chapter Twelve).

However, even in areas where Parliament has legislated, case law is still very important as judges are asked to interpret statutes or delegated legislation in the cases which come before them. For example, in joined cases *R* v *Metropolitan Stipendiary Magistrate, ex p. London Waste Regulation Authority; Berkshire County Council* v *Scott* [1993] 3 All ER 113, the court held that the meaning of the word 'deposit' in the Control of Pollution Act 1974 in relation to waste deposit was not confined to the final resting place of the waste in question. You will find a brief discussion of some of the important rules on statutory interpretation on pp. 29–31.

Given the relevance and importance of case law we have also included a brief discussion of the system of precedent and how it applies in the court structure and you will find this on pp. 27–28.

Equity

Equity is a source of law in England and Wales only. In England and Wales the Court of Chancery originally administered equity which was designed to provide a remedy where there was no common law remedy. Hence parallel common law and equitable jurisdictions developed. However, since the Judicature Acts 1873–1875, which created a unified Supreme Court in England and Wales, both common law and equity have been administered by the same courts. Equity has no application in Scotland.

Soft law

Arguably 'soft law' is not law at all but it certainly influences practice considerably and often statutes require public bodies to take into account 'soft law' in reaching their decisions. 'Soft law' consists of materials such as Guidance, Circulars or Codes of Practice, issued by the Government or other public authorities to explain what the purpose of legislation is or to indicate best practice in terms of complying with legislation. For example, guidance issued by central government includes Planning Policy Guidance notes issued by the Department of the Environment explaining national planning policy in England and Wales (see Chapter Eight); and the Code of Practice issued by the Department of the Environment, Welsh Office and Scottish Office in relation to the statutory duty of care for waste which explains how businesses can take steps to comply with the duty of care by ensuring that waste is properly stored, packaged, transported and disposed of (see Chapter Eight).

Codes of Practice issued by other public bodies include the Commission for Racial Equality's Code of Practice for the elimination of racial discrimination and the promotion of equality of opportunity (1984); and the Equal Opportunities Commission's Code of Practice for the elimination of discrimination on the grounds of sex and marriage and the promotion of equality of opportunity in employment (1985) both of which provide important advice for employers (see Chapter Six).

Soft law is not binding on anyone but its provisions should at the very least be taken into account where relevant. In some cases decision makers such as planning authorities are required to take into account relevant government guidance. A failure to do so may result in their decisions being set aside as unlawful. Codes of Practice on the other hand indicate appropriate standards of behaviour. Breach of such a Code will not usually in itself amount to an unlawful act but it may tend to suggest that unlawful conduct has taken place. The courts will look to such Codes as evidence of required standards of conduct, for example, by employers.

There are also Codes of Practice produced by private bodies or organizations such as the Association of British Travel Agents' Codes of Practice for Tour Operators and Travel Agents (see Chapter Twelve). These are not binding but once again courts may use them to establish what the expected standards of conduct are in a particular business for determining whether there has been a breach of such standards.

A good example of government misuse of guidance in the context of tourism and hospitality is provided by *Laker Airways Ltd* v *Department of Trade* [1977] QB 643. This case concerned Laker's attempts to run a cut price air service known as Skytrain from London to New York. The Civil Aviation Authority (CAA), which regulates scheduled air services into and out of the United Kingdom under the Civil Aviation Act 1971, was bound by s.3(1) of that Act to ensure that the then state-owned British Airways (BA) would not have a monopoly of long-distance air routes and that at least one other British airline could compete with BA. Under s.3(2) of the 1971 Act, the Secretary of State had the power to give guidance to the CAA in relation to its functions. In 1972 the CAA granted a licence to Laker to operate its London–New York service. However, the US authorities delayed granting their consent. In 1975 the government's policy changed and it decided to revoke Laker's licence. The Secretary of State issued new guidance to the CAA which provided that no British airline other than BA should operate long distance routes without BA's consent. Laker challenged the validity of this guidance in the courts, and succeeded in having it quashed by the Court of Appeal which held that the guidance was *'ultra vires'*, that is, it exceeded the Secretary of State's powers under s.3(2) of the 1971 Act since it conflicted with the 1971 Act by giving a monopoly position to BA. A power to issue guidance under an Act therefore does not include a power to alter the objectives of the Act.

Scottish Parliament legislation

Introduction

As a result of the referendum held on 11 September 1997, Scotland is to get its own Parliament. The Government's plans for the Parliament are set out in its White Paper, *Scotland's Parliament* (1997, Cm.3658). The Parliament should be fully operational by the year 2000. The Parliament will be mandated to pass new Acts in relation to 'devolved matters' (see below) or to pass Acts which amend or repeal existing UK Acts of Parliament within the field of 'devolved matters'.

Status of Acts of the Scottish Parliament

The supremacy of Acts of the UK Parliament will not be affected by the establishment of the Scottish Parliament and the UK Parliament will be able to override Acts of the Scottish Parliament or indeed abolish the Scottish Parliament should it so choose. The status of Acts of the Scottish Parliament is therefore similar although not identical to the status of delegated legislation (see below). Such Acts may be challenged in court on the ground that they are *ultra vires*, that is, not within the powers of the Scottish Parliament.

Enactment of Acts of the Scottish Parliament

It will be for the Scottish Parliament to establish its own procedures for passing Acts once it has been set up. However, such Acts will require the Royal Assent, as is the case with Acts of the UK Parliament, and the Government has announced that there will be a short delay before a Scottish Bill is presented for the Royal Assent in order to enable the UK Parliament to satisfy itself that the Bill is *intra vires*, that is, within the powers of the Scottish Parliament.

Devolved matters and reserved matters

The legislation establishing the Scottish Parliament will not specify what matters it may legislate on but will instead specify what matters are to be reserved to the UK Parliament. In its White Paper the Government indicated that the UK Parliament will continue to be responsible for matters including the common market for UK goods and services, consumer protection, vehicle licensing and employment matters.

The White Paper also set out the devolved matters in relation to which the Scottish Parliament will have the power to legislate. For our purposes these include economic development, transport, the promotion of tourism, town and country planning, environmental protection, liquor licensing and food standards in Scotland. Responsibility for prosecutions and the investigation of crime (which is separate in any case at present) is also devolved. It will be possible for the list of devolved matters to be increased or decreased. The Scottish Parliament will also be obliged to ensure the implementation of EC law obligations which relate to devolved matters.

Extent, commencement and structure of Acts of the Scottish Parliament

Acts of the Scottish Parliament will extend to Scotland only. The comments we made above in relation to the commencement and structure of Acts of the UK Parliament (pp. 2–3) are likely to apply to Acts of the Scottish Parliament also.

Welsh Assembly legislation

Introduction

The Government is to establish a Welsh Assembly as a result of the referendum held on 18 September 1997. The Government's plans for the Assembly are set out in its White Paper, *A Voice for Wales* (1997, Cm.3718). The Assembly should be set up by May 1999. The Assembly will have a much more limited law making role than the Scottish Parliament in that it will not be able to amend or repeal Acts of the UK Parliament but only amend, revoke or make delegated legislation within its sphere of competence. Essentially the Assembly will take over the delegated law making role which the Secretary of State for Wales currently exercises. Such delegated legislation will be known as Orders of the Welsh Assembly. Given that it is taking over the functions of the Secretary of State for Wales, the Assembly will have a role in implementing UK Acts of Parliament in so far as they relate to Wales. The Assembly is also to be given a very limited power to amend certain UK Acts of Parliament in order to reform unelected bodies in Wales by subjecting them to a greater degree of democratic control. For our purposes such bodies include the Wales Tourist Board and the new Welsh Economic Development Agency.

Status of Orders of the Welsh Assembly

These will have the same status as delegated legislation (see pp. 3–4).

Enactment of Orders of the Welsh Assembly

Committees within the Welsh Assembly will be responsible for the preparation of Orders. They will consider them in detail and amend them, if thought appropriate, before submitting them to the Assembly for approval.

Welsh Assembly's sphere of competence

The Assembly's sphere of competence will initially encompass all the powers and duties currently exercised or discharged by the Secretary of State for Wales although its functions may be increased or decreased in future. For our purposes, the Assembly will be responsible for bodies and matters including the Wales Tourist Board, for Welsh transport matters and for town and country planning and environmental protection. The Assembly will also be under a duty to ensure the implementation of EC law obligations in so far as they relate to its functions.

CLASSIFICATION OF LAW

Civil law and criminal law

Criminal law deals with wrongful acts or omissions which are harmful to the community and which society through Parliament or the courts has decided merit punishment. It includes both acts which are universally regarded as being inherently wrong (in Latin, *mala in se*), for example, murder or rape, as well as acts which are simply prohibited (*mala prohibita*) for purposes of social utility such as parking on pedestrian crossings. The state is largely responsible for prosecuting criminal conduct although prosecutions by private citizens are possible (see further below at pp. 22–23 and Chapter Five). However, not everything which one might consider to be wrong is regarded as criminal.

Whereas criminal law exists to punish conduct which society has determined merits such punishment, civil law on the other hand exists primarily to uphold obligations which may be incurred voluntarily, such as contracts, or involuntarily, for example tort, that is, the obligation not to cause unintentional harm to another person. Civil law is therefore largely concerned with upholding standards of conduct by ensuring individuals or businesses fulfil their obligations and where they fail to do so, by requiring them to pay compensation or fulfil their obligations as appropriate. Given that it deals with relations between individuals or business organizations, the enforcement of civil law is up to those individuals or business organizations although the state provides the courts to enable the enforcement of such obligations.

You should be aware that a particular act may give rise to both civil and criminal liability. For example, where a road traffic accident has taken place which resulted in injury to a pedestrian because of the driver's negligence, the pedestrian would be able to raise a civil law action for compensation for his/her injuries against the driver, while the public prosecutors might decide to prosecute the driver in the criminal courts for careless or reckless driving under road traffic legislation. An example of this from the hospitality and tourism industries would be where food which does not comply with food safety requirements is sold to someone. If that person is injured by reason of eating such food, they may wish to pursue a civil claim against the supplier for compensation. However, the person who sold the food would face potential criminal liability under s.8 of the Food Safety Act 1990 (see Chapter 10).

Public law and private law

A further classification of law which is also sometimes made is between public law and private law. Public law essentially deals with the relationship between the state and the individual. Therefore, matters of tax, social security benefits, licensing, health and safety, planning, environmental protection, immigration and indeed criminal law are all matters which involve relationships between the state and individuals or business organizations.

On the other hand, private law covers the status, relationships, obligations and property of individuals and business organizations. Therefore, family law, property law, contract and tort (in Scotland, delict) fall within the ambit of private law. You should also note that public authorities are subject to private law, for example, in relation to employment contracts. The distinction between public law and private law is less important in Scotland than in England and Wales since the same principles and remedies are applicable in both public and private spheres in Scotland.

GOING TO LAW

Introduction

We have now examined the sources of law and classification of law and now turn to consider the issue of going to law. This will involve us discussing general issues in relation to litigation such as cost and a discussion of the various courts and tribunals which administer the law. We consider going to law in the civil courts first, then in tribunals, the criminal courts, the European courts and finally alternatives to litigation.

General issues regarding going to law in the civil courts

Introduction

No one is under any obligation to bring a civil law claim. This means that one of the principal disadvantages of the civil courts as a means of solving problems, for example, by obtaining compensation for personal injury, is that many people may be unwilling to take action even if they are entitled to do so and have a strong case. Quite apart from the potential costs and risks of litigating, considerable stress is likely to be involved and for these reasons many people simply choose not to assert their rights in law.

Designation of parties

A person commencing a civil action in private law areas is known as the plaintiff in England and Wales and as the pursuer in Scotland. The respective terms for the party against whom action is taken are defendant and defender. In judicial review cases (see pp. 32–36), the person challenging a decision is known as the applicant in England and Wales and as the petitioner in Scotland. The person whose decision, action or omission is being challenged in a judicial review case is known as the respondent in both jurisdictions.

Courts of first instance and appellate courts

A person may only start an action in a court of first instance such as the County Court or High Court in England and Wales or the Sheriff Court or Outer House of the Court of Session in Scotland. Certain types of actions must be commenced in a particular court. Thus, for example, judicial review cases must be commenced in the Divisional Court of the Queen's Bench Division of the High Court in England and Wales and the Outer House of the Court of Session in Scotland (see also pp. 32–36). We examine this issue in more detail in relation to the various courts below. The other courts are known as appellate courts. Appellate courts are further up the hierarchy of courts and hear appeals from courts of first instance. There is usually more than a single tier of appellate courts (see Figures 1.1 and 1.2). Appeals may be as of right but, in many cases, appeals require leave of the lower court. Legislative provisions normally determine whether an appeal may be based upon issues of fact or law or both. Some courts may operate both as courts of first instance and appellate courts such as the Divisional Court of the Queen's Bench Division of the High Court in England and Wales.

Procedures

We do not intend to provide a detailed discussion of court procedures but merely to highlight some salient developments and features. The courts north and south of the border have made considerable efforts in recent years to speed up procedures and hence reduce both costs and delays. The introduction of small claims systems is a good example of this. In both jurisdictions small claims systems provide a fairly quick and simple method of recovering small value claims, for example, for defective consumer goods, although the applicable limit for claims is rather higher in England and Wales at £3,000 than in Scotland where the limit is only £750.

In England and Wales procedures in the higher courts require full disclosure of expert witness reports in advance of hearings so as to minimize areas of dispute and to reduce the possibility of trial by ambush. This approach is not yet universal north of the border where, however, it may be found in the commercial action procedure for business litigation and the optional procedure for relatively simple personal injury litigation.

Both the Woolf report, *Access to Justice,* and its Scottish counterpart, the Cullen Report, have recently advocated further measures in the courts to reduce costs and delays by, for example, giving judges greater control over the progress of cases.

Costs

Who has not heard a joke or story about lawyers charging excessive costs? Although the notion that lawyers overcharge for their services is by no means always deserved, it is undoubtedly true that potential costs may be one of the greatest disincentives to litigating. However, in order to assess the merits of a case, a person may obtain free advice from Citizens' Advice Bureaux or Law Centres although you should note that there is only a restricted network of Law Centres in Scotland. Many solicitors also provide a free first interview and Legal Aid for preliminary advice on a matter may also be available to those who meet the stringent financial eligibility tests.

If a person decides to commence an action, a fee is payable to the relevant court. The size of the fee depends on the level of court in which the action is raised. Thus, the fee is lowest for an action commenced in the Small Claims Court and highest in the High Court in England and Wales or the Court of Session in Scotland. Further outlays may be payable to the court for various procedural steps as the case progresses. If the plaintiff or pursuer is eligible for Legal Aid it will meet these costs.

Representation in court by a solicitor or barrister (in Scotland, advocate), which is essential, is likely to be costly. Legal Aid may be available to those who meet the relevant test on the merits of the case and stringent financial criteria. In England and Wales the merits test is that there must be a reasonable chance of success, which is 50 per cent or greater. In Scotland the merits test is that the pursuer has a probable cause of action.

The general rule is that costs in civil actions follow success: the unsuccessful party will normally be required to pay the successful party's costs. This can obviously be a major disincentive to taking action. However, it is true to say that even if a party is successful they will not recover all their legal costs from the other side.

To encourage individuals to make use of the small claims system and discourage solicitors from appearing, if the plaintiff loses their action, they do not have to pay the defendant's costs. In Scotland, the position is similar but not identical with the unsuccessful pursuer's liability to pay the defender's expenses generally limited to £75. This considerably reduces the risk of litigating in the small claims courts north and south of the border. Legal Aid is also unavailable for small claims actions as a further measure to discourage solicitors from acting. Given the difficulties which unrepresented parties have in such actions (see below), the fact that Legal Aid is unavailable is hardly satisfactory. Legal Aid is, however, available for appeals from the small claims courts to higher courts.

Legal Aid is also not normally available for proceedings in tribunals for the same reasons. However, it is available for proceedings before an Employment Appeal Tribunal and for proceedings before the courts resulting from a tribunal decision.

Advice and representation

While anyone may in theory bring a civil action, the formality and complexity of many legal and factual issues and the court procedure itself, make it essential to obtain advice at the very least, and representation by a solicitor or barrister (in Scotland, advocate) if court action becomes necessary.

Representation may even be necessary in the small claims courts and tribunals despite the fact that such bodies were designed to be more user friendly for individuals wishing to pursue claims of low value or in relation to specialized issues such as employment matters. Research has shown that in reality these bodies are often much more formal than was intended and that represented parties normally fare considerably better than unrepresented parties (H. Jones *et al.*, *Small Claims in the Sheriff Court in Scotland*, Scottish Office Central Research Unit, Edinburgh, 1991; H. Genn and Y. Genn, *The Effectiveness of Representation at Tribunals*, Lord Chancellor's Department, London, 1989).

In relation to tribunals the complexity of the law which they administer, for example, in the field of employment law with its considerable volume of legislation and case law, means that representation is absolutely necessary (see Chapter Six). In the case of social security and immigration tribunals, research by Genn and Genn (see above) found that parties were best represented by specialist lay representatives from relevant organizations such as the UK Immigration Advisory Service (UKIAS). However, in the case of industrial tribunals it was found that representation by lawyers or specialist lay representatives such as a trade union representative brought an equal chance of success.

Matters of proof

The onus of proof in a civil action lies with the plaintiff (pursuer, in Scotland) and the evidence led must prove the case 'on the balance of probabilities'.

Civil courts in England and Wales

House of Lords

This court is the final appeal court for civil matters in England and Wales. It consists of the Lord Chancellor; the Lords of Appeal in Ordinary, who are often known as 'the law lords'; and peers who hold or have held high judicial office. The quorum for the court is three although five judges normally sit. It hears appeals, with leave, from the Court of Appeal.

Court of Appeal

The day-to-day civil work of this court is carried out by the Master of the Rolls and up to 28 Lords Justices of Appeal. The Court normally sits in groups of three judges. The jurisdiction of the civil division is entirely appellate. As well as hearing appeals from certain tribunals, the Court of Appeal also hears appeals from the High Court of Justice and the County Court. Most civil appeals in England and Wales go no further than the Court of Appeal.

High Court of Justice

The High Court consists of three divisions, the Queen's Bench Division, the Chancery Division and the Family Division. It can sit anywhere in England and Wales although the Lord Chancellor has issued directions as to where the court should sit.

The Queen's Bench Division consists of the Lord Chief Justice and about 54 other judges. The Court has two branches, the Division, in which judges sit alone, and the rather confusingly named Divisional Court of the Division in which two judges usually sit together to hear a case. In the Division, a court of first instance, judges sitting alone have jurisdiction over cases involving commercial matters and the more serious tort cases. The Divisional Court is both a court of first instance and an appellate court. It hears appeals from certain decisions of Magistrates. However, one of its most important functions is to exercise supervisory jurisdiction over inferior bodies, i.e. its judicial review function (see pp. 32–36). This jurisdiction allows the Division to ensure that tribunals and other agencies do not exceed their powers.

The work of the Chancery Division is carried out by the Vice-Chancellor and about a dozen other judges. The Division deals with the law of trusts, wills and estates, partnership, companies and bankruptcies, most tax matters, planning, landlord and tenant cases, equity and with disputes concerning land transactions.

The jurisdiction of the Family Division is apparent from its name. It deals with contested matrimonial cases, adoption and guardianship cases, and consists of the President of the Division and about 16 other judges.

County Court

The County Court is a local court dealing with civil claims. There are over 350 county court districts in England and Wales grouped into circuits each with a circuit judge. The circuit itself is administered by a Registrar. The County Court has express statutory jurisdiction and has exclusive jurisdiction over personal injuries claims below £50,000. Formerly, £50,000 was the upper limit of damages which could be sued for in the County Court but this limit has now been abolished. Certain designated County Courts can also hear undefended matrimonial causes. The County Court provides the informal and inexpensive small claims arbitration procedure which, it should be noted, is not a true arbitration procedure but a simplified court procedure, for claims up to £3,000. Appeals from the County Court go to the Court of Appeal.

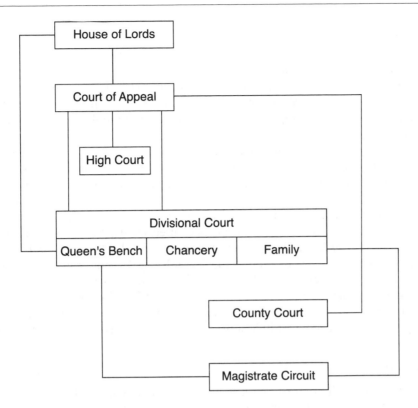

Figure 1.1 Simplified English and Welsh civil court structure

Magistrates' Court

The Magistrates' Court is the lowest court in the hierarchy although it exercises a fairly wide jurisdiction, particularly in relation to criminal matters (see p. 24). It is staffed by local Justices of the Peace. Its jurisdiction covers such matters as non-payment of gas or electricity bills, revocation and renewal of licences (see Chapter 11), and certain types of domestic proceedings. Most appeals go to the Divisional Court of the Queen's Bench Division, although appeals from domestic proceedings go to the Divisional Court of the Family Division (see Figure 1.1).

Civil courts in Scotland

House of Lords

This court is also the supreme court for Scottish civil cases. It hears appeals from the Inner House of the Court of Session. An outline of the composition of the court and its quorum is given in the equivalent section in the English civil courts above (see pp. 17–18). Two of the law lords are normally Scottish judges and every effort is made to ensure that the Scottish judges hear Scottish appeals although this is not always possible.

Court of Session

This court, which is the next most important in the Scottish civil court hierarchy, is split into the Outer House and the Inner House.

The Outer House acts as a court of first instance. The judges who sit in the Outer House are known as Lords Ordinary and sit alone. The jurisdiction of the Outer House includes the more important claims for compensation for personal injuries and judicial review cases. In recent years simplified procedures for certain straightforward personal injury cases (the 'optional procedure') and for commercial actions have been introduced in order to speed up the process of litigation and reduce costs.

The Inner House acts almost exclusively as an appeal court and it is made up of eight senior judges. The Inner House is split up into two divisions of four judges each (although only three usually sit at a hearing), which are known as the First Division and the Second Division. The First Division is chaired by the Lord President, the most senior Scottish judge, and the Second Division is presided over by the Lord Justice Clerk, the second most senior Scottish judge. An Extra Division may also be appointed by the Lord President and has in fact sat regularly in recent years to assist in reducing the backlog of civil appeals. Both the First and Second Divisions and the Extra Division have equal authority and cases are allocated to each at random. The Inner House hears appeals from the decisions of judges of the Outer House and from the Sheriff Court.

Sheriff Court

This is the only civil court of first instance in Scotland which is locally based. Cases are dealt with by a sheriff sitting alone. The Sheriff Court has a very wide jurisdiction dealing with everything from debt to damages actions and there is no upper limit on the sum which can be sued for. Formerly, the Sheriff Court could not hear divorce cases but the provisions of the Divorce Jurisdiction, Court Fees and Legal Aid (Scotland) Act 1983 gave it concurrent jurisdiction with the Court of Session in divorce actions. Moreover, actions valued at less than £1,500 must be brought in the Sheriff Court. However, judicial review cases cannot be brought in the Sheriff Court but must be commenced in the Outer House of the Court of Session.

Actions for between £750 and £1,500 must be brought under the simplified summary cause procedure and those up to £750 in the Small Claims Court which is designed to provide a simple, inexpensive and informal forum for dealing with low value claims, for example, in relation to consumer issues. In both summary cause actions and small claims the normal rules of evidence and procedure are relaxed and there is a restriction on the amount of expenses which can be claimed from the defeated party.

The Ordinary Court, where the procedures have recently been streamlined to try to speed up litigation, hears all other actions.

Scotland is divided into six sheriffdoms, each of which is presided over by a Sheriff Principal. The Sheriff Principal acts both as chief administrator of the court and as an appeal judge for appeals from the Sheriffs within each sheriffdom in civil cases. Appeals from the small claims and summary cause courts must go first to the Sheriff Principal and then to the Inner House of the Court of Session but appeals from the Ordinary Court may go either to the Sheriff Principal and from there to the Inner House of the Court of Sesson or directly to the Inner House (see Figure 1.2).

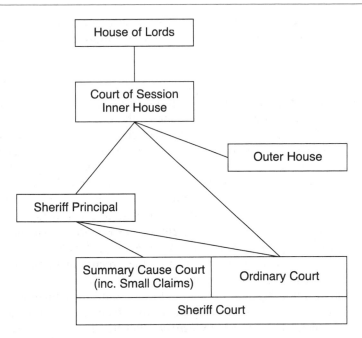

Figure 1.2 Simplified Scottish civil court structure

Tribunals in Great Britain

A very large number of tribunals now exist, dealing with matters ranging from social security benefits to immigration and employment matters. For our purposes the most relevant tribunals are those which deal with employment matters: industrial tribunals. Established in 1964, their jurisdiction covers matters such as unfair dismissal and discrimination in employment. These issues are considered in detail in Chapter 6. Legal Aid is not available for proceedings before industrial tribunals although Legal Aid Advice and Assistance is available for advice from a solicitor prior to bringing proceedings for those who meet the stringent financial criteria. Appeals from industrial tribunals go to the Employment Appeals Tribunal (EAT). Legal Aid is available for proceedings before the EAT. Appeals may be made from the EAT on points of law only to the Court of Appeal in England and Wales and to the Inner House of the Court of Session in Scotland.

General issues regarding going to law in the criminal courts

Summary proceedings and proceedings on indictment

Summary proceedings are those brought in England and Wales before the Magistrates alone with no jury present and if successful will lead to a summary conviction. In Scotland, such proceedings are brought in the District or Sheriff Courts.

Proceedings on indictment are those brought in the Crown Court in England and Wales and in the Sheriff Court or High Court of Justiciary in Scotland where the judge sits with a jury. If successful such proceedings lead to a conviction on indictment. Proceedings on indictment are brought in relation to the more serious crimes and will normally involve heavier penalties than those prosecuted summarily.

Designation of parties

In England and Wales, the vast majority of prosecutions are brought by the Crown Prosecution Service (CPS) and run in the name of the Queen, e.g. *Regina* v *Sunair Holidays Ltd* [1973] 1 WLR 1105 – an unsuccessful prosecution under the Trade Descriptions Act 1968 in relation to a travel brochure. You should note that Regina is abbreviated to R in the citation of cases. Certain prosecutions are required by statute to be commenced by or with the consent of the Director of Public Prosecutions (DPP) and are brought in the name DPP. Private prosecutions, i.e. cases brought by bodies or persons other than the CPS and DPP, run in that body or person's name, for example, *Environment Agency* v *ICI* [1997] 266 ENDS Report 51. The party against whom criminal proceedings are brought is known as the defendant.

In Scotland, most prosecutions are brought by the Procurator Fiscal (PF) and are brought in the PF's own name, for example, *Guild* v *Gateway Foodmarkets Ltd* 1990 SCCR 179 – a prosecution brought in relation to food unfit for human consumption. The more serious crimes are prosecuted by the Lord Advocate and run in the name of Her Majesty's Advocate (HMA): *HMA* v *Raiker* 1989 SCCR 149 – a case involving the defence of coercion. The party against whom proceedings are brought is variously known as the accused, the panel or the defendant.

Public prosecution

Both south and north of the border prosecutions are principally brought by the state, by the Crown Prosecution Service (CPS) or, in certain cases, by the DPP in England and Wales; and by the Procurator Fiscal Service or in the case of more serious cases, by the Lord Advocate, in Scotland.

In both jurisdictions many offences may be prosecuted either summarily or on indictment. In such a case whether an offence is prosecuted in a particular court or prosecuted summarily or on indictment depends on a variety of factors including the nature of the offence and its seriousness. In certain cases, statute provides that a particular offence must be prosecuted in a particular court which has exclusive jurisdiction over that offence. For example, in Scotland, murder cases must be prosecuted in the High Court of Justiciary. In relation to certain statutory offences including health and safety and environmental legislation summary prosecutions in Scotland may only be brought in the Sheriff Court and not in the District Court. However, in England and Wales, in contrast to the position in Scotland, if an offence is triable summarily (i.e. without a jury in the Magistrates' Court) but carries a maximum sentence of over three months imprisonment, the accused may claim the right to a jury trial in which case the Magistrates' Court would commit the person to trial in the Crown Court. No such right exists in Scotland.

Private prosecutions

Prosecutions by private citizens are possible in both jurisdictions. These may be brought if the public authorities refuse or fail to take action. Any penalties imposed following a conviction are exacted by the state. In England and Wales any person has the right to prosecute statutory offences unless the statute expressly excludes this right. This means that a number of public bodies in addition to the CPS bring their own prosecutions, for example, the Health and Safety Executive, the Environment Agency and local authorities. Private citizens and interest groups may also bring prosecutions, for example, *Greenpeace* v *Allbright and Wilson* [1992] 4 LMELR 56; [1991] 3 LMELR 170 – a successful private prosecution brought against a chemical company for water pollution offences.

Although private prosecution is not impossible in Scotland it is very rare since it requires the consent of the Lord Advocate, the government's chief legal officer in Scotland. Should the Lord Advocate refuse such consent, the refusal can be reviewed by the Criminal Appeal Court, but it will not lightly overturn the refusal. As a result of this there have only been a handful of private prosecutions attempted in Scotland this century. In addition, in Scotland, bodies such as the Health and Safety Executive, the Scottish Environment Protection Agency and local authorities cannot bring their own prosecutions but instead, if they wish criminal proceedings to be brought against a person, they must send a report to the Procurator Fiscal. The Procurator Fiscal has discretion as to whether or not proceedings are to be brought.

Courts of first instance and appellate courts

The remarks which we made in relation to the civil courts (see p. 15) are relevant here also. Prosecutions may only be brought in the criminal courts of first instance, i.e. the trial courts. As we noted above, there are rules of law which require certain offences to be prosecuted in particular courts. If a person is convicted in a court of summary jurisdiction or on indictment, they may appeal against their conviction or sentence or both. The appellate courts do, however, have the power to increase a sentence on appeal. The prosecution may appeal against an acquittal or a sentence imposed by a court of summary jurisdiction. They may also appeal against the sentence imposed on a conviction on indictment. However, the prosecution may not appeal against an acquittal by a jury following a prosecution on indictment. Nevertheless following such an acquittal, the prosecution may, if they consider that the law was wrongly applied by the trial court, refer the question of law which arose in the case to an appellate court by way of an Attorney General's Reference in England and Wales and a Lord Advocate's Reference in Scotland. Such a reference in no way affects the acquittal of the defendant.

Costs in criminal cases

Legal Aid is available to most persons facing prosecution especially where there is a possibility of a custodial sentence being imposed.

In England and Wales, but not in Scotland, costs may be recovered by the prosecuting agency in the event of a successful prosecution. For example, in the recent prosecution of Nuclear Electric by the Health and Safety Executive a fine of £250,000 was accompanied by costs of £138,000 ([1995] 248 ENDS Report 46).

Legal Aid is not available for those wishing to bring private prosecutions. If a private prosecution is unsuccessful, the party bringing the prosecution will usually be required to pay the other side's costs as Greenpeace have found to their considerable cost (£28,849) in their unsuccessful prosecutions of ICI. ICI had claimed costs of £72,793 ([1994] 234 ENDS Report 47).

Matters of proof

The onus of proof in a criminal action lies with the prosecution and the evidence must prove 'beyond reasonable doubt' that the offence was committed. This is a higher standard of proof than the civil standard of proof which is 'on the balance of probabilities'. The reason for this is that the consequences of a criminal conviction such as imprisonment or simply having a criminal record may obviously have a very serious impact on a person's life.

Criminal courts in England and Wales

All prosecutions in England and Wales are commenced in the Magistrates' Court although only summary cases are actually tried there. Magistrates' Courts may generally impose sentences of up to six months imprisonment and/or a £5,000 fine. However, the Magistrates' Court also acts as a court of committal for indictable offences. If there is sufficient evidence against an accused, he/she is committed to the Crown Court for trial. The Crown Court tries cases on indictment and has unlimited sentencing powers except where these are restricted by statute.

In summary proceedings appeal lies from the Magistrates' Court either to the Crown Court and thence to the Divisional Court and thereafter the House of Lords or to the Divisional Court (on points of law) and thence to the House of Lords. In proceedings on indictment appeal lies from the Crown Court to the Court of Appeal and thereafter to the House of Lords (see Figure 1.3).

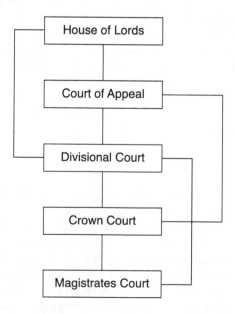

Figure 1.3 Simplified English and Welsh criminal court structure

Criminal courts in Scotland

Court of Criminal Appeal

This court hears appeals from the District Court, the Sheriff Court and the High Court of Justiciary. Normally three judges hear the appeals although larger numbers may sit if the court wishes to depart from one of its earlier decisions. There is no further appeal to any other court, the House of Lords having no role in relation to Scottish criminal appeals. You should also note that the Sheriff Principal has no appellate role in the criminal court structure (see Figure 1.4).

High Court of Justiciary

This is the court in which the most serious crimes in Scotland are tried. Trials in relation to certain crimes including murder, rape and treason must take place in the High Court of Justiciary; in other words the court has what is known as 'exclusive jurisdiction' in relation to these crimes.

   The High Court of Justiciary only acts in proceedings on indictment which are known as solemn proceedings in Scotland and has unlimited sentencing powers except where these are restricted by statute as, for example, in the case of murder where there is a mandatory life sentence.

Sheriff Court

The Sheriff Court may, when acting in summary proceedings, normally impose sentences of up to three months imprisonment and/or a £5,000 fine. In solemn proceedings the Sheriff Court may impose sentences of up to three years imprisonment and/or an unlimited fine.

District Court

The District Court deals with offences of a relatively minor nature such as breach of the peace. It only acts in summary proceedings, i.e. where there is no jury. The judges are justices of the peace.

   Sentences of up to 60 days imprisonment and/or a £2,500 fine may be imposed by the District Court. However, where a stipendiary magistrate has been appointed in the District Court, as has happened in Glasgow, he/she exercises the same powers as a sheriff in summary proceedings.

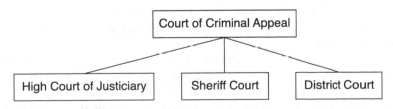

Figure 1.4 Simplified Scottish criminal court structure

European courts

The European Court of Justice

This court, which is located in Luxembourg, does *not* act as an appeal court for domestic courts of member states of the EC. However, in both civil and criminal proceedings, if a point of EC law requires interpretation so that the case may be decided, it is possible for any national court to make a reference to the European Court of Justice (ECJ) for a preliminary ruling on the validity or the interpretation of a piece of EC law under Article 177 of the EC Treaty. A court from which there is no appeal *must* make a reference to the ECJ if it must determine a question of EC law to enable it to decide the case. The ECJ does not decide the case but merely provides authoritative interpretations of the question of EC law posed by the national court which must then decide the case before it.

Other forms of action, for example, under Article 173 of the EC Treaty to annul EC legislation are also competent before the ECJ. Where enforcement proceedings are brought against a member state by the EC Commission under Article 169 of the EC Treaty for failure to implement or comply with EC law, if matters proceed sufficiently far, proceedings may be commenced in the ECJ.

The European Court of Human Rights

The ECJ must not be confused with the European Court of Human Rights which is located in Strasbourg and is an entirely separate institution that was established to adjudicate issues arising out of the European Convention on Human Rights (ECHR). It operates under the auspices of the Council of Europe, a body which is independent of the EC. The ECHR safeguards basic civil and political rights such as the right to privacy (Article 8) and the right to a fair trial (Article 6).

Although the United Kingdom (UK) is a signatory of the ECHR, the Convention had not at the time of writing been enacted as part of domestic law in the UK. This means that a person who alleges that his/her rights under the ECHR have been infringed in either civil or criminal proceedings must first exhaust domestic remedies before being able to go to Strasbourg. Once the petition has been received by the European Commission on Human Rights its admissibility is assessed and, if the Commission determines that it is admissible, attempts will be made to facilitate a settlement between the individual and state concerned. It is only if such efforts fail, that the matter will ultimately come before the European Court of Human Rights for a hearing. As you can imagine, this process is extremely lengthy and will normally not take less than three to four years. The current system therefore does not provide a swift remedy. Indeed you may be interested to learn that many of the successful cases brought against the UK have involved prisoners' rights. This may not be a matter of chance since the process is so lengthy and prisoners may have a considerable amount of time on their hands!

However, at the time of writing the new Labour Government had indicated that a Bill was to be included in its first legislative programme to incorporate the ECHR into domestic law. Such a move would make the ECHR enforceable before any court in the UK and would provide a much swifter remedy for anyone whose rights under the ECHR had been infringed than the current system.

Alternative dispute resolution (ADR)

Alternatives to litigation may be available. Obviously if a satisfactory settlement can be negotiated by an individual or business organization with or without the assistance of a lawyer, potentially lengthy, costly and stressful court action may be avoided. The vast bulk of civil cases never come to court because the parties agree to a settlement. Such a course of action is obviously preferable to litigation. There may, however, be other ways of reaching a satisfactory outcome. Recently, methods of alternative dispute resolution (ADR), such as arbitration, mediation and conciliation have been promoted as a faster and cheaper method of solving disputes than resorting to litigation. The parties are responsible for reaching their own solutions with the help of a neutral third party. Solutions are not imposed on the parties as happens in litigation but the parties work towards their own solutions. ADR is particularly helpful where parties wish to avoid acrimony and continue some form of relationship, as for example, in family or commercial matters. Where there is simply a one-off relationship between the parties as, for example, between a holidaymaker and tour company, ADR may be less appropriate although two examples of ADR which we consider in some detail, the Association of British Travel Agents Conciliation Service and Arbitration Scheme (see Chapter Twelve, pp. 302–303), arise in that context.

There is also some scope for ADR in criminal matters with conciliation being attempted in certain pilot schemes between offenders and their victims. Obviously conciliation would be wholly inappropriate for certain crimes but for issues such as vandalism and petty theft it may be appropriate. For example, part of the scheme could include the offender carrying out work for the victim to repair any damage caused.

THE SYSTEM OF PRECEDENT

Introduction

It is a cardinal principle of both the English and Scottish legal systems that there should be certainty and consistency in the law. This is provided for by requiring the courts at the lower levels in the court hierarchy to follow and apply the decisions of the superior courts (see Figures 1.1 and 1.2). When we talk about 'follow or apply the decisions' we essentially mean follow or apply the legal principle or grounds on which the decision was based. This is known in Latin as the *ratio decidendi*. To give the system some flexibility to adapt to changing or different circumstances it is possible for higher courts to overrule decisions of lower courts and sometimes their own previous decisions (see below). It is also possible for courts to distinguish the decisions of another court rather than follow them. This would involve a judge holding that there was some material difference in circumstance between the case before him and the case which would otherwise be a binding precedent which justified him reaching a different conclusion. The operation of the rules of precedent, therefore, is supposed to provide the certainty and consistency in the law which our legal systems demand together with a degree of flexibility to meet changing circumstances.

Position of the House of Lords

Decisions of the House of Lords bind all lower courts unless of course they can be distinguished from the case before the lower court in question. Before 1966 the House of Lords would not review its own previous decisions. However, in 1966 it announced in a Practice Statement that it would no longer regard itself as bound by its previous decisions. Nevertheless since then the House has been cautious in its approach to reviewing its previous decisions.

Position of lower courts

All other courts are bound by the decision of courts above them in the court hierarchy unless they can distinguish those decisions in some way. However, in some cases lower courts are also often bound by their own previous decisions (unless of course these have been overruled by higher courts). For example, in England and Wales, the Civil Division of the Court of Appeal is bound by decisions of the House of Lords and by its own previous decisions unless it can be shown that these previous decisions were arrived at by a lack of care. In Scotland, the Inner House of the Court of Session is bound to follow decisions of the House of Lords in Scottish cases and is likely to follow one of its own when in point. It will only depart from its own previous decisions if it has been overruled by the House of Lords or if a larger court is prepared to overrule the earlier decision, for example, when seven judges overrule a decision by five judges (e.g. *Reiley* v *Kingslaw Riding School* 1975 SC 28).

English precedents in the Scottish courts

The normal rule of law is that a decision of an English court is not binding upon the Scottish courts and vice versa. However, in areas where the applicable law is very similar in the two systems, for example, in relation to tort in England and Wales and delict in Scotland, or in relation to statutory systems which are common to both jurisdictions such as company law under the Companies Act 1985 or product liability law under the Consumer Protection Act 1987, it is very likely that a Scottish court would follow its English counterpart in construing the law and sometimes vice versa. For example, the famous tort/delict case *Donoghue* v *Stevenson* [1932] AC 562, HL; 1932 SC (HL) 31 is a Scottish House of Lords case but is regarded as a leading authority throughout the United Kingdom and indeed in many other parts of the world (see Chapter Two, pp. 57–58). Indeed, the higher the court from which a decision emanates, the more likely it is that it will be followed in Scotland.

Obiter statements

One word of caution should be mentioned in connection with reading judgments of court cases. The judge, in theory, only deals with the particular legal dispute between the parties and is not concerned with the wider problems of the common law or legislation. However, this does not prevent judges from giving their opinions on hypothetical situations which have not been brought for decision by them. These statements are referred to as *obiter dicta* or simply as *obiter* statements. They may well be of value in providing guidance on a particular issue but should be used cautiously. Indeed, the system of precedent only requires a later judge to follow the *ratio* or crux of previous decisions. Later judges are not bound to follow these extraneous statements.

STATUTORY INTERPRETATION

Introduction

On many occasions when disputes come before courts, the crucial issue is what a particular legislative provision actually means. The court must try to ascertain what Parliament's intention was when it passed the Act and so try to assign a meaning to a particular word or phrase or section or to resolve ambiguities in a statute. The normal approach of the courts is to interpret legislation strictly and literally unless it is absolutely necessary that they should not do so.

Statutory definitions

Meanings of some words are often given in the definition or interpretation provisions of statutes and statutory instruments. These may be exhaustive definitions as, for example: '"food source" *means* any growing crop or live animal, bird or fish from which food is intended to be derived (whether by harvesting, slaughtering, milking, collecting eggs or otherwise' (Food Safety Act 1990, s.1, emphasis added).

Alternatively, a definition may not be exhaustive but simply illustrative: '. . . building operations *include* – (a) demolition of buildings, (b) rebuilding, (c) structural alterations of or additions to buildings, and (d) other operations normally undertaken by a person carrying on business as a builder' (Town and Country Planning Act 1990, s.55(1A); Town and Country Planning (Scotland) Act 1997, s.26(4), emphasis added).

Statutory definitions may extend the normal meaning of a word as, for example: '"horse" includes ass or mule' (Animal Health Act 1981, s.89(1)). Alternatively they may restrict the ordinary meaning of a word: '"animal" means any creature other than a bird or fish' (Food Safety Act 1990, s.53(1)).

Definitions given in statutes often only apply in that statute or even one Part of it. Sometimes an Act will contain interpretation sections in each of its various parts which apply definitions in those parts alone in addition to a general interpretation section which applies to the whole Act. In some instances the same word may be defined in different ways in different parts of the same statute! For example, there are differing definitions of 'harm' in Parts I and IIA of the Environmental Protection Act 1990. Legislation will also on occasion define a word by reference to its definition in another statute, statutory instrument or piece of EC legislation. For example, '"conservancy" authority has the meaning given by section 221(1) of the 1991 Act [Water Resources Act 1991]' (Environment Act 1995, s.56(1)).

Guidance on many important and commonly used words such as 'land', 'month', 'person' and 'Secretary of State', may be found in the Interpretation Act 1978. These definitions apply unless the statute concerned contains its own applicable definition of that word in which case the definition in the 1978 Act does not apply.

Rules of statutory interpretation

Introduction

Over the years the courts have developed a number of rules of interpretation. These include the *eiusdem generis* rule, the literal rule, the golden rule and the mischief rule. Furthermore, the courts are more willing today to look at external aids which might assist in the interpretation of legislation.

Eiusdem generis rule

The *eiusdem generis* rule indicates that where there is a list of words – for example, '"development" means the carrying out of building, engineering, mining or other operations' (Town and Country Planning Act 1990, s.55(1); Town and Country Planning (Scotland) Act 1997, s.26(1)) – the meaning of the general word(s), 'other operations' appearing at the end of the list should be restricted to the context of the more specific words appearing first. Thus the court held in *R* v *Harris* (1836) 7 C & P 446, which involved the interpretation of the Offences Against the Person Act 1828 which made it a felony to shoot at or 'stab, cut or wound' a person, that the word wound had to be construed in the context of the preceding words which all involved injuries caused by an instrument and that therefore wounding did not extend to someone biting off another person's finger!

The literal rule

The literal rule involves giving words and phrases in legislation their literal meaning (e.g. *Black-Clawson International Ltd* v *Papierwerke Waldhof-Aschaffenburg AG* [1975] AC 591).

The golden rule

The golden rule involves the use of a literal interpretation except where this would lead to an absurdity (e.g. *Manson* v *Duke of Westminster* [1981] QB 323).

The mischief rule

Where legislation has been enacted to remedy a specific defect or mischief as is commonly the case, but where the application of literal interpretation would not lead to the remedying of the mischief in question, then the courts will apply this rule, which would involve applying an interpretation which would remedy the mischief. This involves looking at the legislative history of the statute including, for example, previous statutes on the same subject and Law Commission Reports indicating why law reform was necessary to try to ascertain what mischief it was designed to remedy. The mischief rule is an example, albeit on a small scale, of a purposive approach to interpretation.

The ECJ takes a purposive approach to legislation, and you should note that such an approach is common in Europe. EC legislation is prefaced by 'recitals' which indicate what its purpose is. The ECJ is also prepared to look at what is known in

France as *travaux preparatoires* or preparatory works in relation to the particular piece of legislation. Given that courts in Britain are required to adopt a purposive approach to the interpretation of EC law (and indeed international law), it is not surprising that this approach is also becoming more common in relation to domestic legislation.

A good example of a purposive approach to interpretation being applied in a case involving EC law is the Scottish House of Lords case, *Litster* v *Forth Dry Dock & Engineering Co. Ltd* [1990] 1 AC 546, which involved a company which became insolvent and went into receivership. The receiver agreed to sell the assets to another company. In order to try to avoid the provisions of the Transfer of Undertakings (Protection of Employment) Regulations 1981 which are designed to protect the rights of workers in such situations, the receiver dismissed the employees one hour before the assets were transferred, since the regulations purported to apply to persons 'so employed immediately before the transfer'. In these circumstances the House of Lords did not give these words their literal meaning which would have undermined the purpose of the regulations and EC Directive 77/187 which they purported to implement. Instead they looked at the purpose of the legislation, which was to protect the rights of employees in such transfers, and ECJ decisions which had held that where employees were dismissed in such circumstances they were to be treated as though they were still employed by the undertaking at the time of the transfer.

A purposive approach to interpretation is also adopted by the courts in relation to international treaties which have been incorporated into domestic law in the United Kingdom (e.g. *Fothergill* v *Monarch Airlines* [1981] AC 251).

Use of external aids

As our discussion above on the mischief rule demonstrated, the courts are also prepared to look at certain external aids to assist them in interpreting legislation. These include Law Commission reports and, in relation to EC law, *travaux preparatoires*. The courts will also look at dictionary meanings to define a word in a particular context.

However, until recently the British courts were not prepared to look at the publication known as Hansard, which contains a verbatim account of proceedings in Parliament, in order to determine the intended purpose or meaning of a particular legislative provision. This position was changed by the House of Lords' decision in *Pepper* v *Hart* [1992] 3 WLR 1032. The court held that in certain situations the courts are in fact able to consult Hansard to assist them in construing the meaning of a statute. Hansard may be consulted as an aid to interpretation of legislation which is obscure or ambiguous or whose literal meaning leads to absurdity. The use of Hansard was further limited by the court's view that it could not attach meanings to words which they were incapable of having; that importance could only be attached to clear statements in Hansard which showed the intention of the promoter of the Bill (which would normally be the relevant Government Minister); and that there could be no dredging through conflicting statements of intention with a view to discovering the true intention of Parliament. For an example of a situation where use of Hansard might be appropriate, see Chapter Four, p. 99.

JUDICIAL REVIEW

What is judicial review?

Given its importance across most areas of law, we consider that you should be introduced at this stage to the type of action known as judicial review. Judicial review is a method of challenging administrative decision making, principally by public authorities, as well as the validity of delegated legislation and soft law in the courts. It is not possible to challenge the validity of a statute of the UK Parliament by means of judicial review unless it conflicts with EC law (see p. 6).

Judicial review is not a method of appeal against the merits of a decision but is essentially a way of reviewing:

1. whether in taking the decision or making the delegated legislation or soft law the authority exceeded the powers given to it;
2. whether the decision, delegated legislation or soft law was reasonable; and
3. whether in taking the decision or in making the delegated legislation or soft law the authority followed the proper procedure.

Judicial review may also be used to secure the performance of a statutory duty which an authority is not performing. We consider this latter issue under the heading of illegality below.

If a person can exercise statutory appeal rights he/she would normally be expected to make use of those rights rather than resort to judicial review. It is normally only where such rights are not available that a person can make use judicial review.

The grounds of challenge

Introduction

The grounds of challenge are the same in Scotland, England and Wales and are limited to (1) illegality; (2) irrationality; and (3) procedural impropriety. These grounds are clearly discussed in *Council for Civil Service Unions* v *Minister for the Civil Service* [1984] 3 All ER 935, especially by Lord Diplock at pp. 949–951. That case involved the banning of trade union membership at Government Communications Headquarters (GCHQ), the Government's signal intelligence organization, without consultation on the basis of national security considerations. In the past the Government had always consulted unions at GCHQ about changes to their employment conditions but on this occasion they did not do so. The court held that this was a case where the unions had a legitimate expectation that they would be consulted and that this expectation had been breached by the Minister's decision. However, the House of Lords held the decision to be justified on the basis of national security considerations. Such a case would normally be brought before an industrial tribunal (see Chapter Six) but in this case, the jurisdiction of industrial tribunals to hear employment-related complaints by civil servants was excluded. Breach of a legitimate expectation is an example of procedural impropriety.

Illegality

This is the relevant ground of challenge where it is alleged that the authority took a decision which it was not within its powers to take. This is often known as acting *ultra vires,* that is outside one's powers, and sometimes as acting where there is a lack of jurisdiction. Any such decision which is challenged may be quashed by the courts. For example, decisions may be challenged as illegal on the basis that they do not conform to the relevant EC law. For example, in the environmental law case *R v National Rivers Authority, ex p. Moreton* [1996] Env LR 234, a regular user of a beach argued unsuccessfully that in granting a discharge consent for a sewage works near the beach, the National Rivers Authority (now part of the Environment Agency) had not followed the requirements of EC Directive 76/160/EEC on bathing water quality. However, in other cases such arguments have succeeded.

Furthermore, where delegated legislation or soft law has been made under a statutory power, a person may mount a challenge to the legality of the delegated legislation or soft law on the basis that it is *ultra vires,* that is, it exceeds what is permitted by the statutory power. In *Air 2000 v Secretary of State for Scotland (No.2)* 1990 SLT 335 the Secretary of State had made rules (a form of delegated legislation) for Glasgow, Prestwick and Edinburgh airports under a statutory power contained in s.31 of the Airports Act 1986. The rules forced transatlantic flights to stop at Prestwick. Air 2000 successfully challenged these rules as being *ultra vires* the statutory powers given to the Secretary of State in s.31 since they merely provided for the distribution of air traffic between the airports and did not give him a power to force certain types of flight to stop at a particular airport.

The case of *Laker Airways Ltd v Department of Trade* [1977] QB 643 which we discussed above at p. 11 is also relevant in this context. This case involved a successful challenge to soft law guidance issued under a statutory power which purported to change the objectives of the Act in question by giving British Airways a monopoly of the London–New York air route. The Secretary of State had acted *ultra vires.*

Under the heading of illegality we also consider the matter of enforcement of statutory duties. If an authority is under a duty to act and fails to do so, it is essentially acting unlawfully and judicial review may be used to force the authority to discharge its statutory duty. For example, in the environmental case *R v Carrick District Council, ex p. Shelley* [1996] Env LR 273, the pressure group Surfers Against Sewage (SAS) had complained to a local authority about the presence of sewage litter on a beach which they used for surfing. Under Part III of the Environmental Protection Act 1990 a local authority is under a duty to investigate its area for statutory nuisances and if it establishes that a nuisance exists it is under a further duty to serve an abatement notice on the person responsible for the sewage. The SAS argued that the sewage litter constituted a statutory nuisance. The local authority decided to do nothing. The SAS successfully judicially reviewed that decision. The court held that the SAS's complaint triggered the local authority's statutory duty. They had to investigate the issue to establish if the sewage litter did in fact constitute a statutory nuisance and, if they found that it did, they had to serve an abatement notice on the person responsible.

Irrationality

This ground is applicable where it is alleged that a decision is so unreasonable (i.e. perverse) that no reasonable authority would have taken it. This ground is sometimes known as *Wednesbury* unreasonableness after the case *Associated Provincial Picture Houses Ltd* v *Wednesbury Corporation* [1948] 1 KB 233 which involved a decision by a local authority to ban children under a certain age from going to the cinema on Sundays. On the basis of the considerations which are relevant to any decision, there will normally be a range of plausible decisions which it is reasonable for the authority to take. However, where the authority goes beyond the reasonable range of decisions, its decision may be quashed. This ground of challenge also includes taking into account irrelevant considerations or failure to take into account relevant considerations. For example, in the planning case *Trusthouse Forte (UK)* v *Perth and Kinross District Council* 1990 SLT 737, (see also Chapter Eight) multiple planning applications were made to develop a building which had been used as a store to a night-club and discotheque. The owners of an adjacent hotel, Trusthouse Forte, objected to the applications on the basis that the development would affect the amenity of the hotel. The second application, which had been refused, was appealed to the Secretary of State who appointed a reporter to determine the case. A public inquiry was held. At about the same time, when the reporter had not yet issued his decision on the appeal, a fifth and similar planning application was successfully made. Trusthouse Forte judicially reviewed the granting of that application in the Court of Session. They won their case because the local authority had acted unreasonably in granting the fifth application at a time when the appeal on the second application was at such an advanced stage. The outcome of the appeal was a relevant consideration which the local authority ought to have taken into account before reaching their decision on the fifth application. Their failure to take this factor into account meant that their decision was unreasonable.

Procedural impropriety

This ground is applicable where it is alleged that the procedure expressly laid down by statute was not followed, or that the rules of 'natural justice' (i.e. rule against bias and right to a fair hearing) have not been followed, or that a legitimate expectation has been flouted as happened in the *GCHQ* case (see above). Another example of a breach of legitimate expectation occurred in *R* v *Watford Borough Council, ex p. Incorporated West Hertfordshire Golf Club* [1990] 1 EGLR 263. In that case the local authority refused to renew the lease of a golf club because they wanted the club to provide for greater public access and had warned the club that unless this was offered, they might not renew their lease. The club argued that the local authority had made an express and unqualified promise of formal negotiations and thus they had a *legitimate expectation* that the local authority would negotiate with them to see if an agreement could be reached. The local authority argued that any such promise was conditional upon the club presenting improved proposals for greater public access. The court found that the club's legitimate expectation had been breached and quashed the local authority's decision.

Proportionality

You should also be aware that Lord Diplock in the *GCHQ* case (above) suggested that proportionality was another possible ground of challenge in judicial review cases. This would be applicable where a decision, or the action resulting from a decision, was disproportionate to the end which the decision maker was trying to achieve.

Remedies

A wide variety of remedies is available. For example, the court may quash the decision, regulations or soft law (known as *certiorari* in England and Wales; reduction in Scotland), prevent the application of a decision (injunction in England and Wales; interdict in Scotland), or order a body to do something positive (*mandamus* in England and Wales; specific implement or specific performance of statutory duty in Scotland). Damages are available in Scotland and may be available both south and north of the border in cases where an individual has suffered loss or injury as a result of the failure of the United Kingdom to implement an EC Directive or where it has implemented it inadequately.

When a decision or piece of delegated legislation or soft law is quashed, the authority will normally be required to take the decision again or make new regulations or soft law in the light of the judgment in the judicial review.

Procedure

Getting the court right

Judicial review actions must be commenced in the Divisional Court of the Queen's Bench Division of the High Court in England and Wales and in the Outer House of the Court of Session in Scotland.

Requirement to obtain leave in England and Wales

In England and Wales it is necessary for the applicant to obtain leave to bring judicial review proceedings. The requirement to obtain leave is designed to weed out frivolous applications and to ensure that the applicant has sufficient interest in the matter (known as 'standing') and that he/she has, on the face of it, a case to argue. In England and Wales, the courts have conceded the standing of a variety of interest groups to challenge decisions. These include Greenpeace, Friends of the Earth and the World Development Movement.

No requirement to obtain leave in Scotland

Although there is no formal requirement to obtain leave to bring judicial review proceedings in Scotland, nonetheless the court will consider whether the petitioner has title and interest (the Scottish equivalent of standing) and whether the petition has merit. The Scottish courts have taken a rather more restrictive view of standing than their English counterparts and it is not clear that an interest group such as Greenpeace would be able to challenge decisions in Scotland. The requirement to demonstrate interest is not simply a requirement to demonstrate a general public interest in the decision in question but a requirement to demonstrate that the decision somehow affects the applicant personally: *Scottish Old People's Welfare Council, Petitioners* 1987 SLT 179.

Delay

In both jurisdictions a person seeking to challenge a decision should not delay in bringing proceedings. South of the border the Rules of the Supreme Court provide that applications must be brought promptly and in any event within three months from when the grounds for the application first arose. This does not mean that the applicant has three months to commence proceedings; he/she may be refused leave even if the application is brought within three months if it was not brought promptly.

In Scotland the rules of court do not provide for any specific time limits. However, it is still clear that petitions for judicial review must be presented promptly otherwise the court may not be prepared to consider the merits of the petitioner's arguments. For example, in *Hanlon* v *Traffic Commissioner* 1988 SLT 1173, the petitioners delayed ten months before challenging a decision increasing taxi fares, by which time the new fare scale had already been implemented.

Principles of private law 2

INTRODUCTION

The distinction between public law and private law was considered in Chapter One (p. 14). We now consider the core principles of areas of private law relevant to the hospitality and tourism industries, particularly contract, agency and tort (in Scotland, delict). For reasons of space we have decided to exclude a discussion of property law although suggested reading on that subject is provided in the Select Bibliography.

Although the law of persons, another area of private law, which includes family matters such as marriage and divorce and the relationship between parents and children, is generally not of concern to us in this work, two issues from the law of persons are relevant here. First, it should be noted that a person may be an individual, a voluntary association, a partnership or a company. Whenever we refer to a person, it must be remembered that 'person' has this wide definition. Secondly, the law of persons is also relevant in so far as it relates to the issue of legal capacity, for example to enter into contracts. Certain persons are held by law to have limited capacity to contract by reason of their youth or mental capacity. We discuss this issue in more detail below in relation to the formation of contracts.

THE LAW OF CONTRACT

Introduction

Contracts are relevant right across the board in the hospitality and tourism industries. For example, a passenger has a contract with an airline for transporting him/her by aeroplane, a guest at a hotel has a contract with the hotel for accommodation and meals; the hotel may have a contract with a waste disposal company to remove its waste; and a holidaymaker has a contract with a tour operator for a package holiday. However, contracts may be much simpler even than this. For example, buying a magazine in a newsagent's involves a contract.

Contracts are essentially agreements which the courts will enforce. A contract need not be in writing although certain contracts including those involving the sale or purchase of land or buildings must be in writing to be valid. Contracts may also arise out of the actions of the parties where there is no writing or oral agreement. If the courts are asked to determine whether or not a contract exists they will apply an objective test and look at the words and actions of the parties, not at their alleged intentions. However, where a contract was formed orally, it will obviously be difficult to prove this if a dispute arises as to the existence of such a contract or its terms.

The law relating to contract is still substantially based on the common law although Parliament has passed a significant amount of legislation some of which is applicable to a very large number of contracts such as the Unfair Contract Terms Act 1977 (UCTA). Other legislation applies to specific types of contract which are sometimes complex such as the Consumer Credit Act 1974 which governs credit agreements and the Package Travel, Package Holidays and Package Tours Regulations 1992 which deal with package holiday contracts. However, there are basic rules which relate to all contracts which we discuss below. We consider the specific contractual rules relating to employment in Chapter Six; and to package holidays in Chapter Twelve. In this section we discuss, first, the requirements of a valid contract; second, contractual terms; third, the grounds for challenging the validity of a contract; fourth, the need for legality in contracts; fifth, privity of contract; and finally, when contracts come to an end.

Requirements of a valid contract

Introduction

As we mentioned above a contract is essentially an agreement which the law will enforce. There are various requirements for a contract to be recognized as legally valid. First, each party to the contract must have legal capacity to enter into the contract. Secondly, there must actually be an agreement, that is, a valid acceptance which meets a valid offer. Thirdly, the parties must intend to be legally bound. Fourthly, in England and Wales but not in Scotland there is also the requirement of consideration, that is, that one party will not undertake obligations without getting something in return. We consider these various requirements in more detail below.

Capacity

All persons over the age of 18 normally have the capacity to enter into a contract unless they are intoxicated or insane. Young people under the age of 18 in England and Wales, who are known as minors, are subject to common law and statutory restrictions on their capacity to enter into contracts. Under the common law minors may only enter into contracts for necessaries. Necessaries are defined as 'goods suitable to the condition in life of the minor . . . and to his actual requirements at the time of the sale and delivery' (Sale of Goods Act 1979, s.3(3)). This applies to contracts for the sale of goods but not to contracts for services such as booking a holiday although it is likely that the courts would make reference to that definition. We think it is unlikely, however, that the courts would take the view that a hotel or holiday booking was a necessary. The case *Nash* v *Inman* [1908] 2 KB 1 tends to support our view. In that case a court refused to enforce a contract for various items of clothing entered into by a wealthy undergraduate who already had sufficient clothing. The additional clothes were not necessaries. The Minors' Contracts Act 1987 contains certain statutory limitations on the contractual capacity of minors. It provides that a minor may be made liable to repay loans under agreements which he/she has entered into.

In Scotland the Age of Legal Capacity (Scotland) Act 1991 now contains the applicable law. This statute provides that persons over 16 have full contractual capacity except that if a person who is 16 or 17 enters into a contract it can be set aside by a court where it can be shown to be to his or her serious detriment. Persons under 16 are entitled to enter into contracts provided certain conditions are met. These are, first, that the transaction is of the sort which is commonly entered into by a person of that age and circumstances and, secondly, that the terms are reasonable. Such contracts are likely to include, for example, buying magazines or games, but are unlikely to include booking holidays. If these conditions are not met, the contract is a nullity.

An insane person is not legally bound by a contract if he or she is unable to understand the contract due to insanity and the other party is aware of this (*Molton* v *Camroux* (1849) 4 Exch 17). The same is true of a person who is so intoxicated as to be incapable of understanding the contract. In such cases the contract may be set aside by the insane or intoxicated person.

In England and Wales where the other party, that is, the sane or sober person, did not know and had no reason to suspect that the person was suffering from insanity or was intoxicated, the contract will be judged by the same standards as though it were between two persons of sound mind (*Hart* v *O'Connor* [1985] AC 1000). By way of contrast in Scotland, even if the party did not know and had no reason to suspect that the person was suffering from insanity, the contract would not be valid.

Agreement

For there to be an enforceable contract, there must be a valid offer which is met by a valid acceptance. Classified advertisements in newspapers and magazines together with other advertisements such as hotel or holiday brochures, displays of goods and price lists are generally not regarded as offers but as 'invitations to treat' or statements of willingness to negotiate. This is illustrated by the case *Partridge* v *Crittenden* [1968] 1 WLR 1204 in which a person was found not guilty of the offence of offering wild birds for sale, having advertised 'Bramblefinches, 25 shillings each' in a periodical. This was merely an invitation to treat, not an offer. The reason that advertisements are treated this way is because if an advertisement such as a hotel brochure or a shop display were regarded as an offer, anyone who presented the correct money to the hotelier or shopkeeper would be entitled to the accommodation or the article in question. If the hotel ran out of rooms or the shop ran out of such articles, it would be unable to perform its part of the bargain and would be potentially liable in damages for breach of contract to any person who made payment. Therefore to protect those advertising from such a situation, advertisements are not normally regarded as offers (*Grainger & Son* v *Gough* [1896] AC 325; *Fisher* v *Bell* [1961] 1 QB 394). In some cases, however, the language of the advertisement may be so specific that it cannot be anything other than an offer. This is best illustrated by the famous English case *Carlill* v *Carbolic Smokeball Co Ltd* [1893] 1 QB 256. In this case the Carbolic Smokeball Company placed an advertisement in a paper which stated that they would pay a sum of money to anyone who caught a number of specified illnesses including influenza after using one of their smokeballs for a certain period. They claimed to have deposited a sum with a bank to demonstrate their good faith. Mrs Carlill used a smokeball for the specified period but still caught influenza. She sued the Carbolic Smokeball Company and won. The court held that the advertisement went beyond an indication of the company's bargaining position and amounted to an offer. Generally, however, if someone sees a holiday advertised in a travel agency window, usually this is merely an invitation to treat and if the person goes inside to book a holiday, it is he/she who makes the offer and it is open to the travel agent to accept on behalf of the tour operator (on issues of agency, see pp. 54–56).

Offers may be made by a variety of methods, for example, orally in person or by telephone, or in writing by letter or fax or by e-mail. In all cases, however, for an offer to be valid, it must be sufficiently clear and certain otherwise it may be regarded simply as an invitation to treat in the same way that an advertisement normally is. The offer must also be communicated by the person making the offer (the 'offeror') to the person to whom the offer is addressed (the 'offeree') (*Thomson* v *James* (1855) 18 D 1). An offer may also be withdrawn at any time prior to the point at which it is accepted.

For a contract to come into existence, the acceptance must meet the terms set out in the offer and it must be communicated to the offeror. Where an unconditional acceptance meets an offer this is known in Latin as *consensus in idem*, that is, agreement on the same matters or a meeting of minds, and a contract is made. If the acceptance is qualified there will be no contract but a counter-offer which will be open for acceptance by the original offeror (*Gibson* v *Manchester City Council* [1979] 1 All ER 972, HL; *Wolf & Wolf* v *Forfar Potato Co. Ltd* 1984 SLT 100). The old English case *Hyde* v *Wrench* (1840) 3 Beav. 334 illustrates this point well. The defendant offered to sell his farm to the plaintiff for £1,000. The plaintiff responded with an offer of £950. The defendant rejected this. However, the plaintiff then purported to accept the original offer to buy the farm at £1,000. The court held that there was no contract here since the plaintiff's response to the original offer was a counter offer of £950. This counter offer was an implied rejection of the original offer which was accordingly no longer capable of being accepted.

The communication of the acceptance should be in the manner prescribed by the offer otherwise the acceptance may be invalid (*Howell Securities Ltd* v *Hughes* [1974] 1 WLR 155). If the offer does not indicate how acceptance should be made, then the acceptance should generally be made in the same manner as the offer. Where instantaneous communication such as telex, facsimile or e-mail is used the acceptance must actually be communicated to the offeror for the contract to be made (*Entores Ltd* v *Miles Far East Corporation* [1955] 2 All ER 493, CA; *Brinkibon Ltd* v *Stahag Stahl mbH* [1983] 2 AC 34, HL). However, there is an exception to this in the case of postal acceptances. Where the acceptance is made by post, it becomes effective and the contract is made at the time the letter of acceptance is posted, not when it is actually communicated to the offeror. The logical consequence of this is that even if the letter is lost, the contract has still been made (*Household Fire Insurance Co. Ltd* v *Grant* (1879) 4 Ex D 216) although evidence of the lost letter, such as a recorded delivery receipt, would be required. In Scotland a judge has doubted whether the Scottish courts would regard the contract as having been made where the acceptance was lost in the post (*Mason* v *Benhar Coal Co* (1882) 9 R 883).

One issue of which you should be aware is that in the tourism and hospitality industries there is often no opportunity to negotiate a contract because the holiday company or hotel operator uses a standard form contract, that is, the booking form and attached list of conditions which is often found at the end of a holiday or hotel brochure. The booking form amounts to an offer. However, if a person is unwilling to accept its terms there will be no contract, since the conditions are attached by the holiday or hotel company on a 'take it or leave it' basis. If two companies are seeking to contract using their respective standard form contracts, a 'battle of the forms' may take place. So, if one company's standard form contract is used as an offer and is met by another standard form contract, there is no contract. It is the person who sends the last standard form contract which is met by an acceptance by the other party whose contractual terms will prevail (*Butler Machine Tool Co* v *Ex-Cell-O Corporation* [1979] 1 All ER 965).

Intention to create legal relations

Despite what we said above, that agreement is necessary for there to be contract, it is not correct to say that all agreements are contracts. There are some agreements the courts will not enforce because they take the view that the parties did not intend to enter into legal relations with each other. Hence domestic agreements are not enforceable. For example, in *Balfour* v *Balfour* [1919] 2 KB 571, a husband who was posted abroad promised to pay a monthly allowance to his wife who remained behind because of ill health. The Court of Appeal held that he was not bound to pay this amount to his wife. Furthermore, the courts will not enforce social agreements such as an arrangement to share petrol costs where one person is giving another a lift to work (*Coward* v *Motor Insurers Bureau* [1963] 1 QB 259, CA). Collective agreements between trade unions and employers regarding rates of pay and conditions are not themselves legally binding at common law (*Ford Motor Co.* v *AUEFW* [1969] 2 All ER 481) and this is now reflected in statute. However, where such an agreement is incorporated into an individual's employment contract the provisions will be enforceable as part of that contract. Likewise gaming or gambling contracts are not regarded as giving rise to legal relations because the courts regard such matters as too trivial or frivolous to warrant judicial attention. So as the old Scottish case *Wordsworth* v *Pettigrew* (1799) Mor 9524 illustrates, if a person wins a bet they cannot enforce it against the loser or a bookmaker. Likewise football pools are regarded as binding in honour only so that a player may not recover winnings through the courts as the plaintiff attempted to do in *Jones* v *Vernon's Pools* [1938] 2 All ER 626.

Requirement of consideration

In England and Wales there is also a requirement for consideration before a contract will be valid. Each party must agree to provide or do something of value for the other party. English law will not enforce a promise, that is, a unilateral obligation undertaken by one party. So, for example, if a person wishes to stay in a room at a hotel, the consideration provided by the hotelier is the room, while the consideration provided by the guest is payment for that room. Interestingly the law does not require the consideration to be adequate, therefore contracts which involve 'a bargain' or leases involving what is called a 'peppercorn rent' (sometimes literally true!) are valid. An example of this is the House of Lords copyright case *Chappell & Co.* v *Nestle Co. Ltd* [1960] AC 87 in which used chocolate wrappers were part of the consideration towards the purchase of a record.

Although there are many similarities between contract law north and south of the border, one of the principal differences is that there is no requirement for consideration in Scotland. The result of this is that promises or unilateral obligations are enforceable in the Scottish courts. Therefore, if a person undertakes to keep open an offer to sell a property until a certain date, that is an enforceable obligation in Scotland (*Littlejohn* v *Hadwen* (1882) 20 SLR 5). Furthermore, if someone undertakes to pay a reward when a condition is fulfilled, the person fulfilling the condition is legally entitled to the reward in Scotland. For example, in *Petrie* v *Earl of Airlie* (1834) 13 S 68 following the appearance of a poster which accused the Earl of treason by not supporting the Reform Bill in Parliament which extended the voting franchise, he offered a reward for information leading to the detection of the author and printer. The reward was to be payable on conviction. Petrie gave the Earl the information which he was looking for. However, the public authorities declined to prosecute and the Earl did not launch a private prosecution. He refused to pay Petrie because there had been no conviction. However, Petrie successfully sued the Earl for the money. He won because he had fulfilled the condition stipulated by the reward, that is, the supply of information, and could not himself secure a conviction.

Once a promise has been made it cannot be revoked. For a promise to be enforceable in the courts in Scotland, the general rule is that it must be in writing and signed by the person undertaking the unilateral obligation (Requirements of Writing (Scotland) Act 1995). However, even though promises are enforceable north of the border, the Scottish courts still apply a general presumption in favour of analysing cases in terms of offer and acceptance where this is possible (*Malcolm* v *Campbell* (1891) 19 R 278).

Contractual terms

Express terms

The terms of the agreement reached between the parties are known as the express terms. In England and Wales, express terms are further divided into conditions and warranties. Conditions are the most important parts of the contract. If one of the parties is in breach of a condition, the injured party may cancel the contract and claim damages (*Poussard* v *Spiers and Pond* (1876) 1 QBD 410). However, if a warranty is breached this will only result in a claim for damages (*Bettini* v *Gye* (1876) 1 QB 183). Both of these cases involved opera singers who fell ill.

In Scotland no distinction is made between conditions and warranties. If there is a material, that is, a significant breach of the contract by one party, the injured party can cancel the contract (*Wade* v *Waldon* 1909 SC 571). This case involved a comedian who contracted to appear at two Glasgow theatres a year in advance. He failed to supply advertising material for his appearances as required by the contract and the management of the theatres cancelled his booking. He sued them for damages. However, they argued that his failure to supply advertising material was a serious breach of contract entitling them to rescind, that is, cancel the contract. The court did not agree, holding that the failure to supply the advertising material was not a material breach of contract. By refusing to allow the comedian to appear the management had given him a claim for damages against them. Where there is not a material breach, the only remedy is damages.

Implied terms

Certain terms of contracts are so obvious that they are not expressed by the parties. These are known as implied terms (*Shirlaw* v *Southern Foundries (1926) Ltd* [1939] 2 KB 206, CA). For example, if a person books a night in a hotel at a certain price, it is clearly an implied term that the hotel will provide a room and the room will have a bed in it. *The Moorcock* (1889) 14 PD 64 provides a maritime example. In this case wharf owners agreed to allow a vessel to berth at their wharf in consideration of charges for landing and stowing her cargo. However, at low tide the vessel grounded on a hard ridge on the bed of the river and was damaged. The Court of Appeal held that it was an implied term of the contract that the wharf owners should take reasonable care to ensure that the river bottom was not in such a condition as to endanger vessels.

Exclusion and exemption clauses

A person can seek to exclude their liability under contract by inserting an exclusion clause or to exempt themselves in certain circumstances (exemption clause) or to limit liability (limitation clause). In the case of exclusion or exemption clauses in particular this can result in considerable injustice. For example, in the Scottish case *McKay* v *Scottish Airways* 1948 SC 254 the pursuers sought damages against an airline because one of their relatives had been killed in a crash caused by the airline's negligence. The action failed because of an exemption clause in the contract of carriage which exempted the airline from liability for breach of contract for failing to carry a passenger safely as well as exempting the company from its duty to pay damages for harm caused by its negligence. Although such clauses may be negotiable in some cases, in the tourism and hospitality industries there are many cases in which there is no such opportunity because one party uses standard form contracts and the only choice which the other party has is whether to enter the contract or not. Historically the courts have sought to control the use of such clauses at common law. There has now, however, been extensive statutory intervention: the Unfair Contract Terms Act 1977 and, more recently, the Unfair Terms in Contracts Regulations 1994 which implement the EC Directive on Unfair Terms in Consumer Contracts (93/13/EEC). We consider the courts' approach at common law first and then discuss the statutory protection now offered and the relationship between the two.

The courts' approach has been to uphold only those clauses which are incorporated into the contract and which, on a strict construction, actually apply to the situation in question. Signing a document containing the clause in question is evidence that it has been incorporated into the contract even if the clause is legible but in small print (*L'Estrange* v *Graucob* [1934] 2 KB 394). However, the clause may not appear on any document: it might appear on a notice or it might be referred to on a ticket. How then can such terms be incorporated? Essentially where reasonable notice is given of the clause it will be incorporated into the contract. For example, tickets for carriage by rail, air, bus, or sea are usually issued subject to the carrier's terms and conditions which may include exclusion, exemption or limitation clauses. These clauses do not usually appear on the tickets themselves but the tickets will refer to the conditions which may be found in the carrier's standard terms and conditions, which will normally be found in another document. Passengers are bound by these terms even if they did not read them if they were clearly referred to on the ticket although they must be of a kind which could reasonably be expected to apply to such a contract of carriage (*Morris* v *Clan Line* 1925 SLT 321). The fact that the courts have held that there is no requirement for actual notice but only for reasonable notice has on occasion resulted in considerable injustice. For example, in *Thompson* v *London Midland & Scottish Railway* [1930] 1 KB 41, Mrs Thompson was injured alighting from a train because of the LMS's negligence. Mrs Thompson could not read and the ticket was bought for her by a relative. Despite this her claim did not succeed because an exemption clause found on p. 552 of a separate timetable which cost 6d was held to apply! The court took the view that the issue of a railway ticket ought to indicate to a reasonable person that there were conditions attached to it.

However, the law does not always operate so unjustly. Two examples from the tourism and hospitality industries will suffice. In *Chapelton* v *Barry UDC* [1940] 1 KB 532 a person hired two deck chairs from the council. In return he received a ticket which purported to exempt the council from liability for injury caused by deck chairs. However, this condition did not appear on a notice which was posted by the stack of chairs on the beach. The plaintiff was injured because of defective canvas on the chair. The court held the condition to be ineffective as the ticket was merely a voucher or receipt for payment not a contractual document. The notice by the stack of chairs was the offer which was accepted when the plaintiff hired the chairs and the notice did not contain the condition. In *Olley* v *Marlborough Court Ltd* [1949] 1 KB 532 furs were stolen from a guest's hotel bedroom, after the door was locked. On one of the room's walls was a notice purporting to exclude the hotel from liability. When the guest sued the hotel the court decided that the notice had not been incorporated into the contract since the contract was in fact made at reception before the guest was shown the room. This case raises issues of innkeeper's liability which we examine in more detail in Chapter Nine.

However, where there has been a previous course of dealings between the parties, that might be sufficient to incorporate a clause into a contract. For example, if the guest in *Olley* had stayed at the hotel on several previous occasions, the court might well have held that the exclusion clause was incorporated into the contract. It depends on the circumstances what will actually constitute a previous course of dealings but three or four transactions in a five year period is unlikely to be sufficient (*Hollier* v *Rambler Motors* [1972] 2 QB 71).

The courts will also construe the term strictly to make sure it really does cover the situation in question. The general rule is that such clauses are construed *contra proferentem*, that is, against the person seeking to rely on the clause to exclude liability for negligence. For such clauses to succeed they must use express language to exclude liability for negligence or, if they do not, the words they do use must be considered in their ordinary meaning, to establish if they are wide enough to cover negligence and, if they are, then liability for negligence will not be excluded if liability on some other ground than negligence can also be established (*Smith* v *South Wales Switchgear Ltd* [1978] 1 WLR 165). However, the courts will not judge limitation clauses by the same exacting standards. This point is illustrated by the Scottish case *Ailsa Craig Fishing Co.* v *Malvern Fishing Co.* 1982 SLT 377. In this case two fishing boats were tied up together in a harbour at New Year. When the tide came in, the bow of one boat was caught under the pier and it sank. Since it was tied up to the other boat, it too sank. Securicor Ltd had been contracted to patrol the harbour to provide against such an eventuality but their employees were apparently celebrating New Year and the incident was not discovered until it was too late. Securicor relied upon a clause in its contract which limited its liability to £1,000 in respect of any one claim and £10,000 in respect of total claims arising out of any single incident. The House of Lords held the clause to be effective and commented that such clauses were not regarded with such hostility as those which sought to exclude liability.

Limitation clauses in relation to claims for death, personal injury and loss or damage to luggage are very common in the tourism and hospitality industries. For example, carriers, such as airlines, shipping operators and railway operators, normally seek to limit their liability. These limitation clauses have been agreed at an international level as part of the international regulation of civil aviation, shipping, road and rail travel by the Warsaw Convention for the Unification of Certain Rules Regarding Air Transport 1929 (as amended), the Athens Convention relating to the Carriage of Passengers and Their Luggage by Sea 1974, the Convention for the International Carriage of Passengers and Luggage by Rail 1961 and the International Convention for the Carriage of Passengers and Luggage by Road 1974 respectively. It is arguably fair to allow a carrier to place limits on its liability, especially when such limits are internationally agreed, since unlimited liability might lead to the carrier having difficulty in obtaining the necessary insurance coverage to meet any liabilities for personal injury or death or loss or damage to luggage caused by its negligence. Any such clauses are of course still subject to the statutory controls on unfair contract terms which we discuss below.

However, despite the approach adopted by the courts, the potential unfairness of exclusion, exemption and, to a lesser extent, limitation clauses remained all too apparent. Parliament eventually sought to regulate such clauses through the Unfair Contract Terms Act 1977 (UCTA) which has now been supplemented by the Unfair Terms in Consumer Contracts Regulations 1994. UCTA was designed principally as a form of consumer protection legislation. It covers contracts for the sale and supply of goods, employment contracts and contracts for services (UCTA, s.15). It would therefore cover contracts for hotel accommodation, to attend an opera, to book a holiday but it does not apply to insurance contracts or contracts relating to the formation or dissolution of a company or partnership. You should also be aware that it only applies to the attempted exclusion of liability by businesses which is widely defined to include companies, partnerships, sole traders and government bodies (UCTA, s.25(1)). However, UCTA does not apply to attempted exclusion of liability by individuals acting in a personal capacity. Where UCTA does not apply the common law continues to apply. However, even where UCTA does apply the common law rules are still used to determine whether the clause in question has been incorporated into the contract and whether it actually applies to the situation in question.

UCTA makes certain clauses void although it does not prohibit the insertion of such clauses into contracts in the first place. These include clauses which attempt to exclude or restrict liability for death or personal injury caused by reason of negligence (UCTA, s.16). This means that the clause which the airline successfully relied upon in *McKay* v *Scottish Airlines* (see above) would be void if it were included in such a contract today. As regards exclusion or restriction of liability for other forms of harm, that is, property damage or financial loss, UCTA does not make the clause void but subjects it to a 'fair and reasonable' test. We discuss this below.

Not all breaches of contract arise as a result of negligence. A party may simply not perform its side of the bargain or not do so in time and seek to avoid liability by relying on a clause designed to exclude liability for such an eventuality. UCTA does not make such clauses void but once again subjects them to a 'fair and reasonable' test (UCTA, s.17). This provision applies both to clauses in consumer contracts, that is, where one party deals as a business and the other does not hold themselves out as acting in the course of a business, and to standard form contracts, which may obviously be used in contracts between businesses.

In what circumstances, then, will such a clause be 'fair and reasonable'? In applying the test UCTA provides that regard must be had to the circumstances which were or reasonably ought to have been in the contemplation of the parties at the time the contract was made. Where a term purports to restrict liability to a particular sum of money, regard is to be had in particular to (a) the resources which the party seeking to rely on that term could expect to be available to them for the purpose of meeting the liability should it arise; and (b) how far it was open to that party to cover themselves by insurance (UCTA, Sch. 2). The onus of proving that it was fair and reasonable to incorporate a term lies on the party relying on it. Given the doctrine of supremacy of EC law, it is actually likely that the test of unfairness in relation to such clauses in consumer contracts which is found in the Unfair Terms in Consumer Contracts Regulations 1994, which we discuss below, has now in fact supplanted the 'fair and reasonable' test in UCTA in relation to consumer contracts.

The EC has also legislated in this field in the Directive on Unfair Terms in Consumer Contracts (93/13/EEC). This has been implemented in the UK by the Unfair Terms in Consumer Contracts Regulations 1994 and provides protection over and above that provided by UCTA. It applies to contracts for the sale of goods and for the sale and supply of services. It does not apply to employment contracts. Furthermore, it does not apply to core terms of a contract but it does extend to non-contractual notices. The onus of proving that a term was individually negotiated lies with the seller or supplier. A term will be treated as being unfair where it causes a significant imbalance between the rights and obligations of the contracting parties. Such a term is declared to be contrary to the requirement of good faith. In assessing good faith the following factors are relevant:

1. the respective strength of the parties' bargaining positions;
2. any inducement given to the consumer to secure his/her consent to the term;
3. whether the goods or services were made or supplied to the consumer's special order;
4. the extent to which the consumer was dealt with fairly.

In assessing fairness the nature of the goods or services must be taken into account and fairness must be assessed taking into account the circumstances at the time the contract was made. A non-exhaustive list of terms which may be unfair is set out in the Regulations. These include terms which seek to exclude or limit liability for death or personal injury, terms which enable a seller or supplier to vary unilaterally a contract's terms without having to specify a reason for doing so and terms which oblige the consumer to perform his/her part of the bargain but do not impose a similar obligation on the seller or supplier.

If a term is found to be unfair it is unenforceable against the consumer but the contract will continue to exist if it can exist without the term in question. A duty is imposed on sellers and suppliers to put their contracts into 'plain, intelligible language' and where there is doubt about the meaning of the contract it will be construed against the person seeking to rely on it. The Director General of Fair Trading is empowered to seek an injunction (in Scotland, an interdict) against the continued use of an unfair term in a consumer contract where a complaint has been made.

Grounds for challenging validity of contract

Introduction

There are various grounds on which a contract can be set aside. If a contract has been entered into on the basis of misrepresentation or a mistake (known as error in Scotland) or was made under duress (known as force and fear in Scotland) or undue influence or in addition, in Scotland only, facility and circumvention, it may be set aside.

Misrepresentation

An actionable representation is a false statement of fact made by one party to another which induces that party to enter into a contract. What amounts to a misrepresentation? A statement of opinion does not. This is illustrated by *Bisset* v *Wilkinson* [1927] AC 177, PC in which a farm owner stated to a prospective purchaser that he believed the farm would support 2000 sheep although it had not previously been used as a sheep farm. Moreover, a 'trade puff' will not amount to a misrepresentation as the old Scottish case *Bile Bean Manufacturing Co.* v *Davidson* (1906) 8 F 1181 shows. Silence cannot generally amount to a misrepresentation (*Fox* v *MacKreath* (1788) 2 Cox Eq Cas 320) although in certain contracts such as insurance contracts where there is a positive duty of disclosure, silence may amount to a misrepresentation (*The Spathari* 1925 SC (HL) 6). The presence of misrepresentation makes a contract voidable, that is, valid until set aside. A good example of a successful negligent misrepresentation case is *Esso Petroleum* v *Mardon* [1976] QB 801 in which Esso were held liable to a tenant of a petrol station. An experienced Esso employee had induced the contract by negligently misrepresenting the throughput of petrol expected at the filling station. Originally, damages were only available in the case of fraudulent misrepresentations while in the case of negligent misrepresentations the only remedy was to withdraw from the contract. However, as a result of legislation, damages are now also available both north and south of the border in cases of negligent misrepresentation.

Mistake

In certain circumstances a contract may be void on the ground of mistake (known in Scotland as error). This ground of challenge is less common today than it once was since the courts take an objective view of whether or not a contract exists looking at the words and actions of the parties rather than a subjective approach, looking at the parties' intentions. The objective approach is preferable on commercial grounds. People should be bound by what they say not what they think and they should not be able to get out of their obligations simply because they have made a mistake. As the importance of mistake as a ground of challenge has decreased, so that of misrepresentation has increased. Misrepresentation after all is induced mistake which is objectively ascertainable since it results from representations made by one party to another inducing that party to enter a contract and is not concerned with intentions (see above).

There are various types of mistake or error which we can identify. They include a unilateral mistake where one party is mistaken as to some aspect of the contract, a common mistake where both parties make the same mistake and mutual mistake where the parties misapprehend each other's intentions.

An example of a unilateral mistake is provided by *Hartog v Colin & Shields* [1939] 3 All ER 566). In this case the defendants had intended to offer goods to the plaintiff at a certain price per piece. However, in fact they offered them at the same price per pound. The value of a piece was one third that of a pound. The court held that the contract was void since the plaintiffs must have realized the defendants' mistake. Essentially the plaintiffs had sought to take advantage of the defendants' mistake. The Scottish courts have recently refused to grant relief in circumstances where a seller of land believed the land to be subject to a 999 year lease when in fact the land was subject to a more valuable 99 year lease (*Spook Erection (Northern) Ltd v Kaye* 1990 SLT 676). The buyers knew this but the court would not hold the contract void. The sellers ought to have known what they were selling. We think that this is a good decision on commercial grounds since anyone who purchased a bargain might otherwise find themselves facing a legal challenge on the basis that the seller did not realize the true value of what he/she was selling.

Couturier v Hastie (1856) 5 HL Cas 673 provides us with an example of common error. In this case the parties agreed a contract of sale of a cargo of grain which was en route to London. However, neither party knew that the grain had begun to ferment and had to be sold at a port en route. The court held that there was no contract since the subject matter of the sale no longer existed.

A good example of mutual mistake is *Raffles v Wichelhaus* (1864) 2 H & C 906 in which grain was to be transported on a ship called the *Peerless* from Bombay to England. However, there were in fact two ships called *Peerless* sailing from Bombay to England, the first in a few months before the second. The parties did not realize this and the buyer thought the grain was to go on the first *Peerless* while the seller thought it was going on the second *Peerless*. The court held that there was no contract since the parties had misapprehended each other's intentions. However, an objective analysis would have reached the same conclusion: the parties had not reached *consensus in idem*, a meeting of minds, on the key issues and so there was no contract.

Mistakes will be actionable when they relate to essential features of the contract such as its subject matter (as in *Couturier* above) or the identity of the parties, or the price (as in *Hartog* above), or the nature of the contract. *Stewart v Kennedy* (1890) 17 R (HL) 25 demonstrates that the position in Scotland is broadly similar.

Duress and undue influence

The agreement must be voluntary in the sense that it was not entered into in England and Wales as a result of duress (known as force and fear in Scotland), undue influence, or in addition in Scotland only, as a result of facility and circumvention. Where such pressure is present the contract is rendered voidable. Violence either actual or threatened is a clear example of duress (*Cumming* v *Ince* (1847) 11 QB 112). The early Scottish case *Earl of Orkney* v *Vinfra* (1606) Mor 16481 illustrates the point rather dramatically. The Earl sued Vinfra for a sum which he claimed Vinfra owed him under a deed which he had signed. However, the court held that the contract was not valid since the Earl had forced Vinfra to sign, putting his hand on his sword and threatening to kill him if he refused! However, threats need not be of violence. The essence of the plea is coercion of the will, for example, by threatening a hotel proprietor with having her hotel burned down. Economic threats may amount to duress as in *North Ocean Shipping Co. Ltd* v *Hyundai Construction Co. Ltd* [1979] QB 705 in which a shipbuilder demanded 10 per cent more than the agreed price in order to complete a supertanker. The court held that the extra payment could be recovered on the ground of economic duress.

Contracts may also be set aside where undue influence has been brought to bear by one party on another. In England and Wales this doctrine has developed out of equity to cover situations where a plea of duress would be inappropriate. Undue influence is primarily relevant in cases where there is a special fiduciary relationship, that is, a relationship involving trust between the parties, such as parent and child, trustee and beneficiary, doctor and patient and solicitor and client. The House of Lords has held that a presumption of undue influence will arise where there is a fiduciary relationship with a dominant party and the contract in question must be disadvantageous to the weaker party in the relationship (*National Westminster Bank plc* v *Morgan* [1985] AC 686). A presumption of undue influence has even been held to arise between a banker and a farmer who gave the bank a guarantee in respect of his son's overdraft which was secured over his farmhouse (*Lloyds Bank Ltd* v *Bundy* [1975] QB 326). Although such a presumption would not normally arise between a bank and client, it did so here since the farmer placed himself entirely in the hands of the bank and was given no opportunity to seek independent advice. The position in Scotland is similar. In the leading case *Gray* v *Binny* (1879) 7 R 332 a young man sold his inheritance rights for an inadequate amount on the advice of his mother and the family solicitor. The court held that the contract was voidable if he could show that he had entered into it as a result of the advice given. The Scottish courts have held that it is always a question of fact whether a relationship involving authority and trust exists in any given circumstances: such relationships are not confined to the usual categories such as parent and child (*Honeyman's Executors* v *Sharp* 1978 SC 223). The English decision in *Lloyds Bank Ltd* v *Bundy* (above) appears to confirm that this is the position south of the border also.

In addition, in Scotland a contract is voidable if one of the parties can establish facility and circumvention. This involves establishing that a weakminded, that is, facile, person has had the contract unfairly imposed upon them, that is, there has been circumvention, and that they have suffered loss as a result. If the person is insane rather than weakminded, then they would have lacked capacity to enter into a contract at all and there would be no contract (see p. 39). *Mackay* v *Campbell* 1967 SC (HL) 53 establishes that a person who is ill in hospital is not facile for that reason alone. However, *MacGilvary* v *Gilmartin* 1986 SLT 89 suggests that a recently bereaved widow might be in a facile state.

Illegal contracts will not be enforced

As we have seen the courts will not enforce contracts where there is no intention to create legal relations. It is also the case that the courts will not enforce illegal contracts. An illegal contract may be one which is prohibited by statute or one which the courts declare illegal at common law as being contrary to public policy. An example of the former is *Re Mahmoud and Ispahani* [1921] 2 KB 716, CA. In that case the buying or selling of linseed without a licence was declared illegal by legislation. An innocent seller was unable to recover from a defendant buyer who had fraudulently stated that he had a licence: the contract was simply forbidden. However, where the illegality which occurs is incidental to the performance of the contract, the contract may not be illegal at all. Therefore in *St John Shipping Corporation* v *Joseph Rank Ltd* [1957] 1 QB 267 a contract was agreed for the carriage of grain from the USA to Britain. The master of the ship overloaded the ship contrary to maritime safety legislation and was fined for the offence. The charterer of the ship refused to pay part of the shipping costs arguing that it should not be bound when the cargo had been put at risk. When the shipowners brought an action for recovery of these sums, the charterers argued that the contract was illegal. However, the court held that the maritime safety legislation was directed at preventing overloading not at prohibiting contracts. The fact the performance of the contract had been illegal did not prevent the shipowners from recovering the sums due to them.

The courts will also declare certain contracts to be unlawful because they are contrary to public policy as they are somehow injurious to society. For example, an agreement to commit a criminal offence such as fraud which might itself amount to a criminal conspiracy is contrary to public policy. An early example of this is *Everet* v *Williams* (1725) 36 Digest (Repl) 581 which involved an agreement by two highwaymen to ambush a coach which the courts unsurprisingly refused to enforce. Moreover the courts regard contracts involving trading with an enemy during wartime as being illegal because such contracts are obviously prejudicial to public safety.

Contracts which are designed to promote sexual immorality are also regarded as contrary to public policy. You can find an excellent example of this in the old Scottish case *Hamilton* v *Main* (1823) 2 S 356. Hamilton had given the landlord of a public house a promissory note for £60 to cover a seven day stay at Main's public house with a prostitute during which time they consumed 113 bottles of port and Madeira and a large quantity of spirits. The court declined to enforce the promissory note, presumably to deter publicans from promoting such sexual immorality and debauchery as this!

Moreover the courts will not enforce contracts involving bribery. A lesson for those hoping to obtain a licence for a public house may be found in the Scottish case *Barr* v *Crawford* 1983 SLT 481. In this case the licensee died and his wife wanted to take over the licence. However, she was advised that her chances of taking over the licence were not good but that if she made various payments to two individuals, the district licensing board would transfer the licence to her. The board did not transfer the licence to her and she tried to recover the money she had paid but the court held that the payments were a bribe and the transaction was illegal. We consider the proper way to obtain a licence in Chapter Eleven.

In the case of contracts which are illegal as formed the general rule is that it is void and neither party to it can sue upon it. The justice of this approach is readily apparent in cases such as *Barr* v *Crawford* where the parties were equally blameworthy. The approach of the courts in such cases is simply to allow any loss to lie where it falls. However, there may be certain contracts, which are not illegal as formed but illegal in the manner in which they are performed, where the parties are not equally blameworthy. *Archbold's (Freightage) Ltd* v *Spanglett Ltd* [1961] 1 QB 374 involved such an illegality in the manner of performance. In this case whisky was to be transported in the defendants' lorry. However, the lorry was not licensed to carry whisky as required by legislation. This was not known to the plaintiffs. During transit the whisky was stolen and the plaintiffs sued for the value of the whisky. The defendants argued that since the contract was illegal the plaintiffs should not be allowed to recover. However, the Court of Appeal held that the plaintiffs were entitled to recover the value of the whisky as it was only the manner in which the contract was performed which was illegal rather than the making of the contract itself. Therefore in such cases the innocent party may be able to sue upon the contract.

Another important area in this context is the restrictive covenant commonly found in employment contracts, partnership agreements and in sales of businesses. Such covenants are contractual clauses which, for example, might prevent an employee from working in competition with their current employers in a certain area and for a certain period after terminating their current employment. The general rule is that such covenants are void and unenforceable because the courts are reluctant to allow interference with a person's right to earn a living and to permit restrictions on competition. However, such covenants may not always be against the public interest and the courts will uphold them where they are reasonable between the parties and in the public interest. The covenant must also be no more than is required to protect the legitimate interests of the person seeking to enforce it. In employment cases legitimate interests which employers may protect are trade secrets or trade connections. Trade secrets might comprise price and customer lists but will not normally include an employer's scheme of organization and method of business (*Commercial Plastics Ltd* v *Vincent* [1964] 3 All ER 546). An employer is also entitled to preserve trade connections by, for example, preventing an ex-employee from poaching clients. In the Scottish case *Scottish Farmers Dairy Co (Glasgow) Ltd* v *McGhee* 1933 SC 148 a covenant preventing a milkman from competing with his employers for two years within a one mile radius of their place of business was upheld as he would otherwise be able to take advantage of his position in relation to the customers of his former employers since he was their only contact with the customer. However, it is not legitimate for employers to use such covenants to protect themselves from competition alone. In assessing whether the party seeking to enforce the covenant is not going beyond what is necessary to protect legitimate interests the courts consider factors including the spatial extent and the temporal extent of the covenant. What is an acceptable restriction depends to a great extent on the nature of the business. The Scottish courts upheld a two year worldwide restriction in relation to the jeans industry in *Bluebell Apparel* v *Dickson* 1978 SC 16 (involving the manufacture of Wrangler jeans) given the worldwide nature of jeans manufacture involving a tiny number of companies. However, where a market is local in nature with a large number of businesses competing, only much narrower spatial restrictions will be upheld (*Mason* v *Provident Clothing Co. Ltd* [1913] AC 724).

Where a business is sold, one part of the business will be its 'goodwill'. Restrictive covenants are included in contracts for the sale of a business preventing the seller from setting up in competition with the buyer. If it were otherwise the seller could simply start up in the same business again and, relying on the goodwill of the previous business, attract all the former customers back. The goodwill sold to the purchaser would therefore be valueless. While the courts often uphold covenants in such circumstances they will not do so when the restriction is wider than necessary. In *British Reinforced Concrete Co.* v *Schleff* [1921] 2 Ch 563 the plaintiffs made and sold a type of road reinforcement. They purchased the business of the defendants who sold, but did not make, another type of road reinforcement. The defendants covenanted not to compete in the making or selling of road reinforcements in the UK for a certain period. This covenant was held to go beyond what was necessary since it covered not only sale but also manufacture.

Restrictive covenants are also a feature of partnership agreements. You can find an example of such a clause being upheld in the Hong Kong case *Deacons* v *Bridge* [1984] 2 All ER 19 which involved a solicitors' firm. The clause, which prevented the partner from working as a solicitor in Hong Kong for a certain period after he left the partnership, went far beyond what was necessary to protect the firm's interest because the firm was departmentalized and the partner therefore only had knowledge of and contact with a certain number of clients in relation to a particular area of law. However, the court still upheld the clause because of the public interest in facilitating new partners in firms. If a partner was not to be bound by such a provision, it would deter firms from taking on new partners because after the partner had established himself in the firm, he might leave and take his clients with him. However, in Scotland, a covenant which prevented a partner in a firm of solicitors from practising as a solicitor within twenty miles of a spot in central Glasgow was held to be too wide since it probably prevented him from working in about half the solicitors' firms in Scotland (*Dallas, McMillan & Sinclair* v *Simpson* 1989 SLT 454). A much narrower spatial restriction would probably have been acceptable.

The courts are prepared to sever the offending parts of restrictive covenants from contracts (*Carney* v *Herbert* [1985] AC 301). The courts apply what is known as the 'blue pencil test': they will strike out the offending parts of the clause but they will not add new words. What remains after the blue pencil has been applied must make sense.

Privity of contract

In English law the privity of contract is a cardinal rule. This means that it is only the parties to the contract who may enforce it in the courts. However, in the context of holiday cases, there is a partial exception to this very important rule. Since a person may book a holiday for the benefit of their family, the Court of Appeal has held it is possible for a person dissatisfied with a holiday at common law to claim damages for distress suffered by their family as well as themselves although because of the doctrine of privity of contract no one but the person who booked the holiday may sue in court (*Jackson* v *Horizon Holidays* [1975] 3 All ER 92, CA). Another important exception to the rule is when contracts are negotiated by agents (this is discussed on pp. 54–56).

The position at common law in Scotland is very different. North of the border third parties intended to benefit from the contract, do have the right to sue on the contract if there is an express provision in their favour (*Carmichael* v *Carmichael's Executor* 1920 SC (HL) 195).

In the case of package holidays, the position in both jurisdictions has now been modified by the Package Travel, Package Holidays and Package Tours Regulations 1992. The definition of 'consumer' in those regulations includes persons for whose benefit a package was purchased by someone else. Such people are therefore entitled to sue on the package holiday contract just as much as those who paid for it. This is a significant modification of the doctrine of privity of contract and we discuss it further in Chapter Twelve (see p. 288).

Termination of contracts

Introduction

Contracts may come to an end as a result of satisfactory performance, by reason of certain breaches of contract or by what is known as frustration.

Performance

Normally a contract will come to an end when it is performed satisfactorily, for example when holiday transport and accommodation is provided in terms of the contract by a tour operator and the holidaymaker pays the price of the package.

Breach of contract

As we noted above in our discussion of contractual terms, it is only the breach of a term which is regarded as a condition in England and Wales which will justify termination of the contract. In Scotland it is a material breach of contract which will justify termination of the contract. However, a party is not bound to terminate the contract: he/she may indeed affirm the contract.

Frustration

Contracts may also come to an end as a result of what is known as frustration. Frustration of a contract occurs when an event renders the performance of the contract impossible or illegal. For a contract to be frustrated essentially the event causing frustration must be unforeseeable and neither party must be at fault. For example, in *Taylor* v *Caldwell* (1863) 3 B & S 826 the music hall which the plaintiff had agreed to hire from the defendant for the purpose of holding concerts was destroyed by fire before the date of the first concert. In such circumstances the court held that the parties were discharged from their obligations because the contract had been frustrated. However, where performance of a contract has merely been made more onerous, it will not be frustrated as *Tsakiroglou & Co. Ltd* v *Noblee Thorl GmbH* [1962] AC 93 illustrates. In that case the closure of the Suez Canal did not make a contract to carry freight to Britain by ship impossible but simply required the ship to proceed via the Cape of Good Hope. A change in the law or the outbreak of war may frustrate a contract by making its performance illegal. An example of the outbreak of war frustrating a contract is the Scottish House of Lords case *Cantiere San Rocco SA* v *Clyde Shipbuilding & Engineering Co.* [1923] AC 226 which involved a contract between an Austro-Hungarian company and a Scottish company to supply marine engines.

Frustration may also occur when an intervening event means further performance of the contract would remain possible but would be something radically different to what was envisaged. For example, in *Krell* v *Henry* [1903] 2 KB 740 rooms were hired in London overlooking Pall Mall to view King Edward VII's coronation procession. However, the coronation was postponed because the King was ill. The court held that the contract was frustrated since viewing the procession was the essence of the contract. However, in *Herne Bay Steamboat Co.* v *Hutton* [1903] 2 KB 683, a contract to hire a boat to see King Edward's review of the fleet at Spithead as part of his coronation celebrations was not frustrated by reason of the King's absence due to illness since the fleet was present and could still be viewed.

THE LAW OF AGENCY

Nature of agency

Agency describes the relationship when one person (the agent) is appointed by another (the principal) to enter into contracts with third parties on the principal's behalf, normally for a commission. This is one of the biggest exceptions to the rule regarding the privity of contract since the agent negotiates the contract but does not actually enter into it. A contract which results from such negotiations is made between the principal and the third party and once that contract has been concluded the agent withdraws from the scene and is not bound by the contract.

Agency is a very common relationship in business although often the relationship may not be called agency nor may it commonly be realized that a relationship of agency exists. For example, a director is an agent of his/her company (see Chapter Three, p. 89–90), and a partner is an agent of his/her partnership (see Chapter Three, p. 81). In some cases certain persons are incorrectly referred to as agents since no legal relationship of agency exists at all. For example, a car dealer may be called an agent, e.g. a Saab agent, but in fact such a person will sell the car directly to the customer. The dealer is not negotiating on behalf of Saab and should more properly be known as a Saab distributor. One example of agency which we consider in some detail below and in Chapter Twelve (pp. 285–287) is travel agency. A simpler example of agency is the solicitor acting on behalf of his/her client. Solicitors are indeed sometimes called agents or law agents.

However, not every action by an agent will necessarily bind the principal. Whether or not the principal is bound depends on the scope of the agent's authority. If the agent goes beyond the scope of their authority, the principal will not generally be bound. We consider the question of an agent's authority in more detail below. Agency also gives rise to certain rights and duties and these are also considered in more detail below.

Authority of an agent

As we explained above, an agent may enter into contracts which bind the principal when acting within the scope of their authority. Such authority may be actual or ostensible (also known as apparent) or presumed.

Actual authority may be expressly given, for example, in an agency agreement or it may be implied from the conduct of the parties. Travel agents normally have express actual authority given to them by their principals (that is, the various tour operators) under agency agreements. It is good business practice to set out clearly the extent of an agent's authority in such an agreement. A commercial agent and their principal are entitled to a written document setting out the terms of their relationships (Commercial Agents (Council Directive) Regulations 1993, reg. 13).

An agent may also have ostensible authority, that is authority as it appears to other persons to enter into certain contracts on behalf of the principal (*Hely-Hutchison* v *Brayhead Ltd* [1968] 1 QB 549). This will normally only arise where there has been a prior relationship of agency between a principal and agent which has been terminated or altered and the principal behaves or allows the ostensible agent to behave in such a manner that the reasonable inference is that the ostensible agent has actual authority to act in the manner in which he/she is acting. In such circumstances the principal would be bound. An example of this would include a situation where a tour operator had terminated an agency agreement with a travel agent, but the travel agent did not withdraw that operator's advertisements and brochures from display immediately. The travel agent would appear in such a situation to any customer interested in such a holiday to have ostensible authority to bind the operator.

Even where an agent lacks authority, agency may still be constituted by ratification. So, if a person acts for another without any authority, express or implied, agency may still arise if the principal ratifies the act. However, for a principal to ratify such an act, the agent must have acted ostensibly as an agent.

Another situation where agency may also be presumed to exist without any prior authority express or implied is in an emergency situation. An emergency may make action in the manner of agency necessary – this is known as the agency of necessity in England and Wales and by the Latin words *negotiorum gestio* in Scotland. An example of this would be a carrier of perishable goods held up at a channel ferry port by striking French lorry drivers. In such circumstances where delivery is rendered impossible the carrier may dispose of the goods and their actions will bind the owner.

Duties of an agent

In this section we consider briefly some of the important duties which the law imposes on agents. First, an agent is under a duty to exercise reasonable care and skill in performing their duties. The standards expected will be those generally expected in the agent's trade or profession. In England and Wales this is actually a statutory duty (Supply of Goods and Services Act 1982, s.13). However, in Scotland the common law involves an identical requirement.

Secondly, there is a general presumption that an agent cannot delegate tasks. However, whether delegation is permissible is a question to be determined by reference to the particular nature of employment. So, for example, delegation to staff employed by the agent is usually permissible although those staff must be competent.

Thirdly, agency is also a relationship which involves a fiduciary element, that is an element of trust. Several duties flow from this. These include the duty that the agent must not make secret profits or take bribes or misuse confidential information supplied by the principal and that they must not allow their personal interests to conflict with those of the principal. An agent is bound to account to the principal for all money received and should keep money for their principal separate from their own. They must also account to the principal for any incidental advantage which they have obtained from their position as agent without the knowledge of the principal or due to an error by the principal (*Trans Barwil Agencies (UK) Ltd* v *John S Braid & Co.* 1988 SC 222).

Rights of an agent

Although agents have various duties, they also have certain rights in relation to the principal. If the agent has performed the work required by the principal they are entitled to the payment expressly or impliedly agreed with the principal. In the absence of agreement, a commercial agent is entitled to such remuneration as is customarily given to commercial agents selling goods in the relevant place and, if there is not customary practice, to reasonable remuneration (Commercial Agents (Council Directive) Regulations 1993, reg. 6(1)). Furthermore, an agent is entitled to be reimbursed by the principal for all the expenses and liabilities incurred in the due performance of the contract as an agent.

Contracts with third parties

The question of what rights and liabilities arise under a contract entered into by an agent in terms of authority depends on the way in which the agent has contracted. Where the agent discloses the identity of the principal the general rule is that the principal has contracted with the third party and the agent is not liable under and cannot sue on the contract.

However, where an agent contracts as an agent but does not disclose the identity of principal, the agent may incur liability under the contract. Where, in these circumstances, the agent signs a contract buying or selling goods, they are personally liable (*Hichens, Harrison Woolston & Co.* v *Jackson & Sons* [1943] AC 266). Otherwise it may depend on the circumstances whether the person who knows they are dealing with an agent is looking to the credit of the agent or of the unnamed principal (*N & J Vlassopulos Ltd* v *Ney Shipping Ltd* [1977] 1 Lloyd's Rep 478).

Where an agent contracts ostensibly as a principal, the general rule is that both the agent and the principal are liable on the contract and may sue upon it (*Siu Yin Kwan* v *Eastern Insurance Co. Ltd* [1994] 2 AC 199). The third party must elect to find either the agent or the principal liable and once the election has been made it is final.

If an agent enters into a contract without the authority of the principal, the principal is generally not bound. In such a situation the agent would normally be personally bound. However, the principal may ratify the agent's act and thereby incur liability under the contract but this would only apply where the agent actually acted ostensibly as an agent and not as a principal.

As we explained above, a principal may also incur rights and liabilities under a contract where the agent's act was within their ostensible but not actual authority. However, this cannot arise unless there was some previous contractual relationship between the principal and the agent or the principal held the agent out as having such authority (*First Energy (UK) Ltd* v *Hungarian International Bank* [1993] 2 Lloyd's Rep 194).

THE LAW OF TORT

Introduction

Broadly speaking the law of tort (in Scotland, delict) determines when a person must pay another compensation for harm such as personal injury, property damage or financial loss wrongfully caused although it also helps to determine what conduct may be stopped by court order. It is primarily an area of common law based upon decisions of judges in actual cases although there has been considerable statutory intervention. This has included the enactment of the Crown Proceedings Act 1947 to make the Government liable in tort, the introduction of occupiers' liability legislation (see pp. 63–65) and the enactment of the Consumer Protection Act 1987 which has abolished the rule that a person injured by a defective product must demonstrate that the manufacturer was negligent by imposing a system of strict liability (see Chapter Four). In this section we principally examine the torts of negligence and nuisance. We conclude with a brief mention of the tort of trespass. The principles in the areas of negligence and nuisance are broadly similar both north and south of the border although there are some differences particularly in the law of nuisance which we will highlight. There are a number of differences between Scots and English law in relation to trespass. For the sake of simplicity we will hereafter refer to 'tort' rather than referring to 'tort and, in Scotland, delict'.

Tort of negligence

Basic requirements

For a plaintiff to establish a tort of negligence, they must essentially show

- that the defendant owed them a duty of care;
- that the defendant breached that duty, falling below the requisite standard of care by reason of negligence; and
- that the damage, loss or injury allegedly suffered was actually caused by the act complained of.

We discuss these general issues in turn and then consider the issues of vicarious liability, employer's liability, defences available in negligence actions, remedies and finally, occupier's liability.

At this stage you should also note that anyone to whom a duty of care is owed may bring an action in negligence against the person who owed the duty and breached it.

Duty of care

The modern law of negligence is largely based on the Scottish House of Lords case, *Donoghue* v *Stevenson* [1932] AC 562; 1932 SC(HL) 31 which involved a woman drinking ginger beer from an opaque bottle. When the contents of the bottle were poured out, the remains of a snail were visible in the glass and the woman suffered severe shock (and serious gastro enteritis) as a result of seeing the remains of a snail in the ginger beer which she had already drunk. She was held to be entitled to recover damages due to the drinks manufacturer's negligence in allowing the snail to enter the bottle. Today this situation would be covered by the product liability provisions of the Consumer Protection Act 1987 (see Chapter Four). Lord Atkin's judgment contains the famous passage:

> The liability for negligence . . . is no doubt based upon a general public sentiment of moral wrongdoing for which the offender must pay. But acts or omissions which any moral code would censure cannot in a practical world be treated so as to give a right to every person injured by them to demand relief. In this way rules of law arise which limit the range of complainants and the extent of their remedy. The rule that you are to love your neighbour becomes in law, you must not injure your neighbour; and the lawyer's question, Who is my neighbour? receives a restricted reply. You must take reasonable care to avoid acts or omissions which you can reasonably foresee would be likely to injure your neighbour. Who, then, in law is my neighbour? The answer seems to be – persons who are so closely and directly affected by my act that I ought reasonably to have them in contemplation as being so affected when I am directing my mind to the acts or omissions which are called in question.

The crucial principle established by Lord Atkin in this passage is that a person owes their neighbour a duty of care and that the test for establishing who a person's neighbours are in this sense is whether they can reasonably foresee that their conduct will cause harm to them. The approach taken by the courts is to ask whether a reasonable person in the position of the defendant would have foreseen the harm.

A simple example where the tort of negligence would be applicable is that of the car driver. The driver owes a duty of care, more specifically a duty to take reasonable care and to exercise reasonable skill in driving, to all other road users, that is drivers, cyclists or pedestrians: they are the driver's neighbours. Should the driver drive in a careless manner with the result that the car hits a cyclist, then assuming there are no other possible causes of the cyclist's injuries, the car driver will be under an obligation to pay damages to the cyclist for the injuries. An example of this from the tourism industry is *Denyer* v *Heaney,* unreported, Court of Appeal, 19 February 1985. In this case package holidaymakers in Mallorca went to a go-kart track. The plaintiff was a rather timid driver and crawled along on the very outside of the track. The defendant, who was going as fast as possible, made an error of judgment and collided with the plaintiff who suffered a hand injury. The defendant was held liable for damages of £5,500 and costs. Clearly the defendant owed a duty of care to drive with reasonable care and skill even though it was a go-kart track and not a highway or road.

However, a duty of care may arise in a much wider range of situations than this. For example, it may arise where a negligent misrepresentation or misstatement even where the misrepresentation does not result in any physical harm but only economic loss. The leading case on this point is the English House of Lords case *Hedley Byrne & Co. Ltd* v *Heller and Partners* [1964] AC 465 in which advertising consultants relied on creditworthiness checks into their clients carried out by their bankers. The bankers provided negligent advice in relation to a particular client although they escaped liability because of a disclaimer which they had included in their letter to the advertising consultants. However, the House of Lords did establish that there would have been liability in this situation had it not been for the disclaimer. The crucial issue in determining whether a duty of care has arisen is the question of whether there is a special relationship between the parties. Whether there is such a relationship is determined by ascertaining first, if the plaintiff reasonably relied upon the statement made by the defendant; and secondly, if it was reasonable that the defendant should know that the plaintiff would rely on the statement. In *Hedley Byrne* it was the disclaimer which prevented the plaintiffs from reasonably relying upon the statement made by the defendants. This type of liability might attach to a travel agent where they made a negligent misrepresentation which a customer relied upon.

The next question we must ask ourselves is what must be foreseen? In assessing what is reasonably foreseeable it is not necessary to reasonably foresee the exact type of harm which occurred: *Hughes* v *Lord Advocate* 1963 SC (HL) 31. That case involved a Post Office manhole which had been left unattended and was surrounded by paraffin warning lamps and covered by a tarpaulin. Two boys entered the shelter. One picked up a lamp which was knocked over. The paraffin vaporized and exploded. One boy was badly burned. Was the harm to the boy reasonably foreseeable? The House of Lords held that although an explosion might have been unforeseeable, there was a reasonably foreseeable risk of fire in some form and so the boy was entitled to damages. Therefore it is unnecessary reasonably to foresee the exact type of harm. A more recent illustration of this is *Margereson* v *J W Roberts Ltd; Hancock* v *J W Roberts Ltd* [1996] 8 ELM 118. This was a case involving mesosthelioma contracted by people when they were children playing in the vicinity of an asbestos works before the Second World War. The defendants argued that at that time it was not reasonably foreseeable that exposure to asbestos dust would result in mesosthelioma. However, the Court of Appeal held that evidence from as early as 1900 linked exposure to asbestos dust with lung damage and that it was not necessary for the defendants to have foreseen the exact type of injury or damage suffered by the plaintiffs: it was enough that the defendants could reasonably foresee some type of pulmonary injury, not necessarily mesosthelioma.

However, where something is not a known hazard at the time, harm resulting from it cannot be reasonably foreseen. This can be illustrated by the House of Lords case *Cambridge Water Co.* v *Eastern Counties Leather plc* [1994] 1 All ER 53 in which spillages of solvents at the defendants' tannery seeped through a concrete floor, down to the aquifer and contaminated a drinking water borehole operated by the plaintiffs over a mile away. The spillages ceased in 1976. It was held that at that time it was not reasonably foreseeable that the type of harm which was suffered would be suffered. Obviously as the state of scientific knowledge advances a wider range of types of harm including the harm in the *Cambridge Water Co.* case will be regarded as reasonably foreseeable.

Breach of duty

This is where the element of negligence enters our equation. Assuming that a duty of care exists between our plaintiff and defendant, the next question is whether the defendant actually breached that duty, that is, fell below the requisite standard of care or was negligent in the performance of the duty. The general position is that the standard of care to be applied is that of the reasonable person. The court will ask itself the question 'what would the reasonable person have had in contemplation in such circumstances?'. In considering whether precautions need to be taken against a particular risk a court has said that the duty is to weigh on the one hand the magnitude of the risk, the likelihood of an accident happening and the possible seriousness of the consequences if an accident does happen, and on the other hand the difficulty and expense and any other disadvantage of taking precautions (*Morris* v *West Hartlepool Steam Navigation Co Ltd* [1956] AC 552).

Normal practice in a trade is also a factor which will be taken into account although it is not conclusive. The same applies to a trade or industry Code of Practice.

The standard of care required of professional persons or those exercising a special skill is higher than the standard applied in other cases. A professional person is judged by the standards of their profession not of the reasonable man. Nevertheless the standard is the standard of the ordinary practitioner. For example, in the Scottish case *Hunter* v *Hanley* 1955 SLT 213 which involved a doctor using the wrong needle in treating a patient, the court held that

The true test for establishing negligence . . . on the part of a doctor . . . is whether he has proved to be guilty of such failure as no doctor of ordinary skill would be guilty of if acting with ordinary care.

Causation

Where there is a duty of care and the plaintiff has also established a breach of that duty, they must also then prove that the breach was the cause of their loss or injury. The courts have indicated that they approach causation from the point of view of the person in the street, not from the point of view of a scientist or metaphysician (*Yorkshire Dale SS Co.* v *MOWT* [1942] AC 691). As a result of this approach it is sufficient if the breach of duty materially caused the harm. For example, in the Scottish House of Lords case *McGhee* v *NCB* 1973 SC (HL) 37 a man who normally worked in a pipe kiln was sent to work in a brick kiln which was hotter and dustier. He contracted dermatitis and claimed against the NCB on the basis that they failed to provide showers at his work place. The defenders admitted that they had breached their duty to the pursuer and House of Lords found that the breach had materially increased the risk of harm to the pursuer. It is possible for an intervening event to break the causal link between the breach of duty and the harm which occurred.

It may also be the case that the plaintiff is wholly or partly responsible for the harm which they have suffered. If this is so, they are what is known as contributorily negligent. Contributory negligence is a defence to an action in negligence and we examine its scope below.

Vicarious liability

Under the principles of vicarious liability, a person such as an employer may be held liable for harm caused by another person, for example, an employee. So, for example, if a hotel porter drops a case on a guest's foot, the porter's employers may well be liable for any injury caused. If one employee injures another negligently, then the hotel or other employer may also be liable. There are good policy reasons for vicarious liability. Employers will normally have more money available to pay claims than employees and furthermore vicarious liability acts as an incentive to employers to operate safe places of work.

The courts approach the question of whether the employer is vicariously liable by first determining whether the person was an employee and, second, whether the employee was acting within the scope of their employment. Control is an important element in establishing whether a person is an employee but the courts will also look at issues including the intention of the parties, the duration of the contract, how payment is made, whether the tools belong to the employer or employee, and the nature of arrangements for terminating the contract. As our discussion of recent English case law on employment rights in Chapter Six indicates the courts there are looking for a mutuality of obligations between employer and employee to establish whether someone is in fact an employee.

To establish whether an employee is acting within the scope of their employment, the courts do not look simply at an employee's contractual duties. A leading case is *Rose* v *Plenty* [1976] 1 All ER 97 which involved a boy being injured while helping out a milkman with his round. A notice prohibiting the use of boys was posted at the dairy. However, the milkman ignored this and got the boy to help him out, allowing him to ride on the back of his float. The question for the court was whether the milkman was acting within the scope of his employment and hence whether the dairy was vicariously liable since he appeared to be doing his job in a way which had been prohibited by his employers. However, the court held on appeal that the milkman was still doing his job, that is delivering milk, even though he was doing it in a prohibited way and hence his employers were vicariously liable.

Employer's liability

In this section we briefly consider the liability of employers towards their employees when the latter are injured at work. Historically this was governed by the common law of tort but is now the subject of very detailed legislation. An employer's duty at common law was set out in the case *English* v *Wilsons & Clyde Coal Co.* 1937 SC (HL) 46:

> To take reasonable care, and to use reasonable skill, first to provide and maintain proper machinery, plant, appliances and works; secondly, to select properly skilled persons to manage and superintend the business; and thirdly, to provide a proper system of working.

That case involved a splinter from a tool entering a workman's eye. Since the tool had been purchased from a reputable supplier, the workman's claim failed.

However, employer's liability has been heavily regulated by statute. The Factories Act 1961 has been one of the most important statutes in this area of law although it is now being supplanted by new legislation which we discuss in brief below. The Factories Act 1961 imposed various duties on employers. These included a requirement to fence dangerous parts of machinery, a duty to construct soundly and properly maintain floors and steps and to keep them free from obstruction and from any substance likely to cause persons to slip so far as is reasonably practicable and to provide and maintain safe means of access to every place where a person was required to work. There was no requirement on an employee to show negligence. Breach of one of these duties gave rise to strict civil liability.

However, the Factories Act 1961 has been repealed and now only applies to cases outstanding before the new legislation discussed below was brought into force. Safety in the workplace is now regulated under the Management of Health and Safety at Work Regulations 1992, the Workplace (Health, Safety and Welfare) Regulations 1992, the Provision and Use of Work Equipment Regulations 1992, the Personal Protective Equipment at Work Regulations 1992, the Health and Safety (Display Screen Equipment) Regulations 1992 and the Manual Handling Operations Regulations 1992. These Regulations came into effect on 1 January 1993 for all new workplaces and equipment. However, their impact on old workplaces was delayed until 1 January 1996 and on old work equipment until 1 January 1997. Until those dates the provisions of the Factories Act 1961 continued to apply. The Regulations are designed to implement a variety of EC directives on health and safety and were made under the Health and Safety at Work etc Act 1974. Workplace is very widely defined as

> Any premises or part of premises which are not domestic premises and are made available to any person as a place of work, and includes –
>
> (a) any place within the premises to which such person has access while at work; and
> (b) any room, lobby, corridor, staircase, road or other place used as a means of access to or egress from the workplace or where facilities are provided for use in connection with the workplace other than a public highway (road in Scotland). (Workplace (Health, Safety and Welfare) Regulations 1992, reg. 2)

Ships, including ferries and cruise liners, are excluded although there is a considerable amount of maritime safety legislation which applies to them. However, the definition of workplace would clearly encompass the vast majority of tourism and hospitality workplaces such as a travel agency office or hotel. Breach of the duties in these Regulations is a criminal offence and the Health and Safety Executive are responsible for the enforcement of the provisions. However, breach of the Regulations would also appear to give rise to civil liability (Health and Safety at Work etc Act 1974, s. 47(2)) in the same way that a breach of the Factories Act 1961 did. The primary purpose of the provisions is clearly to prevent accidents occurring with criminal and civil liability acting as an incentive to employers to ensure a safe workplace.

Defences

A defendant may obviously advance defences such as there was no duty of care, or if there was that there was no breach of the duty. However, there are certain other defences which might be available to the defendant. These include, first, that the plaintiff was actually wholly or partly responsible for the harm and, secondly, that the plaintiff consented to the actions or omissions of the defendant which caused the harm.

Where the defendant argues that the plaintiff was wholly or partly to blame for the harm suffered, that is, that the plaintiff was contributorily negligent, this is not a complete defence: it simply enables a court to adjust the damages awarded in proportion to the degree to which the plaintiff was contributorily negligent (Law

Reform (Contributory Negligence) Act 1945, s. 1(1)). For example, in *Davies* v *Swan Motor Co.* [1949] 2 KB 291, Davies, a dustbin man, was standing on the running board of his lorry despite instructions not to do so. The lorry collided with a bus and Davies was killed. The award made by the court was reduced by one-fifth because he had contributed to his own injury and death.

Where the plaintiff consents to the defendant's actions or omissions, this may also amount to a defence. The technical legal name for this defence is the Latin phrase *volenti non fit injuria* (there is no legal wrong to a person who was willing). One of the leading cases is the House of Lords case *ICI* v *Shatwell* [1965] AC 656. In this case the plaintiff and his brother, who were employees of ICI, tested detonators without taking the necessary precautions. This was in breach of ICI's instructions and in breach of statutory regulations. The plaintiff was injured in the explosion which took place. His case failed because of the defence of *volenti non fit injuria*: the plaintiff had willingly run the risk of testing the detonators without taking the necessary precautions.

However, the defence of *volenti non fit injuria* does not apply in the case of injuries sustained as a result of involvement in sporting contests. Instead the courts have reduced the standard of care applicable in such cases in relation to players, spectators and the organizer of the event. The lower standard of care suggests that only intentional or reckless conduct will give rise to liability. Hence an error of judgment on the part of a rider causing his horse to take a wrong turn and injuring a photographer standing inside the competition area did not give rise to liability (*Wooldridge* v *Sumner* [1963] 2 QB 43) but a reckless foul tackle by one footballer on another causing injury did (*Condon* v *Basi* [1985] 1 WLR 866).

Remedies

The principal remedy in actions of negligence is damages. These are designed to compensate the plaintiff for pain and suffering, loss of amenity such as inability to participate in a sport which they formerly played and such matters as loss of earnings caused by the injury. In England and Wales but not in Scotland, there are situations in which punitive damages may be awarded which are designed to punish the defendant rather than to compensate the plaintiff for the harm which they have sustained.

Occupiers' liability

Introduction

Another important area where there has been statutory intervention in the law of tort is that of occupiers' liability. The legislation has imposed a duty of care on occupiers towards those who come on to their premises. In England and Wales the relevant statutes are the Occupiers' Liability Acts 1957 and 1984 (OLA 1957; OLA 1984). In Scotland the applicable legislation is the Occupiers' Liability (Scotland) Act 1960 (OLSA 1960). There are some differences in the law applicable north and south of the border, particularly in relation to trespassers, and we will highlight these as we go along.

Occupiers

The duty applies to occupiers. Unfortunately the legislation does not comprehensively define this term. It refers to the person who was in control of the premises at the time of the accident (OLA 1957, s. 1(2), OLSA 1960, s. 1(1)).

The case *Wheat* v *Lacon & Co.* [1966] AC 552 deals with the question of who is an occupier, and particularly the degree of control needed over premises to trigger liability under the legislation. It involved the death of a guest staying in a public house owned by Lacon & Co, a brewery, as a result of a fall on a defective staircase. The guest was staying in a part of the public house occupied by the manager and his wife as their private lodging. The court held that the brewery company did retain sufficient control over the premises to be liable as an occupier although it was also held that the manager was an occupier as well. The brewery had a duty to take care of the structure of the building, including the defective handrail on the staircase and to ensure that there was an efficient system of lighting in the stairway, but they were not responsible for seeing that the lights were properly switched on: that type of day-to-day matter was the responsibility of the manager and his wife as occupiers. You should realize, therefore, that for a person to be an 'occupier' it is not necessary for them to have entire control over the premises. Some degree of control is all that is required and indeed control may be shared with others. There is also no need for an occupier to have a physical presence on the premises.

Premises

Premises are defined as land or other buildings. You can see a simple example involving land in the hospitality and tourism industry context in the Scottish case, *Cairns* v *Butlins* 1989 GWD 40-1879 in which a grandmother tripped in a concealed hole at a Butlins Holiday camp. Butlins denied that the hole existed since they carried out regular inspections. However, the court was persuaded that there was a hole and therefore that the inspections had been negligent.

However, the legislation does not extend simply to occupiers of land or buildings but also to those who have control over any fixed or movable structure, including any vessel, vehicle or aircraft (OLA 1957, s.1(3)(a); OLSA 1960, s.1(3)). Fixed structures might include electricity pylons, theme park rides or diving boards. Movable structures might include ladders.

To whom is the duty owed?

The duty in the OLA 1957 is only owed to lawful visitors. It is not owed to trespassers. In this respect the law in Scotland differs (see below). Lawful visitors would include guests, customers, delivery persons, and salespersons. However, the OLA 1984 sought to extend some degree of protection in England and Wales to trespassers although to a lesser extent than that provided to lawful visitors.

What is the occupier's duty?

The occupier's duty is

to take such care as in all the circumstances of the case is reasonable to see that the visitor will be reasonably safe in using the premises for the purposes for which he is invited or permitted by the occupier to be there. (OLA 1957, s.2(2))

It will be apparent that the duty is not to make the premises safe but to make the visitor safe. The scope of the duty will vary depending on the circumstances of each case. For example, it is reasonable to exercise more care where premises are regularly visited by children. Indeed the Act expressly requires occupiers to be prepared for children to be less careful than adults (OLA 1957, s.2(3)). Liability will not generally arise, however, in the case of tradespeople and contractors carrying out work on the premises since they are expected to carry out their work exercising a reasonable degree of care and skill. The OLA 1957 provides that an occupier may extend, restrict, modify or exclude his liability by agreement or otherwise (s.2(1)). 'Otherwise' suggests means of limiting liability by erecting warning notices and the like. For example, notices could make certain parts of premises off limits to members of the public. However, the Unfair Contract Terms Act 1977 prevents the use of warning notices or contract terms to limit liability for death or personal injury due to negligence. This is limited to business liability and the term or notice must also pass the fair and reasonable test (see pp. 45-47).

As we mentioned above the OLA 1984 extended an occupier's liability to trespassers although the duty is not quite so onerous. The OLA 1984 imposes a duty to take such care as is reasonable in all the circumstances of the case to see that the trespasser does not suffer injury on the premises by reason of the danger concerned. The danger is the risk of suffering injury by reason of any danger due to the state of the premises or to things done or omitted to be done on them. The duty only arises if the occupier is aware of the danger or has reasonable grounds to believe that it exists and if the occupier knows or has reasonable grounds to believe that the other person is in the vicinity of the danger concerned or that he/she may come into the vicinity of the danger. The danger must be one against which in all the circumstances of the case the occupier may reasonably be expected to offer the trespasser some protection. The OLA 1984 provides that the duty can be discharged in an appropriate case by giving warning of the danger or taking steps to discourage the persons from incurring the risk. The OLA 1984 also further narrows the scope of potential liability by indicating that it does not apply to persons using a highway, or to risks which a trespasser has willingly accepted or to loss or damage to property but only to personal injury. Hence burglars, who are clearly trespassers, cannot expect much protection.

In Scotland the standard of care owed by an occupier to lawful visitors and trespassers alike is

such care as in all the circumstances of the case is reasonable to see that that person will not suffer injury or damage by reason of any such danger (OLSA, s.2(1))

The Scottish case *Glasgow Corporation* v *Taylor* [1922] 1 AC 44 provides an example of liability in relation to trespassers albeit before the passing of the OLSA. The pursuer, a seven-year-old child, had died through eating poisonous berries picked from a shrub in public gardens. Glasgow Corporation was held liable even though the child had trespassed to pick the berries.

Tort of nuisance

Introduction – relationship of negligence and nuisance

The tort of nuisance – and here we are referring to what is known as private nuisance in England and Wales – essentially protects the right of an owner or occupier to the 'comfortable enjoyment' of their property. It normally deals with intentional rather than unintentional conduct, unlike the law of negligence. However, there is considerable confusion over the boundaries between liability under nuisance and negligence. If a person's enjoyment of their property is materially affected then they are entitled to a remedy in nuisance. This can extend to nuisances which cause not only inconvenience but those which cause actual physical damage. In the case of physical damage to property there is a clear overlap with negligence. However, there is no overlap in the case of personal injury. If a person suffers injury, the appropriate action is in negligence. To get around this confusion as a matter of practice it is usual to plead both grounds of action in a case. Another relevant issue is that where conduct is continuing, the appropriate action would normally be based on nuisance whereas if it is a one-off accident, then the appropriate action would normally be based on negligence although a one-off incident which causes damage may be a nuisance under normal nuisance principles. An example of this is *Crown River Cruises* v *Kimbolton Fireworks* [1996] 8 ELM 119, QBD in which a 20-minute firework display resulted in burning debris falling onto a barge which caught fire. The fire spread to a passenger vessel, the owners of which sued the firework organizers. It was held that this could amount to a nuisance. In addition in England and Wales, a one-off incident may amount to a nuisance under the rule in *Rylands* v *Fletcher* (see below). It has, however, been held in Scotland that a one-off rave held in an isolated location did not constitute a nuisance: *Cumnock & Doon Valley District Council* v *Dance Energy Associates Ltd* 1992 GWD 25-1441.

In this section we discuss, first, the definition of nuisance; second, the basis of liability in nuisance actions; third, other elements of a nuisance action; fourth, who can bring nuisance actions; fifth, persons who may be liable for nuisance; sixth, defences; seventh, remedies; eighth, the *Rylands* v *Fletcher* rule; ninth, public nuisance; and finally, statutory nuisance.

Definition

A nuisance arises where one person so uses their property as to cause serious disturbance, substantial inconvenience or material damage to a neighbour or a neighbour's property. However, the neighbour need not be somebody who owns or occupies adjacent property: the neighbour might reside at some distance from the source of the nuisance. The disturbance, inconvenience or damage could, for example, be caused by water, smell, noise, vibration or even light. So, for example, in Scotland a recent Sheriff Court decision has established that the glare caused by floodlights at a tennis court shining on a sea-trout fishing pool which prevented fish from being caught since they can only be caught in light levels up to pale moonlight was a nuisance: *Stonehaven & District Angling Association* v *Stonehaven Recreation Ground Trustees & Stonehaven Tennis Club* (1997) 60 SPEL 36. Although this decision is being appealed, it clearly has implications for all those businesses using security lights which might cause some interference to neighbours.

In England and Wales whether conduct constitutes a nuisance essentially depends on whether it is reasonable or not. The court is essentially involved in an exercise to balance the reasonableness of a defendant's activity against a plaintiff's proprietary rights. In Scotland conduct will be actionable as a nuisance when it is more than is reasonably tolerable. Tolerability is judged from the standpoint of the victim and not of the person responsible for the alleged nuisance. In both jurisdictions in assessing whether or not something is unreasonable or more than is reasonably tolerable the courts will take account of all the circumstances and effects of the offensive conduct. The most pertinent factors include:

- the type and seriousness of harm;
- the duration of the harm; and
- the locality where the harm occurred.

Trivial inconvenience will not be actionable but serious inconvenience or disturbance or actual physical damage will normally be. Furthermore, as we noted above a nuisance is normally, although not always, constituted by ongoing conduct. Following on from this it is usually the case that temporary works such as those involving construction or demolition will not constitute a nuisance. This is illustrated by the temporary operation of pumps to drain water from a shaft under construction in *Harrison* v *Southwark and Vauxhall Water Co.* [1891] 2 Ch 409. However, where the defendant fails to take steps to safeguard the plaintiff from unnecessary interference, temporary works may be actionable as a nuisance. For example, in *Andreae* v *Selfridge & Co. Ltd* [1938] Ch 1 the defendant was carrying out demolition works which subjected a hotel proprietor to an unnecessary amount of noise and dust. The hotel proprietor succeeded in recovering damages, partly for business lost as a result of the nuisance.

Locality is also an important factor in determining whether conduct constitutes a nuisance. This point is illustrated by the case *Halsey* v *Esso Petroleum* [1961] 1 WLR 683 in which the plaintiff alleged that the defendants' oil depot was causing an unreasonable degree of noise, smell and acid smuts which were affecting his enjoyment of his house. In determining that this conduct did amount to a nuisance the court took into account the fact that the plaintiff's house was in an area designated for residential development under planning legislation. However, where actual physical damage is caused by a nuisance the position is different. For example, in *St Helens Smelting Co.* v *Tipping* (1865) 11 HL Cas 642 the nuisance complained of was fumes from the defendants' factory which were causing damage to the plaintiff's shrubs. The defendants argued that the area was an industrial one and hence that the plaintiff had to put up with a higher degree of interference with his property by fumes than if he were not in an industrial area. The court rejected this and upheld the plaintiff's claim, taking the view that although locality was an important consideration where the alleged nuisance took the form of interference with comfort and enjoyment of property, it was irrelevant where actual physical damage was caused.

Other factors such as the sensitivity of the plaintiff to harm will also sometimes be considered. If a potential plaintiff is particularly sensitive to one type of nuisance then it will not be actionable unless the nuisance would have affected a reasonable person.

The social utility of the activity from which the harm arises does not mean that it is not a nuisance entitling a plaintiff to a remedy. For example, in the Irish case *Bellew* v

Cement Co. [1948] Ir R 61, the court granted an injunction against the only cement works in Ireland despite the fact that cement was in considerable demand at the time for house building. The fact that the Edinburgh Military Tattoo was a very important tourist event did not prevent a court in Scotland granting an interdict to prevent construction of the grandstand for the event in the noisy manner which had been causing a nuisance (*Webster* v *Lord Advocate* 1984 SLT 13). However, the social utility of an activity may affect the type of remedy granted (see below).

Basis of liability

In England and Wales, liability for nuisance is essentially strict. In most cases the defendant knows of the nuisance in which case they may be regarded as intending it. Furthermore, even if the defendant takes all reasonable precautions they might still be responsible for a nuisance whereas such precautions would usually absolve them from being liable in negligence. However, in Scotland liability for nuisance is based on *culpa* or fault (*RHM Bakeries (Scotland) Ltd* v *Strathclyde Regional Council* 1985 SLT 214). Nevertheless, in Scotland, the escape of a dangerous thing, such as of a pollutant into water, gives rise to a very strong presumption of fault. Proof of fault in Scotland may be supplied by evidence of malice or intentional or reckless conduct causing the nuisance (*Kennedy* v *Glenbelle Ltd* 1996 SLT 1186).

Other elements of a nuisance action

A plaintiff must also establish a causal link between the activity complained of and the harm in question. For example, in the environmental law case *Graham & Graham* v *Rechem International* [1996] Env LR 158 the plaintiffs failed to establish that emissions from the defendants' incinerator had caused harm to their dairy herd since the most plausible explanation was a condition brought on by the plaintiffs' own misfeeding of their animals which is known as Fat Cow Syndrome!

The type of harm suffered by the plaintiff must also be reasonably foreseeable. This was established by the recent House of Lords' decision in *Cambridge Water Co.* v *Eastern Counties Leather plc* [1994] 1 All ER 53, CA, HL. This case involved a claim by the plaintiffs for the cost of the construction of a new drinking water borehole following the discovery in the 1980s that an existing borehole had been contaminated by the spillage of solvents at the defendants' tannery which had occurred up to 1976. The House of Lords held that it was not reasonably foreseeable that at the time spillages of solvents occurred on the defendants' premises they would penetrate the concrete floor of those premises, enter an aquifer and migrate over a mile along the aquifer to contaminate the plaintiffs' drinking water borehole. However, with advancement of knowledge of the behaviour of such substances such damage is now reasonably foreseeable.

Who can bring nuisance actions?

Since nuisance is a remedy connected with the 'comfortable enjoyment' of property, title to sue depends largely on a person having an interest in land. This would obviously include owners but the range of other persons entitled to sue is not so clear. The law has been clarified by the recent House of Lords case *Hunter and Others* v

Canary Wharf Ltd & London Docklands Development Corporation [1997] 2 All ER 426, a case of alleged nuisance by reason of dust and interference with television reception brought by around 500 residents of the London Docklands area against companies involved in developing buildings in the Docklands area, particularly Canary Wharf Tower. Many of those who brought actions were people who occupied property under licence rather than as of proprietary right such as children or spouses or friends. The House of Lords held that only persons with an interest in property such as owners or tenants may bring nuisance actions and not those who merely occupy property under licence.

Persons who may be liable for nuisance

The person who causes the nuisance may obviously be sued. This may often be the occupier of land who is not necessarily the owner. However, it seems clear that owners and licensors may also be liable even if they themselves did not cause the nuisance. For example, in *Sedleigh-Denfield* v *O'Callaghan* [1940] AC 880 the House of Lords held that an occupier of land who had knowledge of a nuisance created by a third party, had a duty, in so far as they were able, to remove it, and if they failed to do so, they would be liable for continuing or adopting the nuisance. That case involved the failure to remove the nuisance by placing a grid over a culvert pipe to stop the accumulation of refuse. In *Leakey* v *National Trust* [1980] QB 485 the National Trust owned and occupied an ancient burial mound. They knew that the mound was liable to cracking and slipping in certain weather conditions because of its soil base but refused to undertake repairs. As a result of this failure the plaintiff's land suffered damage on a number of occasions and the National Trust were held liable in nuisance. It appears that if the defendant ought to know about the nuisance they may still be liable. Therefore a landlord may be liable for a nuisance created by a tenant as in *Tetley* v *Chitty* [1986] 1 All ER 663 in which the landlord permitted go-kart racing on the premises. Reasonable foreseeability of the nuisance is enough to hold the landlord liable. Express prohibition of the creation of a nuisance in a lease was held in *Smith* v *Scott* [1973] Ch 314 to exempt the landlords, a local authority, from liability in circumstances where a house had been let to an anti-social family who harassed their neighbours, the plaintiffs. However, in Scotland in *Webster* v *Lord Advocate* 1984 SLT 13 the Secretary of State licensed the erection of the Edinburgh Military Tattoo grandstand (which caused noise disturbing the pursuer's enjoyment of her flat) and obliged the contractors not to cause a nuisance. However, he took no steps to enforce this contractual provision and the court found against him. The distinction between the *Smith* and *Webster* cases may lie in the fact that one was simply a residential lease whereas the other involved a commercial contract. It is likely that the *Webster* approach would be followed in commercial leases and construction contracts where there are anti-nuisance clauses which are not monitored or enforced.

The principles of vicarious liability which we explained in relation to the tort of negligence above apply equally in the case of private nuisance.

Defences

Various defences may be open to the defendant. These would obviously include arguments that the alleged nuisance was not actually a nuisance and/or that someone other than the defendant had caused the nuisance. However, in addition, or alternatively, it might be open to the defendant to argue that the nuisance was actually authorized by statute or that the plaintiff had lost the right to complain about the nuisance.

Where a person is performing a statutory duty they will not be liable for nuisance in undertaking the duty in the absence of negligence. In the case of the exercise of a statutory power, the defendant will not be liable for a nuisance in the absence of negligence if the statute expressly excludes liability for nuisance or is silent on the matter. However, the defendant will be liable for the creation of a nuisance in the exercise of a statutory power even in the absence of negligence where the statute expressly makes them liable or expressly does not exempt them from liability (*Department of Transport* v *North West Water Board* [1984] AC 336). Where a nuisance is the inevitable result of carrying out statutory authority such as the power to operate an oil refinery, the defendant will not be liable for it (*Allen* v *Gulf Oil Refining Ltd* [1981] AC 1001). However, the possession of a licence such as planning permission from a regulatory body is not the equivalent of statutory authority and is not necessarily a defence (*Wheeler* v *JJ Saunders Ltd* [1995] Env LR 286).

It is doubtful whether a person can acquire a right to commit a nuisance by virtue of the operation of the doctrine of prescription, that is, by 20 years of committing the acts in question. In *Sturges* v *Bridgman* (1879) 11 ChD 852, the defendant, a confectioner, had used a noisy mortar and pestle for over 20 years. There had not been any complaints during that period but a doctor residing at the back of the site had built a new consulting room close to the defendant's operational area and the noise became a problem. Prescription did not operate as a defence here because the noise only became a nuisance after the construction of the new consulting room. It seems more correct to say that individuals with an interest in property may lose their rights to take action if they acquiesce in the nuisance for 20 years. However, they would still be able to complain about an increase in the level of pollution as the case *Kennaway* v *Thompson* [1981] QB 88 illustrates. In that case noise levels caused by water skiing on a lake increased over time. Even though the plaintiff was not able to prevent all water skiing taking place, she did obtain an injunction preventing a considerable amount of the increased noise levels.

It is, however, no defence that a person came to a nuisance and so must put up with it. *Sturges* v *Bridgman* (see above) illustrates this point since the extension of the doctor's property brought him to the nuisance. However, this did not deprive him of a remedy. The plaintiff is certainly under a duty to mitigate his/her loss as is normally the case in tort but need only take reasonable action and would not be required to take abnormal steps to protect him/herself from the effects of a nuisance.

Furthermore, as we explained above it is not possible for a defendant to argue that the social utility of the activity complained of acts as a defence (see pp. 67–68).

Remedies

If a person is enduring noise or smells the most effective remedy is simply an injunction (in Scotland, an interdict) to prevent the conduct or activity complained of from continuing or from being repeated or even from commencing. Where an interim injunction or interdict is sought to prevent an alleged nuisance continuing pending a hearing to determine whether the conduct does amount to a nuisance, the court will consider what is known as the balance of convenience. It is in this situation that the social utility of the activity complained of may affect the remedy which the court is prepared to grant. For example, in the Scottish case *Barr & Stroud* v *West of Scotland Water Authority* 1996 GWD 36-2126 the court would not grant an interim interdict preventing the operation of a sewage works, which was allegedly causing an odour nuisance interfering with a neighbouring business, because the social utility of continuing to operate the sewage works and hence not having raw sewage overflowing into two rivers outweighed the business interest affected. However, this did not mean that a remedy in damages would not be potentially available.

Damages are available when actual physical damage loss or harm occurs. In Scotland *culpa*, that is, fault, must be proved if damages are claimed. The plaintiff may recover for physical damage to property, for depreciation in the value of the property and for loss of business resulting from the nuisance although in the latter case, the plaintiff may not recover the whole amount of the loss if the court considers that some loss would have been suffered even though no actionable nuisance had been committed. Thus in *Andreae* v *Selfridge & Co. Ltd* (see above) the court quantified the amount which the plaintiff's hotel would have lost in any case had the demolition works in question not constituted a nuisance and deducted that amount from the total damages representing the loss of business which they in fact suffered. The principle applied in that case would also appear to apply to cases involving depreciation of the plaintiff's land.

The Rylands v Fletcher rule

This is a special type of nuisance and derives from the judgment in *Rylands* v *Fletcher* (1865) 3 H & C 774. The case involved the construction of a reservoir on land belonging to the defendant. The contractors failed to seal mine shafts under the reservoir with the result that water flooded a mine belonging to the plaintiff. The House of Lords found the defendant strictly liable. The essence of the rule is that a person will be strictly liable for damage caused by the escape of dangerous materials which he/she has brought onto his/her land. The application of the rule has been limited by the requirement that the use of the land must be non-natural for the rule to apply and, more recently, by the requirement that the type of damage which occurs must be reasonably foreseeable: *Cambridge Water Co.* v *Eastern Counties Leather plc* (see above). The *Cambridge Water Co.* case also established that the *Rylands* v *Fletcher* rule was an aspect of the tort of nuisance. You should note that the *Rylands* v *Fletcher* rule only applies in England and Wales.

Public nuisance

There is also a type of nuisance in England and Wales (but not in Scotland) known as public nuisance. A public nuisance has been defined by a judge as 'any nuisance "which materially affects the reasonable comfort and convenience of life of a class of Her Majesty's subjects"' (*Attorney-General* v *PYA Quarries* [1957] 2 QB 169). That case involved quarrying which was affecting neighbouring houses by vibrations and dust. The quarrying was held to constitute a public nuisance. Public nuisance actually derives from the criminal law. A member of the public who can prove that he/she has suffered special damage from the defendant's commission of the common law crime of public nuisance may sue the defendant in tort. The tort does not require interference with private property but annoyance of the public by, for example, obstruction of the highway or pollution of the public water supply.

Any person may bring an action in public nuisance but in order to succeed he or she must show special damage has been suffered that is greater than that suffered by the public. Personal injury or property damage would clearly amount to special damage. However, it is possible for actions to be brought in the public interest by the Attorney-General as in the case mentioned above or by a private individual suing in the name of the Attorney-General and with the Attorney-General's consent. This latter type of action is known as a 'relator' action.

Liability in public nuisance is generally fault-based although there is an exception which we deal with below. The fault consists of unreasonable conduct on the defendant's part.

The most common type of public nuisance is obstruction of the highway. This could be caused by people queueing on the pavement and obstructing businesses. Where the queuing is avoidable, for example, by opening the doors to a theatre or cinema earlier (*Lyons, Sons & Co.* v *Gulliver* [1914] 1 Ch 631) or by selling ice cream inside a shop rather than through a window (*Fabbri* v *Morris* [1947] 1 All ER 315) public nuisance will be established.

If premises on a highway become dangerous because they have not been repaired and a passer-by or neighbour is injured, that would constitute a public nuisance with the occupier or the owner (if the latter had covenanted to repair the building) being held liable (*Wringe* v *Cohen* [1940] 1 KB 229). Liability in this type of public nuisance is strict.

It is possible to claim damages for personal injury as well as for property damage in public nuisance and indeed for pure economic loss, such as loss of profits caused by an obstruction of the highway. An example of this is *Wilkes* v *Hungerford Market* (1835) 2 Brig NC 281 where the plaintiff was able to recover loss of profits arising from interference with public access to his shop caused by such an obstruction. The ability to sue for pure economic loss is an advantage over the tort of negligence where such losses are not generally recoverable.

Statutory nuisance

Largely as a result of problems with the common law as a means of dealing with nuisances, such as the need for a plaintiff who was willing and able to take action and the non-availability of remedies to clean up nuisances, from the middle of the nineteenth century Parliament legislated to impose duties on local authorities to inspect their areas for statutory nuisances and to take action to abate any such nuisances which were found. Statutory nuisance provisions for England, Wales and Scotland are now contained in Part III of the Environmental Protection Act 1990 (EPA 1990). The matters which may constitute a statutory nuisance are defined in the statute. They include smoke, fumes or gases, dust, steam or smell, noise or premises in such a state so as to be prejudicial to health or a nuisance (EPA 1990, s.79(1)). Local authorities must inspect their areas from time to time for statutory nuisances (EPA 1990, s.79) and, if they find such a nuisance, they must serve an abatement notice on the person responsible for the nuisance (EPA 1990, s.80(1)). They must also investigate if a statutory nuisance exists following a complaint. These duties are enforceable in the courts and do not leave the local authority with any discretion (*R* v *Carrick*

District Council, ex p. Shelley and Another [1996] Env LR 273). Contravention of an abatement notice is a criminal offence (EPA 1990, s.80(4)).

While local authorities have the primary role in abating statutory nuisances, individuals may also take action in the Magistrates' Court (in Scotland, the Sheriff Court) to enforce the abatement of a statutory nuisance (EPA 1990, s.82).

Tort of trespass

In this final section we provide a very brief outline of the tort of trespass. Trespass is the oldest tort and may be committed against a person or land. Trespass against goods is now a matter of statute, in England and Wales.

An example of trespass against the person in our context was the unlawful imprisonment of the plantiff in a public house in *Warner* v *Riddifor* (1858) 4 CBNS 180. He was employed there on one month's notice, but was dismissed with one week's notice. When he refused to leave without the extra pay to which he was entitled, the police were called and he was prevented from going upstairs for some time in case he took money from the till. He won his case and was awarded substantial damages.

Trespass to land is probably the best known of various types of trespass. Someone in lawful possession of land may prevent persons who trespass on their land from doing so by means of an injunction. Damages may also be obtained if the trespasser causes damage. Nominal damages may also be available for the act of trespass itself (*Hickman* v *Maisey* [1900] 1 QB 752). Reasonable force may be used to remove trespassers who have refused to leave following a request. The danger of this approach is that it may expose the landowner to criminal charges of assault or an action in tort of trespass to the person.

It is commonly believed that there is no law of trespass in Scotland. However, this view is incorrect (*Wood* v *North British Railway Co.* (1899) 2 F 1) as it is possible to obtain an interdict, the Scottish equivalent of an injunction, against a trespasser and to obtain damages where the trespasser causes damage. Nominal damages for the act of trespass are not available in contrast to the position south of the border. If a trespasser who has been ordered off a property refuses to leave no greater force than is reasonably necessary in the circumstance may be used to remove the trespasser (*Wood* v *North British Railway Co.* (see above). However, as we explained above using reasonable force is fraught with difficulty (*Bell* v *Shand* (1870) 7 SLR 267). The reason why a belief has grown up that there is no law of trespass in Scotland is because it is very difficult to enforce. An interdict may only be served on a named person and will only be granted by a court in Scotland if there is a reasonable apprehension that the trespass will be committed again. By way of contrast in England and Wales an injunction will hold good against any person who has notice of it.

There are various circumstances where trespass has been made a criminal offence by statute. However, in general trespass is not a criminal offence and hence if you see a notice saying 'Trespassers will be prosecuted', it is unlikely to be correct. However, certain bodies have statutory powers to make trespass on their property a criminal offence including Railtrack plc (formerly the British Railways Board) in relation to operational railway land and the Ministry of Defence in relation to defence establishments or lands. Furthermore, certain types of trespass, for example, by travelling people, anti-roads protestors, anti-hunt sabboteurs and groups of ramblers trying to demonstrate that a path is a right of way have recently and controversially been criminalized by the Criminal Justice and Public Order Act 1994. In Scotland in addition it is technically a criminal offence to camp or light fires on private property without permission under the Trespass (Scotland) Act 1865, a statue which was aimed at travelling people.

Trespass to goods, that is the wrongful interference by one person with another's goods, is now the subject of statutory regulation by virtue of the Torts (Interference with Goods) Act 1977. For example, if a person wrongly took another's luggage, this could constitute trespass under the Act. This statute does not apply in Scotland where this situation would be governed by the common law.

Forms of business organizations | 3

INTRODUCTION

In this chapter we discuss the three forms of organization which are normally used for carrying on business activity: the sole trader, the partnership or the company. Choice of organization depends on a variety of factors including the nature of the business; obtaining finance for the business; the persons involved; and tax matters. It should be noted that for reasons of space we do not consider the issue of bankruptcy or insolvency of business organizations.

However, before we proceed to consider the various business organizations and their relative merits it is worth mentioning two preliminary matters.

First, when the law refers to a person, this may in fact be a reference to a company. Persons in law can be natural persons (i.e. individuals) or legal persons, (i.e. companies and, in Scotland, partnerships). See also Chapter Two, p. 37.

Secondly, there are certain limitations which the law imposes on the names which a business (whether sole trader, partnership or company) may use. Since these provisions apply to all business organizations, this is discussed in the next section before we consider the various forms of business organizations themselves.

BUSINESS NAMES

Purpose of law on business names

The objectives of the law on business names are essentially twofold: (1) to ensure that persons are aware of the true identity of businesses where it is not apparent from the name of the business; and (2) to prevent the use of prohibited and undesirable names. The principal piece of legislation in this area is the Business Names Act 1985 (BNA).

Disclosure of business name

In order to achieve the first objective the BNA requires that all persons who trade under a name different from their own:

1. must state the business's name (in the case of a sole trader, clearly state the trader's name; in the case of a partnership, the name of every partner (except where there

are more than twenty partners); and, in the case of a company, the registered name of the company) on all business letters, invoices, receipts, orders etc.;

2. must also state, in relation to every person named, an address in Great Britain at which documents may be served;
3. must prominently display the names and addresses in the premises where business is carried on; and
4. must supply such names and addresses in writing on request.

Failure to comply with any of these provisions is a criminal offence (Business Names Act 1985, s.4(6)). In the case of companies, the Companies Act 1985 (CA) reinforces these provisions by requiring companies to paint or affix their names in a conspicuous position and in letters which are easily legible outside every office or place in which business is carried on (CA, s.348(1)) and to mention their names on all business documents including correspondence, cheques, invoices and receipts (CA, s.349(1)). One of the principal reasons for these provisions is to enable court action to be taken against the correct person.

Names which require permission

The second objective is achieved by requiring that certain names may only be used with permission of the Secretary of State or the Government Department or public authority concerned. This is achieved by a variety of statutory provisions and in some cases the prohibition on the use of certain names is absolute. For example, it is unlawful to use the words 'Boy Scouts' in any circumstances (Chartered Associations (Protection of Names and Uniforms) Act 1926, s.1); 'Red Cross' without the permission of the Army Council (Geneva Convention Act 1957, s.6); the word 'bank' unless the company has been authorized by the Bank of England (Banking Act 1987, s.67); 'building society' without being registered as such (Building Societies Act 1986, s.107); words requiring the written approval of the Secretary of State or other public authority under the Company and Business Names Regulations 1981 (as amended) which include 'England', 'Wales', 'Scotland', 'Ireland', 'Great Britain', 'council', 'association', 'group' and 'holding' (BNA, s.6); and any words which would be likely to give the impression that the business is connected with central and local government (BNA, ss 2–3). If a person seeks to register a company with such a name without obtaining the requisite permission, registration will be refused (CA 1985, s.26).

Passing off

For practical purposes, it is also advisable that the business name should not be like that of an existing business otherwise the public might confuse the two. Furthermore, there may be a danger of the person with the similar name raising a court action on the basis that 'passing off' is occurring. Passing off is where one person seeks to take advantage of the name and goodwill of another business by imitating its name. If the court establishes that passing off is occurring, it can grant an injunction (in Scotland, an interdict) to prevent the business continuing to trade in that name and may award damages. For example, in *Exxon Corporation* v *Exxon Insurance Consultants International Ltd.* [1982] Ch 119, the court granted an injunction preventing the defendants from passing off by using the word Exxon and an injunction preventing them from allowing any name containing Exxon to remain on the register of companies. This would have required them to change the name of the company or to dissolve it.

SOLE TRADER

Establishment of the business

A sole trader is a person who goes into business on his/her own account. All profits which are made are retained by a sole trader and he/she is personally liable for all losses. To set up as a sole trader there is no statutory requirement to register as is the case with incorporating a company or to go through any other legal formalities. However, when acquiring or leasing premises and commencing business, a sole trader should be aware that all relevant regulations must be complied with including those relating to health and safety, planning and environmental matters. Furthermore, as we mentioned above, the provisions of the BNA impose some limitations on the names which a sole trader may adopt when proposing to trade in a name other than his/her own.

Merits of being a sole trader

Sole traders are obviously subject to fewer regulations as to the conduct of their business than companies. There is no requirement to hold an annual general meeting or to lodge an annual return and annual accounts with the registrar of companies as is the case with companies. However, accounts must be prepared on an annual basis for tax purposes.

Sole traders may also cease business whenever they like. There is no special legal procedure which must be gone through before the business may cease operating in contrast to the position with companies, which must be dissolved. In the event of a trader's death, his/her successor may wish to carry on the business or may sell it as a going concern or sell the assets to other businesses after settling its liabilities.

However, sole traders are at a disadvantage compared to both partnerships and companies in terms of raising capital. This is because they put their own money into their businesses and although they may be able to convince a lending institution to give them a loan they cannot bring in partners with capital nor can they raise funds through share issues. The forms of security which they can grant to lending institutions to secure loans are also more limited than those which a company can grant.

Furthermore a sole trader's liability for debts is also potentially unlimited so that private property, such as a house, may be needed to pay off debts. Transferring property to a spouse is not necessarily an option if it can be shown that this was done to defeat creditors.

PARTNERSHIPS

Nature of partnerships

Partnerships are regulated by the provisions of the Partnership Act 1890 (PA). This statute defines a partnership as 'the relation which subsists between persons carrying on a business in common with a view of profit' (PA, s.1).

This definition clearly requires some form of business activity to be carried on even if only for a short duration and the business must be a commercial venture aiming at a profit. Joint ventures are partnerships of limited purpose and duration, for example, for a construction project. In practice, in many cases the partners in a joint venture are in fact companies rather than individuals.

The number of partners in a partnership cannot exceed twenty except in professional partnerships such as solicitors or accountants (Companies Act 1985, s.716).

In England and Wales a partnership is not a legal person separate from the partners of which it is composed. However, in Scotland, although partnerships are also governed by the PA, a partnership is, to a certain extent, treated by law as a legal person in its own right, distinct from its partners (*Jardine-Paterson* v *Fraser* 1974 SLT 93). This has significant consequences in relation to ownership of property except for land and buildings and partnership liabilities for debts and obligations. A Scottish partnership can also sue and be sued in its own name although the Rules of the Supreme Court in England and Wales have been amended to enable this to be done. We consider these issues in more detail below.

Finally, as you may be aware, partnerships are commonly referred to as firms.

Establishing a partnership

Rules for determining whether a partnership exists

Whether a partnership exists is a question of the intention of the parties as they appear from all the circumstances of the case. Section 2 of the PA provides some rules to assist in determining whether or not a partnership exists. For example, joint tenancy or ownership does not of itself create a partnership but receipt of a share of the profits of a business is *prima facie* evidence that the recipient is a partner.

Partnership deed or agreement

The relationship between the partners is contractual and the rules about the formation of contracts and capacity to enter into contracts discussed in Chapter 2 at pp. 38–42 are applicable in this context. There is no requirement that the partnership agreement should be in writing although it is good practice to have a written agreement. This is usually known as a 'partnership deed' in England and Wales and a 'partnership agreement' in Scotland. This document should at the very least deal with:

1. the partnership name;
2. how the business is to be financed;
3. management of the business;
4. how profits are to be shared by the partners;

5. the partners' rights and duties;
6. accountancy procedures;
7. how disputes between partners are to be dealt with; and
8. the ways in which the partnership may be terminated.

Restrictions on partnership name

As we mentioned above, the BNA's provisions impose some limitations on partnerships where they intend to trade in a name other than the name of the partners. Hence, the names and addresses of all the partners must be displayed on a prominent notice and on all business letters and documents. However, there is no legal requirement for registration of the partnership with any government body in contrast to the position with companies (see pp. 85–86).

Relations between the partners

Introduction

Relations between the partners may be regulated expressly or impliedly. Where there is a partnership deed or agreement its provisions should expressly regulate relations between the partners. Such relations may be varied by the consent of all the partners which need not be given expressly but may be inferred (PA, s.19).

Anti-discrimination provisions

The Race Relations Act 1976 (RRA) and the Sex Discrimination Act 1975 (SDA 1975) (as amended) apply to partnerships with six or more partners and make it unlawful to discriminate against a person on the grounds of race or sex either in the arrangements made for offering a partnership, or in the terms of position offered, or by refusing such a position, or by expelling a person from the partnership (RRA, s.10; SDA 1975, s.11; see also Chapter Seven for a general discussion of discrimination).

Partners' rights

Where there is no agreement to the contrary s.24 of the PA provides that partners will have certain basic rights including the right to share profits and losses equally (PA, s.24(1); e.g. *Garner* v *Murray* [1904] 1 Ch.57); the right to an equal share in the firm's property (PA, s.24(1)); the right to participate in the management of the business (PA, s.24(5)); and the right to veto any new partner being introduced to the partnership (PA, s.24(7)). However, you should note that no partner is entitled to a salary (PA, s.24(6)).

Consequences of the fiduciary relationship between partners

Since the relationship between partners is characterized like agency as being a fiduciary relationship involving the utmost good faith (in Latin, *uberrimae fidei*), it is necessary for all partners to render true accounts and disclose all relevant information to their fellow partners (PA, s.28). Likewise if secret profits are made from dealings with outsiders, a partner must account for these to the other partners (PA, s.29). They are entitled to a share of these profits in accordance with the terms of the partnership agreement or, if it is silent on the matter, to an equal share of the profits (PA, s.24(1)). The fiduciary relationship also requires that partners do not enter into competition with their firm (PA, s.30).

Partnership property

There is no requirement that partners contribute capital or property to the partnership. However, any property brought into the firm by a partner when it was established or which has been acquired subsequently is partnership property (PA, s.20). It is also the case that property bought with partnership money is presumed to have been bought for the partnership although this presumption may be rebutted (PA, s.21).

As noted above, where there is no provision to the contrary in the partnership deed or agreement all partners are entitled to an equal share in the partnership property (PA, s.24(1)).

In Scotland, again as a result of the fact that partnerships have a limited separate legal personality, the partnership may hold property in its own name with the exception of land and buildings which must be held in trust by the partners for the firm (PA, s.20(2)).

Expulsion of a partner

It is not possible to expel a partner by majority unless a power to do so is conferred expressly by the partnership deed or agreement (PA, s.25). Such provisions are construed strictly by the courts which may refuse to enforce them where they have been invoked for private reasons and are not in the interests of the partnership (*Green v Howell* [1901] 1 Ch 495). Since partnerships are based on good faith, there are not usually provisions relating to dismissal in partnership agreements.

Relations between the partnership and third parties

General provisions on partners' liabilities

In England and Wales, a partner is jointly liable together with all the other partners for the firm's debts and liabilities incurred while a partner. However, in Scotland, since a partnership has, to a limited extent, a separate legal personality from the partners, the debt must be constituted against the firm (e.g. *Highland Engineering Ltd v Anderson* 1979 SLT 122). If the firm cannot pay, payment of the debt may be sought from one or more of the partners who are jointly and severally liable for debts incurred by the firm (PA, s.9) subject to a *pro rata* right of relief against each other (PA, s.4(2)). This means that each partner is individually liable for the whole debts and liabilities of the firm but that the partner(s) sued may seek to recover the share of the debt owed by the other partner(s).

In the case of new, retiring or deceased or bankrupt partners there are exceptions to the above general rules. First, in the event of a new partner, he/she will not normally be liable for any debts or liabilities incurred before joining the partnership (PA, s.17(1)). Secondly, a retiring partner does not cease to be liable for debts and liabilities incurred before retirement (PA, s.17(2)). However, retiring partners are not liable for debts or liabilities incurred after retirement unless they hold out, that is, represent, that they are continuing as a partner (PA, s.14(1)). In *Tower Cabinet Co.* v *Ingram* [1949] 2 KB 397 the court held that where a partner retired and the remaining partner continued to use notepaper belonging to the partnership contrary to an agreement that it would be destroyed on the dissolution of the partnership, the retired partner did not knowingly suffer himself to be held out as a partner. Finally, where a partner dies or becomes bankrupt, his or her estate ceases to be liable (PA, s.36(3)).

Contract

In terms of contractual relationships with third parties, the general law of agency applies (see Chapter Two, pp. 54–56). The actual authority of a partner to enter into contracts which bind the firm may be regulated by the partnership deed or agreement. However, even where a partner lacks actual authority, he/she may still have ostensible or apparent authority to enter into contracts which may still bind the firm. Therefore where a partner enters into a contract 'in carrying on in the usual way business of a kind carried on by the firm' he/she will bind the firm unless he/she in fact have no authority and the person with whom they are dealing knows this (PA, s.5; *United Bank of Kuwait* v *Hammoud* [1988] 1 WLR 1051). Thus, it is important to agree what areas of responsibility each partner has. If the partners do agree any restrictions on their power, such restrictions have to be notified to all persons who deal with the firm otherwise third parties may rely on the fact that the partner can bind the firm and other partners for all acts which are done in the course of the firm's business. Any partner who contravenes such an agreement, where persons dealing with the firm were aware of the restrictions on their power, will be personally bound on that contract with the third party (*Fortune* v *Young* 1918 SC 1).

Tort/delict

A partnership is vicariously liable for the tortious (in Scotland, delictual) acts or omissions of any partner acting in the usual course of its business (PA, s.10). This means that a partnership must take out insurance to cover all its potential tortious liabilities. It is not enough for a partner to take out insurance in relation to his or her own careless acts. Claimants may bring their actions against the firm and/or the individual partner who caused the claimant's loss. If the firm pays compensation to the claimant it may then seek to recover that amount from the partner whose actions or omissions caused the loss. In Scotland claimants must first bring an action against the firm and if it cannot pay they may then bring actions against the partner(s) whose negligence caused the claimant's loss. It must be remembered that partners are jointly and severally liable in Scotland and have a *pro rata* right of relief against the other partners (PA, s.12). For a general discussion of the law of tort, see Chapter Two, pp. 54–74.

Misapplication of third party funds

If a partner misapplies funds received from a third party, for example a client, the firm is liable (PA, s.11). However, if a partner misapplies trust funds, the other partners are not liable unless they had notice of the breach of trust but the trust money may be recovered from the firm if it is still within the firm's control (PA, s.13).

Dissolution of partnership

This may be regulated by the partnership deed or agreement. However, subject to any such provision in the partnership agreement s.32 of the PA provides that:

1. a partnership established for a fixed term will be dissolved on the expiry of that term;
2. a partnership established for a single undertaking will be dissolved on the termination of that undertaking; or
3. if entered into for an undefined period, by a partner giving notice to the others of his/her intention to dissolve the partnership.

In the case of a partnership established for a fixed term which carries on business beyond the expiry of the term, the law will infer the continued existence of the partnership. This is known as 'tacit relocation'. The terms of the original partnership agreement will continue to be valid in so far as they are consistent with the continuing partnership (PA, s.27).

A partnership is also dissolved by the death or bankruptcy of one of the parties unless the partnership deed or agreement provides otherwise (PA, s.33). However, the retirement of a partner does not necessarily dissolve a partnership if there is a provision to that effect in the partnership deed or agreement or all partners otherwise consent.

A partnership will also be dissolved where it becomes unlawful for the firm or its members to carry on the business (PA, s.34), for example, where one of the partners becomes an enemy alien following a declaration of war (*Stevenson* v *Cartonnagen-Industrie* [1918] AC 239). The court may also dissolve a partnership on an application from a partner on various grounds including where a partner becomes permanently incapable of performing his/her partnership duties or where a partner persistently breaches the partnership deed or agreement or where the business can only be carried on at a loss (PA, s.35).

Limited partnerships

The Limited Partnership Act 1907 provides for a form of limited liability for partners known as limited partners. A limited partnership comprises at least one full partner together with limited partners. In return for an investment of a fixed sum of money in a firm, the limited partner's liability for the firm's debts is restricted to the amount which is invested provided that he/she complies with two conditions. These are that the sum must remain invested in the partnership and that he/she does not participate in the management of the business. Participation in the management of the firm will render a limited partner liable for all the debts of the firm along with any full partners.

This type of partnership is not commonly found, although a number of farming enterprises operate as limited partnerships. It is not clear why it is not used to a greater extent given the considerable protection from liability for the firm's debts which is afforded to limited partners.

Merits of partnership

There are considerable advantages of establishing a partnership. For example, there are no legal formalities required for setting up a partnership in contrast to incorporating a company although the drafting of a partnership deed or agreement will normally involve paying solicitors' fees. In terms of ongoing formalities, there are no requirements to hold annual general meetings or lodge annual returns and accounts with a government body in contrast to companies. Obviously, however, a partnership must still prepare accounts since it is not exempt from the scrutiny of the tax authorities, HM Inland Revenue and HM Customs and Excise. Nonetheless the great advantage of partnerships over companies is privacy. Whereas the documents which a company is required to submit to the registrar of companies on its incorporation and its annual return and accounts are available for public inspection, there are no similar requirements in relation to a partnership. In Scotland, the limited separate legal personality which partnerships possess, may also shield the partners to an extent from liability, although if the firm cannot pay its debts, then the partners will be jointly and severally liable.

There is access to greater capital than is the case with a sole trader since more than one person can invest in the firm, although the methods by which a partnership may grant forms of security to lenders to raise capital are also more limited than in the case of companies.

However, any partner's personal assets are at risk if the partnership has considerable liabilities. In England and Wales partners are jointly liable for a firm's debts and obligations. However, in Scotland, if the firm cannot pay its debts, the partners are jointly and severally liable. Although limited partnerships provide considerable protection from liability for limited partners, even greater protection is provided by incorporating a company which is a completely separate legal person from its investors.

COMPANIES

Introduction

Companies are principally established under statute. However, bodies may also be incorporated by Royal Charter, for example, the British Broadcasting Corporation, the University of Strathclyde and many others. You should also note that many public bodies established under specific statutes are bodies corporate. Such bodies include local authorities, the Environment Agency (established by the Environment Act 1995), the Countryside Council for Wales (established by the Environmental Protection Act 1990) and Scottish Natural Heritage (established by the Natural Heritage (Scotland) Act 1991).

The principal statute governing companies presently is the Companies Act 1985 (CA). However, several other important statutes are relevant. We have already considered the Business Names Act 1985 (BNA). In addition the Insolvency Act 1986, the Company Directors (Disqualification) Act 1986 and the Companies Act 1989 are among the important Acts which are relevant in this field.

Corporate personality

Separate personality and its consequences

A company is a distinct legal person. This is very important and means that it has a separate personality from its promoters, directors and shareholders and that claims against the company, for example for debts, are not claims against those individuals. Therefore, the fact that one individual takes all a company's profits, does not make that person liable for the company's debts beyond the amount unpaid on shares which he/she has in the company.

The leading case on this point is *Salomon v Salomon & Co.* [1897] AC 22. Salomon, a bootmaker, incorporated a company in which he held 20 001 shares and six family members held one share each. He then entered into an agreement with the company for the sale of his bootmaking business to the company. He loaned back to the company £10,000 of the purchase price secured over the company's assets. This meant that if the company went into liquidation its assets would be applied to repay this loan. The company went into liquidation with assets of £6,000 and debts of £8,000 to unsecured creditors. These creditors claimed that the company's assets should be used to repay the debts owed to them and should not be used to repay Salomon because he and the company were in reality the same person and it was not possible to lend money to oneself. However, the House of Lords decided that the loan transaction between the company and Salomon was valid as it was a separate person from Salomon. Hence Salomon was entitled to the company's remaining assets rather than the unsecured creditors.

This approach may cause serious problems for creditors in situations where the company is insolvent but its directors and shareholders are solvent. It also means that when a person deals with a company, they are not dealing with its subsidiaries or parents. Thus, for example, where a company is wholly owned by a parent company, when a person deals with the subsidiary and it goes out of business, they acquire no rights against the parent company.

Since a company has a personality of its own, the death of shareholders and/or directors does not affect its existence in a strict sense. A company can only cease to have an existence by a formal legal process involving winding up and dissolution. Various provisions permit dissolution in certain circumstances. The most common is s.652 of the CA which permits the registrar of companies to strike defunct companies off the register of companies and dissolve them.

Piercing the corporate veil: looking behind corporate personality

There are, however, limited circumstances in which the courts may be prepared to look behind the facade of the company's personality to the individuals who lie behind it (known as 'piercing the corporate veil'), although they are usually reluctant to do this. These circumstances are principally as follows:

- If a company is being wound up, s.212 of the Insolvency Act 1986 imposes certain liabilities on any officer of the company (including the company secretary and directors) who has 'misapplied or retained, or become accountable for' any funds or property of the company or broken their fiduciary duties (i.e., their duty of good faith – see p. 90). Such an officer must restore the same or pay compensation. Regardless of the company's own personality, therefore, any company director may be required to account when things go wrong.

- If in the course of a winding up there is an allegation of wrongful trading under s.214 of the Insolvency Act 1986, a court is entitled to investigate whether the directors were responsible for that wrongful trading. This is a very important principle for all those who are dealing with a company and, more importantly, for those who are or intend to become directors of a company. Under s.214, a director is trading wrongfully if a company has gone into insolvent liquidation (i.e. its assets are insufficient for the payment of its debts and other liabilities) and at some time prior to the commencement of the winding up the director knew or ought to have concluded that there was no reasonable prospect that the company would avoid going into insolvent liquidation. No dishonesty need be involved; it is sufficient for the director to be negligent or to have behaved unreasonably. The court may order any director involved in such conduct to 'make such contributions (if any) to the company's assets as the court thinks proper'. However, if a director took every step to minimize the loss to the company's creditors, he/she will not be liable.

Corporate personality and criminal liability

Since a company is a legal person it may be criminally liable although its potential liability is more limited than that of an individual. This is because a company cannot normally have the *mens rea* (guilty mind) which is a necessary requirement for conviction of defendants in all but statutory strict liability offences. There are, however, many such offences, for example, in the areas of health and safety, environmental protection, food safety and licensing legislation. You should note that many such regulatory statutes make provision for the criminal conviction of company officers including directors, company secretaries and other similar officers where they consented to or connived at the commission of the offence by the company or the offence was committed by reason of their negligence, for example, s.37 of the Health and Safety at Work Act 1974. We provide a more detailed discussion of the criminal responsibility of companies and their officers in Chapter Five.

Types of company

Introduction

Companies may be classified in various ways. The following discussion attempts to outline the principal methods of classification and at the same time to clarify the various distinctions between types of companies.

Registered companies

The principal form of business organization in Great Britain is the registered company. If a company is incorporated under the CA it must be registered prior to its incorporation (CA, s.1). If it is not registered it will not have the status of a company. The company name and various information about the company are actually placed on a register which is open to public inspection and held by the registrar of companies. The location of a company's registered office determines where it is registered (CA, s.2). Companies with their registered offices in England and Wales are registered in Cardiff, and those with their registered offices in Scotland are registered in Edinburgh. We briefly consider the requirements of registration below (see pp. 87–89).

Unregistered companies

Certain companies are not registered because they are not incorporated under the Companies Acts but by specific statutes or by Royal Charter. These are not important in the context of the hospitality and tourism industries.

Limited and unlimited companies

Section 1 of the CA allows registration of limited or unlimited liability companies. Limited liability companies are not a means of avoiding payment of debts. Companies have a separate legal personality and this means that even if they are what is known as limited liability companies they have unlimited liability to pay all their debts. The limitation on liability does not refer to the company's liabilities but to its shareholders' (who are known in company law as 'members') liabilities. If a company is registered as a limited company what is meant is that its shareholders' liability to meet the company's debts, where it is being wound up in an insolvency, is limited to the nominal value of their shareholdings.

Where a company is unlimited, this means that the liability of its shareholders to pay the debts of the company when it is being wound up if, for example, it has become insolvent, is unlimited. This potential for unrestricted personal liability in the event of a winding up is obviously a disincentive for being a member of an unlimited company. However, there is one major advantage which unlimited companies have which is that they are not required to file annual accounts with the registrar of companies which limited companies must do. This enables the internal affairs of the company to be kept secret since the accounts of limited companies are publicly available.

The reason for limiting liability is essentially to encourage business activity. Without it individuals might feel constrained from investing in business because of the potential liabilities to which they might be subject.

Companies limited by shares

This is by far the most common type of company. In a company limited by shares, the liability of the shareholders when the company is being wound up in an insolvency is limited to the nominal value of their shares. They cannot be required to make further contributions in relation to their shareholdings even if their shares in fact have a much higher value than their nominal value. For example, if a person holds 1000 shares with a nominal value of £1 each, and they have paid for the shares, they will not be liable to pay anything in the event of an insolvency even if the shares are worth £10 each on the market. If they have not paid for the shares they will only be liable to pay £1,000, again regardless of the market value of the shares. Persons who have partly paid for shares will only have to pay the outstanding sum due in the event of insolvency. However, it should be remembered that the Insolvency Act 1986 does provide that company officers who may also be shareholders may need to make further contributions if they have, for example, been trading fraudulently or wrongfully (Insolvency Act 1986, ss 213, 214).

Companies limited by guarantee

This form of company is usually adopted by clubs or associations or charitable or other non-trading organizations. It is not a vehicle which is normally used for commercial purposes. The members agree to limit their liability by guaranteeing to pay an agreed amount in the event of the company being wound up (CA, s.1(2)(b). This is simply not practical for business organizations.

Private companies

A private company must indicate that it is a private company by adding the word 'Limited' or its abbreviated form 'Ltd' to its name (CA, s.25(2)). It can register without a minimum share capital, unlike a public company (see below). It may begin trading as soon as it receives its certificate of incorporation from the registrar of companies.

The Government's deregulation initiative has ensured in recent years that the requirements of submitting annual returns and accounts to the registrar of companies have been considerably simplified. For example, companies with a turnover of less than £1,400,000 and a balance sheet total of less than £700,000 or fewer than 50 employees file abridged accounts. A medium sized company, that is, one whose balance sheet is under £2,800,000 or which employs fewer than 250 people, need not submit details of turnover or gross profit margins.

As a result of the EC Twelfth Company Law Directive (89/667/EEC), since 15 July 1992 it has been possible for a private company to have a single member (i.e. shareholder). Previously it was not so easy for sole traders to incorporate since they required at least one other member. Now that restriction has been abolished, it is easier for sole traders to incorporate their businesses.

Public companies

The use of the words 'public limited company' or the abbreviation 'plc' indicates that a company is a public company and it is a statutory requirement to use them (CA, s.25(1)). Public companies must have at least two shareholders and a minimum contributed share capital. This provision implements the EC Second Company Law Directive (77/91/EEC). The minimum level of contributed share capital may be prescribed by the Secretary of State (CA, s.118). The current level is set at £50,000 (CA, s.11). Public limited companies cannot be limited by guarantee but only by shares.

Incorporating a company limited by shares

It is possible to buy 'off-the-shelf companies' which may have been set up by solicitors' firms or businesses specializing in such corporate matters.

Registered companies must provide the registrar of companies with two documents which together form the company's constitution: (1) the memorandum of association; and (2) the articles of association (CA, ss 10 and 12). We discuss the contents of these documents further below.

A statement of the first directors, company secretary and the company's intended registered office must also be submitted to the registrar (CA, s.10; Sch. 1) together with a statement of capital (Finance Act 1973, s.47), a statutory declaration of compliance signed by a solicitor involved in the incorporation of the company or a person named as director or company secretary (CA, s.10) and the appropriate registration fee.

On registering the memorandum, the registrar allocates a number to the company and issues a certificate of incorporation which is essentially the company's birth certificate. The certificate is conclusive evidence that the company has complied with the requirements of registration, is authorized and has been properly registered (CA, ss 10,12,13).

The provisions of the Business Names Act 1985 and the CA impose limitations on the names which a company might use. We discuss this above at pp. 75–77.

Constitution of a company

The memorandum of association

Model memoranda of association are provided in the CA and it is possible to adapt these to the particular purpose required. However, s.2 of the CA requires that all memoranda of association must include the following information:

- company name;
- whether the company's registered office is in England, Wales, Scotland or Northern Ireland;
- the objects of the company, i.e. what the company is in business to do. This used to be of considerable importance as the company could not do things which exceeded its objects, i.e. were *ultra vires*. However this rule has in effect been abolished and indeed it is now possible for the company to go into business as a general commercial company;
- a statement whether the liability of the members is limited and whether by shares or by guarantee;
- where the liability of the company's members is limited by shares, a statement of the amount of authorized share capital of the company and how many shares the company is authorized to issue and the value of each share, e.g. £1,000,000 authorized share capital of 1,000,000 £1 shares; and
- in the case of a public company, it must state that it is a public company.

The memorandum must be signed by at least two persons in the case of public or unlimited companies but, in the case of private companies, need only be signed by a single subscriber. Each signatory must subscribe for at least one share and the signature must be attested by at least one witness (CA, s.2(5)–(6)).

Articles of association

The articles of association regulate the internal management of the company governing matters such as the appointment and retirement of directors and their powers, the rights attaching to various types of shares, and the conduct of company general meetings. The CA provides that if no articles are submitted to the registrar by the incorporators the statutory articles which appear in the CA, Table A, will apply.

Alterations to the memorandum or articles

Both the memorandum and articles may be altered by the company in general meeting although this may only be done by what is known as special resolution and, in the case of the memorandum of association, there is also the requirement that the special resolution may require confirmation by the court if it is challenged by members holding at least 15 per cent in nominal value of the company's issued share capital (CA 1985, ss 4 and 9). These restrictions are designed to safeguard the interests of members and creditors.

Directors

Directors as a company's agents

Although a company is a separate legal person it obviously cannot itself act. Essentially a company acts through its directors to whom its management is assigned (*Ferguson* v *Wilson* (1866) LR 2 Ch App 77). They are its agents and it is therefore important to consider what their powers are (see below). A discussion of the general principles of the law of agency may be found in Chapter Two on pp. 54–56. Shareholders have no authority to bind a company at all (*Ernest* v *Nicholls* (1857) 6 HL Cas 401).

Minimum number of directors; appointment and retirement

Every company must have at least two directors except a private company which needs only one director (CA, s.282). Every company also needs a secretary and a sole director cannot also be a secretary (CA, s.283). Appointment and retirement of directors is governed by the company's articles of association.

Authority to bind the company

If the company has more than one director, the various directors may well be allocated specific functions. Where a director has a specific function, for example to enter into a particular type of contract (such as buying stock), and it is within the objects of the company as set out in the memorandum, then any such contract entered into will bind the company. However, where a director enters into a contract which is beyond his/her actual powers, the contract will still bind the company if it is a contract which a third party would expect to be within the ordinary ambit of authority of such a director or is within the apparent or ostensible authority of such a director (*Freeman & Lockyer* v *Buckhurst Park Properties (Mangal) Ltd and Another* [1964] All ER 630).

Furthermore, the company will be bound by a contract which is not outside the powers laid down in the memorandum and articles even if there has been some irregularity in internal arrangements (*Royal British Bank* v *Turquand* (1856) 6 E & B 327). In that case the company's articles gave the directors the power to borrow money on the company's behalf but only after obtaining a resolution passed by the company in general meeting. Money was borrowed from a bank without the requisite resolution being obtained. The court held that since the bank had no way of knowing whether or not the resolution had been passed it was entitled to assume that the resolution had been passed and the contract was therefore held to be binding on the company. However, where a third party has been notified that the director has no authority to bind the company, then the company is not bound by the transaction.

Similarly where a company holds out or represents that a director has more authority than he or she actually has the company is bound by any contracts entered into by that director, since once again the third party cannot know of the internal irregularity.

Company's liability in tort for directors' actions or omissions

Aside from giving rise to contractual liability, a director's actions or omissions may give rise to tortious (in Scotland, delictual) liability which renders the company liable to pay compensation to a third party.

Directors' duties

Since directors are agents of the company they owe a fiduciary duty to the company. This means that if they make unauthorized profits as a result of their position as directors they must account to the company for them. They are not allowed to make secret profits from their position (*Cook* v *Deeks* [1916] AC 544). Directors are required to act honestly in the performance of their duties, and to exercise a reasonable degree of diligence, care and skill (*Re City Equitable Fire Insurance Co.* [1925] 1 Ch 407).

Shareholders

Membership of a company

A company's shareholders are known as its members in company law (CA, s.22). It is, however, possible for a person to be a member without having shares in a company. A person who believed that he had been allotted shares and had purchased further shares from another member and whose name had been entered on the register of members was held by the Court of Appeal to be a member even though the shares did not in fact exist as a result of procedural irregularities in increasing the company's authorized share capital (*Re Nuneaton Borough Association Football Club Ltd* [1989] BCLC 454, CA).

Every company must keep a register of its members including details of their shareholdings and whether these are fully paid up or not (CA, s.352).

Shareholders' rights

The members have no responsibility for managing the company. That responsibility is assigned to the company's directors (see above). The members' principal entitlements are to an annual dividend on their shares when the company is making a profit and, if the company is wound up while solvent, to a share of the surplus assets in proportion to their shareholdings. However, the members do have significant powers over the company.

At the company's annual general meeting (CA, s.366) the members have an opportunity to question the management of the company over the previous year. The annual general meeting will normally consider the annual accounts and directors' and auditors' reports; the re-appointment of auditors or the appointment of new auditors; the re-appointment or replacement of directors retiring; and resolutions to pay the auditors and directors the fees proposed. Clearly discontent with management of the company may be reflected by votes on issues such as re-appointment of directors and resolutions to pay the directors' fees. Recent shareholder (and public) concern over 'fat cat' directors paying themselves very large bonuses in the utility companies has resulted in rowdy scenes at some company annual general meetings.

There are also provisions for the holding of extraordinary general meetings to consider particular issues. Under the Table A articles only the company's directors have the power to call an extraordinary general meeting. However, members holding at least 10 per cent of the company's paid up share capital have a statutory right to requisition an extraordinary general meeting (CA, s.368).

Corporate administration

The CA imposes considerable administrative requirements on companies. These include the requirement to hold an annual general meeting of members (CA, s.366); the requirement to submit an annual return to the registrar of companies (CA, s.363(1)) which must contain prescribed information about the company; and the requirement to submit annual accounts and directors' and auditors' reports to the registrar of companies (CA, s.242(1)).

The Government's deregulation initiative has simplified these requirements somewhat in that it is now possible for private companies to dispense with the requirement to hold an annual general meeting (CA, s.366A), and it is possible for small and medium sized companies to submit abbreviated annual accounts and reports to the registrar of companies (CA, s.246(1)).

Merits of incorporation

Although there are obviously considerable legal formalities in establishing and administering a company which necessarily involve some expense, these disadvantages are outweighed by the considerable advantages which incorporation brings. First, corporate personality provides protection for those investing in a company by way of shares. Where the company's liability is limited, if the company becomes insolvent shareholders are only liable to pay any unpaid balance on the shares which they hold which minimizes the risk associated with investment in contrast to the position with sole traders and partnerships.

Secondly, corporate personality brings the advantage of continuity. A company does not cease to exist when a shareholder or director dies. Unlike sole traders and partnerships its existence is unaffected by the death of persons lying behind it. It continues to exist until it is formally wound up and dissolved.

Thirdly, ownership of property is very simple. The company may own property of any kind in its own name. The company officers, unlike partners, have no legal interest in the company's property: it does not belong to them.

Fourthly, a company has considerable advantages over other forms of business organization in terms of raising capital. It may do so by issuing shares or by borrowing. If it offers shares to the public (which only public companies may do) the pool of investors is very wide and members of the public may be attracted by the relatively low investment risk. Where it borrows, it is able to grant lenders a wider range of securities over its assets than a sole trader or a partnership. In particular, it may grant what is known as a floating charge over all its assets which neither a sole trader nor a partnership may do. A floating charge is a form of security which 'floats' over all a company's assets such as land, buildings, plant and stock. If the company goes into receivership, the floating charge 'crystallizes' and attaches to the company's assets at that time. Although certain debts such as employee wages and sums due to the Inland Revenue and Customs and Excise must be paid in a receivership prior to other debts, debts secured by floating charges are given priority after those debts. For these reasons they are a very attractive form of security for banks and other investment institutions.

Product liability $\boxed{4}$

DEVELOPMENT OF PRODUCT LIABILITY

Introduction

The law of product liability is essentially concerned with the protection of consumers. In present day society, we expect to enjoy the myriad of manufactured goods which are now a part of everyday life. We also expect from these goods reasonable serviceability and absolute safety. If injury arises through the use of defective goods, the consumption of sub-standard foods or the ingestion of unsafe medicines, we expect substantial compensation to be paid to the injured person and preferably prosecution of the party responsible for the production of the offending article.

The law prior to *Donoghue* v *Stevenson*

However it was not always so and a student coming to this topic of law anew is usually surprised to find that the protection we now expect from the law as a matter of course was considered impossible only seventy years ago. In 1929 a Scottish judge, considering a case in which two children had been injured after drinking a bottle of ginger beer which contained the remains of a dead mouse (*Mullen* v *Barr & Co.* 1929 SC 461), refused to hold the producers of the ginger beer liable, saying,

> It would seem little short of outrageous to make them responsible to members of the public for the condition of the contents of every bottle which issues from their works. It is obvious that, if such responsibility attached to the defenders, they might be called on to meet claims of damages which they could not possibly investigate or answer.

The impact of *Donoghue* v *Stevenson*

Thankfully, this view, which had existed from time immemorial, was soon to change. Only three years later in the famous Scottish case of *Donoghue* v *Stevenson* [1932] AC 562, (which is discussed in more detail in Chapter Two on pp. 57–58) in remarkably similar circumstances – a decomposed snail found in a bottle of ginger beer – the House of Lords found the producer to be liable in damages to the injured consumer. The liability of the producer was based on negligence under the law of delict in Scotland. A similar principle is applied under the law of tort in England.

Tort/delict is discussed in more detail in Chapter Two. Thus was born the law of product liability in the United Kingdom and its principles have been followed in similar form in most industrialized countries.

The move from a fault-based to a strict liability system

Remarkably, even though this branch of the law is relatively modern, it was soon found to be inadequate to protect consumers in many of the circumstances which arise in a modern industrialized society. Further consideration was given as to how best to protect consumers and a system based on strict liability of the producer was established – in the UK under the Consumer Protection Act 1987 (CPA) – and throughout the European Community since the new law is based on an EC Directive (Council Directive 85/374/EEC) known as the Product Liability Directive. A strict liability system does not require any proof of fault or negligence and hence in theory should make claims by consumers easier.

The new law supplemented rather than replaced the existing common law and both sets of provisions remain available, with an injured consumer being able to base a claim on either system.

In product liability law we therefore require to consider two different bases for the protection in law of the consumer of goods:

- protection under the common law through the principle of negligence as understood by the law of tort in England and Wales and the law of delict in Scotland, and
- statutory protection under Part I of the CPA.

Since the provisions of the CPA, founded on strict liability of the producer, were intended to provide greater protection to consumers, it may be anticipated that most claims would be made under those provisions. However, in a break with the true intentions of strict liability, various defences are made available to producers who may thus escape liability under the CPA. There may therefore be circumstances where an injured party may still find it desirable to pursue their claim on the older common law provisions. We shall therefore briefly consider the common law provisions before looking in detail at the more recent statutory provision and its foundation in EC law.

THE COMMON LAW

Introduction

In addition to the difficulties raised for consumers by the presence of defences under the CPA which allow producers to escape liability in certain circumstances (see pp. 101–103), there is the additional problem that the CPA does not affect the liability of products which were supplied prior to 1 March 1988 when the CPA came into force. The common law of tort, or delict in Scotland, therefore continues to have force alongside the 1987 legislation.

Under tortious or delictual law, the consumer will have to establish that there was a harm caused by a legal wrong and that that wrong was caused by the fault of the producer or manufacturer of the defective goods.

It is, of course, also possible for contract law to apply in cases of product liability and indeed a claim brought under contract law does not require proof of fault. Actions can also be raised under the sale of goods law, which is covered by the Sale and Supply of Goods Act 1994. However, a consumer will normally have a contract only with the retailer who sold them the goods, rather than with the manufacturer. Moreover, a person who receives goods as a gift from a third party has a contract neither with the manufacturer nor with the retailer. This was the case in *Donoghue* v *Stevenson* (see above where Mrs Donoghue could not raise an action against the cafe owner who sold the ginger beer because it was in fact sold to her friend). In such circumstances, the only option is to bring an action in tort or delict.

Requirements for a successful common law action

Donoghue v *Stevenson* established the principle that a manufacturer of goods owes a duty of care to the ultimate consumer. That duty is to take reasonable care in the circumstances. Lord Atkin stated what is now his famous 'neighbourhood principle' in this case. He said,

> the rule that you are to love your neighbour becomes, in law, you must not injure your neighbour; and the lawyer's question, Who is my neighbour? receives a restricted reply. You must take reasonable care to avoid acts or omissions which you can reasonably foresee would be likely to injure your neighbour. Who, then, in law is my neighbour? The answer seems to be – persons who are so closely and directly affected by my act that I ought reasonably to have them in contemplation as being so affected when I am directing my mind to the acts or omissions which are called in question.

In tort or delict, it must be reasonably foreseeable that the manufacturer's acts or omissions were likely to harm the consumer. Problems can arise when raising an action under tort or delict in showing that the duty of care was in fact breached by the manufacturer and that the breach actually caused the harm. Showing that it was the manufacturer who breached the duty of care can be problematic if there are a number of others involved through the chain of supply, such as wholesalers, importers, employers and retailers. Further difficulties can arise in even identifying the manufacturer if the product is made in a small factory in another country, perhaps even outside Europe, such as in China or Korea.

If the consumer can overcome such difficulties and show that the manufacturer breached the duty of care which was owed, he or she must then show that there is a link between this breach and the harm that was caused. Consumers face difficulties in showing such a link when, for example, there is an element of delay in a case or where the defect does not come to light until some time after the product has been used.

Difficulties in linking breach of duty with harm caused where defect remains hidden until some time after product used

Thalidomide

This situation arose in the Thalidomide tragedy in the 1960s which is widely recognized as having been the catalyst for the modern development of product liability law generally. The Thalidomide tragedy was a result of drugs having been given to pregnant women in the late 1950s/early 1960s to relieve morning sickness. The defect in the drug did not become apparent until the children were born. Upon birth the children were found to have suffered various limb deformities, caused by their mothers having taken the drug. The problem for the children and their families lay in proving that the manufacturer of the drug had been negligent since no one could have known of the side effect of the drug until after a child was born to a mother who had taken the drug. It was impossible to prove negligence and there was widespread concern that the law would not assist the public in obtaining compensation in these tragic circumstances. The children did eventually receive some compensation but only because the public outcry forced the Government and manufacturers to establish a compensation fund. There was in fact no legal obligation upon the manufacturers to do so.

As a result of this situation Commissions were established in the UK and Europe to consider review of the law of product liability. Eventually these reports led to the EC Directive (Council Directive 85/374/EEC) and the CPA.

The response of the US courts

The problem of a defect in a product not surfacing until some time after the product has been used is also illustrated by the US case of *Sindell* v *Abbott Laboratories* 26 Cal. 3d 588. The case involved the drug Diethylstilbestrol (DES) which was given to pregnant mothers to prevent miscarriage. The drug, however, caused cancerous vaginal and cervical growths in many of the daughters who were born to these mothers. The defect in the drug only became apparent some ten to twenty years later when the daughters developed these cancerous growths. The lengthy delay clearly poses problems for an injured party trying to prove fault by the manufacturers so many years before the harm occurred. A further difficulty in this case was that over 200 companies had produced the drug and the mothers faced the task of identifying which manufacturers should be held liable. The US Courts finally made each of the five producers who were ultimately involved as defenders in the action liable. Their decision was based on the somewhat unusual basis of percentage of market share. This principle has not been accepted in the UK.

Cases against cigarette manufacturers

Similar problems also arise in actions which are taken against cigarette manufacturers where the consumer has to show that smoking cigarettes caused the cancer they now have. The recent trend in raising such actions against tobacco manufacturers is also an example of consumers using the common law because the product, that is, the cigarettes, was supplied before 1 March 1988 when the CPA came into force.

The widely publicized Scottish case of *McTear* v *Imperial Tobacco Ltd* 1995 SCLR 611; 1997 SLT 175 was raised by a man who had contracted lung cancer. The case was taken over by his widow when Mr McTear later died from the cancer. Mrs McTear alleged that the lung cancer was caused by her husband smoking cigarettes over a number of years. Mr McTear had started smoking in 1964; health warning notices did not appear on cigarette packets until 1971. Today, the Tobacco Products Labelling (Safety) Regulations 1991 give the requirements for warnings on cigarette packets. Mrs McTear argued that the tobacco manufacturers were aware of the dangers of smoking prior to 1964 and that they had breached their duty to warn those using their product of the dangers of lung cancer. By the time the tobacco manufacturers were warning of the dangers, Mr McTear, it was argued, was already addicted to the cigarettes and was unable to give them up. The cigarette manufacturers however claimed that despite the lack of warnings, the dangers of smoking were publicly known by 1960. They also denied the link between smoking and cancer. The manufacturers had pleas of *volenti non fit injuria* (that is, that Mr McTear had voluntarily assumed the risk) and of contributory negligence.

In the United States where similar cases are being raised, a smoker's decision to continue smoking even after warnings were given made her 80 per cent contributorily negligent (*Cippolone* v *Liggett Group Inc.* 120 LEd. 2d 407; 112 SCt 2608).

Unfortunately, Mrs McTear's case will not be decided in court because Mrs McTear was refused funding by the Scottish Legal Aid Board to continue her action. It is, however, only a matter of time until a similar case is brought before the UK courts, funded either privately or with a different decision from the Legal Aid Board.

THE CONSUMER PROTECTION ACT 1987

Introduction

The effect of the CPA is to introduce, with certain limitations, a situation whereby the producer will always be liable to pay compensation without proof of fault on the producer's part where someone has been injured or killed or a private consumer's property has been damaged by a defective product. Section 2 of the CPA sets out the principal basis of liability. The CPA does not permit producers to exclude or reduce their liability by contractual provision or in any other way (CPA 1987, s.7) but does specify certain specific defences which may permit producers to escape liability if the appropriate circumstances can be established (CPA 1987, s.4). It is therefore necessary to consider the following:

- What kind of damage is covered?
- Who is potentially liable?
- What products are covered?
- When is a product defective?
- What defences are available to a producer?

What kind of damage is covered?

Section 2(1) of the CPA refers to liability for 'damage'. Section 5 contains the definitions which make clear what damage is covered by the Act:

1. Death;
2. Personal injury, including any disease and any other impairment of a person's physical or mental condition;
3. Damage to property, including land and buildings as well as movable property. The property must be for private use, occupation or consumption, thus excluding such

items as company cars, but claims are excluded if the value of the property does not exceed £275. This is to prevent too many trivial cases for property damage. If more than £275 worth of damage is done to property the full sum will, of course, be recoverable, including the first £275.

You should, however, note that 'damage' does not cover damage to, or destruction of, the defective product itself. It is also impossible to recover compensation from the producer of a product if damage is caused to the product by a defective component part, unless the main product was supplied with that component part comprised within it.

Pure economic loss is not covered by the statute and if the consumer suffers a financial loss because of the damage to their property or person, they will be unable to recover it from the producer. If, for example, a defective car phone bursts into flames, damaging the car, the consumer, although able to claim the cost of repairing the car, would be unable to claim the cost of renting an alternative vehicle while her own car was being repaired. Such loss would be recoverable under the common law of tort or delict (*Spartan & Steel Alloys* v *Martin* [1973] 1 QB 27).

Although the wording of the statute would appear on the same basis to exclude wage loss resulting from personal injury which is caused by a defective product, the original European Directive which the CPA implements makes it clear that such wage loss would be recoverable.

Who is potentially liable?

This is one area in which the CPA makes clear its intention of expanding protection of the consumer. Not only is the producer made liable but also the importer and 'own brander' and any member of the chain of supply unless they can identify either the producer or the person who supplied them. The intention is to remove from the consumer the problem of identifying the producer of the goods, who may for example be a small obscure factory in Taiwan or Korea. Thus, s.2 extends liability to:

1. the manufacturer (including the manufacturer of any component) and the abstracter if the product is a raw material;
2. an importer into the European Community, in the course of business. This does not cover those who import products from one member state into another;
3. an 'own brander', that is someone who holds out to be the producer by putting their name or mark on the product. 'Own branders' can be easily illustrated by the example of supermarket chains who now sell many products with their logos printed on them. If such supermarkets, 'hold themselves out as' the producer of these goods, then they will be caught under the CPA. If, however, the supermarket states on the product that someone else manufactured the item, then they would escape liability here. They may, however, be covered by the next section of the CPA, that is, as a supplier of the product;
4. any supplier of the product, but subject to the provision that they will not be liable if within a reasonable time of request by the injured party they provide the identity of the producer, own brander or importer. Provided a supplier can point to the producer, own brander or importer, they will escape liability, even if that person is now untraceable or even bankrupt. This will force suppliers to keep detailed records of all sources of supply, in order to avoid liability.

The CPA provides that where two or more persons are liable under this section for the same damage, the liability is joint and several. This means that the consumer can choose to either claim the damages solely from one of the defendants or split the compensation payable to them equally between them.

What products are covered?

What is covered

The term 'product' is given a very wide meaning to cover essentially any goods including any component or raw material incorporated in them (CPA, ss 1(2) and 45). Although buildings are not covered by the CPA, the component parts used to build them such as the bricks and cement will be. Department of Trade and Industry guidance (Guide to the Consumer Protection Act 1987, Product Liability and Safety Provisions) states that the CPA is not intended to cover printed material, except in the case of warnings or instructions on a product, in which case the producer of the product will be liable. 'Product' is also extended to include gas, electricity and water; any substances and things comprised in land by virtue of being attached to it; and any ship, aircraft or vehicle (CPA, ss 1(2) and 45(1)).

What is not covered

A notable exception from the term 'product' is agricultural produce and game unless it has undergone an industrial process (CPA, s.2(4)). Agricultural produce is defined as 'any produce of the soil, of stock farming or fisheries' (CPA, s.1(2)). Thus, all primary agricultural produce is excluded from the terms of the Act unless it has undergone an industrial process (CPA, s.2(4)). This is clearly a major exception. The term 'industrial process' is not defined in the CPA. This is unfortunate in view of the wide variety of processes which are carried out daily on agricultural produce and game. Fruit and vegetables, for example, are treated with pesticides and other chemicals, meat and vegetables are frozen and milk is pasteurized. The lack of definition in the statute has led to uncertainty over which processes are covered and which are not. It is likely that the industrial process will have to give the product essential characteristics before it is covered by the statute. During the debate on the CPA in Parliament, 'industrial process' was defined by one Minister as 'mechanical and large scale'. The case of *Pepper* v *Hart* now allows such statements made by Ministers in Parliament to be relied upon in interpreting a statutory phrase in any court proceedings (see Chapter One, p. 31). However, the exception of primary agricultural produce is now under review. Consumers suffering injury following consumption of food products will of course also have recourse under the terms of the Food Safety Act 1990 (see Chapter Ten).

When is a product defective?

Consumer expectation test

The general test for a defective product is set out in s.3(1) of the CPA and is known as the 'consumer expectation' test. A product will be defective if the safety of that product is 'not such as persons generally are entitled to expect'. This is an objective test and does not refer to the specific consumer nor to the specific producer.

In this context, 'safety' includes the safety of products comprised in the main product. It also covers not only the context of risk of death or personal injury, but also includes risks of damaged property. Determining what safety standards will generally be expected is a difficult task due to the CPA's vague language. All the circumstances should be taken into account. The CPA gives a non-exhaustive list of some of the factors to be considered. These are:

- The way in which and the purposes for which, the product has been marketed, its get-up, the use of any mark in relation to the product and any instructions for, or warnings with respect to, doing or refraining from doing with or in relation to the product (CPA, s.3(2)(a));
- What might reasonably be expected to be done with or in relation to the product (CPA, s.3(2)(b)); and
- The time when the product was supplied by its producer to another (CPA, s.3(2)(c)).

Nothing in s.3 requires a defect to be inferred solely from the fact that the safety of a 'product which is supplied after that time is greater than the safety of the product in question' (CPA, s.3(2)(c)).

These provisions ensure that products such as cleaning fluid, which are obviously not intended to be eaten or drunk by children, are nonetheless caught under the CPA if manufacturers could have anticipated that children might eat or drink them, even though this is an unreasonable thing to do. In the US case, *Spruill* v *Boyd Midwhay Incorporated*, US Court of Appeal, 4th Circuit 1962, 308 F 2d 79 it was stated that the manufacturer must

> be expected to anticipate the environment which is normal for the use of his product and where, as here, that environment is the home, he must anticipate the reasonably foreseeable risk of the uses of his product in such an environment . . . and to warn them, though such risks may be incidental to the actual use for which the product was intended.

Use of warnings

Manufacturers must provide warnings on products where the dangers of that product are not obvious and which arise from its intended use or foreseeable misuse. This obligation follows from the general safety requirement contained in the CPA (s.10). It is an offence for a person to supply, offer, agree to supply, expose or possess consumer goods which fail to comply with the general safety requirement (CPA, s.10(1)). Such a failure occurs if the goods are not reasonably safe having regard to all the circumstances including the use of any instructions or warnings which are given in relation to the use or consumption of the goods (CPA, s.10(2)(a)). There is no obligation to warn of dangers which were unknown and undiscoverable at the time of supply. Any warning which is given to a consumer must be adequate; if a user does not read and understand the warning, it cannot influence their behaviour, and so is of no use. Warnings should generally be proportionate to the degree of danger involved, be non-removable, be in a prominent position on the product and be clear and unambiguous. Manufacturers, however, must be careful not to simply produce defective products and cover them with warnings, instead they should redesign them to be safer. Warnings shift the responsibility for accident prevention from the manufacturer to the consumer; shifting it back to the manufacturer wherever possible is a more effective way of avoiding accidents.

There are generally considered to be three types of defects that a product may have. These are design defects, manufacturing defects and inherent risks which are unavoidable and require no warning. An example of such a product that cannot have its inherent risk designed out of it, is a knife. There will, however, be some inherent risks which should be warned of, for example the toxic effect of a cleaning fluid.

There has been much publicity surrounding the recent trend in so called 'alcopops' and 'extra strength' beers. These products contain a much higher percentage of alcohol than consumers might normally expect. While premium beers or lagers generally have an alcoholic content of around 5 per cent, stronger beers can have as high a volume as 8 or 9 per cent.

The new alcopop drinks have been heavily criticized for potentially misleading the public. Despite the facts that the bottles give the alcoholic content and state that they are 'alcoholic drinks', they have been criticized for giving the appearance of being a soft drink but with an alcoholic content of around 5 per cent.

Despite the high levels of alcohol in these drinks which may surprise many consumers, warnings advising of the dangers of excess consumption are not generally given on such products. It remains to be seen whether such lack of warning will render these products defective or whether such dangers shall be deemed to be 'obvious' or 'known'.

The Portman Group was set up by the Government to monitor this area within the drinks industry which has caused so much public concern.

If, then, the safety of the product is not of a standard which persons generally are entitled to expect, taking account of such factors as warnings, the seriousness of the defect and the number of consumers affected by the defect, the product will be defective.

In the context of food safety (see Chapter Ten) disclosing the presence of an injurious ingredient on a food label was held not to constitute a defence to rendering food injurious to health (*Haigh* v *Aerated Bread Co. Ltd* [1916] 1 KB 878).

What defences are available to the producer?

Development risks defence

There are a wide variety of defences available to producers in terms of the CPA, the most controversial of which is the 'development risks' defence. We propose to begin with a discussion of this defence before considering some of the others open to producers.

The European Product Liability Directive (Directive 85/374/EEC), which the CPA implements, left open the option to member states of whether or not to include the development risks or 'state of the art' defence in their legislation. The UK opted to include it and it is given in s.4(1)(e) of the CPA. The defence has been criticized for reducing the CPA's strict liability system to little more than a fault- or negligence-based liability system. The UK Government's implementation of the defence has also been criticized for being more lenient on producers than the Product Liability Directive intended. However, it has been decided by the European Court of Justice that there is no obvious conflict between the Product Liability Directive and the UK implementing legislation (*EC Commission v UK*, C-300/95 [1997] All ER (EC) 481).

The CPA provides a defence to anyone proceeded against under its provisions if that person can show that:

> the state of scientific and technical knowledge at the relevant time was not such that a producer of products of the same description as the products in question might be expected to have discovered the defect if it had existed in his products while they were under his control (CPA, s.4(1)(e)).

In order to succeed under this defence, the defects which are later shown to exist in the product must not have been reasonably discoverable by the manufacturer under the knowledge existing at that time.

The defence is of considerable importance to many manufacturers whose products are discovered to have harmed consumers. Food manufacturers, for example, whose use of additives in their products causes physical injury to consumers will have a defence if they can show that at the time of their supply the state of scientific and technical knowledge would not have allowed a similar producer who produced the same food to be expected to have discovered the defect. For the consumer this, along with the various other defences, is an unfortunate addition to the CPA. The statute was originally intended to have a scheme of strict liability. This would have meant that such consumers who suffered physical injuries from food additives would have been able to hold the producer liable for the harm caused to them, without the need to establish fault on the part of the manufacturer or to overcome this defence.

The state of knowledge is not the particular industry's standard as this would encourage manufacturers to minimize their research work and hence escape liability through an excuse of ignorance. On the other hand, manufacturers are not expected to be aware of every piece of obscure research which is being carried out in their field of manufacture. A manufacturer's state of knowledge will be judged according to what experts in the particular field generally consider to have been known at the relevant time.

This is likely of course to lead to lengthy debates about what information was available around the world and is hardly helpful to an injured consumer. The ironic result of the availability of the development risks defence is that it appears that the CPA would not help injured parties in a Thalidomide type case as the manufacturers would again be able to argue that the defects in the drug could not have reasonably been discovered by any manufacturer. This defence is therefore widely regarded as having significantly weakened the benefit of the CPA to the consumers.

Compliance with legislation

No liability will fall upon the producer if the defect in their product can be attributed to compliance with any legislation or regulation which is in force (CPA, s.4(1)(a)). In order to succeed with this defence, however, a producer will have to show that there was no way to comply with the other legislation and exclude the defect: it is not enough merely to have complied with the legislation.

The producer did not supply the product to another

It is a defence for a manufacturer to show that he or she did not supply the product (CPA, s.4(1)(b)). This position could arise for example if a manufacturer's goods are stolen or fraudulently copied and supplied to a consumer.

Goods not supplied in the course of a business or with a view to profit

If goods are not supplied in the course of a business and are not supplied with a view to profit, this provides a valid defence (CPA, s.4(1)(c)). This situation clearly arises when DIY enthusiasts donate their work to charitable events or to family and friends!

The defect did not exist at the time of supply

A manufacturer also has a defence if the defect did not exist in the product when it left the manufacturer (CPA, s.4(1)(d)). This allows the manufacturer to claim that the defect arose as a result of the actions of another down the line of supply, for example, the retailer.

Defective design

The producer of a component part of a product can escape liability if the defect in the final product is due to the design of the main product (CPA, s.4(1)(f)). This producer also has a defence if he/she complies with the main producer's instructions and it is these instructions which are defective.

Establishing the defences: burden of proof

The burden of proof in each of the defences, including the development risk defence, is on the defendant. This means that the producer of goods must bring themselves within one of the defences. In the case of the development risks defence for example, the law presumes that the producer knew of the defect in the product and it is for the producer to show otherwise. This reversal of the burden of proof is greatly beneficial to the injured consumer and is a clear example of the intention that the CPA should assist the consumer seeking to claim against a manufacturer.

Time limits for raising actions

Schedule 1 of the CPA gives important time limits for actions raised under the statute. Generally, an action must be raised within three years of the incident complained of. In England and Wales, the consumer must bring an action within three years of either (i) the date of the incident or (ii) the date the plaintiffs knew the incident was sufficiently serious to justify an action, that the damage was caused by the defect and the identity of the defendant, whichever is the later.

The time limit is extended where a person dies within the three year period from personal injuries they sustained as a result of the incident. Similar provisions on time limits apply in Scotland.

Schedule 1 further provides that a producer's potential liability for a defective product is extinguished after ten years from the relevant date if no claim is brought. This is an unfortunate addition to the legislation for consumers, particularly for those who use a product whose defect does not come to light until a number of years after the product has been put on the market, such as those consumers who used the DES drug, detailed on p. 96. Such consumers will have their right to claim against the producer extinguished even before their three year period can begin to run.

Enforcement

Prohibition notices

Schedule 2 of the CPA makes provision to allow the Secretary of State to issue prohibition notices for products that he/she considers unsafe. The notice must give the reasons for its issue, state the day it comes into force and allow the trader to make written representations to show that the goods are safe. If such representations are made, the Secretary of State must consider whether the notice should be revoked.

Notice to warn

Part II of Schedule 2 of the CPA gives the Secretary of State the power to issue notices to warn on goods he/she considers to be unsafe. Before doing so, however, the Secretary of State must issue a notification which contains a draft of the proposed notice, gives notification of the intention to issue a notice, states that the Secretary of State considers the goods unsafe, giving the reasons for this view and allows the person to make representations to the Secretary of State to show that the goods are in fact safe. The actual notice to warn will only be served if no representations are made to the Secretary of State or once any such representations have been considered. The Secretary of State has the power to revoke notices to warn.

Conclusion

The traditional view in product liability law led for a time to the consideration of liability in cases on a cost/benefit basis. This theory required an assessment to be made of the level of risk to the public from the existence and use of the product and the potential cost of eliminating this risk weighed against the general benefit to consumers of having the product available at a reasonable cost. Thus, a certain element of risk to the public could be found to be acceptable. This was highlighted in the judgment of Lord Reid in the House of Lords case, *Morris* v *West Hartlepool Steam Navigation Company* [1956] AC 552 when he said it was the duty of an employer in considering if some precaution should be taken against a foreseeable risk, to weigh, on the one hand, the magnitude of the risk, the likelihood of an accident happening and the possible seriousness of the consequences if an accident does happen, and on the other hand, the difficulty and expense and any other disadvantage of taking the precaution. In this case, a seaman successfully claimed damages for personal injuries he sustained on falling some 40 feet into the hold of a ship. The shipowners were ultimately found to be negligent in not providing guard-rails despite the fact that it was common practice within the shipping industry not to provide them.

The view in modern society has evolved to the point that it is argued that no risk to the general public is acceptable and the consumer should be protected at all costs. Since defects in goods and accidents are always likely to be possible this leads to a change in the distribution of the cost of an accident. Under the cost/benefit system it is accepted that a few consumers might be injured and will thus lose financially (as a result of physical injury) but the large majority of consumers will benefit through the availability of the product. This can perhaps best be envisaged through consideration of the effect of the availability of certain pharmaceutical drugs.

However, if one moves to a true strict liability system then no consumer should suffer financial loss. Although the consumer might still suffer injury he will always receive compensation for this as the producer will always be liable. This places an additional cost on the producer who must arrange product liability insurance to cover the cost of claims. The cost of this insurance is added to the price of the goods and thus effectively the cost of compensation for the few parties suffering injury is spread across society as a whole.

A strict liability system therefore arguably offers greater protection to the public and spreads the risk of financial loss equitably. Unfortunately the producers are unhappy about this situation as they are liable even if they could not have foreseen the problem. The cost of their goods is increased and this can lead to them being less competitive in the market place particularly if they have to compete against producers from countries where strict liability does not exist.

It is this fear of damaging national industries which led to the inclusion of defences in the Product Liability Directive and the CPA and thus prevented the creation of the true strict liability system which had at one time been anticipated. We would argue, however, that the scheme introduced by the CPA does approach a strict liability scheme and does provide enhanced protection to consumers at large.

Remarkably, there are no reported decisions of cases where claims have been based upon the CPA in the nine years since it came into force. We are not certain why this is so but it may be, and we hope that it is, because the stronger bargaining position given to claimants by the terms of the CPA has led to manufacturers and their insurers settling claims before they come to court.

Criminal responsibility $\boxed{5}$

INTRODUCTION

While organizations plan to make binding legal relationships under the civil law, they plan to avoid criminal liability. Nevertheless much of the law regulating business is enforced through criminal sanctions, and it is inevitable that businesses will have to consider directly the issue of criminal responsibility. This will involve protecting an organization, its employees and clients against being the victims of crime as well as ensuring that the organization itself does not attract criminal penalty. This chapter considers the potential criminal responsibility of the organization and those who are part of it. Many of the other chapters mention possible criminal penalties, and there is a potentially enormous amount of applicable criminal law. For that reason in this chapter we concentrate on the legal principles which differentiate criminal from civil law.

REAL AND REGULATORY CRIME

Legal writers often make a distinction between real crime and regulatory crime. On the one hand there is what is often called 'traditional crime' or 'street crime', such as theft, assault, rape, and on the other hand there is the regulatory crime which does not appear to be criminal in quite the same way, such as illegal parking, licensing offences and the rest. There is no legal distinction between the two forms of crime and sometimes it can be difficult to distinguish between them. Embezzlement is not a street crime but it is almost indistinguishable from theft. It is not clear that it is appropriate to try to make such a distinction between real and regulatory crime. Sometimes the effects of some breaches of regulatory law can be at least as devastating as real crime. A false trade description may result in someone spending a lot of money for little or no return, more than the amount lost to the petty thief. A breach of food safety regulations might lead to serious illness and death, compared with the shock of a minor assault.

It is sometimes suggested that the criminal law is not an appropriate way to enforce many of the laws in the business sphere, and it is the case that in many areas there is an additional, complementary means of enforcement, by statutory regulatory bodies, such as the Health and Safety Executive which oversees health and safety at work issues, and the local authority trading standards and environmental health departments, which oversee their respective areas. The relevant legislation gives such bodies powers of inspection and search, and often their own administrative powers, such as prohibition notices (powers available to the regulatory bodies in the spheres of health and safety at work and consumer safety). However, these bodies always retain the ultimate back up of prosecution. Prosecution is used by most of these regulatory bodies as a sanction of last resort, where persuasion, warnings and the use of other statutory powers have failed to bring compliance with the statute.

Although most crimes committed in the course of business will be statutory or regulatory crimes, nevertheless traditional crime may also arise. This can be traditional crime for personal benefit, like theft and embezzlement, but it may also be organizational crime, where, for example, an organization can in theory be prosecuted for culpable homicide or manslaughter where its gross negligence causes death. The criminal law of England and Wales on the one hand and Scotland on the other is very different in respect of the traditional crimes and it is not intended to refer to these other than in passing. The statutes which regulate organizations tend to be either UK statutes common to both jurisdictions or separate statutes making broadly similar provision.

CRIMINAL RESPONSIBILITY

Criminal law aims to prevent or control behaviour rather than, as the civil law does, to compensate the victim or enforce obligations. The state is principally responsible for enforcing criminal law (see Chapter One, pp. 22–23) which involves stigmatization of the individual and compulsory measures of punishment. For this reason the criminal law concentrates more on the behaviour of the alleged offender (rather than on the wrong done to the victim) and traditionally great importance is placed on ensuring that only those who are responsible for their actions are punished. The victim may seek redress through the civil courts: it is through the criminal law that society condemns the behaviour.

MENS REA

Because of the emphasis in criminal law on the need to establish responsibility for the criminal act, there is a basic principle that only those whose mental attitude shows criminal fault can be held to account. Criminal fault is often given the Latin tag of *mens rea*, the guilty mind, and only someone who can be said to have had such a guilty mind can be convicted. This is a rule which applies to virtually all traditional offences, although we shall see that it does not apply to a large number of statutory offences in the sphere of business. It is always presumed that *mens rea* is an essential part of a crime, unless it is excluded expressly in a statute or by necessary implication.

The difference between civil fault and criminal fault is essentially that while simple negligence can amount to fault under civil law (and in breach of contract fault is irrelevant – the fact that the contract has been breached is all that matters), under criminal law more than simple negligence has to be proved.

Each crime has its own particular *mens rea*. Some crimes must be committed intentionally. This is the most traditional form of *mens rea* and probably coincides with most people's idea of what criminal behaviour is ('he/she meant to do it'). For example, theft (a common law offence in Scotland and a statutory offence under the Theft Act 1968 in England and Wales) is a crime of intention, involving the appropriation of another's property intending to deprive them of it. For some other crimes it may be necessary to prove a particular guilty knowledge. For example, reset is a crime requiring knowledge: it involves the possession of stolen goods, knowing that the goods are stolen. Yet other crimes may require proof of recklessness (in some cases this may be an alternative to intention). There is a difference in the meaning of recklessness between Scotland and England, and between different crimes in England. In Scotland recklessness includes both deliberate risk taking and gross negligence (*Allan* v *Patterson* 1980 SLT 77). In England some crimes of recklessness can only be committed by deliberate risk taking (*R* v *Cunningham* [1957] 2 QB 396), while others may be committed by a failure to think about the possibility of risk which has been created by the accused's behaviour, similar but not identical to gross negligence (*R* v *Caldwell* [1982] AC 341). In both countries gross negligence is a sufficient *mens rea* for manslaughter (England) or culpable homicide (Scotland). This is not simple negligence such as would be sufficient to establish liability under tort (in Scotland, delict) but a more extreme negligence.

The *mens rea* element of a crime must coincide with the behavioural element (this is often called the *actus reus* – the guilty act). It is no use having the requisite criminal intention some time before or some time after the criminal act; the act must be committed along with the accompanying necessary mental attitude. Section 14 of the Trade Descriptions Act 1968 has given rise to some good examples of this point. Under this section it is an offence for someone in the course of trade or business to make a statement which they know to be false, or recklessly to make a false statement, regarding the provision of services, accommodation or facilities. This is an offence therefore with two alternative forms of *mens rea*: either the accused must have known that the statement was false or they must have been reckless as to whether it was false or not. In *Sunair Holidays* v *Dodd* [1970] 2 All ER 410 the company was charged with an offence under s.14 in relation to their advertising of a holiday. They had stated in a brochure that all twin-bedded rooms in a hotel had certain facilities including a terrace. The company had a contract with the hotel that their clients would be accommodated in rooms of that standard. In relation to the booking complained of, however, the clients were allocated a room without a terrace. The company were convicted in the first place because the justices found that they had been careless in their dealings with the hotel. However, the appeal court overturned this conviction since they found that any carelessness had occurred in the monitoring of the arrangement with the hotel: at the time the statement was made it was accurate.

However, if a statement continues to be issued in a leaflet or brochure, the *actus reus* is not simply the issuing of the statement, but is also the keeping of it in circulation. Thus, if the falsity of such a statement is discovered after its issue and the brochures are not recalled effectively, *mens rea* will coincide with the *actus reus* from that date. This happened in *Wings Ltd* v *Ellis* [1984] 3 WLR 965. This brochure advertised a hotel as air-conditioned. This was in fact false but at the time of issuing the brochure the company believed that the statement was true. They subsequently discovered that it was false and advised customers dealing with them direct and travel agents of the change. However, not all customers were informed and many brochures continued unamended in circulation. The case was appealed to the House of Lords which held that an offence was committed when the false statement was read by a member of the public who was interested in travelling, and on the date complained of, the company knew it was false.

Before leaving s.14 of the Trade Descriptions Act 1968 it is worth noting how the phrase 'recklessly' has been interpreted by the courts. In this context a person acts recklessly if he or she does not give any thought to whether the statement is false or not: it does not have to be shown that he/she deliberately ran the risk of its being false. In *MFI* v *Nattrass* [1973] 1 All ER 762 a managing director approved in 5–10 minutes an advertisement which offered free delivery of sliding door gear but which did not indicate that this was only available when the gear was sold with a door. The appeal court agreed that he had been reckless since he had not thought through the implications of the advertisement and had not had regard to its falsity or otherwise. The court felt that Parliament in s.14 had placed a positive obligation on businesses to have regard to whether their advertisements were true or false.

STRICT LIABILITY

Strict liability is the name given to criminal liability which does not require proof of criminal fault. Some statutes provide a definition of a crime which only has a behavioural component and has no mental component. Thus the crime is 'doing X', not 'intentionally doing X', nor 'knowingly doing X', nor 'recklessly doing X'. Such offences are most commonly found in the regulation of businesses, particularly in areas of consumer protection, employee safety, environmental protection and the licensing and control of particular activities. Because strict liability is contrary to basic principles of criminal law there is a presumption that a statutory offence requires *mens rea* on the basis that it is wrong to stigmatize someone as criminal who has not been morally culpable.

The words of the statute must clearly displace this presumption. If any word such as 'knowingly' or 'recklessly' is used it is impossible for there to be strict liability. Certain other words also imply a kind of *mens rea*. For example, where a statute criminalizes the possession of an article, it must be shown not only that the accused had the article under their control (e.g. in their pocket) but also that they knew they had it. Similarly if the offence consists of permitting something to take place, it is necessary to show that the accused knew that it was taking place, or at any rate that he/she should have known but was 'wilfully blind' to the issue. In *Brown* v *Burns Tractors Ltd* 1986 SCCR 146 the company was charged with permitting a person to drive in breach of tachograph regulations. The court held that knowledge of the breach was required, but that it was met in this case by a form of inadequate supervision which amounted to 'shutting one's eyes to the obvious'.

One of the main justifications of strict liability offences, particularly in the business sphere, is that their existence will promote a greater vigilance. This is most likely in business offences, where there are likely to be many layers of an organization in carrying out an activity. An example of a strict liability offence is s.1 of the Trade Descriptions Act 1968 which makes it an offence in the course of trade or business to apply a false trade description to goods or to supply goods with a false trade description attached to them. Unlike s.14 of that Act which applies to false descriptions of services, accommodation and facilities, there is no need to prove that the false statement was made knowingly or recklessly. So also s.20 of the Consumer Protection Act 1987 imposes strict liability for the offence of giving to a consumer in the course of business a misleading indication as to the price of any goods, services, accommodation or facilities.

DUE DILIGENCE DEFENCE

Many statutes which impose strict liability mitigate the effect of this by providing for a due diligence defence. The burden is on the accused to prove such a defence (on the balance of probabilities, not beyond a reasonable doubt as the prosecution must do). Such a defence must be expressly stated in the statute – if it is not, there is no such opportunity available to the accused. There is such a defence in the Consumer Protection Act 1987 (s.39), in the Trade Descriptions Act 1968 (s.24) and in the Licensing (Scotland) Act 1976 (s.67). Such defences are in general construed fairly narrowly: they usually require the accused to have exercised 'all' due diligence to avoid the offence being committed. In *Byrne* v *Tudhope* 1983 SCCR 337 a licence holder was prosecuted for breach of the Licensing Acts, by selling liquor outside the permitted hours. The actual sale had been made by the manager of the bar while the licence holder was absent. The licence holder put forward the due diligence defence on the basis that he had told the manager what the permitted hours were, and that it was illegal to sell outside these. The defence was unsuccessful, however, since he had not advised the manager about the specific provision of the legislation, nor had he given the manager a 'portfolio' of information which he had available but had not got round to passing on.

One effect of a due diligence defence is usually that if an employer has exercised all due diligence, the failure of an employee will not be attributed to the organization, so long as the employee is of a junior level in relation to the organization as a whole. In *Tesco Supermarkets Ltd* v *Nattrass* [1972] AC 153 a store manager had advertised soap powder in breach of the Trade Descriptions Act. Tesco convinced the court that they had a good system to ensure that this did not happen. The House of Lords found that the error of the store manager was not that of the company, because he was not at a senior policy level in the company as a whole. Similarly in *Readers Digest Association* v *Pirie* 1973 JC 42, although the issue was not due diligence, the organization was charged with an offence under the Unsolicited Goods and Services Act 1971, for demanding payment not having reasonable cause to believe that there was a right to payment. Readers Digest convinced the court that they had a good system to check that this did not happen, and that it was the mistake of a junior employee who should have known that there was no right to payment. Since the company could not be said to have not had reasonable cause to believe it had the right to demand payment it was not guilty.

WHO IS RESPONSIBLE?

In keeping with the basic principle of criminal responsibility, liability for crime is essentially personal. An individual may be personally responsible for a criminal act either because they have committed the crime or because they have participated in or assisted in a common plan to commit the crime. This latter form of personal liability is known as accessorial, or art and part in Scotland. The main difference between the two jurisdictions is that in Scotland, unlike England and Wales, it is not possible to become liable for a crime after it has been committed: the concept of the accessory after the fact is part of English, but not Scottish, law.

This emphasis on personal responsibility means that the principle of vicarious liability is alien to the criminal law. There is no vicarious liability for traditional crime. However, just as the traditional requirement for *mens rea* may be excluded in a statute, so also vicarious liability (which is a form of strict liability, that is, liability without fault) can arise under statute. There are two ways in which this might occur. First, (and unusually) the statute might expressly provide for this. For example, the Licensing Acts do this. Section 67 of the Licensing (Scotland) Act 1976 provides for vicarious liability on the part of a licence holder for the acts of an employee or agent for the offences listed in a Schedule to the Act. Forty-two of the sections of this Act impose vicarious liability on the licence holder (subject, of course, to the due diligence defence).

More likely, vicarious liability will arise by necessary implication. This means that the statute would be unworkable without the imposition of vicarious liability. In areas such as consumer protection or other business situations, where it is likely that the behaviour controlled would be carried on by employees or agents for employers, it will be necessary in many cases to imply vicarious liability. This usually applies to strict liability offences but it may also apply to offences involving *mens rea* if the statute would be unworkable otherwise. An example is *Tesco Stores Ltd* v *Brent London Borough Council* [1993] 2 All ER 718 where the company was charged under s.11 of the Video Recordings Act 1984 which makes it an offence to supply a video recording contrary to its classification to someone who is not of the age specified in the classification certificate. It is a defence that the accused neither knew nor had reasonable grounds to believe that the person concerned had not attained the relevant age. The company in this case had sold an '18' video recording to a 14-year-old boy. The trial court found that the company's cashier had reasonable grounds to believe that the boy was not 18. The company argued that it could not be guilty since its senior officers did not have reasonable grounds for this belief. The appeal court held that it was the cashier's knowledge and belief that was relevant since it was through her that the company supplied the video recording. 'Were it otherwise', said Lord Justice Staughton, 'the statute would be wholly ineffective in the case of a large company, unless by the merest chance, a youthful purchaser were known to the board of directors' (p. 721). It is important that you note that there is no due diligence defence in this statute: if there had been, the approach adopted in *Tesco* v *Nattrass* (above) would have applied. It is presumably because a due diligence defence would make the statute unworkable that one was not included in the statute.

CORPORATE LIABILITY

Prosecution of companies for statutory offences involving strict liability is routine and unproblematic. This is not so with traditional crimes involving *mens rea*. The difficulty is that companies have no true existence: they are legal fictions. Where *mens rea* is an issue, vicarious liability is legally unacceptable, without clear statutory provision. Somehow companies have to have personal liability attributed to them. This has been done in the English courts by using the 'controlling mind' theory; Scottish criminal courts have not developed their own approach but appear to approve the English approach although they have not applied it. For example, the controlling mind theory was quoted approvingly in *Purcell Meats* v *McLeod* 1986 SCCR 672 in relation to a charge of attempted fraud. However, Scottish cases relating to statutory crimes suggest that Scottish courts may be more willing to accept an employee to whom authority has been delegated as a controlling mind. The controlling mind theory is an artificial theory by which a company is identified with its controlling officers. The theory originated in a civil case, *Lennard's Carrying Co. Ltd* v *Asiatic Petroleum Co. Ltd* [1915] AC 705, and was applied to criminal cases in *Tesco* v *Nattrass* (above). In that case the company was able to blame its store manager and not itself because he was not one of the controlling minds of the company. Lord Reid defined these as 'the board of directors, the managing director and perhaps other superior officers of a company . . .' and those to whom '. . . the board of directors may delegate some part of their functions of management giving to their delegate full discretion to act independently of instructions from them' (p. 171). One of the main problems with this theory is that it applies well and logically to a small company, essentially owned and controlled by one person (as was the case in the original *Lennards* case) but it is difficult to apply to a large company with a complex corporate structure. In practice the controlling mind theory means that for a company to be liable it must be proved that a director (or similar) is a controlling mind of the company and that he or she is guilty of the offence. If that cannot be done, the company cannot be liable. The theory operated to convict a small company (and its managing and sole director) in the unreported case of *R* v *OLL Ltd and Kite* (1994). This case concerned the prosecution for manslaughter of a company, its managing director and its manager (an employee who was acquitted of the charge). OLL Ltd was a company (formerly called Active Leisure and Learning Ltd) whose business was the running of a leisure activity centre. Four young people died on a canoe trip in Lyme Bay organized by the company. Both the managing director and the company were convicted in the first successful prosecution of a company for manslaughter or culpable homicide in the UK. The managing director received a sentence of three years imprisonment (reduced to two years on appeal), while the company was fined £60,000.

On the other hand there was no conviction in the case of *R* v *P & O European Ferries (Dover) Ltd and Others* (1990) which is also unreported. This was a prosecution for manslaughter arising out of the deaths of passengers on the ferry, the *Herald of Free Enterprise*, which sank when it became waterlogged when its bow doors were not closed. Two employees, five directors and the company were prosecuted. For the company to be convicted at least one of the directors would have to have been found to be guilty. In the event the judge withdrew the case from the jury because there was insufficient proof of gross negligence on the part of the directors, and the Crown dropped the charges against the two employees as a result.

Even if it is possible to impute the actions and mental attitude of a controlling mind to a company, or to hold a company vicariously responsible for the actions of its employees or agents in respect of certain statutory crimes, the courts are not prepared to hold that a company can be convicted of every crime. Some crimes are seen as involving too strong an element of human agency to be capable of being committed by a company. A company cannot be convicted of an offence which is defined as driving in a particular way, since only a human being can drive (*Richmond London Borough Council* v *Pinn and Wheeler Ltd* [1989] RTR 354). However, a company can be convicted of an offence of causing or permitting a vehicle to be driven in a particular way. In *Docherty* v *Stakis Hotels Ltd* 1991 SCCR 6 the company was charged with offences under the Food Hygiene (Scotland) Regulations 1959 in relation to the kitchen in one of the hotels owned by the company. The Regulations placed the obligations on 'the owner or other person having the management and control of a food business carried on in any premises'. The appeal court held that since a company had to operate through natural persons it was incapable of having management and control of a business and accordingly it could not be convicted of this offence.

DIRECTORS AND EMPLOYEES

Individuals are personally responsible for the criminal actions which they commit. Some statutory crimes can only be committed by the person on whom a duty is placed by the statute. Some statutes which impose offences on employers or owners of businesses contain provisions for which these people alone can be responsible. Section 20 of the Consumer Protection Act 1987 makes it an offence for any person to give a misleading price indication to consumers 'in the course of any business *of his*'. Thus only the person whose business it is may be prosecuted under this section. A prosecution was raised under this section against the manager of a shop in *Warwickshire County Council* v *Johnson* [1993] 1 All ER 299, but was held to be incompetent since the manager, although acting in the course of business, had not been acting 'in the course of a business of his'. Whether or not this is the case depends on the precise wording of the statute. In the case of the Trade Descriptions Act 1968, if an organization wishes to rely on a due diligence defence under s.24, it must prove that, as well as having exercised all due diligence, the commission of the offence was due to a mistake, reliance on information supplied by another or to the act or default of another person, an accident or some other cause beyond the organization's control. If the defence is based on its being another's fault, such as an employee's (as was the case in *Tesco* v *Nattrass* (above)), this cannot be relied on without leave of the court unless the accused has given such information which will identify that other person seven days before the hearing (s.24(2)). If the offence was due to someone's act or default, that person can be prosecuted (s.23).

Many statutes provide that where a company is convicted of an offence under the Act, if the offence was committed with the consent or connivance of, or is attributable to the neglect of, a director, manager, secretary or other similar officer of the company, that person as well as the company shall be guilty of the offence and can be prosecuted accordingly. While the scope of such provisions as regards directors and company secretaries is clear, their scope in relation to 'managers' and 'other similar officers' is much less clear. The fact that a corporate officer is called a manager or even general manager is not conclusive (*R* v *Boal* [1992] 3 All ER 177). What is crucial is the authority which the officer in fact exercises within the company or other body corporate. Liability under such provisions will only attach to officers in a position of real authority such that they are in a position to determine corporate policy (*R* v *Boal* (above); *Armour* v *Skeen* [1976] IRLR 310).

MANSLAUGHTER/CULPABLE HOMICIDE

Although prosecutions for manslaughter or culpable homicide arising out of business activity are rare, whether against an individual or a company, there is increased public awareness of the possibility of this offence being relevant. When death results unintentionally from legitimate activity it may still be a criminal offence if the death was caused by the gross negligence of the accused (*Paton* v *HMA* 1936 JC 19 (Scotland); *Adomako* [1995] 1AC 171 (England and Wales)). In *R* v *P & O European Ferries (Dover) Ltd and Others* (above) it was the failure of the prosecution to establish that there had been gross negligence on the part of the directors which led the judge to withdraw the case from the jury and order the acquittal of the directors and the company. The Report of the Sheen Inquiry into the sinking of the ferry had concluded that the company was 'riddled with sloppiness from top to bottom'. Sloppiness is not, however, sufficient for a criminal conviction: individuals must be proved to have been grossly negligent, to have overlooked obvious and serious danger. Where death results there may have been a breach of health and safety legislation, most of which impose strict liability offences, and prosecution under the relevant statutory provision is more likely to be successful.

Employment in the hospitality and tourism industries | 6

INTRODUCTION

The relationship between employer and employee may be very personal where the business is small and the employer active within it, or it may be extremely impersonal where the business is large or an employer is inactive. The relationship may be conducted very formally, or very informally; it may be conducted according to advanced management principles or it may be conducted on no more complex basis than mutual respect. Whatever the practical and theoretical basis of employment, and regardless of size and complexity of undertaking, the legal basis of the relationship is the same. Although the same law applies to the small and large employer alike, what is reasonable behaviour in unfair dismissal law may vary according to the size of the employer (Employment Rights Act 1996 (ERA), s.98(6)).

As we will see the legal basis of employment is the contract between employer and employee. However, except in the smallest of undertakings, employment is usually a collective experience, often involving collective rather than individual negotiation with an employer. There has been a tradition in Great Britain that collective resolution of employment relations is the most effective, so that rather than looking to the individual contract a collective agreement would be a more important source of employee rights and obligations. Since 1980 there has been some erosion of this tradition and an increasing emphasis on individual rights and duties.

Since the mid-1960s there has been an enormous expansion in the amount of statutory regulation in employment, covering employment security, health and safety, maternity, discrimination, industrial action and a wide range of individual rights. It is beyond the scope of this book to examine the complete range of employment issues regulated by law. This chapter will concentrate on a smaller number of fundamental issues concerned primarily with individual employment rights and employment security, thus highlighting the legal relationship between the employer and the employee.

THE EMPLOYER/EMPLOYEE RELATIONSHIP

Contract of service/contract for services

The term 'employ' does not necessarily relate to employment as an employee but also includes employment of individuals on a more casual basis to perform services personally, as contractors. Such individuals would refer to themselves as self-employed: as far as the law is concerned they are 'independent contractors'. At common law there is a distinction made between a *contract of service* (which regulates employment as an employee) and a *contract for services* (which regulates employment as an independent contractor). A contract of employment is a contract of service. Section 235(1) of the ERA defines an employee as someone who works, or has worked, under a contract of employment, and further defines a contract of employment as a contract of service (or of apprenticeship). The essential difference between the two types of contract is that an employee agrees to put his/her ability to work at the disposal of the employer in return for a wage, while an independent contractor agrees to perform certain services for the employer under the terms of the contract.

While employment of independent contractors may more traditionally have been used for short term contracts, such contracts have been used much more in the last decade, for longer term employment as well as short term. It is important to distinguish between the two, since they have very different legal effects. First, many statutory employment protection rights only apply to those who are employed under a contract of service: for example, only employees are entitled to statutory unfair dismissal protection, statutory redundancy pay or statutory maternity rights which are all governed by the ERA. There are, however, a number of statutory employment protection rights which also extend to those employed under contracts for services: for example, actions relating to equal pay (Equal Pay Act 1970 (EPA 1970)), sex discrimination (Sex Discrimination Acts 1975 and 1986 (SDA 1975; SDA 1986)), race discrimination (Race Relations Act 1976 (RRA)), disability discrimination (Disability Discrimination Act 1995 (DDA)) and deductions from wages (ERA).

Secondly, employers have more specific and more extensive duties in relation to the health and safety of their employees both at common law and under the Health and Safety at Work etc. Act 1974 (HSWA), s.2. Employees and independent contractors are taxed differently, while employers are only responsible for the national insurance contributions of employees. A final important difference is that employers are vicariously liable for the negligent actions of their employees carried out in the course of their employment (see Chapter Two, pp. 60–61).

How to tell the difference

In most cases identifying whether or not someone is employed as an employee or an independent contractor will be a straightforward matter: the parties will have clearly described the nature of their relationship and the reality will accord with that. However, sometimes the matter may be left unclear and each party may have a different interpretation of the nature of the contract, or, alternatively, both parties may have entered into a relationship they have described in a particular way (probably that it is not an employment relationship) but the reality may be different. Problems can arise in these cases where an action for unfair dismissal or a claim for redundancy pay is raised, or where a failure to pay tax or national insurance is questioned, or where an employer is sued for damages after an accident. What the parties have called their contract is not decisive: after all if it were simply a case of stating in a contract 'X is not an employee' it would be a simple matter to minimize national insurance and taxation responsibilities.

In *Withers* v *Flackwell Heath Football Supporters' Club* [1981] IRLR 307 a bar steward accepted employment on a self-employed basis. The tribunal found that he was indeed self-employed and thus barred from raising an action for unfair dismissal, being particularly influenced by the fact that the contract described him as self-employed and left him to regulate his own taxes. However the Employment Appeal Tribunal (EAT) held that he was in fact an employee, observing: 'That both parties put the self contradictory label "self-employed" on their relationship is far from conclusive and is to be disregarded when the reality is that the label, and the fiscal consequences which flow from its use, are adopted simply for fiscal reasons.' On the other hand, in cases where it becomes impossible to tell the difference, where there has been a genuine agreement between employer and employed the tribunal or court will be entitled to rely on the parties' description of the contract (*Massey* v *Crown Life Assurance Co.* [1978] ICR 590).

While historically the courts have adopted single factor tests to decide whether or not a contract is one of service or one for services, such as the 'control test' or the 'organization/integration test', the complexities of modern employment have ensured that no one factor can be used as a universal indicator of whether a contract is one of employment or not. The courts use a multi-factor approach, sometimes called the 'multiple test', by which they look at the substance of the relationship, including how wages are paid, what hours are worked, the ownership of any tools, the extent of control of working methods, tax arrangements, and taking all of these into account will decide whether the predominant nature of the contract is that of employment or not (*Ready Mixed Concrete (SE) Ltd* v *Minister of Pensions and National Insurance* [1968] 2 QB 497).

It is easy to see that this approach depends very much on the precise factors in each case and also the weighting given to any factor. In applying the multiple test the courts probably are trying to establish whether or not the alleged employee is in fact in business on their own account or is in fact in business on the employer's account. This is sometimes called the 'small businessman' test and was first articulated in *Market Investigations* v *Minister for Social Security* [1969] 2 QB 173. There the alleged employee was a market researcher who was described in her contract as self-employed. In deciding that she was in fact an employee the court adopted the multiple test approach, stating that they were looking to see if she was on business on her own account, looking in particular to see whether the employee provided her own equipment (she did not), whether the employee hired her own helpers (she did not), whether the employee took any financial risk (she did not) and whether she took any responsibility for investment or management (she did not). This approach was put in down to earth terms by the EAT in *Withers* v *Flackwell Heath Football Supporters' Club* (above) by suggesting that the question to ask the worker (in that case a bar steward) was 'Are you your own boss?'. The EAT felt that in the circumstances of this case Mr Withers's answer would certainly have been 'No', and that he was an employee.

A good example of the courts using the multiple test, although it is debatable whether the result would be replicated in an identical case today, is *O'Kelly* v *Trusthouse Forte plc* [1983] IRLR 370. Appeals from industrial tribunals may only be based on a point of law, so that as long as a tribunal does not apply the wrong law or make a perverse decision its decision cannot be overturned (see below). In this case the employer dismissed a number of 'regular casuals' who staffed their banqueting department and who had been given preference in hiring and were regularly employed in that capacity. They were dismissed when they joined a trade union. Trusthouse Forte argued that they were not employees and therefore not entitled to claim unfair dismissal. The tribunal looked at the factors affecting their employment and divided them up into three categories: factors which were consistent with employment as employees; factors which were not inconsistent with employment as employees; and factors which were inconsistent with employment as employees. Let us look at how they allocated each factor.

First, the tribunal felt that the following were *consistent with employment as employees*: their services were provided in return for a wage; the work was performed under the direction and control of Trusthouse Forte; the workers' clothing and equipment was provided to them; payment of wages was made in arrears after payment of tax and national insurance contributions; there was a disciplinary and grievance procedure to which the workers were subject. Secondly, the tribunal considered that the following were *not inconsistent with employment as employees*: the workers did not receive a regular salary and were paid for work actually performed; the workers were not paid on the same basis as regular staff and had no sick pay or pension rights; and there were no regular hours. Finally, the tribunal took the view that the following were *inconsistent with employment as employees*: neither party had to give any notice of termination; the workers had the right whether or not to accept work; the employers did not have to provide work; there was a custom in the industry that casual workers were self-employed. Using the multiple test and balancing all these factors together, the tribunal and ultimately the Court of Appeal held that the workers were not employees.

The factors which tipped the balance were the facts of the custom and that neither workers nor employer were under any obligation to offer or accept work. Normally the essence of an employment contract is the mutual obligation to both provide work (or a wage) and to perform the work, and here this 'mutuality of obligation' was missing since although the employers always offered the banqueting work to the casuals on their register they were not obliged to, and nor were the regulars obliged to accept although they always did. Some other cases have found this mutuality of obligation to arise out of a course of dealing between the parties (e.g. *Nethermere (St Neots) Ltd* v *Taverna and Gardiner* [1984] IRLR 240).

It may be that different aspects of the contract will be highlighted depending on why the existence of the contract is being challenged or sought to be established. It is certainly the case that most of the emphasis on the 'business on your own account test' has arisen in the context of questions of tax and national insurance (*Market Investigations* v *Minister for Social Security* (above)), while 'mutuality of obligation' has been emphasized in the context of unfair dismissal (*O'Kelly* v *Trusthouse Forte plc,* above), and the issue of control has traditionally been seen as being of importance where vicarious liability or the employer's safety responsibility is in issue (*Ferguson* v *John Dawson and Partners (Contractors) Ltd*

[1976] 3 All ER 817). However, while individual tribunals or courts may emphasize certain aspects more in one case rather than another, it would seem that a unitary approach to what is a contract of service is what the courts aspire to (see, e.g., *Lane* v *Shire Roofing Co. (Oxford) Ltd* [1995] IRLR 493 and *Lee* v *Chung* [1990] IRLR 237).

There are certain cases where a worker may be formally employed by one employer but may be under the practical control of another employer and here it will depend on what the subject matter of the dispute is. An employee might be loaned by the employer to another employer: perhaps equipment is being hired and an employee who can work the equipment is loaned with the equipment. Assuming that all else remains the same, the worker will remain in the employment of the permanent employer. However, the worker will also be considered to be in what is known in Latin as the *pro hac vice* employment of the temporary employer (i.e. the employment of the temporary employer on that occasion) and this concept has an important consequence so far as vicarious liability and safety liability are concerned. The employer owes the same duty of care that is owed to his/her own employees to *pro hac vice* employees, so long as the temporary employer has control over the method of work of the employee (*Garrard* v *Southey* [1952] 2 QB 174): otherwise responsibility for safety remains with the permanent employer.

Similarly an employer is also vicariously liable for the negligent acts of *pro hac vice* employees committed in the course of their employment, again only so long as the temporary employer has control over the method of work of the employee. This principle was applied in the case of *Sime* v *Sutcliffe Catering (Scotland) Ltd* [1990] IRLR 228. A company contracted out its catering operations to the defender; existing canteen workers continued to be employed by the company, while new workers were employed by the defender. Mrs Sime was injured when she slipped on a piece of aspic which had fallen from a plate of salmon being carried by a fellow-worker. She was successful in her claim for damages against the defender on the basis that, whether the aspic had been dropped by a person directly employed by them or by a person employed by the company, they would still be vicariously liable since the canteen workers not directly employed by them were in *pro hac vice* employment with them. The whole day to day management of the catering operation including staff was carried out by the defenders, their canteen manager having complete control over the way all canteen workers did their jobs. However, Mrs Sime was not entirely successful: her damages were reduced by 25 per cent because of her contributory negligence in failing to notice the aspic!

The employer

An employee, therefore, is someone who is employed under a contract of service. The employer is the person who is the other party to that contract, or, in the context of an independent contractor, is the other party to a contract for services. While an employee must always be an individual person, since the essence of employment is the obligation to perform personally, this is not the case for the employer. In fact, in larger scale employment it is unlikely that the employer will be an individual: it is far more likely that the employer will be a limited company or a partnership (see Chapter Three for a discussion of the forms of business organization). As we saw in Chapter Three limited companies have their own legal personality, which is completely independent of their directors or shareholders, and it is the company which is held to account in any contracts, so that it is the company's assets which must be used as compensation. Companies of course can only operate through individuals, and companies are vicariously liable for the actions of their employees acting in the course of their employment, including high level employees. Companies are also bound by the actions of their directors. Thus in cases where an employee wishes to take action against an employer for breach of duty, the appropriate person to sue is the 'person' that owns the business, an individual if it is a sole trader business, the firm if it is a partnership and the company if it is a company.

In the case of certain employment rights it may be possible to take action against individuals other than the employer. The individual who has been negligent is always responsible for his or her own actions, so that the negligent employee may be sued (instead of the vicariously liable employer) where he or she has injured another. In cases of sex and race discrimination, it is possible to sue, in addition to the employer, someone who has instructed another to discriminate (perhaps a supervisor) (SDA 1975, s.39; RRA, s.30) or who has knowingly aided discrimination (that includes the person who has actually committed the discriminatory act such as harassment (SDA 1975, s.42; RRA, s.33) or who has induced another to discriminate by offering them a benefit or detriment (again perhaps a supervisor, or perhaps a trade union) (SDA 1975, s.40; RRA, s.31).

CONTRACT OF EMPLOYMENT

Constituting the contract

A contract of employment, like any other contract, is an agreement between the two parties to it. Like most other contracts it need not be in writing, but may be formed by verbal or written agreement, or may be implied from the actions of the parties. The only exceptions to this general rule are Scottish fixed term contracts for a year or more and contracts of apprenticeship, both of which must be in writing to be binding (*Grant* v *Ramage & Ferguson* (1897) 25 R 75). At common law a fixed term contract of employment is one which is entered into for a definite term, and which cannot be terminated by either party before that term ends, unless there is a material breach of contract by the other. Contracts which are terminable by either party on giving notice (probably the most common form of contract of employment) are usually known as periodic contracts. Such contracts are not expressed as being indefinite and indeed, on the face of it, they run for a fixed term or period, such as one month. However, in effect they will continue automatically unless one party gives notice. This automatic continuation is known as *tacit relocation*.

All the general rules of contract apply (see Chapter Two, pp. 37–54). One which has raised a number of interesting issues is the rule that a contract, to be valid, must not be illegal or tainted by illegality (see Chapter Two, pp. 50–52). A contract is illegal or tainted by illegality where it is for an illegal purpose, or where it is agreed to be carried out in an illegal way. In a number of cases where applications have been made to industrial tribunals, the employer's defence has been that the contract is not valid because it is illegal. The majority of such cases have involved contracts where the employee has been paid free of tax, in order to defraud the Inland Revenue. Although the contract may be valid in every other respect the worker would not satisfy the requirement of statute of being employed under a valid contract of employment.

However, two cases show the limits of the rule. In *Coral Leisure Group Ltd* v *Barnet* [1981] IRLR 204 the employee was a PR executive whose job included entertainment of clients. As part of this he procured prostitutes for clients. When his employers claimed in a defence to a tribunal action that the contract was tainted by this illegality, it was held that it was not, since the contract was not entered into for that purpose. Similarly, in another case involving illegal performance of an initially legal contract, *Hewcastle Catering Ltd* v *Ahmed and Elkamah* [1991] IRLR 473, the employer had been involved in VAT fraud, in which the waiters participated. The waiters informed HM Customs and Excise who are responsible for administering VAT, and were then dismissed. The court found that the fraud had benefited the employer alone and therefore the employment contracts were not tainted. The Court of Appeal said that the *pactum illicitum* (illegal contract) rule is a public policy rule, and so it would not be applied if to do so would affront conscience and would appear to assist or encourage illegality.

It is important to make a distinction between tax avoidance and tax evasion, the former being a perfectly legal method of minimizing the amount of tax which is due to be paid, while the latter is an illegal method of arranging not to pay tax which is due. While a payment method which is solely devised to evade tax will invalidate the contract, a payment method which is a genuine arrangement, which is or could be openly disclosed to the Inland Revenue, to minimize tax liability will not. The EAT made this distinction in *Lightfoot* v *D and J Sporting Ltd* [1996] IRLR 64. Mr Lightfoot was employed as head gamekeeper, and was assisted by his wife. For most of his employment she had received no payment from the company. A few months before his dismissal Mr Lightfoot and the company had agreed that part of his wage would be paid to his wife. As a consequence, because she was not liable for tax, the amount coming into their household increased. When he was dismissed the company claimed that this arrangement was a dishonest attempt to evade income tax, and accordingly the tribunal held that his contract was tainted by illegality. The EAT, however, referred the matter to a different tribunal to consider whether or not it was a legitimate tax avoidance scheme which had been or would be disclosed to the Inland Revenue. If it was, it would not be illegal.

Statutory written particulars of employment

While there is no requirement for writing to constitute a contract of employment, there is a statutory requirement for an employer to provide employees with a written statement of the major terms and conditions of their employment (ERA, ss 1–7). The content and form of the written statement were revised to ensure compliance with EC law. If there is a written contract which fulfils all the requirements of the written statement there will probably be no need to issue a written statement in addition, although the current legislation does not make this explicit as the previous legislation did.

There is an important legal distinction between a contract of employment and the statutory written statement. Like all contracts, a contract of employment is legally binding and can be enforced. The written statement on the other hand is not contractual and therefore not binding in its own right. This is true even where the written statement is signed by the employee since usually signing in this situation is simply signing as a receipt. However, if the employee is asked to sign the statement on the basis that it constitutes the contract, this can give the written statement contractual effect (*Gascol Conversions* v *Mercer* [1974] ICR 420). A written statement which has not been objected to by the employee, and which is subsequently disputed, will be viewed by any tribunal or court as providing evidence of what the contract is, but not conclusive evidence. Thus, if an employee can produce other evidence of what was agreed between herself and the employer – in, for example, a letter of appointment, or in what was said at an interview – the tribunal or court will apply the contractual term and not the term in the statutory written statement (*Robertson and Jackson* v *British Gas Corporation* [1983] IRLR 302).

Nevertheless the written statement is strong evidence of the terms of the contract, and this is especially so where the employer seeks to establish that the written statement does not represent the terms of the contract (*System Floors (UK) Ltd* v *Daniel* [1981] IRLR 475). In *Trusthouse Forte (Catering) Ltd* v *Adonis* [1984] IRLR 382 the employer had posted a notice stating that anyone caught smoking in the no smoking area would be dismissed for gross misconduct. Ten days later Mr Adonis's written particulars were reissued. In the disciplinary rules attached, smoking in a no smoking area was included in the list of offences which merited dismissal upon repetition after a warning: there was also a list of offences which amounted to gross misconduct justifying dismissal without warning which did not include smoking in a no smoking area. Six months later Mr Adonis was dismissed for smoking in a no smoking area: he had not previously been warned. It was held that the dismissal was in breach of contract. The employer was unable to convince the tribunal or the EAT that the written particulars (issued after the notice) did not represent the contractual position.

An employer must provide a written statement to an employee who works eight hours or more a week and who is to be employed for one month or more, unless they work wholly or mainly outside Great Britain. The written statement must be provided within two months of starting work, and if there are any changes to the terms and conditions they must be notified to the employee within a month. You should note that employers cannot unilaterally vary contracts simply by issuing notices of change (see also p. 130).

The statement must specify:

1. the name and address of the employer,
2. the name of the employee,
3. the date when employment began, and
4. the date when continuous employment began, if it is different from 3.

This might arise where previous employment with a previous owner of the business or with an associated employer (i.e. a company which is owned by the same person(s)) is being counted for the purposes of the current employment (where an employee requires a certain period of continuous employment to raise an action, the period of continuous employment must be calculated according to ERA, ss 210–218 Transfer of Undertaking (Protection of Employment) Regulations 1981 (TUPE81) as amended by the Collective Redundancies and Transfers of Undertakings (Protection of Employment) Regulations 1995: *Secretary of State for Employment* v *Globe Elastic Thread Co. Ltd* [1979] IRLR 327), which can be important when calculating entitlement to, for example, maternity or redundancy pay.

The statement must then go on to state certain terms of the contract (or if there are none it must state so). These are:

1. scale or rate of remuneration and intervals of remuneration;
2. the hours of work, including 'normal working hours' if there are such;
3. terms relating to holidays including pay and public holidays and method of calculating accrued pay;
4. terms relating to incapacity for work including sick pay;
5. terms relating to pensions;
6. the length of notice the employee and employer must give to terminate employment;
7. the job title or brief description of the job the employee is employed to do;
8. if the employment is not to be permanent, how long it will last, or if fixed term the date it will end;
9. the place of work of the employee, or if the employee is required to work at more than one place, a statement of that and the employer's address;
10. any collective agreements which affect the terms and conditions of employment;
11. where the employee is required to work outside the UK for more than one month, a statement of the period of absence from the UK, the currency of remuneration, any additional remuneration while abroad, and conditions relating to return to the UK.

The employer can fulfil the requirement relating to 4 and 5, sickness and pensions, by referring the employee to another document, such as a handbook, so long as it is reasonably available. The requirement relating to 6, notice periods, can be met by referring the employee to the relevant legislation (ERA, s.86).

In addition, the employer must also supply the employee with a note specifying:

1. any disciplinary rules (or the employee may be referred to a reasonably accessible document for this information);
2. the person to whom the employee should appeal against a disciplinary decision, and the person to whom the employee should address any grievance, and how any such applications should be made;
3. any further steps necessary for such an application (or reference to a reasonably accessible document).

This last note does not have to be given out by an employer where the total number of employees employed at the time employment began was less than 20, taking account of the combined number of the employer and any associated employer.

If the written statement is wrong, or is not provided, or is partial, the employee may apply to an industrial tribunal. The tribunal has the power to add to or amend the statement to reflect the true contractual position when it finds that they vary. However, if they find that there is a gap in the contract in respect of one of the 'non-mandatory' terms, that is the terms which are not essential for there to be a contract of employment in existence such as sick pay or pensions, the tribunal is only empowered to declare that there is no term, and cannot draw up their own term (*Eagland* v *British Telecommunications plc* [1992] IRLR 323).

Sources of the terms of a contract of employment

The terms of most contracts of employment come from a number of different sources: even where there is a comprehensive written contract of employment it is likely that other sources will be relevant.

Agreed terms

The primary legal source of any contract of employment, like any contract, is the terms agreed between the parties. With the exceptions noted earlier, the agreement may be verbal or written. The terms agreed take precedence over any other term, and those agreed in writing take precedence over all other terms (but remember that some writings may not be contractual, such as the statutory written statement, and will simply be evidence of the contract) (*Robertson and Jackson* v *British Gas Corporation,* above).

Implied terms

As well as the terms expressly agreed between the employer and employee, there may also be terms agreed by implication. Such terms may be implied into the contract through the parties acting in such a way as to imply agreement. For example, an employee might comply with the employer's required hours of work, or the employer might pay the employee at the rate requested without formal agreement. A term might also be implied into a contract because it is needed to make the contract work effectively: this is often known as the *business efficacy* test. Or a term might be implied into a contract because it is obvious that if the parties had thought about it at the time they were entering into the contract they would have included it: this is often known as the *officious bystander* test (if a bystander had suggested to the employer and employee that they include the term the two would have told the bystander – politely – that it was obvious). These two approaches have been used in cases which have had to decide if an employer had the right to require the employee to move his or her place of work, where the contract itself did not contain an express mobility clause. A right to transfer may be implied if the court is 'satisfied that the implied term is one which the parties would probably have agreed if they were being reasonable' (*Courtaulds Northern Spinning Ltd* v *Sibson* [1988] IRLR 305 at p. 309), but it will not be implied if the employee is asked to work outside reasonable daily travelling distance (*O'Brien* v *Associated Fire Alarms Ltd* [1969] 1 All ER 93), and it will depend on the nature of the employer's business how necessary any mobility clause is, so that it may be necessary for an employer whose work involves specialist engineering work (*Jones* v *Associate Tunnelling Co. Ltd* [1981] IRLR 477), but not for the employer whose business is a chain of stores (*Aparu* v *Iceland Frozen Foods plc,* [1996] IRLR 119). In other words if the nature of the work means that it is likely to be short term in any one place such a clause is more likely to be implied. It is, of course, better to cover the matter expressly.

Custom and practice

A custom in a trade or industry or a local custom may become part of a contract if it has been followed for a long time in practice, and is 'reasonable, certain and notorious' (*Devonald* v *Rosser & Sons Ltd* [1906] 2 KB 728). Not all practices adopted by an employer will have contractual effect, and may remain an exercise of an employer's discretion. Important factors to take into account to decide whether a practice has become a contractual entitlement include whether the policy has been drawn to the attention of the employees and whether it has been followed without exception for a substantial period (*Quinn* v *Calder Industrial Materials Ltd* [1996] IRLR 126). *Quinn* (above) established that the fact that the employers had paid an enhanced redundancy pay rate on the four occasions they had declared redundancies over a seven year period did not in itself make the enhanced payment a contractual entitlement.

Terms of collective agreements

A collective agreement is an agreement between a trade union or group of trade unions and an employer or group of employers. The collective agreement itself is not legally enforceable by the parties to it (the trade union(s) and the employer(s)) unless it is in writing and contains a statement that the parties intend it to be legally enforceable (Trade Union and Labour Relations (Consolidation) Act 1992 (TULRCA92), s.179), which is unusual.

Although the collective agreement itself is unenforceable certain of its terms may become part of the individual contracts of employment in the industries or workplaces regulated by the collective agreement. Therefore an employee who works in a business where pay rates are determined by agreement between the trade union and the employer may be able to enforce the pay rise agreed collectively on the basis that it has become part of his/her contract of employment. The terms of a collective agreement may be incorporated into the individual contract by express agreement: this is certainly the most satisfactory way. Remember that the statutory written statement must state if there is a collective agreement affecting terms and conditions at work (see p. 125). This incorporation is effective whether or not the employee is a member of the trade union concerned, and also irrespective of whether or not the employer is itself a party to the collective agreement. The terms of a collective agreement might also be incorporated by implication into the employee's contract, in the same way as a custom might become part of the contract. Also, in certain cases, a union might act on behalf of particular individuals as their agent and any agreement made on their behalf could be enforced by them (*Edwards* v *Skyways Ltd* [1964] 1 All ER 494).

Common law terms: the employee's duties

Certain duties are implied into each contract of employment on each side. First, there are the *employee's common law duties*. An employee must be willing to give *personal service*: the employee cannot, for example, send along a replacement if he/she is unwell or unwilling (*Ready Mixed Concrete (SE) Ltd* v *Minister of Pensions and National Insurance* [1968] 2 QB 497). An employee must obey the lawful orders of the employer, so long as they are within the scope of the contract, so long as they are not illegal and so long as they do not place the employee in personal danger (*Ottoman Bank* v *Chakarian* [1930] AC 277). The employee must *take reasonable care* in performing his/her duties. What is reasonable depends on the job and qualifications of the employee. A professional or skilled employee must exercise the care and skill to be expected of a reasonably competent member of the profession or trade concerned. An employee who causes his/her employer loss by breach of this duty may be liable to compensate the employer (*Lister* v *Romford Ice and Cold Storage Co. Ltd* [1957] AC 555). Finally the employee owes a duty *to give faithful service* to the employer.

The duty to give faithful service is the employee's side of the *mutual* duty of trust and confidence, the employer's side of which is dealt with below. On the employee's side this can be looked at as a number of linked duties. The employee should serve the employer's best interests while working (*Secretary of State for Employment* v *ASLEF* (No 2) [1972] 2 All ER 949). The employee must not let his/her own interests conflict with those of the employer, so that although employees may do what they like in their own time in general, during their employer's time they should work only on their employer's account, and in their own time should not do any work which involves a conflict with their employer's interests. Thus if an employee agrees to work for a competitor of the employer in his/her own time, the employer may be able to object to this if there is a danger that confidential information might be given to the competitor regardless of whether or not the employee is likely to breach confidence (*Hivac Ltd* v *Park Royal Scientific Instruments Ltd* [1946] 1 Ch 169).

The employee must not make a secret profit out of employment: this involves not simply prohibiting the taking of bribes by the employee to influence the performance of the employment, but also requires an employee to disclose to and, if requested, account to the employer for any gift or benefit received in the course of employment, however innocently given or taken (*Boston Deep Sea Fishing & Ice Co.* v *Ansell* (1888) Ch D 339). The employee must not disclose confidential information, and to an extent this duty extends beyond employment. Confidential information is information the employer believes would be prejudicial if released, and which the employer reasonably believes is secret, judged by trade practice (*Thomas Marshall (Exports) Ltd* v *Guinle* [1979] 1 Ch 227). A distinction is made between on the one hand confidential information which is learned as part of the employee's work, which should not be disclosed during employment, but which as part of the employee's own skill and knowledge can be disclosed after employment ends; and on the other hand information regarding specific trade secrets which are so confidential that they cannot be disclosed either during or after employment (*Faccenda Chicken Ltd* v *Fowler* [1986] IRLR 69).

An employer who wishes to protect his/her business against possible disclosure by an ex-employee, however, would be best to do so by means of a *restrictive covenant* in the contract of employment. Such a restriction should be no more than is necessary, in terms of area covered, time it lasts, and sphere of employment covered, to protect the employer's legitimate interests in protecting customers and confidential information. Such a restrictive covenant can be more effective from the employer's point of view, since it can prohibit the employee actually setting up in opposition or working for a competitor for a specified time and place, whereas the implied duty can only prohibit unlawful disclosure which it may be difficult to prove (*Living Design (Home Improvements) Ltd* v *Davidson* [1994] IRLR 69).

Finally, the common law rule that the employee must give the employer the benefit of any inventions made in the course of employment is now regulated by the Patents Act 1977 (ss 39–45) and the Copyright, Designs and Patents Act 1988 (s.11(2)).

Common law terms: the employer's duties

The duties owed by the employer are the counterpart of the employee's duties. These duties express the 'wage/work' bargain whereby one agrees to work in return for payment from the other. The employer's primary duty is to *pay wages*, usually the agreed sum, or if none is agreed a reasonable sum. In general the employer does not have a duty to provide work, so long as he/she continues to pay wages. As a judge said more than fifty years ago: 'Provided I pay my cook her wages regularly, she cannot complain if I choose to take any or all of my meals out'! (*Collier* v *Sunday Referee Publishing Co. Ltd* [1940] 4 All ER 234, p. 236) An employee, however, might be able to insist on being provided with work, if failure to provide work would affect the employee's reputation (as with an actor), or where the failure led to a reduction in wages, such as where someone is paid on the basis of work done. Someone who was paid entirely by commission, or gratuity from customers, might be able to use this exception, but where the commission or gratuity supplements a basic wage it is unlikely to be applicable (*Turner* v *Sawdon* [1901] 2 KB 653). In addition to wages the employer must *reimburse the employee for any losses or expenses* incurred in the course of employment.

An important duty which the employer owes the employee is the *duty to take reasonable care for the employee's safety*. This is a duty which also applies under the law of tort (in Scotland, delict), and indeed since damages for pain and suffering can be obtained under tort, but not contract, it is not likely that an action for compensation by an injured employee would be based on contract (for a discussion of tort and delict, see Chapter Two, pp. 57–63). The employer's duty involves a duty to employ competent and safe co-workers (*Hudson* v *Ridge Manufacturing Co. Ltd* [1957] 2 QB 348); a duty to provide and maintain safe plant and machinery; a duty to provide and maintain safe premises; and a duty to provide and maintain a safe system of work (*English* v *Wilsons and Clyde Coal Co. Ltd* 1937 SC(HL) 46). Detailed consideration of health and safety at work is beyond the scope of this book.

The employer also has a duty to take care when providing a reference. There is no obligation on an employer to provide a reference, but if it is provided reasonable care must be taken to see that the reference is fair and just (*Spring* v *Guardian Assurance plc* [1994] IRLR 460).

Finally there is the *mutual duty of trust and confidence*, which from the employee's side is essentially a duty of loyalty or faithful service. The employer's side of this duty is not so specific as the employee's, and it is essentially to do nothing which would forfeit the employee's loyalty. This duty has been most important in cases of constructive dismissal which is dealt with below, where an employee may resign because of an employer's breach of contract and treat the resignation as if it were a dismissal. An employer who treats an employee with contempt, or with complete disregard for their position, will probably be in breach of contract. The worse the employer's behaviour the more likely it is to justify the employee's resignation. In *Isle of Wight Tourist Board* v *Coombes* [1976] IRLR 413 a director who had insulted his secretary in front of other staff by calling her 'an intolerable bitch' was held to be in breach of contract justifying the secretary in resigning. In *Hilton International Hotels (UK) Ltd* v *Protopapa* [1990] IRLR 316 the behaviour of a line manager in reprimanding a telephone supervisor about an absence in front of other employees was found to have 'humiliated, intimidated and degraded [the employee] to such an extent that there was a breach of trust and confidence which went to the root of the contract.' In *Palmanor Ltd t/a Chaplins Night Club* v *Cedron* [1978] IRLR 303 the behaviour of the club manager in using foul language to an employee was held to go beyond the bounds of what was reasonable. The EAT made the point that in the heat of the moment people can say things which they later regret and which should not be taken too seriously, but that there comes a time when even in the heat of anger an employee cannot be expected to tolerate the behaviour.

Altering the contract of employment

Since a contract is an agreement, it can only be altered by agreement. An employer, therefore, cannot unilaterally vary the terms of the contract without the employee's consent. The employee's consent may be given expressly, or it may be given implicitly, by for example working in conformity with the new terms. However, simply not objecting to a proposed change which does not have immediate practical effect does not necessarily imply acceptance (*Aparu* v *Iceland Frozen Foods plc* [1996] IRLR 119). Some things which an employer wishes to change might not be contractual terms but might fall within the scope of the employer's control of employment, such as certain employment practices, and may thus be varied by the employer (*Secretary of State for Employment* v *ASLEF (No 2)* [1972] 2 All ER 949). If an employer decides that contractual change is necessary and is unable to obtain the employee's acceptance of the change, the employer can only effect change by dismissing the employee and offering employment under the new terms. In doing this the employer may be liable for unfair dismissal compensation (see pp. 136–147).

TERMINATION OF THE CONTRACT OF EMPLOYMENT

Introduction

Resignation (by the employee) and dismissal (by the employer) are not the only ways in which the employment relationship may be terminated. The question of what amounts to dismissal and resignation will be looked at more closely in the context of unfair dismissal below (see pp. 136–147).

A number of events may cause termination. *Expiry of the contract* may bring about the end of employment. So, if a contract is formed to carry out a particular task, it will expire on completion of the task. If it is formed for a specific time period it expires on completion of the time. It will also end in the event of the *death* of either employer or employee, and in the case of *dissolution of a partnership* (see Chapter Three, p. 82). While dissolution of a partnership can terminate the contracts of employees of the firm, if the business is acquired as a going concern TUPE81 (as amended by the Collective Redundancies and Transfers of Undertakings (Protection of Employment) Regulations 1995) will operate to transfer the contracts of existing employees to the new employer. The *sequestration or winding up of a company* will also end the contract. Bankruptcy or insolvency of the employer is breach of contract and allows the employee to terminate the contract. If the business is acquired as a going concern under TUPE81 contracts of employment will be transferred to the new employer.

The contract may end because of the doctrine of *frustration of contract* where, without fault of either party, the contract becomes impossible to perform or becomes a substantially different one from that agreed, it terminates automatically (see also Chapter Two, pp. 53–54). Where the employer and employee mutually agree that the contract be terminated, employment ends by *agreement*.

Termination by notice

Unless the contract is expressly stated to be *ad vitam aut culpam* (till death or gross misconduct), or unless it is for a fixed period, it may be terminated by either party on giving notice, or by the employer paying wages in lieu of notice.

The appropriate notice is what the parties have contractually agreed, or if there is no agreement what is reasonable in all the circumstances. In no cases, however, can the notice be less than the minima specified in ERA, s.86: namely that after one month's employment an employee is entitled to one week's notice, and that after two year's employment she is entitled to one week for every year worked to a maximum of twelve weeks; after one month's employment an employee must give the employer one week's notice of termination.

Termination in the case of breach

Where one party materially (seriously) breaches the contract – often called repudiation of contract – the other (innocent) party is entitled to terminate the contract without notice. This is called *summary dismissal* where the employer dismisses the employee without notice. It is called *constructive dismissal* where the employee resigns on account of the employer's repudiation.

Where someone materially breaches the contract they are not deemed to have ended it themselves. When one party repudiates the contract, it ends only if the innocent party decides to 'accept' the repudiation and terminate the contract (*London Transport Executive* v *Clarke* [1981] ICR 355).

REMEDIES FOR BREACH OF CONTRACT

Specific performance/implement and injunction/interdict

These are remedies by which in the former case a court orders someone to perform their legal obligations and in the latter a court orders them to stop breaching their obligations. Such remedies are not available to compel either employer or employee unwillingly into a contract of employment. The contract is personal and voluntary. Statute reinforces this common law rule (TULRCA92 s.236).

However there are circumstances where it may be possible to obtain an injunction (in Scotland, interdict). An *employee* may be able to obtain an injunction to prohibit an employer acting in breach of contract to enforce a notice period, or to enforce a contractual disciplinary period, if an employer tries to dismiss without notice or without going through the disciplinary procedure. This remedy can only hold off a contractually proper dismissal, not avert it altogether. It is a discretionary remedy. A judge will not award it if it is clear that the employer has lost all trust and confidence in the employee (*Hughes* v *London Borough of Brent* [1988] IRLR 55).

An *employer* may be able to obtain an injunction to prohibit an employee from working for another in breach of an express or implied contractual term. This will not be granted unless it is necessary to protect the legitimate interests of the employer, and unless the employer is prepared to continue with his/her side of the contract (carry on with the duty to pay wages) (*GFI Group* v *Eaglestone* [1994] IRLR 119).

Damages for breach of contract

Where an employee has been summarily dismissed (i.e. without notice) without there being lawful grounds for this (lawful grounds being material breach of contract by the employee), the employee is entitled to raise an action of *wrongful dismissal*. The only remedy for wrongful dismissal is damages. The measure of damages is what is needed to compensate the employee for the financial loss suffered as a result of the summary dismissal. This is limited to a sum to reflect the amount of notice that should have been given, and an amount to reflect any other breach by the employer which is relevant, such as an amount to reflect the time a contractual disciplinary procedure would have taken (*Dietman* v *London Borough of Brent* [1988] ICR 842), and probably also, where if contractual notice had been given the employee would have been entitled to claim unfair dismissal, the amount of compensation the employee might have won to reflect that lost opportunity (*Robert Cort & Son Limited* v *Charman* [1981] IRLR 437).

Withholding wages

If an employee refuses to carry out a material part of the employment contract, this is a repudiation of contract; legally the employer could terminate it. The employee who refuses to perform the contract is in breach of the duty to be ready and willing to work. Since contracts are mutual, this releases the employer from the duty to pay wages. The employer who decides not to pay wages would have to tell the employee that he/she was not prepared to accept partial performance of the contract (*Wiluszynski* v *London Borough of Tower Hamlets* [1989] IRLR 259).

STATUTORY EMPLOYMENT PROTECTION RIGHTS

Employment protection legislation has given employees rights additional to any contained in the contract of employment. Some of these rights apply only to people who are employees and not independent contractors (such as unfair dismissal and redundancy pay), while others apply to independent contractors as well as employees (such as discrimination). Some rights require a qualification period of employment while others do not.

Most employment protection rights are enforced not in the ordinary courts but in front of industrial tribunals. These were first established in 1964 (Industrial Training Act 1964, s.12), and their jurisdiction has been much extended since then. The jurisdiction of the industrial tribunals is mainly statutory. Major statutes which provide for reference to industrial tribunals include ERA, EPA 1970, SDA 1975, SDA

1986, RRA and the DDA. Certain common law actions for breach of contract may also be raised in industrial tribunals. Claims for damages for breach of a contract of employment or of another contract connected with employment may be raised, but only on termination of the contract of employment. Claims may not go to an industrial tribunal which relate to copyright, patents or trademarks, or to restrictive covenants or to terms imposing obligations of confidence.

A panel of three, a chairperson and two others drawn from a pool of persons appointed by the Secretary of State, hears cases in industrial tribunals. Chairpersons are lawyers of at least seven years' standing. Organizations representing employers and workers nominate the others. Appeals go from industrial tribunals to the EAT (and from there to the Court of Appeal (in Scotland, to the Inner House of the Court of Session) and on to the House of Lords) on a point of law, that is that the tribunal misdirected itself as to law, or that the decision of the tribunal was so perverse or 'so very clearly wrong that it just cannot stand' or 'so outrageous in its defiance of logic or of accepted standards of industrial relations that no sensible person who has applied his mind to the question with the necessary experience could have arrived at it' (*Berkshire Health Authority* v *Matadeen* [1992] IRLR 336 at p. 342).

Each statute will specify the time within which the relevant application must be made. For example in an unfair dismissal case an application must be made within three months of dismissal unless it is not reasonably practicable to do so; in sex or race discrimination employment cases an application must be made within three months of the date of the act complained of unless the tribunal considers it just and equitable to hear it out of time.

There are many rights and obligations imposed on employee and employer. The next chapter will consider those concerned with discrimination. The remainder of this chapter will concentrate on a small number of key employment rights. You should consult the specialist employment law textbooks referred to in the further reading section for this chapter for the full range of rights and duties.

DEDUCTIONS FROM WAGES

General

The contract of employment – and thus primarily by the agreement of employer and employee – governs the issue of what wages are due and how they are to be paid. There is specific statutory protection afforded to an employee against non-contractual deductions, permitting deductions only according to the provisions of the ERA. The ERA does not, however, make any provision about the reasonableness of any contractual provision for deduction; that is a matter for the parties.

An employer may not make a deduction from wages or, equivalently, demand a payment from a worker unless either it is *required or authorized by statute*, or it is *required or authorized by the worker's contract* or the worker has *previously signified in writing her agreement to the deduction* (ERA, s.13(1)). Worker in this context includes employees, apprentices and independent contractors (ERA, s.230(3)).

Where the *contract* authorizes the deduction, the term may be either a written term of a contract which the worker received a copy of before the deduction was made, or it may be any term of a contract, whether express or implied, verbal or written, which the worker has been notified of before the deduction was made (ERA, s.13(2)). Thus the crucial point is that the employee must have agreed to the possibility of deduction, and that there must have been a written record of the agreement, of which the employee has been notified.

Wages includes any sum payable to a worker in connection with employment, including any bonus or holiday pay whether contractual or otherwise, and sums payable under statute or tribunal order (maternity pay, statutory sick pay) (ERA, s.27(1)), and vouchers which have a fixed monetary value and which can be exchanged for money, goods or services (ERA, s.27(5)). Wages, however, does not include a payment in advance for a loan by the employer, nor payment in respect of expenses, or a pension or gratuity regarding retirement, nor payment regarding redundancy, nor any payment other than in the worker's capacity as worker (ERA, s.27(2)). Unauthorized deduction from wages is contrary to the ERA, as is non-payment of wages. The latter is not explicitly mentioned in the ERA and an over-literal interpretation of the word 'deduction' led to the view that total non-payment could not be covered since deduction implied partial payment. The Court of Appeal rejected this view (*Delaney* v *Staples* [1991] IRLR 112): if the deduction is total and results in a refusal to pay, it may be challenged under the ERA (*Bruce* v *Wiggins Teape (Stationery) Ltd* [1994] IRLR 536).

The ERA does not cover some deductions from wages: those in respect of overpayment of wages or expenses; statutory deductions to a statutory authority (e.g. taxation) or arising out of a statutory disciplinary proceeding; authorized deductions to a third party (such as a trade union); those in respect of any strike or industrial action the worker took part in; and those in respect of a court or tribunal order to make payment to the employer (ERA, ss.14–16). Any dispute about these has to be dealt with under the general law, and can only be taken to an industrial tribunal if employment has ended.

Workers in retail employment

There are two additional protections for workers in retail employment against deductions relating to cash shortages and stock deficiencies. This applies not just to those who work in the retail sector, but to workers who carry out a retail function, whether or not they do so on a regular basis. Retail employment means the carrying out of 'retail transactions' (the supply of goods or services) directly with members of the public or with fellow workers or other individuals personally, or the collection of money payable in connection with such transactions (ERA, s.17(2)).

The ERA does not regulate the reasonableness of any contractual provision for such a deduction: it simply regulates the form of any such deduction. The first additional protection is that any deduction must be made within 12 months of the employer establishing the need to made the deduction. If there is to be a series of deductions the first must be made within the 12 month period (ERA, s.18(3)). If the employer tries to recover money not by deduction but by demanding a payment from the employee, the general provisions relating to deductions must apply and in addition the worker must be notified in writing of the total liability for the shortage or deficiency. The employer must issue a written demand for payment, the demand being issued on a pay day, which must occur after the notification but before the 12 months is up (ERA, s.20).

The second additional protection is that the amount of any deductions must not exceed one tenth of the total amount of wages payable to the worker on the pay day in question, except in the case of a final instalment of wages (ERA, s.18(1), s.20(5)). Deductions may therefore have to be made in instalments.

SICK PAY

Statutory sick pay

There is a statutory entitlement to 28 weeks statutory sick pay (Social Security Contributions and Benefits Act 1992, ss 151–163) and the Statutory Sick Pay Act 1994 which the contract of employment cannot restrict. It is payable to the employee by the employer, who may recover 80 per cent of the amount paid from national insurance contributions. There is one level of statutory sick pay and the Secretary of State keeps the amount under review.

Contractual sick pay

The contract of employment may give an additional right to be paid full (or a percentage of) pay. If there is no express agreement, there may be an implied agreement depending on the conduct of the parties or custom and practice (*Mears* v *Safecar Security Ltd* [1982] ICR 626).

HOURS OF WORK

Recent EC legislation has introduced restrictions on the hours that employees can be required to work, in the interests of health and safety (Working Time Directive 93/104/EEC). The UK Government mounted an unsuccessful challenge to the legality of this legislation, which ought to have been brought into force in the member states in November 1996. The attitude of the Government elected in May 1997, however, is more positive towards measures to protect employees. UK legislation is expected during the course of 1998.

The Directive lays down minimum daily and weekly rest periods and paid annual holidays, maximum weekly working time and provisions relating to night work. The Directive excludes a number of sectors of activity completely from its operation including air, rail, road, sea, inland waterway and lake transport. In addition to this general exclusion, there are a number of other specific possible exemptions from parts of the Directive which national legislation may include.

The minimum daily rest period is 11 consecutive hours in a 24 hour period. Where the working day is longer than 6 hours, there must be a rest break to be agreed by collective bargaining or contained in legislation. The minimum weekly rest period is an uninterrupted period of 24 hours in addition to the daily 11 hours. The maximum weekly working time is an average of 48 hours for each 7 day period, over a reference period of no more than 4 months. The minimum amount of paid leave is 4 weeks which may not be replaced by payment in lieu. The normal hours of night workers should not exceed an average of 8 hours in a 24 hour period: for especially hazardous or stressful work it should not exceed 8 hours in any 24 hour period.

At the option of the member states, national legislation may provide for certain groups of workers to be exempt from these requirements. This includes the exemption of people whose working time cannot be measured, such as managing executives and family workers, from all of the above except the annual leave entitlement. Legislation or collective agreement may also exempt a number of other workers, so long as they are afforded appropriate protection, from the daily and weekly rest and break requirements and the night work limit (but not the maximum weekly working time). This includes activities where the worker's work and residence or different places of work are distant from each other; security and surveillance activities requiring a permanent presence; dock or airport workers; work where there is a foreseeable surge of activity such as tourism. There may be exemption from the daily and weekly rest requirement and the night work limit for workers such as cleaning staff whose work is split up over the day.

The Directive also allows national legislation to permit individual employees to agree to work more than 48 hours a week, subject to monitoring requirements and subject to protection against pressure to agree to do so, and also in certain circumstances to extend the reference period to 6 months, or under collectively agreed arrangements to 12 months. The necessary UK legislation giving effect to this is likely to be introduced in the course of 1998.

UNFAIR DISMISSAL

Introduction

The ERA re-enacts a right not to be unfairly dismissed (ERA, s.94). It widens the scope to claim compensation on dismissal firstly because, unlike the common law action for wrongful dismissal, it is available both in the case of summary dismissal and in the case of dismissal by notice; secondly it may be available in the case of non-renewal of a fixed term contract; and thirdly compensation is available for loss of earnings in addition to failure to issue notice. However, there is a maximum limit on unfair dismissal compensation, so that the person who is dismissed from a common law fixed term contract and whose loss would amount to more than the statutory maximum should pursue the common law claim, not the statutory one.

It is not possible to contract out of the right not to be unfairly dismissed, so that any term in a contract of employment restricting the right to claim unfair dismissal is invalid (ERA, s.203). However, an employee who works under a *fixed term contract of one year or more* may sign away the right, if he/she has agreed in writing before the expiry of the contract to exclude unfair dismissal rights, so long as the dismissal is simply the expiry of the contract (ERA, s.197).

Excluded employees

Not all employees are entitled to raise an action. Among those who are excluded from exercising this right are employees with less than two years' continuous employment with the employer (ERA, s.108). This exclusion does not apply to certain types of dismissal, such as pregnancy dismissals, health and safety dismissals, trade union dismissals or dismissals for asserting a statutory right. For other types of dismissal absence of the necessary continuity of employment is an absolute bar to a claim. The rules for establishing continuity are contained in ERA and TUPE81. At the time of writing there has been a successful challenge to the two year qualification which is subject to appeal to the House of Lords (*R* v *Secretary of State for Employment ex p. Seymour Smith and Perez* [1995] IRLR 464). The Court of Appeal held that the raising of the qualification from one year to two years in 1985 was contrary to the Equal Treatment Directive 76/207 and possibly also Article 119 of the EC Treaty in that it amounts to indirect sex discrimination (for the meaning of indirect discrimination see Chapter Seven) against women (who are more likely to have shorter employment times because of breaks for family reasons). The House of Lords has referred this case to the European Court of Justice ([1997] IRLR 315). We consider that legislation should be introduced to clarify the position.

Also excluded from unfair dismissal protection are employees who have reached the *normal retirement age* for employees in their position in the undertaking in which they are employed, or if there is no normal retirement age those aged 65 or over are excluded (ERA, s.109). *Normal* will usually mean contractual, and the tribunal will start from a presumption that this is the case. However, if an employee can show that in practice the contractual retirement age is significantly departed from and that retirement is in practice at a different age, normal will mean that age (*Barclays Bank plc* v *O'Brien* [1994] ICR 865). This alteration to the contractual retirement age can only apply where the alteration is to a higher, not lower, age (*Bratko* v *Beloit Walmsley Ltd* [1995] IRLR 629). The tribunal will be guided by the reasonable expectations of the group to which the employee belongs (*Brooks* v *British Telecommunications plc* [1992] IRLR 66).

Employees who under their contract of employment ordinarily work outside Great Britain are excluded (ERA, s.196). In cases where the employee works abroad and in Great Britain, preponderance of employment might be decisive, but in cases of difficulty the base the individual works from may be considered. In *Todd* v *British Midland Airways Ltd* [1978] IRLR 370 since the employee flew out of a British airport, his employment was held to be in Great Britain. In contrast, in *Wood* v *Cunard Line* [1989] IRLR 431, the employee worked on a cruise ship in the Caribbean, flying to join the ship from Great Britain, his employers giving him a return flight to Great Britain or anywhere else. The Court of Appeal held that this employment was 'wholly outside' Great Britain. Merchant sailors employed on a ship registered in the UK ordinarily work in Great Britain unless the employment is wholly outside Great Britain or they are not ordinarily resident in Great Britain (ERA, s.196).

Dismissal

An action of unfair dismissal can only be raised if an employee has been dismissed, not (usually) if he/she has resigned or agreed to go. If there is any doubt about the matter it is up to the employee to prove that there was a dismissal. Dismissal has a broad meaning and can occur in three ways (ERA, s.95). It may be by termination of the contract by the employer, with or without notice. It may be by expiry of a fixed term contract without renewal. Or it may be by termination by the employee with or without notice in circumstances such that he/she is entitled to terminate it without notice by reason of the employer's conduct (usually known as 'constructive dismissal'). What these three types of termination have in common is that they are all caused by the employer, even though they may not take the traditional form of dismissal.

Dismissal: termination by the employer

The courts have been careful to look at the reality of situations rather than going simply on the form of words used. Thus while frustration of contract, agreement and resignation are not dismissal, the courts look carefully to see if in reality the termination was at the instance of the employer.

In cases of long term absence due to ill health it is possible to argue that the contract is frustrated where it looks as if the employee may be incapable of work for an extended or indefinite period. However, the attitude of the courts to this is expressed by the EAT in this warning in *Williams* v *Watsons Luxury Coaches* [1990] IRLR 165: '. . . the courts must guard against too easy an application of the doctrine, more especially when redundancy occurs and also when the true situation may be a dismissal by reason of disability.' If an employer dismisses because of ill health it will be fair if the employer has arrived at the decision to dismiss reasonably (see p. 142).

If an employer issues an ultimatum to an employee to resign or be dismissed, or in any way puts the employee in such a position that they have no real option but to resign, the resulting resignation will in fact be an employer termination or dismissal (*Robertson* v *Securicor Transport Ltd* [1972] IRLR 70). Similarly if the employee is pressurized to agree to leave employment, the agreement will also be an employer termination. Thus volunteering to be dismissed in response to a request for volunteers is a dismissal (*Burton, Alton and Johnson Ltd* v *Peck* [1975] IRLR 87).

Dismissal: non-renewal of a fixed term contract

A fixed term contract here includes not only a common law fixed term contract which cannot be terminated by notice before its term, but also a contract with a fixed termination date which can also be terminated by notice before that date (*Dixon* v *BBC* [1979] IRLR 114).

Dismissal: constructive dismissal

Only where the employer breaches the contract can the employee be justified in resigning without notice, and the breach must be a material breach (*Western Excavating (EC) Ltd* v *Sharp* [1978] IRLR 27). The breach may be of an express or an implied term of the contract, including the employer's duty of trust and confidence (for examples in relation to the employer's common law duty see above at pp. 129–130). Interpretation of the contract may be very important here. In *Pederson* v *London Borough of Camden* [1981] IRLR 173 the employee had been appointed as a bar steward/catering assistant, on the basis that he would be doing bar duty unless he was not required to do so. For four years he did mainly bar duty, and was then told that his job would be solely catering. The Court of Appeal held that there had been a fundamental breach of contract regarding the duties he had been appointed to perform so that he had been constructively dismissed. To exercise the right to claim unfair dismissal, the employee must actually resign, and must not delay in resigning after the breach by the employer or the employee will be held to have acquiesced to the change, unless it is a continuing breach (*Lewis* v *Motorwold Garages Ltd* [1985] IRLR 385).

Fairness

Once it has been established that there has been a dismissal, that is not the end of the matter. The tribunal must go on to establish what the reason was for the dismissal, and whether the dismissal was reasonable or unreasonable.

Fairness: the reason for the dismissal

While the burden of proof was on the employee to prove that there was a dismissal, it is for the employer to prove what the reason, or the principal reason, was for the dismissal. In *A Hanlon* v *Allied Breweries (UK) Ltd* [1975] IRLR 321 the employer's only answer to the employee's claim was that they had not dismissed her. The applicant was a barmaid who had been suspended on full pay after an argument with her manager: she resigned when her employer failed to pay her during this period. The tribunal held that she was entitled to resign, and had been constructively dismissed. Since the employer had not given any reason for the failure, the dismissal was automatically unfair.

The employer may only dismiss the employee on the basis of one of the five statutory reasons. These are: the *capability or qualification* of the employee for the work he/she was employed to do; the *conduct* of the employee; *redundancy*; that there would be a *contravention of statute* if the employee continued to work in his/her position; or *some other substantial reason* which justifies dismissing the employee (ERA, s.98). The employer cannot substitute a reason which was not in mind at the time of dismissal (*Hotson* v *Wisbech Conservative Club* [1984] IRLR 422).

An employee who has been dismissed may request the employer for a *written statement of reasons* for the dismissal. If the employer does not comply within two weeks the employee may apply to an industrial tribunal (ERA, s.92).

Fairness: the reasonableness of the dismissal

Introduction

Once the reason is established, the tribunal can then turn to the issue of fairness. In deciding whether the dismissal for the reason established was fair, the tribunal has to decide whether in the circumstances the employer acted reasonably or unreasonably in treating the reason as sufficient for dismissing the employee (ERA, s.98). There is no burden of proof on either employee or employer. What is reasonable depends partly on the size and administrative resources of the employer's undertaking (ERA, s.98). While it would be reasonable to expect a large national organization to have an exhaustive disciplinary procedure which is fully independent and allows for an appeal, this may not be possible for the very small business. The most important question is what is reasonable in the individual case.

Judging what is reasonable

The tribunal has to decide whether they consider that a reasonable employer would have acted as the employer did in the circumstances. The tribunal must not look at it from the point of view of what it would have done in the circumstances, but it must use the perspective that there may be more than one reasonable response in a situation and so long as the employer's decision to dismiss is within the 'band of reasonable responses' which a reasonable employer might have adopted, it will be a reasonable decision (*British Leyland* v *Swift* [1981] IRLR 91). There may be occasions where some employers might think it too harsh to dismiss for certain conduct, but others might think it appropriate: if there is a genuine range of possible reasonable responses it is not up to a tribunal to decide between them. This difference of opinion occurred in *Trust Houses Forte Hotels Ltd* v *Murphy* [1977] IRLR 186. A night porter admitted to having used £8 worth of his employer's liquor for which he was responsible, for his own use, intending to replace it, and was dismissed. Although a tribunal found that his dismissal was unfair, the EAT held that it could not be said that a reasonable employer could not have decided to dismiss in cases where there had been theft of property entrusted to an employee's care.

In deciding whether or not an employer's decision to dismiss an employee is reasonable the tribunal must take account of both the *sufficiency of reason* and the *procedure* used by the employer in taking the decision to dismiss. Procedure is not simply a technicality but is an essential aspect of deciding whether the employer's action in dismissing the employee was reasonable in all the circumstances. Therefore, even if it would have made no difference to the outcome for the employer to have followed a proper procedure, the very fact of not doing so is a strong indicator that the employer has behaved unreasonably (*Polkey* v *AE Dayton Services Ltd* [1987] IRLR 503).

Reasonable procedure

What amounts to a reasonable procedure depends on the circumstances and the reason for the dismissal, so that in cases of redundancy there may be an emphasis on consultation and warning; in cases of capability an emphasis on hearing the employee and giving assistance; in cases of ill-health an emphasis on consultation, informed assessment and compassion; in cases of misconduct an emphasis on hearing the employee and giving fair warning. Whatever the reason for the dismissal, the reasonable employer should be fair to the employee.

Reasonableness: conduct dismissals

Introduction

There has been a great deal of case law on reasonableness in conduct dismissals, much of which is applicable to capability dismissals as well. The Advisory Conciliation and Arbitration Service (ACAS), has issued a *Code of Practice on Discipline Practice and Procedures in Employment* (1977). Like all Codes of Practice it is not legally binding in itself, but it is taken account of by tribunals in assessing whether the terms of the statute have been complied with (see also Chapter One pp. 10–11). It is therefore a good basis for developing a proper procedure for handling discipline matters, including conduct dismissals.

To provide sufficient reason for dismissal the relevant conduct will usually, but not always, be conduct inside employment. Misconduct outside employment, including conviction for a crime, may constitute a sufficient reason depending on the link between the offence and the employment. According to the ACAS Code of Practice 'The main considerations should be whether the offence is one that makes the individual unsuitable for his or her type of work or unacceptable to other employees' (para.15.c). One instance of gross misconduct may be sufficient grounds for dismissal, depending on the circumstances, while for lesser misconduct any dismissal should usually follow on repetition after warning (para.12).

In conduct dismissals the approach adopted by the EAT in *British Home Stores Ltd v Burchell* [1980] ICR 303 has been followed consistently. The employer's dismissal of an employee who was suspected of stealing from them but against whom there was insufficient evidence to prosecute was held to be reasonable. The employers had satisfied three key requirements: they had a genuine belief in the guilt of the employee; this belief was based upon reasonable grounds; and they had carried out a reasonable investigation. Thus an employer does not have to have proof of misconduct to the criminal standard of proof, that is, proof beyond reasonable doubt. Genuine belief is sufficient, so long as it is based on reasonable grounds derived from a reasonable investigation. Thus the law approaches the question from the perspective of the employer's behaviour – was it reasonable? – and not from the perspective of justice to the employee – did he/she do it?

Contractual provision

Where there is a contractual procedure, while failure to follow it in every respect does not automatically render a dismissal unfair, nevertheless a reasonable employer can be expected to comply with the requirements of its own disciplinary code (*Westminster City Council* v *Cabaj* [1996] IRLR 399).

Facts known at the time

The reasonableness of dismissal can only be assessed in the light of the facts known by the employer at the time of the dismissal. If subsequently facts come to light which would have justified the dismissal, these cannot retrospectively make an unfair decision fair, although they may justify a reduced award of compensation (*W Devis & Sons Ltd* v *Atkins* [1977] IRLR 314).

Reasonable investigation

What is necessary in the way of investigation will depend on all the circumstances, including the type of evidence available to the employer. The more circumstantial the evidence, the more investigation will be needed (*ILEA* v *Gravett* [1988] IRLR 499).

Hearing the employee

Many cases emphasize the importance of giving the employee an opportunity to be heard. The Court of Appeal has described a failure to allow a hearing to an employee who had been dismissed after a conviction for assault without a hearing as a breach of an 'immutable standard of fairness' (*McLaren* v *NCB* [1988] IRLR 215). Any hearing should be meaningful. If the employers have made their mind up before the hearing it is not meaningful. It is a crucial part of a fair disciplinary procedure that an employee knows the case against him/her (*Spink* v *Express Foods Group Ltd* [1990] IRLR 320). A hearing should be unbiased, and while a minor breach of justice might be overlooked, it cannot be if fairness to the employee is prejudiced absolutely. In *Moyes* v *Hylton Castle Working Men's Social Club and Institute Ltd* [1986] IRLR 482 a bar steward was dismissed after two incidents of alleged sexual harassment of a barmaid, the incident having been witnessed by the chairman and assistant secretary of the club. These two officials were part of the committee of five which investigated the incident and were present at the full committee of the club which decided to dismiss. The EAT held that the dismissal was unfair since it was clearly unnecessary for the two to be both witnesses and judges (since there were enough personnel available) and thus justice did not appear to be done, nor was it done.

Consistency

Fairness involves being consistent. The ERA emphasizes 'equity and the substantial merits of the case' (ERA, s.98). Inconsistent treatment of similar offences may show that the employer has been unreasonable, perhaps by leading the employee to believe certain behaviour would be overlooked, or by suggesting that the employer is overreacting or that there is another underlying reason for dismissal. However, employers do not have to treat all offences in the same way as each case will depend on its own individual facts. In *Hadjioannou* v *Coral Casinos Ltd* [1981] IRLR 352, contrary to company rules, a blackjack inspector had socialized with a member and borrowed money from a guest. He argued that other employees had not been dismissed for breach of this rule. The EAT supported the tribunal's finding that the dismissal was unfair, emphasizing that each case must be looked at on its own merits.

Reasonableness: capability

Dismissals because of capability (which include ill health dismissals) are not misconduct dismissals so that a disciplinary approach is not appropriate. However, the principles of fair warning and hearing the employee apply equally to this category of dismissal. An employer should have a genuine belief on reasonable grounds that the employee is incapable of carrying out the job together with a reasonable procedure to establish that belief and to provide any reasonable assistance (*Taylor* v *Alidair Ltd* [1978] IRLR 82). Trainee employees and recently promoted employees should be given particular support and consideration (*The Post Office* v *Mughal* [1977] IRLR 178).

In cases of long term illness, in deciding whether to dismiss, the employer should take account of the nature of the illness, the likely length of the continuing absence and the need of the business to have the work done. A reasonable employer might consider transfer to another job. A reasonable employer will take proper account of medical advice, and will consult with the employee unless there are exceptional circumstances (*Spencer* v *Paragon Wallpapers Ltd* [1980] IRLR 259; *Eclipse Blinds Ltd* v *Wright* [1992] IRLR 133). Employers must also take account of the provisions of the DDA (see Chapter Seven).

Reasonableness: redundancy

Some redundancy dismissals are automatically unfair, without the need to consider whether the employer acted reasonably or unreasonably. Such dismissals are: where the grounds for selection are an inadmissible reason, that is pregnancy, health and safety, assertion of a statutory right (for the meaning of these grounds, see below at pp. 144–145); where the grounds for selection are trade union membership or non-membership or taking part in trade union activities (TULRCA, s.153).

In other cases the relevant consideration is whether or not the employer acted reasonably. A reasonable procedure of consultation should be followed wherever possible. This may include objective selection criteria; fair application of criteria; investigation of the possibility of transfer to other jobs; warning or consulting employees; and consulting trade unions (*Williams* v *Compair Maxam Ltd* [1982] ICR 156). Small employers should also consult, even if only informally (*Boulton and Paul Ltd* v *Arnold* [1994] IRLR 532).

Reasonableness: contravention of statute

This is where continuation of employment, for example as a driver, would be contrary to statute, because for example the employee had lost his/her licence. Reasonableness can still be an issue, since transfer might be a possibility.

Reasonableness: some other substantial reason

This can include a wide range of reasons, usually involving situations where a reasonable employer would think it necessary to dismiss in the best interests of the business. There may, however, be cases where the perceived interests of the business conflict with justice to the employee. In *Saunders* v *Scottish National Camps Association* [1981] IRLR 277, the EAT upheld a tribunal finding that dismissing a homosexual maintenance worker from his employment at a children's camp was for a substantial reason. The tribunal decision turned on their perception that a considerable proportion of employers would think this necessary (applying the 'band of reasonable responses' test), so that it may be thought that other tribunals would not take this approach. In *Bouchaala* v *Trust House Forte Hotels Ltd* [1980] IRLR 363 the employers dismissed the employee because they believed, on advice from the Department of Employment, that he would not qualify for a work permit, advice which was erroneous. It was held that this genuine belief that dismissal was necessary was a substantial reason.

There have been a number of cases involving dismissals as part of business reorganization. For reorganization to justify dismissal the employer has to prove that the reorganization was necessary for the business, and that there was adequate consultation about the reorganization and its consequences with the employee (*Chubb*

Fire Security Ltd v *Harper* [1983] IRLR 143). In *Ladbroke Courage Holidays Ltd* v *Asten* [1981] IRLR 59 the employers failed to justify their decision not to retain a seasonal bar manager because of pressure on the wages bill, because they did not show why it was necessary to reduce the wages bill, and did not discuss the matter with the employee before dismissing him.

Dismissals on the transfer of the business

Under TUPE81 (as amended) dismissals because of a transfer of a business are presumed to be unfair. Where an employee is dismissed either before or after a transfer of a business, if the principal reason for the dismissal is the transfer or is connected with the transfer, the dismissal is unfair (TUPE81, reg. 8). However, the employer may prove in defence that the reason for the dismissal was an 'economic, technical or organizational reason entailing changes in the workforce of either the transferor or the transferee before or after a relevant transfer' (an ETOR). Such a reason is a 'substantial reason' in terms of ERA, s.57. The ETOR must relate to the conduct of the business, and not to making the business more attractive to a potential buyer (*Wheeler* v *Patel* [1987] IRLR 211). In *Gateway Hotels Ltd* v *Stewart* [1988] IRLR 287 the sellers of a hotel received an offer to purchase which made the sale conditional on the dismissal of all the existing employees. They tried to negotiate the removal of the condition but when they failed they dismissed their employees. It was held that this was connected with the transfer and was not an 'economic' reason in the sense intended by TUPE81 in that it was not connected specifically with the conduct of the business. Accordingly the dismissals were unfair. The decision to dismiss for an ETOR must also meet the general test of fairness in ERA, s.57(3).

Automatically unfair dismissals

Introduction

There are a number of grounds for dismissal which are treated as automatically unfair. This has two consequences: first there is no requirement for any period of continuous employment, and all employees may rely on these grounds; secondly, the question of reasonableness is irrelevant. The dismissal is simply unfair if it is for one of the following reasons.

Pregnancy dismissals

Dismissals because of pregnancy are automatically unfair and we deal with them in more detail in the next chapter (ERA, s.99).

Health and safety dismissals

It is automatically unfair to dismiss an employee on one of the following grounds: (a) for carrying out or proposing to carry out designated health and safety duties; (b) for performing or proposing to perform any functions as a safety representative or member of a safety committee; (c) where there is no safety representative or committee or it was not reasonably practicable to raise the matter with them, for bringing harmful or potentially harmful matters to the employer's attention or proposing to do so; (d) where there is danger which is reasonably believed to be serious and imminent and which could not reasonably have been averted, for leaving the place of work or refusing to return or proposing to do so; (e) where there is danger which is reasonably believed to be serious and imminent, for taking appropriate steps to protect him/herself or others or proposing to do so. What is appropriate depends on the circumstances, in particular the employee's knowledge and the facilities and advice available to him/her (ERA, s.104).

If the dismissal arises under (e), it will not be unfair if the employer shows that the employee was negligent in the steps taken and that a reasonable employer might have dismissed for that reason.

In the case of dismissals under (a) and (b) a special award of compensation will be made in addition to the usual awards.

Dismissal for assertion of a statutory right

It is automatically unfair to dismiss an employee for either bringing proceedings against an employer to enforce certain statutory rights, or alleging that the employer had breached certain statutory rights. This includes all rights under ERA and certain provisions of TULRCA. If the claim or allegation is ill-founded the employee is still entitled to the benefit of this right so long as he/she acted in good faith (ERA, s.104).

Trade union dismissals

A dismissal is automatically unfair if the reason for it is:

1. that the employee was or proposed to become a member of a trade union;
2. that the employee took part or was going to take part in the activities of an independent trade union at the appropriate time;
3. that the employee was not a member of a union or particular union or was refusing to join or was proposing to resign (TULRCA, s.152).

Trade union activity is appropriate where it takes place outside working hours or during working hours with the agreement of the employer.

Dismissal during industrial action

The legislation disallows an employee from making an application to an industrial tribunal if the dismissal occurred while the employee was taking part in a strike or other industrial action at the time of the dismissal (TULRCA, ss 237–238). Industrial action is any collective action taken to put pressure on the employer (*Power Packaging Casemakers* v *Faust* [1983] IRLR 117). In the case of unofficial industrial action the loss of the right to claim is absolute, unless the reason for the dismissal was health and safety or pregnancy. Whether the action is official or unofficial is determined according to whether or not the action has been authorized or endorsed by the union (TULRCA, s.20).

In the case of official industrial action a dismissed employee could raise an action if the dismissal was selective. A dismissal is selective if any other employee who works at the same establishment as the dismissed employee and who was taking part in the industrial action when he/she was dismissed has not been dismissed. It is also selective if such an employee was dismissed but was later offered re-engagement within three months of the applicant's dismissal if the applicant was not.

Remedies for unfair dismissal

A dismissed employee may raise a claim at an industrial tribunal that he/she was unfairly dismissed within three months of the effective date of termination. The effective date of termination is the date dismissal takes effect: the end of the notice period if notice is given, the date of dismissal in the case of summary dismissal. In the case of unjustified summary dismissal, the notice period required by statute (one week for someone with under two years' employment) should be added on (ERA, s.92).

All applications for unfair dismissal are sent to ACAS whose duty is to try to get the parties to reach agreement without going to a tribunal. ACAS settles around a third of applications, while another third are withdrawn and the remainder proceed to tribunal (see, e.g., ACAS *Annual Report* 1995).

Order for re-instatement or re-engagement

The tribunal must explain what orders for re-instatement and re-engagement are and ask the applicant if he/she wishes such an order to be made. In the case of *re-instatement* the effect is that the employer must treat the employee as if he/she had not been dismissed: the order will specify the arrears and benefits which are due to the employee (ERA, s.112). In the case of re-engagement the effect is that the employer or an associated employer must re-employ the applicant in comparable or other suitable employment: the tribunal will specify the employer, the nature of employment, the remuneration and any other benefits.

If the applicant requests it, the tribunal will consider first re-instatement and then re-engagement, taking account of the applicant's wishes, the practicability of making an order, and in the light of the applicant's contribution to the dismissal whether an order would be just. Although the legislation places these orders as the primary remedies for unfair dismissal, in practice less than one per cent of successful applicants have such an order made in their favour (see, e.g., Department of Employment *Gazette* October 1994). Even where an order is made, because of the common law rule that a contract of employment cannot be enforced, in the event of the employer refusing to comply the tribunal can only order an increase in compensation (see below).

Compensation

Introduction

If no order for re-instatement or re-engagement has been made there are three possible awards of compensation for the successful applicant; if such an order has been made there is an additional award. The placing of maximum limits on the awards lessens the effectiveness of the provision.

Basic award

This is ordered for all types of dismissal, and is calculated according to the formula: one and a half weeks' pay for every year the applicant was in employment and aged over 41; one week's pay for every year where the applicant was aged between 22 and 41; half a week's pay for every year where the applicant was aged between 18 and 22. The maximum number of years to be counted is 20. The maximum week's pay is fixed by statutory instrument. Where dismissal is for trade union reasons there is also a minimum.

The basic award can be reduced by any redundancy pay; by a 'just and equitable' amount if the employee unreasonably refused an offer of re-instatement; by a 'just and equitable' amount if the employee's conduct before dismissal merits it; and where the employee was over 64 on dismissal by one-twelfth for every month that he/she was past his/her 64th birthday (ERA, s.122).

Compensatory award

This is ordered for all types of dismissal. It is the amount which the tribunal thinks is just and equitable in all the circumstances as compensation for the financial loss suffered as a result of the dismissal. This award can be reduced by any excess of redundancy pay left after setting it against the basic award; by a just and equitable amount if the employee caused or contributed to his/her dismissal; and if the employee failed to mitigate his/her loss (ERA, s.123) by, for example, not looking diligently for work (*Scottish and Newcastle Breweries plc* v *Halliday* [1986] IRLR 291). The maximum amount of the compensatory award is also set by statutory instrument.

Additional award

Where the employer has failed to comply with an order for re-instatement or re-engagement, the tribunal will order payment of a basic and compensatory award and unless it was not practicable to implement the order it will make an additional award of between 13 and 26 weeks' pay, or if the dismissal involved sex or race discrimination of between 26 and 52 weeks' pay (ERA, s.117).

Special award

This is an extra award to be paid in certain automatically unfair dismissal cases including certain health and safety dismissals and trade union dismissals (ERA, ss 118 and 125; TULRCA, s.157).

REDUNDANCY PAY

Introduction

There is a statutory right to redundancy pay for employees who are dismissed because of redundancy (ERA, s.135). The statutory pay is a minimum which can be enhanced either by contractual arrangement or voluntarily by the employer. A contract of employment cannot exclude the right to statutory redundancy pay unless it is a fixed term contract for two years or more and the employee has agreed in writing before the end of the contract to waive the right to redundancy pay (ERA, s.197).

Excluded employees

There is a similar, but not identical, list of exclusions as there is for unfair dismissal protection. Employees must have two years' continuous employment, but in this case employment only starts to count once the employee is over 18. Employees who are over normal retirement age or over 65 are not entitled to statutory redundancy pay. To qualify for the payment an employee must ordinarily work inside Great Britain or be working in Great Britain when dismissed. In addition employees who have pension rights which commence immediately on dismissal are wholly or partially excluded (ERA, s.158).

If an employer dismisses an employee whom he/she is entitled to dismiss without notice (because of the employee's material breach of contract or gross misconduct), even though the employee may also be redundant the employer does not have to pay redundancy pay. If the employer decides to give the employee the notice he/she would have been entitled to were it not for the misconduct, it must be accompanied by a statement telling the employee the situation (ERA, s.140(1)).

Dismissal

Although colloquially we talk about 'taking' redundancy and 'making' people redundant, the reality is that redundancy involves dismissal. Only those who are dismissed are entitled to redundancy pay. Dismissal has the same extended meaning as it has for unfair dismissal (ERA, s.136(2)) including employer termination, failure to renew a fixed term contract and constructive dismissal. An employee who resigns in anticipation of an impending redundancy but who has not been given notice of dismissal will not be entitled to claim statutory redundancy pay (*Doble* v *Firestone Tyre and Rubber Co. Ltd* [1981] IRLR 300).

Once notice of dismissal has been given the employer and employee may always agree that the employee could leave early and still claim redundancy pay (*CPS Recruitment Ltd* v *Bowen and the Secretary of State for Employment* [1982] IRLR 54). There is also a statutory provision for an employee who has been given notice, to resign before the notice expires and claim redundancy pay (ERA, s.85). The employer might object to this and contest the right to redundancy pay: if the employee still resigned it would be up to a tribunal to decide whether redundancy pay should be paid.

Redundancy

Introduction

The dismissal must be because the employee was redundant. Redundancy may either be because of a *cessation of business* or a *diminution in the requirements of business* (ERA, s.139).

Cessation of business

Redundancy can arise when the employer ceases or is going to cease carrying on the business the employee is employed in, or it may arise when the employer is ceasing the business in the place where the employee is employed. The place where an employee is employed is the place where they actually work, and not wherever they could be required to work under the terms of their contract. In *Bass Leisure Ltd* v *Thomas* [1994] IRLR 104 an employee had worked as a fruit machine collector, based at the Coventry depot. Her contract contained a mobility clause which entitled her employers to transfer her. The Coventry depot closed and Mrs Thomas was relocated to a town 20 miles away. When she found the transfer unsatisfactory she resigned and claimed redundancy pay. The tribunal and EAT rejected the employer's argument that they had not ceased business in the place she worked: they said that the test was primarily a factual one of where the employee actually worked, not where she might be asked to work.

An employer, of course, could avoid paying redundancy pay by requiring the employee to move under the terms of a mobility clause (including an implied obligation to move). In *Bass Leisure Ltd* v *Thomas* (above) the company had not complied properly with the mobility clause which had provided that the transfer should be to 'suitable' alternative work, that domestic circumstances would be taken account of, and that the area should be reasonably accessible from her normal residence. The move was unsuitable for her domestic arrangements and was not reasonably accessible from her home.

Diminution in requirements of business

This form of redundancy can arise when the employer's requirements for employees to carry out work of a particular kind have ceased or diminished or are going to, or where they have ceased or diminished in the place where the employee was employed. This diminution is likely to arise out of a decline in work, but might also arise out of a reorganization or change in work patterns, including the introduction of new technology which may not be due to economic decline. The question is simply: 'Have the employer's requirements for a certain kind of work ceased or diminished?' Thus, changing shift times does not change the requirements for the work and does not make those who worked the old shift times and who do not wish to work the new shift times redundant (*Lesney Products & Co. Ltd* v *Nolan* [1977] IRLR 77; *Johnson* v *Notts Combined Police Authority* [1974] IRLR 20).

The ERA does not state that it is the requirements for the work the employee is actually doing which must have diminished. If an employee is dismissed to make way for another employee whose job is redundant, the dismissal of what is sometimes called the 'bumped' employee may be for redundancy. However, this argument did not work in *Babar Indian Restaurant* v *Rawat* [1985] IRLR 57, where a kitchen assistant in a restaurant was dismissed to make way for an employee who had been employed in a frozen food concern also owned by the owners of the restaurant and which had been closed down. It was held that the businesses were separate, and that there had been no diminution in the requirements for employees in the restaurant.

Link with unfair dismissal

Dismissal on grounds of redundancy entitles an employee to a redundancy payment. If the dismissal is automatically unfair or unreasonable the employee will also be entitled to claim unfair dismissal.

Lay off or short time

Redundancy pay can also be claimed by an employee who has been laid off (no pay) or employed on short time (less than half pay) for four or more consecutive weeks, or for six out of thirteen weeks. Within four weeks the employee can serve a notice on the employer that he/she intends to claim redundancy pay, and within seven days he/she must resign (ERA, s.148). An employer may issue a counter notice that thirteen weeks work can be provided within the next four weeks. If the employee still resigns a tribunal must decide if redundancy pay is due.

Renewal of contract or re-engagement

If the employer offers to renew the employee's contract or to re-engage the employee in suitable alternative employment to take effect within four weeks of the old contract ending, there will be no entitlement to redundancy pay if the employee accepts or unreasonably refuses the offer (ERA, s.141).

In assessing whether or not the offer was 'suitable' the matter is looked at objectively to assess whether the new job could reasonably be considered suitable for a person in the position of the employee. In assessing whether or not the employee's refusal was unreasonable the matter is looked at subjectively, and the personal circumstances of the employee can be taken into account (*Cambridge & District Cooperative Society* v *Ruse* [1993] IRLR 156). The question of reasonableness of refusal should only be considered if the offer is considered to have been reasonable (*Hindes* v *Supersine Ltd* [1979] IRLR 105).

If the new contract differs from the old there is a trial period from the end of the old contract until four weeks into the new contract, or longer if agreed in writing (ERA, s.138). If the employee resigns or is dismissed because of a change to the new contract during the trial period, he/she is considered to have been dismissed because of the original redundancy.

Strike action

If an employee takes strike action during the notice period and is dismissed as a consequence, the employee does not lose the right to redundancy pay, but the employer may serve a *notice of extension* requiring the employee to make up the days lost (ERA, s.143).

Misconduct

If an employee is dismissed (properly) for misconduct during the notice period he/she will not automatically lose entitlement to redundancy pay, but it will be up to an industrial tribunal to decide what proportion, if any, of the pay he/she should obtain (ERA, s.140). Redundancy pay is in recognition of past service.

Calculation of redundancy pay

Redundancy pay is calculated according to the same formula as the basic award in unfair dismissal, that is, one and a half weeks' pay for every year the applicant was over 41; one week's pay for every year the applicant was between 22 and 41; half a week's pay for every year the applicant was between 18 and 22, up to a maximum of 20 years. There is the same maximum imposed by statutory instrument.

The employer must give a *written statement* as to how redundancy pay is made up and is guilty of a criminal offence if he/she does not do so (ERA, s.165).

Consultation

Both UK and EC law impose obligations on employers to consult with employee representatives about proposed redundancies. There are similar obligations also to consult about proposed business transfers.

When an employer is proposing to dismiss 20 or more employees from the same establishment all within a 90 day period, the employer must consult with the appropriate representatives (TULRCA, s.188). There is no duty to consult where less than 20 at one establishment are being dismissed, except as is necessary not to fall foul of unfair dismissal law. The appropriate representatives are either union representatives or employee representatives, elected by fellow-workers to represent them, either specifically for the redundancy consultation or more generally. They must be consulted 'in good time', and no later than 30 days before the first dismissal where between 20 and 100 are being dismissed, and no later than 90 days before where 100 or more are being dismissed. In the case of failure to consult, a tribunal can make a *protective award* which will have the effect of protecting the employees' wages for a period.

Discrimination in employment and service provision

7

INTRODUCTION

Discrimination may be generally rather than legally described as treating a person unfavourably not because of their individual qualities but because they have a particular characteristic or belong to a particular group. Such treatment denies justice to the individual who is subjected to it. There is no common law against discrimination, but there are a number of modern statutes which prohibit certain forms of discrimination. There is no statutory prohibition against discrimination in general, simply a series of prohibitions: this of course does not morally justify discrimination in other ways. The statutes which prohibit discrimination in Great Britain are the Sex Discrimination Acts 1975 and 1986 (SDA 1975; SDA 1986), the Equal Pay Act 1970 (EPA), the Race Relations Act 1976 (RRA) and the Disability Discrimination Act 1995 (DDA). There is similar provision in Northern Ireland in respect of sex and race discrimination while there is unique legislation against religious and political discrimination. There is also extensive EC law relating to sex discrimination in employment (Article 119 of the Treaty of Rome 1957 (equal pay); and the Equal Treatment Directive 76/207/EEC). The British statutes apply to both employment and the provision of services. Many of the statutory provisions utilize similar concepts, in particular the RRA and SDA. It is appropriate to deal, so far as is possible, with these two statutes together. The provisions relating to disability are significantly different in many respects so that these relatively new provisions will be looked at separately. Finally, we will deal separately with employment rights to equal pay and maternity rights, enacted under the EPA and the Employment Rights Act 1996 (ERA).

PROHIBITED DISCRIMINATION

Race discrimination

The RRA prohibits discrimination on racial grounds. The term race has a very imprecise meaning and the RRA defines racial grounds as meaning a person's colour, or race, or nationality, or their national origins or their ethnic origins (RRA, s.1).

Thus it is unlawful to treat someone unfavourably because of their skin colour. It is also unlawful to discriminate because of a person's nationality regardless of skin colour. A person may be of British nationality but be treated unfavourably, for example, because of their parent's nationality, i.e. their national origins: that too is unlawful. The concept of ethnic origins is more complex. Before discussing what it means, it is important that you note that the RRA is limited to the categories of race included in the Act and does not extend to religious discrimination or political discrimination, factors which are often associated with nationality and race and with a person's desire to come to Britain. As we noted above, there is legislation in Northern Ireland which prohibits discrimination on religious or political grounds but this does not apply in the rest of the United Kingdom.

Religion and other cultural factors may, however, indirectly form racial grounds under the RRA if they contribute to the formation of a distinct ethnic origin. It is unlawful to discriminate against a Jewish person (*Seide* v *Gillete Industries* [1980] IRLR 427), even though their Jewishness may not be covered by race, colour, nationality or national origins. The House of Lords defined the term 'ethnic origins' in a case involving the refusal to admit a Sikh boy to a private school unless he agreed to forgo the Sikh turban and wear the school cap (*Mandla* v *Lee* [1983] 2 AC 548). Sikhism is a religion and Sikhs do not have a unique race, colour or nationality. Lord Fraser found that Sikhs were, however, an ethnic group, and suggested that for a group to be an ethnic group it should possess in particular a long shared history and its own cultural tradition (often but not necessarily associated with religious observance). Other additional relevant characteristics were common geographical origin, common language, common literature of their own, common religion different from its neighbours and being a minority, oppressed or dominant group within a larger community. Thus Sikhs are a group with a common ethnic origin, as are Jewish people. So also are gypsies: in *Commission for Racial Equality* v *Dutton* [1989] IRLR 8 the Court of Appeal was considering the legality of a sign in a public house which stated 'No travellers', and held that the sign could constitute discrimination against gypsies who were a racial group by virtue of their ethnic origins. Rastafarians have been held not to be such a group (*Dawkins* v *Crown Supplies (PSA)* [1993] IRLR 294), and it is generally accepted that members of more universal religions such as Islam or Christianity are not members of ethnic groups by virtue only of their religion. The Commission for Racial Equality (CRE) has recommended the passing of separate religious discrimination legislation.

The RRA prohibits discrimination on racial grounds whether or not it relates to the race of the victim of the discrimination. Thus in *Showboat Entertainment Centre Ltd* v *Owens* [1984] IRLR 65 the manager of an amusement centre was dismissed when he refused to obey an instruction from his employers to exclude black youths from the centre. It was held that he had been unlawfully discriminated against on racial grounds even though he himself was white since the unfavourable treatment afforded to him was caused by racial considerations.

Sex discrimination

The SDA prohibits discrimination on grounds of a person's sex. It also prohibits discrimination on the grounds that a person is married (SDA 1975, s.3). The SDA 1975 does not prohibit discrimination against a person because they are single, but the EC Equal Treatment Directive makes a wider prohibition against discrimination on grounds of marital or family status (Art. 2.1). Like the RRA which applies to everyone regardless of race, the SDA 1975 applies to men as well as women (SDA 1975, s.2(1)) and there have always been a large number of complaints under the SDA 1975 brought by men. The ECJ has also ruled that the Equal Treatment Directive 76/207 applies to discrimination against transsexuals, since that discrimination is essentially based on the sex of the person concerned (*P* v *S and Cornwall County Council* [1996] IRLR 347).

The SDA 1975 refers to discrimination because of sex, and the UK courts take the view that this does not include sexuality or sexual preference (*R* v *Ministry of Defence ex p. Smith and Others* [1996] IRLR 100). In *Smith* v *Gardner Merchant Ltd* [1996] IRLR 342 the Employment Appeals Tribunal (EAT) held that they had no jurisdiction to hear a case of sex discrimination brought by a barman on the grounds that he had been sexually harassed and dismissed because of his homosexuality. The EAT considered that the injustice suffered by homosexuals in Mr Smith's situation would have to be dealt with under unfair dismissal legislation: but whereas there is no qualification period necessary to establish a discrimination claim, such a qualification period is necessary for unfair dismissal claims.

Disability discrimination

The DDA prohibits discrimination against disabled persons, that is, someone with a disability and those who have had a disability in the past (DDA, s.2). Disability is defined as a physical or mental impairment which has a substantial and long term adverse effect on the person's ability to carry out normal day-to-day activities (not their ability to do the job) (DDA, s.1). How this very complex concept is to be interpreted is further defined in the DDA itself (DDA, Sch.1), in the Disability Discrimination (Meaning of Disability) Regulations 1996 and in a Guidance Note issued under the DDA by the Government (Department for Education and Employment Guidance and Codes of Practice: Document 1: Guidance on matters to be taken into account in determining questions relating to the definition of disability).

Mental *impairment* includes the impairment of mental functioning (such as learning difficulties) and also mental illness, but only if the illness is a clinically well-recognised illness, that is, recognized by a respected body of medical opinion. Certain things are also excluded from being considered impairments, such as substance addiction (unless it is an addiction caused by medical prescription of drugs) and including addiction to alcohol, hayfever (unless it exacerbates other conditions), and certain 'tendencies' to steal, set fires, abuse people, to exhibition and voyeurism.

A severe disfigurement is to be treated as an impairment which has the necessary substantial adverse day to day effect. However this provision excludes tattoos and piercings.

A *substantial adverse effect* is one which is more than minor or trivial: it may have an effect on the time taken to carry out an activity, or the way in which the person carries out the activity, or the cumulative effects of a number of more minor adverse effects might add up to a substantial effect. If a person is being treated by medication which successfully controls the adverse effects of the impairment, the medication is to be disregarded, so that the level of disability of a person with a hearing impairment who uses a hearing aid would be judged by reference to their hearing without the aid, as would a sufferer from diabetes be judged without reference to any medication they were taking. However, someone whose impaired eyesight is corrected by spectacles or contact lenses does not come within the definition of 'disabled'.

Anyone who suffers from a progressive condition, such as cancer, multiple sclerosis or HIV infection, which is likely to result in substantial adverse effect, but which has not reached that stage, is to be assessed as having an impairment with a substantial adverse effect. However, it appears that there must be some symptoms which are having an adverse affect before the protection of the DDA applies (DDA, Sch.1, para. 8(1)(b)), so that someone who is suffering from HIV infection which has not yet produced any symptoms will not be covered by the protection of the DDA. Less favourable treatment of such a person would only be unlawful if it contravened some other legislation, such as the unfair dismissal provisions of the ERA.

An effect is *long term* if it has lasted at least 12 months; or is likely to last for at least 12 months; or is likely to last for the rest of the person's life. The effects do not have to continue throughout the whole 12 month or more period, so long as they are likely to recur. Where someone has recovered or the effects of a disability have receded so that they are no longer substantial, such a person will be protected as a person with a past disability so long as the disability originally lasted for or recurred within 12 months.

The DDA defines *normal day-to-day activities* by the following exclusive list of activities: mobility; manual dexterity; physical coordination; continence; ability to lift, carry or otherwise move everyday objects; speech, hearing or eyesight; memory or ability to concentrate, learn or understand; or perception of the risk of physical danger. The impairment might directly affect the activity by, for example, making it impossible or difficult to walk, or it might do so indirectly so that while walking might be perfectly possible, nevertheless the pain or tiredness resulting from the impairment might make it difficult.

The concept is not intended to cover specialized work or highly skilled sporting people whose impairment does not affect their normal day-to-day activity, but does affect their ability to do a particular form of work, including their own profession or trade. The Guidance gives some examples of inabilities which it would be reasonable to consider having a substantial adverse effect on normal day-to-day activities as well as some which it would not. For example, in relation to the ability to lift, carry or otherwise move everyday objects, the Guidance suggests that it would be reasonable to regard as having a substantial adverse effect: an inability to pick up objects of moderate weight with one hand; and an inability to carry a moderately loaded tray steadily. On the other hand it would not be reasonable to regard as having a substantial adverse effect: an inability to carry heavy luggage without assistance; or an inability to move heavy objects without a mechanical aid.

UNLAWFUL DISCRIMINATION

The SDA 1975 and RRA on the one hand and the DDA on the other have different structures, although there are some similarities between the legislation. Since both the SDA 1975 and the RRA have the same broad definitions and structure, we will deal with them together. Both these Acts contain the provisions proscribing certain forms of act as unlawful discrimination in three Parts (I, II and III). Part I of each Act defines what is meant by discrimination; Part II deals with discrimination in employment, while Part III deals with discrimination in service provision. It is important that you note this structure of the Acts since in order for someone to establish a claim of unlawful discrimination under either Act they must establish *both* that an act of discrimination (as defined in Part I) has occurred *and* that this act of discrimination has occurred in respect of an activity proscribed (in either Part II or Part III). The Acts do not, therefore, strike at every act of discrimination. Rather they are essentially limited to discrimination in employment and service provision, and do not apply to discrimination in other private or public spheres. An example of discrimination which unfortunately slipped through the net of the RRA is *Hector* v *Smethwick Labour Club and Another* [1988] RDLR 1988/167. The doorman of the club had told a group of people who wished to enter to collect for charity, in relation to Mr Hector who was black, that 'the black lad can't'. Although the Court of Appeal strongly deprecated the behaviour, it found that there was no unlawful discrimination since the facility the club was alleged not to have provided to Mr Hector (allowing entry to collect for charity) was not something it was in the business of providing as required by RRA, s.20.

The structure of the DDA is different in that, while the activities which are proscribed are essentially the same as those which are proscribed in the SDA 1975 and RRA, discrimination is defined differently in relation to employment on the one hand and the provision of goods, facilities and services on the other hand. Part I of the DDA defines disability; Part II defines discrimination in employment; Part III defines discrimination in service provision.

We go on to consider the definition of discrimination in sex and race cases first, and follow this with a review of employment discrimination firstly in sex and race cases and secondly in disability cases, and lastly a review of discrimination in service provision in each area.

RACE AND SEX DISCRIMINATION

Introduction

There are three forms that discrimination might take under Part I of the SDA 1975 and RRA. These are direct discrimination; indirect discrimination; and victimization. Victimization is discussed along with DDA victimization below. Neither the RRA nor the SDA 1975 uses the terms direct and indirect discrimination, although the definitions of discrimination in s.1 of each Act are recognized as such. By contrast, the EC legislation uses the terms direct and indirect discrimination but does not define them (Directive 76/207/EEC, Art. 2.1).

On the other hand, under the DDA, there is only one form of discrimination, that is direct discrimination but this is different from direct discrimination under the RRA and SDA 1975. We will deal with discrimination under the DDA in the context of the specific areas of discrimination.

Direct discrimination

Less favourable treatment

Direct sex discrimination is treating a woman less favourably on grounds of her sex than a man is or would be treated (SDA 1975, s.1(1)(a)) and vice versa. Direct race discrimination is treating a person less favourably on racial grounds than another is or would be treated (RRA, s.1(1)(a)). One of the factors which makes this legislation difficult to use is that it is necessary for the applicant not just to show that he or she was treated less favourably than someone else was treated and that there is a difference of gender or race, but the applicant must also prove that the ground for this treatment was sex or race. Having sex or race as a ground for treatment is not the same as looking for the motive of the alleged discriminator: motive is irrelevant. *Peake* v *Automotive Products Ltd* [1977] IRLR 365, an early case in which Lord Denning held that letting women and disabled men away five minutes before the rest of the men was not sex discrimination because it was an exercise of gallantry and was in the interests of safety, was subsequently disapproved – by Lord Denning himself! – in *Ministry of Defence* v *Jeremiah* [1979] IRLR 436. Since then the House of Lords has clarified that the question of whether sex or race was the ground of treatment should be looked at from the perspective of whether the sex or race was the cause of the treatment. Thus, in trying to assess whether or not an employer or service provider has treated someone less favourably on grounds of sex or race the appropriate question to ask is whether the person would have received more favourable treatment *but for* their sex or race. This approach was established in *James* v *Eastleigh Borough Council* [1990] ICR 554. The Council had instituted a policy of free entry to the public swimming baths for all those over state pension age (at the time, unlike occupational retirement age, discriminatory at 60 for women and 65 for men). Mr James was a 61 year old retired man who had to pay 75p to enter the baths (unlike his wife, a 61 year old retired woman who was admitted free). The High Court and Court of Appeal had found that the ground or reason for this treatment of Mr James was the desire to alleviate poverty within the borough. Nevertheless the House of Lords rejected this approach. That question related to the motive for the implementation of the policy. The correct approach was to ask the question: 'Would the plaintiff, a man of 61, have received the same treatment as his wife but for his sex?' the answer to that question was clearly 'Yes'. There were other, non-discriminatory ways in which the Council could have pursued their objective, such as opening the baths free to all who had retired, or all who were over a certain age.

This case, which concerned payment of 75p, also strongly suggests that any attempt to argue, as was done in *Peake* v *Automotive Products Ltd* [1977] IRLR 365, that some discrimination is too trivial to be actionable is misguided. Similarly in *McConomy* v *Croft Inns Ltd* [1992] IRLR 561 the Northern Ireland Court of Appeal upheld a complaint of sex discrimination when a man had been ejected from a public house for refusing to remove an earring. The company argued that since the earring could have been removed and replaced in seconds any detriment suffered was too trivial to be litigated upon. The court pointed out that where Parliament has declared behaviour to be unlawful the courts should be very wary of treating examples of such behaviour as trivial.

Comparatively less favourable treatment

Discrimination is being treated less favourably than someone who is not of the same sex or race as the applicant. A comparison can be made with an actual person who has received more favourable treatment, or it may be made with a hypothetical person who would have received more favourable treatment. This comparator, whether actual or hypothetical, must be someone whose relevant circumstances are the same or not materially different (SDA 1975, s.5; RRA s.3). Thus in *Hurley* v *Mustoe* [1981] IRLR 203 where a waitress had been dismissed on her first day of starting work when her employer discovered she was the mother of under-school age children, it was not necessary for the applicant to compare herself with an actual male employee who was the father of under-school age children: she compared her treatment with the treatment her employer would have given her if she had been a man in the same circumstances as herself.

Discrimination against a woman because she is pregnant is also sex discrimination even though there is obviously not a man to compare her with. For many years the UK courts considered it appropriate to compare a pregnant woman with the nearest male equivalent, usually described as a sick man, or a man needing time off work for physical reasons (e.g. *Hayes* v *Malleable Working Men's Club* [1985] ICR 703), so that in any case the issue was whether the woman had been treated less favourably than such a comparable man had been or would be treated. The ECJ, however, held that since only women become pregnant, discrimination on grounds of pregnancy is sex discrimination without the need for any comparison (*Webb* v *EMO Air Cargo UK Ltd* [1994] IRLR 382 (ECJ); [1995] IRLR 645 (HL)).

Proof of direct discrimination

In any tribunal or court case the burden is on the complainant to prove that the less favourable treatment was on ground of race or sex. It may be difficult to do this by direct evidence and so the complainant may prove the case by producing evidence which allows the tribunal to draw an inference of unlawful discrimination. If the applicant can prove a *prima facie* case of discrimination (such as that she was the best qualified and most experienced applicant and yet she was not shortlisted, being black, and all those shortlisted were white), the court or tribunal will look to the respondent to give a non-discriminatory explanation of the unfavourable treatment. If the respondent does not give a satisfactory explanation a tribunal may draw an inference of unlawful discrimination (*King* v *The Great Britain China Centre* [1991] IRLR 513). Inferences may also be drawn from statistical evidence of a more general nature. Evidence of a respondent's record in dealing with women, or members of racial groups, may be relevant to establishing an inference of unlawful discrimination (or may help to establish that such discrimination is unlikely) (*Singh* v *West Midlands Passenger Transport Executive* [1988] IRLR 186).

Indirect discrimination

Definition

Indirect sex discrimination under UK law occurs where a requirement or condition is applied equally to men and women but which is such that the proportion of women who can comply with it is considerably smaller than the proportion of men who can comply and vice versa, where the condition cannot be shown to be justifiable irrespective of sex, and where it is to the applicant's detriment that they cannot comply with the condition (SDA 1975, s.1(1)(b)). Similarly indirect race discrimination occurs where a requirement or condition is applied equally to all racial groups but which is such that the proportion of members of a racial group who can comply with it is considerably smaller than the proportion of those not of that racial group who can comply, where the condition cannot be shown to be justifiable irrespective of race, and where it is to the applicant's detriment that they cannot comply with the condition (RRA s.1(1)(b)).

The applicant must prove that there was a requirement or condition which was being applied; that the proportion of women (or members of the racial group) who can comply with the condition is considerably smaller than the proportion of men (or people who are not members of the racial group) who can comply; and that it is to their detriment that they cannot comply. Then it is up to the respondent to prove that the requirement or condition is justifiable.

Requirement or condition

There must be a requirement or condition being applied which the applicant cannot comply with. There is a difference between how UK and EC law defines indirect discrimination. While under UK law there must be a condition, that is something which is mandatory and not a guideline (*Perera* v *Civil Service Commission* [1982] ICR 350), EC law also includes the situation where the respondent has adopted a practice which has a discriminatory effect (*Enderby* v *Frenchay Health Authority and the Secretary of State for Health* [1993] IRLR 591). Any condition might be the subject of a complaint so long as the applicant can show that it adversely affects women (or the members of the racial group) and cannot be justified. In its Code of Practice (Code of Practice for the elimination of racial discrimination and the promotion of equality of opportunity (1984), p. 6) the CRE gives possible examples of such conditions – a rule about clothing or uniforms which disproportionately disadvantages a racial group and cannot be justified; an employer who requires higher language standards than are needed for the safe and effective performance of the job. In its Code of Practice (Code of Practice for the elimination of discrimination on the grounds of sex and marriage and the promotion of equality of opportunity in employment (1985), p. 19) the Equal Opportunities Commission (EOC) suggests that a requirement to be mobile might bar more women than men and more married than single women. Other conditions which might be indirectly discriminatory could include an age requirement which would prevent women who were raising young families from applying for a job (*Price* v *Civil Service Commission* [1977] IRLR 291) or a condition that a job was only available to someone who was prepared to do it on a full time basis which would have a similar effect (*Home Office* v *Holmes* [1984] IRLR 200); or a condition that holidays could not be taken on certain dates which would disadvantage certain ethnic groups (*J H Walkers Ltd* v *Hussain* [1996] IRLR 11).

A considerably smaller proportion can comply

The applicant will have to prove, probably by means of relevant statistics, that the proportion of women (or members of the racial group) who can comply is considerably smaller than the proportion of men. The applicant does not need to prove that they could not physically comply with the requirement, so long as they can show that in terms of social and cultural factors it is less likely that they would be able to comply (*Price* v *Civil Service Commission* (above)). A Sikh man could physically remove his turban and a woman could decide that in spite of family commitments she was prepared to work full time, but in most cases because of social and cultural factors they are far less likely to decide to do this than their non-Sikh, or male, counterparts.

Proof will be by taking the relevant group, say, in the case of a dispute about a requirement to work full time as a Tourist Officer working for a local authority, all those qualified to work as Tourist Officers in the area of the authority, and comparing the percentage of men in that group who can comply with the condition with the percentage of women in that group who can comply with the condition. If the difference is considerable, the first hurdle of proving indirect discrimination will have been overcome (*Jones* v *Chief Adjudication Officer* [1990] IRLR 533). It is up to the tribunal or court to decide what is the appropriate group for comparison: in some cases it might be all those qualified for a job; in cases involving promotion it might be all those working for an employer; in some cases it might be all men and all women.

Justification

The respondent must show that the requirement is justified irrespective of sex or race. The UK courts have developed their own definition of justifiability in connection with discrimination which is similar, but not identical, to the approach of the ECJ. The EC approach is that the respondent must show that indirect discrimination is objectively justified on economic grounds and that the imposition of the condition or practice corresponds to a real need on the part of the organization and is appropriate and necessary to attain that end (*Bilka Kaufhaus Bmbh* v *Von Hartz* [1986] IRLR 317). In the UK cases a tribunal or court should approach the issue by balancing the discriminatory effect of the condition against the discriminator's reasonable need to impose it (*Ojutiku* v *MSC* [1982] IRLR 148 (RRA); *Webb* v *EMO Air Cargo (UK) Ltd* [1993] IRLR 27). The requirements of food safety were held to justify an employer in applying a prohibition against beards in relation to employees preparing food, a prohibition which had a considerably greater effect on Sikhs (*Panesar* v *Nestle Co. Ltd* [1980] ICR 60).

RACE AND SEX DISCRIMINATION IN EMPLOYMENT

Introduction

Part II of the RRA and of the SDA 1975 prohibits discrimination in employment. Their major provisions relate to acts of discrimination carried out by or on behalf of employers at establishments in Great Britain. All employees are bound by the Acts.

The exemption of those who employed five employees or less from the SDA 1975 was repealed by s.1 of the SDA 1986. In addition it extends to discrimination by partnerships against partners (RRA, s.10; SDA 1975, s.11); principals against contract workers (RRA, s.7; SDA 1975, s.9); trade unions, employers' organizations and professional organizations against their members (RRA, s.11; SDA 1975, s.12); 'qualifying bodies' (bodies whose authorization is needed for entry into a particular profession or trade) against those wishing to qualify for the profession or trade (RRA, s.12; SDA 1975, s.13); vocational training bodies and employment agencies against potential trainees or job applicants (RRA, ss 13–14; SDA, ss 14–15).

The employer's duty not to discriminate against those he/she employs extends not just to employees but also to those employed under a contract personally to carry out work (RRA, s.78; SDA 1975, s.82). Thus a self-employed worker whose employment was terminated because of her pregnancy had no rights under employment protection legislation but was able to raise a successful action alleging sex discrimination against her former employers (*Caruana* v *Manchester Airport* [1996] IRLR 378).

Job applicants

It is unlawful for an employer to discriminate against an applicant for a job in the arrangements made for deciding who should be offered employment (SDA 1975, s.6(1)(a); RRA, s.4(1)(a)). This can include drawing up a short list of applicants to be interviewed based on discriminatory criteria. It may involve the questions asked at the interview. Asking a candidate for a promoted post whether their racial background would inhibit their ability to do the job was held to be racially discriminatory (*City of Bradford Metropolitan County* v *Arora* [1989] IRLR 442). In *Saunders* v *Richmond upon Thames Borough Council* [1978] ICR 75, an early case under the SDA 1975, a woman golf professional lost her claim alleging sex discrimination in the recruitment process, but the EAT referred to a question 'Do you think men respond as well to a woman golf professional as to a man?' as reflecting 'what is now an out-of-date and proscribed attitude of mind'.

There is a separate procedure for dealing with discriminatory advertisements. The CRE and EOC have the statutory responsibility for taking action against those who publish advertisements which indicate or could reasonably be understood to indicate an intention to discriminate unlawfully (SDA 1975, s.38; RRA, s.29). The SDA 1975 provides that using a job description with a sexual connotation such as 'waiter', 'postman' or 'stewardess' is to be taken to indicate an intention to discriminate unless the advertisement contains an indication to the contrary (SDA 1975, s.38(3)). If someone wishes to complain about an advertisement they must inform the appropriate body who may take enforcement action. The individual can only raise an action in an industrial tribunal on their own behalf if, in spite of the advertisement, they persist in applying for a job and are refused (*Cardiff Women's Aid* v *Hartup* [1994] IRLR 391).

It is unlawful to discriminate in the terms on which employment is offered (SDA 1975, s.6(1)(b); RRA, s.4(1)(b)) and also to refuse or deliberately omit to offer employment on discriminatory grounds (SDA 1975, s.6(1)(c); RRA, s.4(1)(c)). The latter is appropriate where the applicant claims that they would have been offered the job but for their sex or race. If, however, the applicant accepts or the tribunal finds, that they would not have been offered the job in any case, the appropriate ground for action would be under SDA 1975, s.6(1)(a). The applicant may have been treated badly at the interview or elsewhere in the selection process, even though they were not the best candidate for the job.

Genuine Occupational Qualification (GOQ)

Both the RRA and SDA 1975 provide for exceptions to the rule that sex or race cannot be a basis for selection (SDA 1975 s.7; RRA s.5). There are certain circumstances where an employer may be able to assert that sex or race is a genuine qualification for the job. The categories of such qualifications are defined in the RRA and SDA 1975 and relate to the job, not the applicant.

The sex GOQs are:

1. the essential nature of the job calls for a man (or woman) because of physiology (but excluding physical strength or stamina) or in a dramatic performance or other entertainment for authenticity;
2. the job needs to be held by a man (or woman) to preserve decency or privacy, because it might involve physical contact with men (or women) in circumstances when they might reasonably object to having women (or men) present or because men (or women) are likely to be undressed or are using sanitary facilities;
3. the job is likely to involve the holder working in a private home and objection might be taken to a woman (or man) having the likely degree of physical or social contact with a knowledge of intimate details of the person living in the home;
4. the nature of the establishment makes it impracticable to live elsewhere than on the employer's premises and the only sleeping accommodation is used by men (or women) and does not have separate sanitary accommodation for women (or men) and it is not reasonable to expect the employer to equip the premises;
5. the establishment is a hospital, prison or other establishment or people needing special care and they are all men (or women) and it is reasonable that the job be held by a man (or woman);
6. the holder of the job provides personal services promoting welfare or education or similar services and those can be most effectively provided by a man (or woman);
7. the job needs to be held by a man (or woman) because of legal restrictions on the employment of women (or men);
8. the job has to be held by a man (or woman) because it is likely to involve work outside the UK in a country whose law or customs are such that the duties could not be performed effectively by a woman (or man);
9. the job is one of two to be held by a married couple.

If, however, an employer already has sufficient employees to carry out the work to which the GOQ might apply without inconvenience, the GOQ will not apply (*Etam plc* v *Rowan* [1989] IRLR 150), so that for example although it might be necessary for there to be a number of female workers in a gym or swimming baths, if there are enough already working there to preserve decency being a woman would not be a GOQ for a vacancy.

The race GOQs are:

1. the job involves participation in a dramatic performance or any other entertainment, for authenticity;

2. the job involves participation as an artist's or photographic model in the production of a work of art or visual image, for authenticity;
3. the job involves working where food and drink is provided and consumed by members of the public in a particular setting, for authenticity;
4. the holder of the job provides people of that racial group with personal services promoting their welfare and those can be most effectively provided by a member of that racial group.

In the case of the GOQs which refer to the effective provision of personal welfare services, the RRA and SDA 1975 do not require that an employer shows that these services can only be provided by a person of the particular sex or racial group: the requirement is that they be most effectively provided by such a person (*Tottenham Green Under 5s Centre* v *Marshall* [1991] IRLR 162). However, the job concerned must involve direct personal contact with clients, so that in *London Borough of Lambeth* v *CRE* [1990] IRLR 281 it was held that a job in an administrative capacity in a department which delivered welfare services would not attract a GOQ.

Discrimination against employees

The RRA prohibits discrimination against employees in respect of the contractual terms of employment (RRA s.4(2)(a)). In relation to sex discrimination, the primary legislation regarding contractual terms is the EPA 1970 (see below). Actions under the SDA 1975 in respect of pay are not competent (SDA 1975 s.6(5)–(6)), but contractual terms other than pay may be dealt with under either the SDA 1975 or the EPA 1970. However, the action must be brought under the EPA 1970 if it is possible to bring them under that Act (if there is an actual male comparator for the woman to compare herself with).

Both the RRA and SDA 1975 prohibit discrimination in the way access is afforded to opportunities for promotion, transfer or training or to any other benefits, facilities or services or deliberately omitting to afford access to them. The definition of benefits includes benefits not provided directly by the employer but which the employer facilitates access to (SDA 1975 s.6(2)(a); RRA s.4(2)(b)), such as, for example, health insurance. Retirement ages were also brought within the sex discrimination legislation by the SDA 1986 (ss 2–4). That Act also repealed most of the restrictions on women's hours of work. It is unlawful discrimination under both the RRA and SDA 1975 to dismiss an employee on discriminatory grounds, or to subject them to a detriment (SDA 1975, s.6(2)(b); RRA s.4(2)(c)). Detriment means 'putting at a disadvantage' *(Ministry of Defence* v *Jeremiah* [1979] IRLR 436), and can include any treatment which has that effect.

Harassment at work

The term 'harassment' is not found in either the RRA or SDA 1975, but where someone is subjected to a detriment by treatment which is grounded in race or sex this will constitute unlawful discrimination. The case which established that sexual harassment was actionable under the SDA 1975 was *Porcelli* v *Strathclyde Regional Council* [1984] IRLR 467 when a woman who had endured persistent insults and suggestive remarks from two male colleagues until she felt compelled to apply for a transfer was successful in her claim under the SDA 1975.

The detriment need not amount to dismissal or demotion or some other tangible detriment. Although the applicant in *De Souza* v *AA* [1986] IRLR 103 failed in her action to prove race discrimination, that case established that detriment in this context could involve creating a disadvantage for the harassed employee where she 'could justifiably complain about his or her working conditions or environment.' This approach places a duty on employers not to cause or permit harassment to occur when they can control whether it happens or not. In *Burton and Rhule* v *De Vere Hotels* [1996] IRLR 596 two black waitresses were made the butt of sexist and racist remarks at a dinner held in a hotel at which Bernard Manning, a comedian notorious for including sexist and racist jokes in his material, was the speaker. An assistant manager of the hotel helped one of the waitresses and the manager apologized to them fully next day. An industrial tribunal did not uphold their complaint of racial discrimination against the hotel because it did not consider that the hotel had subjected them to the detriment, but rather the customers and Mr Manning had. However, the EAT held that the question was whether the employer could control the situation and could have prevented or reduced the harassment by good employment practice. Good employment practice here would have been for the manager to have instructed the assistant managers to look out for the interests of the waitresses (since it could be anticipated that some harassment might arise in the presence of Mr Manning) and to remove them from the hall if things became unpleasant. Since they failed to take these precautions they had permitted racial harassment to occur. The court emphasized that the employer's duty would be most extensive in circumstances like this where the employer could exercise control over the situation of his/her employees, comparing it to the position of a bus or railway company who might be able to foresee that harassment might occur at times to their drivers or conductors and yet be able to do little to control this, apart from making their attitude to the harassment known to the customers and offering employees support if harassment occurred.

Harassment, whether racial or sexual, may consist of conduct including assault (*Jones* v *Tower Boot Co. Ltd* [1997] IRLR 168) or verbal harassment. So far as sexual harassment is concerned the law is strengthened by an EC Code of Practice, *Recommendation on the protection of the dignity of women and men at work* (29.11.91) and *Protecting the dignity of women and men at work: a code of practice on measures to combat sexual harassment*, which although not binding on tribunals in the UK has been used for interpretation of UK law, for example, in *Insitu Cleaning Ltd* v *Heads* [1995] IRLR 5. This Code contains a definition of harassment and also guidelines as to good practice in relation to prevention of harassment and dealing with complaints. The Code defines sexual harassment as 'unwanted conduct of a sexual nature or other conduct based on sex affecting the dignity of women and men at work. This can include unwelcome physical, verbal or non-verbal conduct . . .'. One sufficiently serious incident may constitute harassment.

The victim of harassment may also be able to utilize the criminal law against the individual harasser if, for example, an assault or a sexual offence has been committed. In England and Wales there is a statutory summary offence of harassment (Protection from Harassment Act 1997) where there has been a course of conduct which amounts to harassment and which the perpetrator knew or ought to have known amounts to harassment. This Act also introduces in both England and Wales, and Scotland a tort/delict of harassment which enables a victim to take civil action to stop the harassment taking place. You will find our general discussion of tort (in Scotland, delict) in Chapter Two.

Clothing and appearance at work

We have already noted that certain clothing requirements might amount to indirect race discrimination. A uniform which required men to wear a particular cap and which made no allowances for the fact that a Sikh man would not be prepared to remove his turban and wear the cap instead would be discriminatory, unless it could be justified as being reasonably necessary for the employer's business. Similarly a uniform policy for women which took no account of the fact that certain national or ethnic groups would not be prepared to have their legs uncovered could also be racially discriminatory.

Different clothing requirements for men and women could also amount to direct sex discrimination, but this will not be so if the clothing requirements though different are comparable. In *Schmidt* v *Austicks Bookshops Ltd* [1977] IRLR 360 a rule that women had to wear skirts rather than trousers when in the public area of a bookshop was found to be comparable with restrictions on male employees which prohibited the wearing of tee-shirts or 'out-of-the-way clothing'. A rule, which did not apply to the men, that the women had to wear an overall in the public area was held not to be serious enough to amount to a detriment under the SDA 1975. The EAT felt that an employer was entitled to a large measure of discretion in controlling the image of the establishment including the appearance of staff; an approach which the Court of Appeal more recently adopted in *Safeway plc* v *Smith* [1996] IRLR 456 where it held that a rule prohibiting male members of staff from having long hair which would not fit under the cap, when female staff were allowed to wear their long hair in a pony tail, was not discriminatory. The EAT felt that this was within the reasonable discretion of the employers, but emphasized that where the appearance code may affect the employee outside work, as here, it should be looked at more carefully. The key element seems to be that comparable standards of dress and appearance are required for both sexes, not that the dress be identical.

DISABILITY DISCRIMINATION IN EMPLOYMENT

Introduction

The provisions of Part 2 of the DDA are similar in many ways to their counterparts in the RRA and SDA 1975. The DDA relates to employment at an establishment in Great Britain; and the employer's duty not to discriminate extends to employees and to those employed under a contract personally to carry out work (DDA, s.68). Discrimination against applicants in relation to arrangements for selection, terms of an offer of employment and refusal of employment is prohibited; as is discrimination against employees in respect of employment terms, opportunities for promotion, transfer, training or other benefits, dismissal or any other detriment (DDA, s.4). A major difference, however, lies in the exemption for small businesses from the obligations imposed by DDA (DDA, s.7). A small business is defined in relation to the number of employees, and the initial level of employees at which the DDA applies is 20 or more. This number may be amended, but only downwards, and must be reviewed by the Secretary of State no later than 2 December 2000.

There are two ways in which an employer might discriminate against an employee. These correspond to, but are significantly different from, the concepts of direct and indirect discrimination in the RRA and SDA 1975.

Less favourable treatment

It is discrimination to treat a disabled person less favourably for a reason which relates to that person's disability than another person is treated or would be treated, where the employer cannot show that the treatment is justified (DDA, s.5). The treatment must be because of matters relating to the person's disability, and must involve a comparison between the treatment afforded the disabled person and the treatment afforded someone who does not suffer from the disability, or the treatment which would have been afforded to them had they not suffered from the disability. A major difference between this form of discrimination and direct discrimination under the RRA and SDA 1975 is that under those Acts direct discrimination (less favourable treatment) cannot be justified. Under the DDA such treatment can be justified but only if the reason for it is both material to the circumstances of the particular case and substantial (DDA, s.5(3)). This definition is broader than that of direct discrimination under SDA 1975 and RRA since it extends to less favourable treatment which 'relates to' the disability.

Justification

The Code of Practice for the elimination of discrimination in the field of employment against disabled persons or persons who have had a disability explains that this means that the reason for the less favourable treatment has to relate to the individual circumstances in question and not just be trivial or minor. The Code also gives a number of examples including the following contrasting examples. First, a situation where an employer who turns down a clerical worker 'solely on the ground that other employees would be uncomfortable working alongside him. This will be unlawful because such a reaction by other employees will not in itself justify less favourable treatment of this sort – it is not substantial. The same would apply if it were thought that a customer would feel uncomfortable.' The second example is of an applicant for a job who suffers from psoriasis who is rejected for a job modelling cosmetics on a part of the body 'which in his case is severely disfigured by the condition. That would be lawful if his appearance would be incompatible with the purpose of the work. This is a substantial reason which is clearly related – material – to the individual circumstances.'

Where an employee is receiving less pay because the form of pay is performance related, the Disability Discrimination (Employment) Regulations 1996, which were made under the DDA, specifically provide that this will be justified, so long as all employees, or all employees of the class to which the disabled employee belongs (so long as the class is not defined according to disability), are paid according to the same performance related method (reg. 3).

Duty to make adjustments

The second form of discrimination is an unjustified failure to make reasonable adjustments to the workplace or to working arrangements where these are necessary (DDA, s.5(2)). A duty to make adjustments arises where either working arrangements or any physical feature of the premises places the disabled person concerned at a substantial disadvantage to those who are not disabled. An employer should take such steps as are reasonable in all the circumstances of the case to prevent the arrangements or feature having that effect (DDA, s.6). Working arrangements means the arrangements for determining who should be appointed to a job, and the arrangements for offering employment, promotion, transfer, training or any other benefit (but not occupational pension schemes or any retirement, sickness or accident benefit). The Disability Discrimination (Employment) Regulations 1996 define physical features as including any feature arising from the design or construction of a building; any feature of any approach to, exits from or access to a building; any fixtures, fittings, furnishings, furniture, equipment or materials on the premises; and any other physical element or quality of any land (reg. 9).

The duty is not a general one and only arises in relation to the individual disabled person. Where the problem arises in relation to the arrangements for recruitment, the duty only applies where a disabled person has notified the employer that they may be an applicant for a job, and in any case does not arise unless the employer knows or could reasonably be expected to know that the applicant or employee has a disability and is likely to be caused substantial disadvantage. Thus if an employee decides to keep his/her disability a secret from the employer, the employer cannot be under any duty until he/she is informed of the situation. If anyone in the organization knows of the disability as a result of their job, for example as a personnel officer or line manager, that is the equivalent of the organization knowing it.

Adjustments

The DDA gives non-exclusive examples of the sort of steps which an employer might have to take to comply with the duty to make adjustments:

1. making adjustments to premises;
2. allocating some of the disabled person's duties to another person;
3. transferring the disabled person to fill an existing vacancy;
4. altering working hours;
5. assigning the disabled person to a different place of work;
6. allowing the disabled person to be absent during working hours for rehabilitation, assessment or treatment;
7. giving, or arranging for the disabled person to be given, training;
8. acquiring or modifying equipment;
9. modifying instructions or reference manuals;
10. modifying procedures for testing or assessment;
11. providing a reader or interpreter;
12. providing supervision.

Reasonable steps

The employer's duty to make adjustments is not absolute, but a duty to do what is reasonable. To decide what is reasonable, regard must be had to the extent to which taking a step would prevent the disadvantage and the extent to which it is practicable for the employer to take the step, as well as financial considerations (DDA, s.6(4)). A disabled person could not be required to contribute to the cost of an adjustment but if he/she has specially adapted equipment which he/she is prepared to use it may be reasonable for the employer to allow use of it (and also to take some other step). The Code of Practice gives an example of how this might work in the case of an employee working in a job where a company car is essential, but whose disability means that a specially adapted car would be necessary. The Code suggests

> If she has an adapted car of her own which she is willing to use on business, it might well be reasonable for the employer to allow this and pay her an allowance to cover the cost of doing so even if it would not have been reasonable for him to provide an adapted company car, or to pay an allowance to cover alternative travel arrangements in the absence of an adapted car (para. 4.31).

An employer can only justify a failure to make reasonable adjustments which are necessary if the reason for the failure is material to the circumstances of the case and substantial. The examples which the Code of Practice gives are of circumstances in which the employee has failed to cooperate with adjustments or occupational medical advice (para. 4.34).

An employer who is attempting to justify the first form of discrimination (less favourable treatment) cannot do so unless he/she has complied with the duty to make reasonable adjustments.

You can take the view that the duty to make reasonable adjustments corresponds to the concept of indirect discrimination. By making working arrangements which place a disabled person at a substantial disadvantage, there is the same practical discrimination, as there is in the case of indirect race or sex discrimination. The concepts are different, however, in that with indirect discrimination the concept is a statistical one applying where the category of women or members of a racial group are disadvantaged, while the duty to make reasonable adjustments applies where the individual disabled person is disadvantaged.

POSITIVE ACTION IN EMPLOYMENT

Race and sex discrimination

The philosophy behind the RRA and SDA 1975 is to ensure that people are not treated unfavourably because of their gender or race. Their general approach is one of gender and race neutrality, so that discrimination in favour of members of disadvantaged or discriminated against groups is prohibited. The SDA 1975 explicitly applies its provisions to men (SDA 1975, s.2), while the RRA makes reference to racial grounds and racial groups generally and not to minority groups. In *Mecca Leisure Group plc* v *Chatprachong* [1993] IRLR 531 a tribunal had upheld two claims of race discrimination by the applicant, one that he had been racially abused by a manager who had addressed him and referred to him in insulting and degrading terms, and the second that his employers had failed to provide him with opportunities for promotion by failing to give him training in improving his English language skills. The EAT upheld the claim in respect of the abuse, but overturned the second finding. There was no indication that the employers were giving English language training to any other groups of workers, and there is no duty on an employer to give such training.

This general approach seems to be in accord with EC law. In *Kalenke* v *Freie Hansestadt Bremen* [1995] IRLR 660 the ECJ held a law which allowed gender preference in recruitment and which did not leave room for consideration of the individual situation to be contrary to EC law. It is unclear whether this makes it unlawful under EC law to make provision for gender in a 'tie-break' situation: that is where there is no difference between male and female applicants. In any event it is contrary to current UK law.

However, the RRA and SDA 1975 provide for action to be taken in relation to training. Both Acts permit training bodies and employers to offer training courses specifically for one sex or a particular racial group where they have been under-represented in or completely absent from a particular type of work or particular post (SDA 1975 ss 47–48; RRA ss 37–38). This does not allow preferential hiring.

Disability discrimination

While the terms of the SDA 1975 and RRA prohibit any preferential treatment being given on the basis of sex or race, there is no such prohibition in the DDA. The Disabled Persons (Employment) Act 1944, now repealed by the DDA, provided for a quota of registered disabled employees to be attained by larger employers. Few employers ever attained their quota under this law. The duty to make adjustments under the DDA requires an employer to make special arrangements for disabled applicants and employees, but these arrangements are only to eliminate the disadvantage that disabled persons suffer by reason of their disability. The DDA specifically states that, apart from the duty to make adjustments, an employer is not required to treat a disabled person more favourably than he treats or would treat others (DDA, s.6(7)): there is, however, nothing to stop such favourable treatment.

RACE AND SEX DISCRIMINATION IN SERVICE PROVISION

Introduction

It is unlawful for anyone who is concerned with the provision of goods, facilities or services to the public or a section of the public (whether for payment or not) to discriminate in relation to their provision (SDA 1975 s.29; RRA s.20). This could take the form of refusing or deliberately omitting to provide them; or refusing or deliberately omitting to provide goods, facilities or services of like quality or to that normally provided; or refusing or deliberately omitting to provide them on like terms or in like manner as normal. Thus in *Gill* v *El Vino Co. Ltd* [1983] QB 425 refusing to serve women in a wine bar unless they were seated at a table, when men could also be served at the bar, was unlawful discrimination.

Facilities and services

There is no definition of goods, facilities and services so that all such are included. The SDA 1975 and RRA give examples of facilities and services (SDA 1975 s.29(2); RRA s.20(2)), including access to and use of any place which members of the public or a section of the public are permitted to enter; accommodation in a hotel, boarding house or other similar establishment; facilities for entertainment, recreation or refreshment; facilities for transport or travel; the services of any profession or trade, or any local or other public authority. This also includes facilities and services not provided by the person himself, but which it is within that person's powers to facilitate access to (RRA s.40; SDA 1975 s.50).

Public provision

The RRA and SDA 1975 only apply where the provision is to the public or a section of the public. Private clubs (ones which select members personally) do not provide services to the public or a section of the public: accordingly such clubs, in relation to members, are outwith the SDA 1975. There is special provision in the RRA: such clubs with a membership of 25 or more are brought within the remit of the Act. Clubs which are commercial ventures and do not regulate membership by personal selection are subject to the RRA and SDA 1975 like any other enterprise. Where private clubs offer services to the public they are bound by the terms of the RRA and SDA like anyone else.

Exemptions

The RRA and SDA 1975 exempt 'small premises' (RRA s.22; SDA 1975 s.32) from the requirements relating to the provision of accommodation. This exemption applies where the premises are occupied by the provider of the accommodation or a near relative (i.e. wife, husband, parent, child, grandparent, grandchild, brother or sister) and part of the accommodation on the premises is shared with other residents on the premises, so long as there is not normally residential accommodation on the premises for more than an additional six people. Alternatively, if there are separate letting arrangements for the accommodation on the premises, the premises are small if there is not normally accommodation for more than two households apart from that of the provider or relative.

The SDA 1975 makes it clear that service providers do not have to provide a service for men and women when these are commonly provided in a different way. If a particular skill is commonly exercised in a different way for men and women, it is not discrimination for a service provider who normally only exercises his/her skill for one gender to insist on exercising his/her skill for the other gender in the same way, or even, if he/she reasonably considers it impractical, to refuse to exercise it altogether (SDA 1975, s.29(3)). Thus, for example, a female beauty consultant whose skill was in advising women about cosmetics would not be obliged to learn a different range of skills to enable her to give equivalent advice to men.

It is possible to restrict facilities or services to one gender under the SDA 1975 in certain circumstances (SDA 1975, s.35). These are where the facilities or services are to be used by two or more at the same time and either they are such that male users are likely to suffer serious embarrassment at the presence of a woman or vice versa; or that users are likely to be undressed and might reasonably object to the presence of a member of the opposite sex; or that physical contact between users is likely, and a male user might reasonably object to such contact with a female user or vice versa. Thus single sex swimming arrangements should not contravene the SDA 1975.

The SDA 1986 removed most areas of possible lawful sex discrimination. In *Greater London Council* v *Farrar* [1980] ICR 266, the GLC had granted an entertainment licence subject to a restriction that no women wrestlers be employed. This condition was held to be lawful under s.51 of the SDA 1975 since the order was an exercise of statutory authority. The SDA 1986 overturned this decision by providing that public entertainment licences cannot require unlawful discrimination in employment (SDA 1986, s.5).

DISABILITY DISCRIMINATION IN SERVICE PROVISION

Introduction

It is unlawful for a provider of services to discriminate against a disabled person in the provision of goods, facilities and services, whether for payment or not (DDA, s.19). It is only those who provide services to the public or a section of the public who owe the duty not to discriminate, so that producers and manufacturers are under no duty in relation to their products, and private membership clubs are also excluded from the operation of the DDA. However this exclusion does not operate where a private club provides a service to the public. The Code of Practice Rights of Access Goods, Facilities, Services and Premises, 1996, states: '. . . a private golf club hiring out its facilities for a wedding reception – the Act applies to those services' (para. 2.6). Unlike the provisions in relation to employment there is no small business exemption for service providers.

The unlawful discrimination might take the form of refusing to provide or deliberately not providing a service to the disabled person which is provided to members of the public; or the discrimination might be in the standard of service provided or the manner in which it is provided; or it might arise from the terms on which the service is provided. The Code of Practice gives some examples of these from the entertainment and hospitality sector. Two examples of unlawful refusal of service are: 'A group of deaf people is refused entry to a night club because the doorman thinks that communication using sign language might be seen as threatening . . .' and 'A hotel pretends that all rooms are taken in order to refuse a booking from a mentally ill customer'. The example given of unlawful standard or manner of service is: 'A restaurant tells a severely disfigured person he must sit at a table out of sight of other customers, despite other tables being free'. An example of an unlawful provision of service on worse terms is: 'A travel agent asks a person who is deaf and blind for a larger deposit than she requires from others because she assumes without good reason that the customer will be more likely to cancel his holiday' (paras. 3.3–3.8).

There is a fourth form of unlawful discrimination which is to fail to comply with the duty to make adjustments. This duty, unlike the rest of the duties, was not in force at the time of writing and is unlikely to be in force until around 2005.

Goods, facilities and services

As with the RRA and SDA 1975 the DDA gives a list of services which it covers, although the list is not exhaustive. It includes access to, and use of, any place which members of the public are permitted to enter; accommodation in a hotel, boarding house or other similar establishment; facilities for entertainment, recreation or refreshment; the services of any profession or trade, or any local or other public authority. The DDA excludes the use of transport from the operation of this part of the Act (DDA, s.19(5)(b)). Nevertheless other facilities and services provided by transport providers other than the transport itself should be covered, such as access to platforms, ticket offices and waiting areas. Part V of the DDA, however, makes provision for making Regulations to secure accessibility of taxis and public services and rail vehicles to disabled passengers. This part of the DDA was not in force at the time of writing.

Less favourable treatment

Discrimination in this part of the DDA is treatment of a disabled person for a reason which relates to his/her disability which is less favourable than the treatment of someone who does not have that disability or is less favourable than the treatment would be if the person did not have the disability and which the service provider cannot justify (DDA, s.20). Although the definition of discrimination is similar to that of discrimination in relation to employment, there is a difference in the defence of justification which the service provider may put forward.

Justification

Treating a disabled person less favourably may be justified if the service provider reasonably forms the opinion that one of a number of statutory conditions apply. The service provider would have to prove that he/she held the opinion that one of the conditions applied and that it was reasonable to hold that opinion. The first of the statutory conditions is that the discriminatory treatment was necessary in order not to endanger the health and safety of anyone including the disabled person. Restrictions must be necessary and must be based on information. For example, where a cinema manager turns away a wheelchair user because he/she assumes, without checking, that the disabled person could be in danger in the event of a fire although there are in fact adequate means of escape, the test of justification would not be met because the opinion formed by the provider was unreasonable (Code of Practice, para. 5.6). The Code of Practice also makes a more general point that 'Every opportunity should be taken, as far as practicable, to enable disabled people to use cinemas, theatres, leisure centres and other entertainment venues. Equally, disabled people should not be prevented from living where they choose through unfounded concerns for safety' (para. 5.7).

Secondly, the service provider may reasonably form the opinion that the disabled person is incapable of entering into an enforceable contract. This would only arise where the service provider reasonably held the opinion that the disabled person was incapable of understanding the meaning of the obligations he/she was being asked to enter into. Disabled persons should be assumed to be able to enter into any contract unless there is clear evidence to the contrary (Code of Practice, para. 5.9). We discuss the general rules regarding capacity to enter into contracts in Chapter Two, pp. 38–39.

Thirdly, the service provider may reasonably form the opinion that, unless he/she refuses to serve the disabled person, he/she will be unable to provide the service to other members of the public. The public would have to be effectively denied service before this justification applied: simply being inconvenienced would not give rise to a justification. This justification might arise where, for example, a tour guide who refuses to allow an unaccompanied wheelchair user on a tour of old city walls 'because he has well-founded reasons to believe that the extra help he has to give her would prevent the party from completing the tour' (Code of Practice, para. 5.11). Note that the belief must be well founded.

Fourthly, it may be justifiable to provide service to a lower standard, or on different terms, if it is necessary to be able to provide the service at all either to the disabled person or to other members of the public. So, for example, it would be justifiable discrimination for a hotel to restrict wheelchair users to ground floor rooms because rooms on other floors were not accessible since this restriction was necessary to provide the service to the wheelchair user (Code of Practice, para. 5.11).

Finally, it may be justifiable to provide the service to the disabled person on different terms (such as, additional cost) but only if the difference reflects an actual greater cost of providing the service to the disabled person. However, once the duty to make adjustments come into effect it will not be justifiable to make any extra charge to a disabled person to reflect the cost of complying with that duty.

Duty to make adjustments

Once the duty to make adjustments comes into force, failure to comply with that duty will also amount to discrimination, subject to the justification defence just outlined. Placing this duty on service providers is necessary to give disabled people effective access to services. There are three circumstances in which a service provider will have to take action to adjust the services provided. First, where a service provider has a practice, policy or procedure which makes it impossible or unreasonably difficult for disabled persons to make use of a service provided to the public, it is his/her duty to take such steps as are reasonable in the particular circumstances to change the practice, policy or procedure so that it no longer has that effect. For example, policies which restrict access to wheelchair users would have to be reconsidered.

Secondly, where a physical feature, arising for example from the design of a building or the access to it, makes it impossible or unreasonably difficult for disabled persons to use the service, the service provider has a duty to take what steps are reasonable in the circumstances to remedy the situation. The duty may take the form of removing the feature in question; altering it so that it no longer has the disadvantaging effect on disabled persons; providing a reasonable means of avoiding the feature; or providing a reasonable alternative method of making the service in question available to disabled persons (DDA s.21(2)). Future regulations may provide exemptions from the duty to make adjustments, although it is not expected that this power will be used widely, and may also give guidance as to what would be a 'reasonable' means of either avoiding the feature or making an alternative provision of service.

Thirdly, the DDA places a duty on a service provider to take reasonable steps to provide an auxiliary aid or service if such a provision would enable disabled persons to make use of or facilitate their use of the service, for example, by the provision of a sign language interpreter or of information on audio tape (DDA, s.21(4)).

Financial considerations are also relevant. The DDA does not require a service provider to undertake expenditure which would be over a maximum limit to be provided by Regulations. Moreover, the DDA does not require a service provider to take any steps which would fundamentally alter the nature of the service or of the nature of the trade, profession or business.

VICTIMIZATION

Victimization is a form of unlawful treatment by which a person is treated less favourably by reason of their behaviour in challenging alleged discrimination by, for example, bringing proceedings against the alleged discriminator under the RRA, SDA 1975 or EPA 1970 or DDA; or giving evidence or information in connection with proceedings under the Acts brought against the alleged discriminator; or alleging that the discriminator or someone else has committed an act which would be a breach of the Acts; or has done anything relating to the Acts in relation to the alleged discriminator (RRA s.2; SDA 1975 s.4; DDA s.55). This last category could include trying to gather information for possible tribunal or court action. Where a person deliberately makes a false allegation, he/she is not protected by these provisions.

RESPONSIBILITY FOR DISCRIMINATION

Primary responsibility for complying with the legislation rests with the employer. Principals are responsible for discrimination carried out with their authority by their agents. Employers are liable for the discriminatory actions of their employees which are done in the course of their employment whether or not it is done with their knowledge or approval (SDA 1975 s.41; RRA s.32; DDA s.58). Although this is a similar phrase to that used in defining the concept of vicarious liability in the context of tort (in Scotland, delict; see also Chapter Two, pp. 60–61), the Court of Appeal in England has decided that it does not have the same meaning under the RRA (and by implication the SDA 1975 and DDA). In *Jones* v *Tower Boot Ltd* (above) a young black worker was subjected to racist assault and abuse for the six weeks he worked for the company before his resignation. While the EAT applied the common law approach to vicarious liability and held that since the assault and abuse were not authorized forms of employment the employers were not liable, the Court of Appeal, however, held that since the Acts placed a duty on an employer to ensure that no discrimination took place at work, a broader approach should be taken so that conduct arising out of work should be included. Thus the employers were vicariously liable for the assaults and abuse suffered by Mr Jones.

The Acts provide a defence for an employer who can prove that he had taken such steps as were reasonably practicable to stop the behaviour or behaviour of that kind (SDA 1975 s.41(3); RRA s.32(3); DDA s.58(5)). This is another incentive, if one were needed, for employers to ensure that they have an equal opportunities policy and that they monitor and enforce it.

While the primary responsibility under the Acts rests on the employer, the Acts also allow the employee or agent whose action the principal is responsible for (or would have been if the employer had not been able to take advantage of the defence referred to in the previous paragraph) to be sued (SDA 1975, s.42; RRA, s.33; DDA s.57).

REMEDIES FOR DISCRIMINATION

In the case of discrimination under all three Acts in relation to employment the aggrieved employee or applicant may present a complaint to an industrial tribunal within three months of the alleged act of discrimination (SDA 1975 s.76; RRA s.68; DDA s.8). There is no Legal Aid for representation at a tribunal. Applicants may apply for financial assistance from the CRE (RRA) or the EOC (SDA 1975 and EPA 1970) but there is no equivalent provision for the DDA. A tribunal has the power to make a declaration of the rights of the parties, to award compensation and to make recommendations that the respondent should take a course of action to reduce any adverse effect on the applicant (SDA 1975, s.65; RRA, s.56; DDA, s.8). Compensation, unlike the position with unfair dismissal compensation, may include an amount to represent any injury to feelings suffered by the applicant. Also in contrast to unfair dismissal claims, there is no upper limit on the amount of compensation that may be awarded. If an unsuccessful respondent fails to comply with a recommendation, an order for compensation or an increase in compensation may be made.

Actions based on discrimination in service provision must be brought before a County Court in England and Wales or a Sheriff Court in Scotland within six months of the alleged act of discrimination (SDA 1975 s.67; RRA s.57; DDA s.25). Legal Aid may be available in these cases, and again individuals may apply for assistance to the CRE or EOC. The court may make any order available to the High Court in England and Wales or the Court of Session in Scotland, including an award of damages without an upper limit. We discuss general issues in relation to going to law in the courts and tribunals in Chapter One, pp. 15–27.

EQUAL PAY

Introduction

The EPA 1970 (as amended by the Equal Pay (Amendment) Regulations 1983), not the SDA 1975, governs the right to equal pay regardless of gender. The relevant EC law, Article 119 of the EC Treaty and the Equal Pay Directive 1975, has been very influential in the development of this field. This law has been particularly important because Article 119 is of direct effect and thus can be relied on by all employees regardless of sector of employment (for a discussion of direct effect see Chapter One, pp. 6–7). Thus, in *Defrenne* v *Sabena* [1978] 3 CMLR 312 an air stewardess was able to base a claim for equal pay with a male air steward on Article 119 even though there was no equal pay legislation in Belgium.

In spite of its name, the EPA 1970 applies not just to pay but also to all contractual terms of employment. There is an overlap with the SDA 1975. The SDA 1975 does not apply to issues of pay, but does apply to both contractual terms and non-contractual terms other than pay. But the EPA 1970 takes precedence if it is possible to use either Act (SDA 1975, s.6).

Equality clause

The way in which the EPA 1970 operates is by implying an 'equality clause' into a woman's contract of employment, which has the effect of equalizing the terms of her contract with any more favourable terms in the man's contract (EPA 1970, s.1(1)). This applies to each individual term of employment so that a tribunal does not look at the overall package but at the equalization of terms. In *Hayward* v *Cammell Laird Shipbuilders* [1986] IRLR 287 a female cook had successfully obtained a finding of equal pay for work of equal value with a male joiner. The employers argued that, since her sick pay benefits were superior to his, this neutralized the effect of his higher pay: the House of Lords rejected this argument since the equality clause equalizes each individual term of the contract.

In an equal pay case a woman must compare herself with an actual man, unlike SDA 1975 claims where comparison can be made with a hypothetical man. This comparator must be a man in the same employment as the woman, either employed currently or as a predecessor in employment (EPA 1970, s.1(6)). It is up to the woman to choose her own comparator, and she may choose any number of comparators. Ms Hayward had in fact successfully compared herself not just with a joiner, but also with a lagger and a painter.

Equal pay may be claimed on one of three grounds: that the woman and her comparator are doing like work; that the woman and her comparator are doing work which has been rated as equivalent; that the woman and her comparator are doing work of equal value.

Like work

A woman is employed on like work with her comparator not only if the work is the same, but also if it is broadly similar and any differences between her work and his are not of practical importance (EPA 1970, s.1(2)(a) and (4)). Differences merely on paper, which are in the contract but do not occur in practice are not significant. In *Capper Pass* v *Lawton* [1976] IRLR 368 a female 'cook' successfully established like work with two male assistant 'chefs'. She worked alone in the company kitchen preparing meals for the directors and their guests; the two comparators worked under a head chef preparing meals in the company canteen. She did not have to prepare meals on such a large scale as they did, nor were there so many sittings involved for her as for them. Nevertheless since the work was broadly similar and the differences between them were not of practical importance, she and they were doing like work.

An unsuccessful attempt to use contractual duties which did not apply in practice as a defence to an equal pay claim was made in *Shields* v *E Coomes (Holdings) Ltd* [1978] IRLR 263. A female counterhand in a betting shop claimed equal pay with a male counterhand. In addition to the jobs which women counterhands did, male counterhands were also expected to open the betting shops, to take money between shops and to the head office, and to deal with any problems until the police arrived although in fact there were no such problems. The differences between the woman's and man's work were held not to be of practical importance because part of the differences were contractual only and did not arise in practice; and in addition the only reason the men were asked to undertake the additional duties was because they were men, not because they had any special training or expertise in that area.

Work rated as equivalent

Where an employer has voluntarily undertaken a job evaluation survey which has rated the woman's job and her comparator's as being of equal value to each other, this survey may be relied on by the employee if the employer does not enforce it (EPA 1970, s.1(2)(b)). This is not an important provision in practice. When the EPA 1970 was first enacted, there were only two grounds of equal pay, like work and work rated as equivalent. Because it only applied when the employer voluntarily conducted such a survey, the ECJ found that the UK law was not effective (*EC Commission v UK* [1982] IRLR 333) and as a result the next ground, that of work of equal value, was introduced.

Work of equal value

A woman does not have to compare herself with someone with whom she is doing like work. She may choose a comparator who is doing different work which she believes makes equivalent demands on him as her work does on her (EPA 1970, s.1(2)(c)). In cases where the woman is claiming equal pay for work of equal value, the procedure can be more complex than that for like work, or work rated as equivalent (EPA 1970, s.2A). At a first hearing the tribunal decides if there are no reasonable grounds for finding the work is of equal value. If it does not decide thus the tribunal itself may decide the claim, or they may order the appointment of an independent expert who makes a report to the tribunal. Until 1996 there could only be a finding in favour of the woman if an independent expert was appointed, and it remains to be seen how common it will be for tribunals to decide the issue themselves. If they do commission such a report, it is not binding on the tribunal. There is then a second hearing at which the issue is determined taking account of the report and any other evidence. If an employer has conducted his own job evaluation survey, so long as it is not discriminatory, its results will operate to exclude a claim of equal value (EPA 1970, s.2A(2) and (3)). Under equal value claims, a cook has compared herself to a painter, joiner and lagger (*Hayward v Cammell Laird Shipbuilders,* above); other cooks have compared themselves to clerical workers and surface mineworkers (*British Coal Corporation v Smith* [1996] IRLR 404); and 'dinner ladies' have compared themselves with gardeners, roadsweepers, refuse collectors and leisure attendants (*Ratcliffe v North Yorkshire County Council* [1995] ICR 883). The reason for the provision is that over the years a system of 'job segregation' has built up with certain jobs being seen as predominantly women's and others as predominantly men's, with the women's jobs tending to be lower paid than the men's, largely because they are done by women and thus perceived as being of lower status.

Employer's defence

Once the applicant has established that she does like work with her comparator, or that her work has been rated as equivalent, or that it is of equal value, the burden shifts to the employer. Unlike the SDA 1975 an applicant need not show that the ground of difference in pay is sex: however, the employer may defend an action by proving that the reason for the inequality in pay is a genuine material factor other than sex (EPA 1970, s.1(3)). Material means that the reason must be relevant and significant (*Rainey* v *Greater Glasgow Health Board Eastern Division* 1987 SLT 146). Any such reason which is not tainted by sex discrimination may amount to a material factor. For example, seniority or experience may amount to such a factor, or it may be that labour shortage may require an employer to pay a premium for a worker, but in the latter case not only must this be a genuine reason untainted by sex, but it is only the difference which has to be paid to attract the worker which will be justified (any premium over that would not be) (*Enderby* v *Frenchay Health Authority and Secretary of State for Health* [1993] IRLR 591).

The material factor defence is a similar concept to that of justification of indirect discrimination looked at above. The UK courts view it as different, however, on the basis that where there is no indirect discrimination it is not necessary to seek objective justification on economic grounds: it is enough that the reason for the different payment is not based on sex, is significant and relevant. Thus, for example, over-payment of a man because of genuine mistake that he was more experienced than a woman doing like work would operate as a defence (*Tyldsley* v *TML Plastics Ltd* [1996] IRLR 395). It is not clear that this distinction is justified in terms of EC law.

MATERNITY RIGHTS

Introduction

Women employees have a number of maternity rights under the ERA. Workers who are not employed under a contract of employment may use the SDA 1975 if they are discriminated against because of their pregnancy since less favourable treatment on grounds of pregnancy is direct sex discrimination (*Caruana* v *Manchester Airport* [1996] IRLR 378). Similarly, refusal to employ a woman because of pregnancy would also amount to direct sex discrimination (unless, perhaps, the contract was a short fixed term contract which was due to be performed at a time she would be on maternity leave) (*Dekker* v *Stichting Vorminscentrum Voor Jonge Volwasen (VJV Centrum) Plus* [1991] IRLR 27; *Webb* v *EMO Air Cargo (UK) Ltd* [1994] IRLR 482). Women employees do not have to rely on the SDA 1975 since they have specific rights under the ERA.

The EC Pregnant Workers Directive 92/85 also led to a major revision of UK law, including the introduction of a new universal right to maternity leave and the equalization of statutory maternity pay with statutory sick pay.

Parental leave

There is an EC Directive on paternity leave 96/34 which provides for a minimum entitlement to parental leave for men and women workers on the birth or adoption of a child to allow them to take care of the child, for at least three months, until up to eight years old. This Directive did not originally apply to the UK since the UK had opted out of the relevant EC law. The UK Government has abandoned its opt-out measures to comply with the Directive should be introduced in 1998.

Right to time off for ante-natal care

A pregnant employee has the right to reasonable, paid time off to attend ante-natal appointments (ERA, s.55).

Right not to be unfairly dismissed on grounds of pregnancy

All employees, regardless of length of service, have the right not to be dismissed on grounds of pregnancy or childbirth. It is automatically unfair to dismiss a woman for any of the following reasons:

1. where the reason (or principal reason) for the dismissal is that the woman is pregnant or any other reason connected with her pregnancy (which has been held to include a worker's need to take time off for illness or for maternity leave and the employer's need to hire a replacement (*Brown* v *Stockton on Tees Borough Council* [1988] IRLR 263); and the dismissal of a single woman who became pregnant from her job as a teacher in a Roman Catholic school because the governors disapproved of the morality involved (*O'Neill* v *Governors of Thomas More RCVA Upper School and Bedfordshire County Council* [1996] IRLR 372));
2. where a maternity leave period is ended by dismissal the reason for which is that the employee has given birth or any other reason connected with having given birth;
3. where the employee's contract is terminated after the maternity leave period because she took maternity leave;
4. where the reason for the dismissal is giving birth or a reason connected with that and:
   (a) before the end of maternity leave the woman gave her employer a medical certificate saying she was incapable of work;
   (b) she was dismissed during the four week period after the end of maternity leave while the certificate was still effective;
5. the reason for dismissal is a requirement or recommendation in relation to the suspension from work provisions, looked at more closely below;
6. the maternity leave is ended by dismissal for redundancy and the employee has not been made an offer of suitable alternative employment (ERA, s.99).

It is also automatically unfair to select a woman for redundancy for any of the reasons above.

This does not mean that it will always be automatically unfair to dismiss a woman who is pregnant or on maternity leave: the reason for the dismissal must be one of those prescribed. The employer must have known that the woman was pregnant or of the other connected factor.

Suspension from work on maternity grounds

Where a statute or code of practice requires or recommends that a woman who is pregnant, has recently given birth or is breastfeeding, is suspended from work, the employer must pay her during the suspension unless she unreasonably refuses suitable and appropriate alternative work (ERA, s.66). This provision, derived from the EC Directive, replaces earlier law which allowed an employer to dismiss an employee who was incapable of working for such a reason. Where an employer dismisses a woman in these circumstances it is automatically unfair dismissal.

Right to statutory maternity pay

To qualify for statutory maternity pay the woman must have been working for her employer for 26 weeks up to and including the 15th week before the expected week of confinement (EWC) (i.e. the week during which the woman is due to give birth), and her average earnings in the last 8 weeks must have been not less than the lower national insurance earnings limit. To claim statutory maternity pay she must work up until the 11th week before EWC, she must produce a certificate of EWC and must give the employer at least 21 days notice (in writing if requested) that she is to be absent because of pregnancy or confinement – or as soon as reasonably practicable (Social Security Maternity Benefits and Statutory Sick Pay (Amendment) Regulations 1994).

The maternity pay period is a maximum of 18 continuous weeks. It starts in the week after the woman stops work (having worked past the 11th week and given her employer the requisite notice): the latest date it can begin is in the week after confinement. If a woman is off work sick because of a pregnancy related reason on or after the sixth week before EWC the maternity pay period starts automatically.

There are two rates of maternity pay. The first six weeks are payable at the rate of 90 per cent of normal weekly earnings. The remaining 12 weeks are payable at a flat rate which is the same as the higher rate of statutory sick pay.

Right to maternity allowance

A woman who is not entitled to maternity pay is entitled to claim maternity allowance so long as she works to the 11th week before EWC, she has been in employment or been a self-employed earner in 26 out of the 66 weeks immediately before EWC and she has paid 26 weeks' standard rate national insurance contributions in the 66 week period before EWC. There are also two rates of maternity allowance.

The employer is entitled to be compensated (out of contributions to the National Insurance Fund) for any maternity payments made. However, only small businesses (defined by total amount of national insurance contribution) will be compensated in full.

Right to maternity leave

All pregnant employees irrespective of length of service have the right to 14 weeks maternity leave (ERA, ss 71–78). A woman cannot start her leave before the 11th week before the EWC and if she has not elected to start the leave by then, it will be triggered by an absence from work because of the pregnancy occurring after the beginning of the sixth week before EWC. There is a compulsory two weeks absence after childbirth. The employee must give her employer 21 days notice that she is going to take her leave, or give notice as soon as reasonably practicable.

If an employee becomes redundant during the 14 weeks and it is not practicable to continue to employ her under her existing contract she is entitled if there is a suitable vacancy to be offered alternative employment.

A woman on maternity leave has a right to retain the benefits of the terms and conditions of employment except pay which she would have been entitled to if she had not been absent on maternity leave, such as a right to continue to use a company car. A woman who also has a contractual right to maternity leave may take advantage of whichever right is in any particular respect the more favourable.

Right to return to work

This right is in addition to the general right to maternity leave. Only those who have been continuously employed by the employer for two years at the beginning of the 11th week before EWC can qualify for this right (ERA, ss 79–85). She must give her employer at least 21 days notice in writing that she will be absent from work because of pregnancy or confinement; that she intends to return to work with the employer; and of the EWC (or, if it has already occurred, the date of confinement).

If the employer requests it in writing, not earlier than 49 days after EWC or the notified date, she must give written confirmation that she intends to return to work, replying within 14 days or as soon as is reasonably practicable.

The employee can exercise the right at any time before the end of 29 weeks from the week of confinement subject to the following procedure. She must give 21 days written notice to the employer of her 'notified day of return' (NDR). The employer may postpone the return to work for specified reasons for up to 4 weeks after NDR. The employee may postpone the return to work for up to 4 weeks on production of a medical certificate.

The statutory procedure must be strictly complied with. However, if the employee has not properly exercised her statutory rights, but has nevertheless acted under an agreement with her employer, she will be able to take advantage of that agreement (*Lucas* v *Norton of London Ltd* [1984] IRLR 86).

The right is to return to 'the job in which she was employed under the original contract of employment and on terms and conditions not less favourable than those which would have been applicable to her if she had not been so absent'. Thus she may not get her exact previous job back, but she must not be put in a less favourable position. As regards seniority, pension rights and other similar rights the period of employment after absence is to be regarded as continuous with employment before absence.

If it is not practicable for the employer to allow her to return to work because of redundancy the employer must offer her suitable alternative employment where there is a suitable alternative vacancy. An employee who is not allowed to exercise her right to return to work has been unfairly dismissed. However, where five or less are employed and it is not reasonably practicable to permit a return to work, the employer is exempt from such a claim, as also is the employer where it is not reasonably practicable for a reason other than redundancy to permit return and the employee has unreasonably refused an offer of alternative employment.

An employee who has a contractual right to return and qualifies for the statutory right may in returning to work take advantage of whichever right is, in any particular respect, the more favourable.

Of all the employment rights which have been examined in this and the preceding chapter, the maternity rights are among the least straightforward. Indeed the statutory provisions for the right to return to work have been roundly criticized by the EAT as being of 'inordinate complexity' (*Lavery* v *Plessey Telecommunications Ltd* [1983] ICR 534). As the court pointed out this is particularly regrettable because employment rights relate to everyday obligations of ordinary employers and employees.

Planning, environmental and health and safety law | 8

INTRODUCTION

The chapter focuses principally on planning and environmental law and explains the relevance of these to the tourism and hospitality industry. The chapter concludes with a very brief outline of the requirements of health and safety law. You should note that we also discuss aspects of an employer's liability towards employees for unsafe workplaces in Chapter Two (pp. 61–62).

PLANNING LAW

Introduction

Planning law essentially provides a framework for decisions as to what development may or may not be permitted within a policy context together with a range of controls to regulate development operations and to take enforcement action where unauthorized developments occur. Hospitality and tourism industry developments will normally be subject to planning controls.

Objectives of planning law

There are no statutory objectives for planning. The legislation is essentially a framework through which policy objectives can be applied. It has been said that 'planning seeks to preserve the environment while improving it by careful control of development, moving towards the ultimate goal of a healthy and civilised life' (Collar, *Planning Law*, 1994). In Planning Policy Guidance Note 1 (PPG1) *General Policy and Principles*, para. 2 the Government indicates that

> The town and country planning system is designed to regulate the development and use of land in the public interest. The system has served the country well. It is an important instrument for protecting and enhancing the environment in town and country, preserving the built and natural heritage, conserving the rural landscape and maintaining Green Belt.

In Scotland the principal objectives of the planning system are similar but not identical to those in PPG1, placing emphasis in addition upon the encouragement of economic, social and environmental regeneration (NPPG 1 *The Planning System*,

1994, para. 4). In the context of tourism, preserving the built and natural heritage is a very important planning function, since many tourists visit Great Britain precisely because of the high quality of its heritage. Planning controls play a major part in preserving that heritage. For example, controls under the Planning (Listed Buildings and Conservation Areas) Act 1990, its Scottish equivalent of 1997 and the Ancient Monuments and Archaeological Areas Act 1979 ensure a high degree of protection is afforded to buildings of historic or architectural importance and ancient monuments.

Currently, one of the main policy objectives for the planning system is making a contribution towards sustainable development (PPG 1, para. 3; NPPG 1, paras. 5–7). Sustainable development has been defined as:

> Development which meets the needs of the present without compromising the ability of future generations to meet their own needs (World Commission on Environment and Development, *Our Common Future,* 1987).

The Government's strategy on sustainable development is set out in *Sustainable Development: The UK Strategy*, Cm 2426, 1994. It envisages the planning system being used to promote the re-use of brownfield sites rather than permitting development on greenfield sites, by protecting sites of significant ecological merit, by encouraging less use of transport by siting shops and workplaces closer to people's homes or, where transport is necessary, by encouraging use of public transport. As far as the hospitality and tourism industries are concerned, the planning system could, for example, be used to restrict development in sensitive areas which might forever be spoiled (and so lost to future generations) if a hotel complex was built or to ensure that such a development was carried out in the most sensitive way.

The legislation

The principal legislation governing planning in England and Wales is the Town and Country Planning Act 1990 and, in Scotland, it is the Town and Country Planning (Scotland) Act 1997. There are other associated statutes covering related issues such as hazardous substances controls and buildings which are listed for historical or architectural reasons. In addition there are a large number of statutory instruments made by the Secretary of State which cover issues such as what development is permitted without the need for planning permission and the procedure for making and dealing with planning applications.

This section examines:

1. the administration of planning in England, Wales and Scotland, in particular the respective roles of the Secretary of State, local authorities and the courts;
2. the role of development plans in the planning system;
3. what exactly requires planning permission, namely development and what this term actually encompasses;
4. what development does not require planning permission;
5. applications for planning permission;
6. the determination of planning applications;
7. conditions in grants of planning permission;
8. the role of planning agreements in the planning system; and

9. the extensive enforcement powers available to planning authorities to ensure that planning controls are adhered to.

Administration of planning law

The Secretary of State

The Secretary of State has overall responsibility for the administration of the planning system. In practice these functions are exercised by the Secretary of State for the Environment in England, the Secretary for State for Wales in Wales and the Secretary of State for Scotland in Scotland. For the sake of convenience, we simply refer to the Secretary of State hereafter. The functions of the Secretary of State are:

- Establishment of national planning policies through Planning Policy Guidance Notes (PPGs) in England and Wales and National Planning Policy Guidelines (NPPGs) in Scotland, preparation of associated guidance and circulars on the meaning and effect of new legislation.
- Call-in powers in relation to development plans. In Scotland, the Secretary of State's approval is still required for structure plans.
- Call-in powers in relation to planning applications. This will normally be done only where the application is of national importance or in the interests of procedural fairness.
- Determination of appeals against decisions of local planning authorities (in Scotland, planning authorities). The determination of such appeals will normally be delegated to Inspectors from the Planning Inspectorate in England and Wales and to Reporters from the Scottish Office Inquiry Reporters' Unit in Scotland. For the sake of simplicity we hereafter refer to 'inspectors' although you should take this to mean 'inspectors and, in Scotland, reporters' unless the context indicates otherwise.

Where possible the Secretary of State will seek to apply national policy through policies in structure plans, determination of called-in applications and in appeals. However, policy does not have the binding force of law and so each plan, application and appeal must be looked at on its own merits.

Local government

England
In Greater London and other metropolitan areas all local authority planning functions are exercised by the relevant London borough council or metropolitan borough council (TCPA, s.1(2)). However, outside those areas, local authority planning functions are split between county councils and district councils (TCPA, s.1(1)(a)-(b)). In some cases planning functions have been transferred by Parliament to Joint Boards (TCPA, s.2), National Park Authorities (Environment Act 1995, s.63) and Urban Development Corporations (Local Government, Planning and Land Act 1980, Part XVI).

Wales and Scotland
In Wales and Scotland the unitary local authorities established by the Local Government (Wales) Act 1994 and the Local Government etc. (Scotland) Act 1994

respectively exercise all local authority planning functions (TCPA, s.1(1B); TCPSA, s.1). In Wales they are known as local planning authorities but in Scotland, simply as planning authorities.

There are three principal planning functions of local government: the preparation of development plans (see pp. 189–190); the determination of planning applications (see pp. 197–201); and the enforcement of planning controls (see pp. 205–207). In Wales and Scotland these functions are all performed by the new unitary local authorities. However, in England, in non-metropolitan areas, the functions are divided between county and district councils (TCPA, Sch. 1; Town and Country Planning (Prescription of County Matters) Regulations 1980, reg. 2). County councils are responsible for preparing structure plans, mineral plans and waste plans and also for developments relating to minerals, mineral extraction and waste disposal. District councils are responsible for the preparation of local plans, determining all other planning applications and the enforcement of planning controls. For the sake of simplicity hereafter we refer to local planning authorities in England and Wales and planning authorities in Scotland as 'planning authorities'.

Appeals and the role of the courts

Appeals to the Secretary of State

A person whose application for planning permission has been refused by a planning authority has the right to appeal to the Secretary of State (TCPA, s.78; TCPSA, s.47). Likewise, persons against whom planning enforcement action is taken normally have a right of appeal to the Secretary of State. The Secretary of State will normally delegate their determination to an inspector (TCPA, s.79(7), Sch. 6, para. 1; TCPSA, Sch. 4). However, in cases where the Secretary of State decides to make the decision, an inspector will make findings at the inquiry and will recommend a decision to the Secretary of State. The Secretary of State is not bound to follow the recommendation of the inspector in such cases because the power to make the decision is vested in the Secretary of State not the inspector.

Appeals against decisions of the Secretary of State to the courts

It is possible to appeal against decisions of the Secretary of State to the courts. However, it is not possible to review the merits of the decision but only its legality, that is, that the Secretary of State has somehow failed to act as required by statute and the decision is therefore invalid (TCPA, s.288; TCPSA, ss 238–239). This is because the power to make the decision is vested by law in the Secretary of State, not the court. Therefore, provided that the Secretary of State has acted within the framework of the legal powers prescribed in the relevant legislation, the decision cannot be overturned by the court because the effect of that would be to switch the power to make the ultimate decision from the Secretary of State to the court.

Not only are the grounds of appeal to the courts on fairly narrow points of law, there are also restrictions on the persons who may appeal against a decision of the Secretary of State. The planning legislation provides that only persons aggrieved by a decision of the Secretary of State may appeal to the High Court in England and Wales or, in Scotland, to the Court of Session (TCPA, s.288; TCPSA, ss 238–239). Persons aggrieved could include the applicant if the Secretary of State refused an appeal by the applicant; or the planning authority if the Secretary of State granted an appeal by the applicant; or in certain cases it could include a third party such as an objector or even someone who has failed to make objections for a valid reason where the Secretary of State's decision has somehow prejudiced that person's interests (*Buxton* v *Minister of Housing and Local Government* [1961] 1 QB 278). However, a third party who is merely dissatisfied with a decision would not be regarded as an aggrieved person (*Buxton* (see above)).

Judicial review

Where a person does not have a statutory right of appeal, the only means of recourse to the courts will be by way of judicial review (see Chapter One above). For example, where planning permission is granted by a local authority, a third party such as an objector has no statutory appeal rights and therefore may only challenge the decision by way of judicial review. In Chapter One we discussed the case *Trusthouse Forte (UK)* v *Perth & Kinross District Council* 1990 SLT 737 where a hotel, objecting to various applications to develop a night club in neighbouring premises, successfully challenged the grant of planning permission for a night club in judicial review proceedings.

However, you should note that persons who have statutory appeal rights, namely applicants refused planning permission by a planning authority and persons aggrieved by a decision of the Secretary of State, may also be able to have recourse to judicial review although normally the courts would require such persons to exercise the statutory appeal rights which they have.

The grounds of judicial review are essentially identical to the grounds for statutory review (see pp. 32–35). Therefore the merits of any decision are not reviewed. The court will only examine the legality, rationality and procedural propriety of the decision. Once again the court does not substitute its decision for that of the planning authority which enjoys the decision making power.

Criminal matters

The courts also have a role in determining whether offences have been committed where there is a contravention of planning enforcement powers. Prosecutions for contravention of planning controls are rare. Enforcement issues are considered in more detail on pp. 205–207.

Development plans

Introduction

The development plan essentially consists of the structure plan and the local plan. Its purpose is to guide development by indicating a local authority's policies on issues affecting development and indicating what types of development will be acceptable in various locations.

The importance of the development plan has recently been enhanced by the creation of a presumption in favour of development in accordance with the development plan unless material considerations indicate otherwise (TCPA, s.54A; TCPSA s.25). We consider the significance of this new presumption further on pp. 197–198.

Structure plans

The structure plan is actually a written statement rather than a 'plan' in the diagrammatic sense. It is the planning authority's statement of planning policy for their territory designed more as general guidelines for the local level implementation of the policy when they are dealing with specific proposals. It is therefore unlikely that the contents would be sufficiently detailed to provide anyone with information which they could identify as having an adverse effect on their own property. However, the plans can serve as a useful guide to developers in the hospitality and other industries especially given the presumption in favour of development in accordance with the plan (see pp. 197–198). Policies on issues such as tourism and recreation would be included in the plan. In England and Wales county councils now have the power to adopt structure plans although they must have regard to regional and strategic planning guidance on the preparation of such plans issued by the Secretary of State (TCPA, s.31(6)(a)). The Secretary of State also has reserve powers to direct that a structure plan or any part of it is submitted for approval (TCPA, s.35A(1)). In Scotland, structure plans must still be submitted to the Secretary of State for approval (TCPSA, s.10). Public consultation is required in the preparation of the structure plan. This, however, does not of course mean that the planning authority has to accept the views of the public. But they must give due consideration to any views expressed and in due course explain what effect the views have had on their deliberations.

Local plans

In contrast with the structure plan, a local plan is usually map- or drawing-based. It set out detailed policies for development and use of land within the broader policies of the structure plan. Preparation of local plans used to be a discretionary matter but, following changes made by the Planning and Compensation Act 1991, it is now mandatory for planning authorities to prepare such plans. In England and Wales, a single district-wide plan must be prepared, but in Scotland it is still possible for planning authorities to prepare different local plans dealing with different subjects or areas within their districts. For example, four Scottish local authorities prepared the *Loch Lomond Local (Subject) Plan for Tourism, Recreation and Conservation* (August 1986) which also illustrates the fact that councils may collaborate in producing local plans. Thus it may be that in Scotland there are several different plans in force at any time in respect of a particular property.

When the planning authority proposes to institute one, the procedure is much the same as for a structure plan (TCPA, s.43; TCPSA, ss 11–17). However, both north and south of the border the Secretary of State has reserve powers in relation to local plans (TCPA, ss 44–45; TCPSA, ss 18–19). If there are objections, there must either be a public local inquiry or agreement reached with the objector(s) by negotiation.

Development

Introduction

As a general rule, if what is proposed constitutes development within the legal meaning, then planning permission will be required. That does not necessarily mean that the would-be developer must apply for and obtain planning permission from the planning authority; consent may be automatically conferred as we shall see below. But it is important to make the distinction between projects which are not 'development' and therefore do not require permission at all, and those which are 'development' but do not need planning permission because it has already been granted. We consider these distinctions further below.

The legislation does not provide an exhaustive definition of development but states that it includes (1) various types of *operations* including building, engineering and mining operations; and (2) *material changes in use* of land where no structural operation need be involved (TCPA, s.55; TCPSA, s.26).

Operational development – building operations

Some guidance as to what constitutes a building operation was provided in *Barvis Ltd.* v *Secretary of State for the Environment* (1971) 22 P & CR 710, a case involving the erection of a tower crane, which was held to constitute a building operation in the circumstances. The court suggested that the following factors should be taken into account when determining whether an object is a building or structure:

1. size;
2. whether it was constructed on site or brought on to the site ready-made;
3. degree of permanence;
4. whether it was physically attached to land.

The erection of rides for a visiting fair is not likely therefore to constitute a building operation (*James* v *Brecon County Council* (1963) 15 P & CR 20).

It is obvious that if a business wished to build a new hotel or leisure complex from scratch it would require planning permission. However, if a business wished to carry out alterations to its hotel premises, it is less clear whether planning permission would be required. Alterations which are internal and which do not alter the use to which a building is put will not normally require planning permission, although, in the case of listed buildings, they may require listed building consent, whereas internal alterations which do alter the use to which the building is put or structural alterations or external alterations which materially affect the external appearance of the building would usually require planning permission.

Whether particular works materially affect the external appearance of a building is a question of fact. In *Kensington & Chelsea Royal London Borough Council* v *GC Hotels* (1980) 41 P & CR 40 the court held that the installation of floodlights on the ground and first floor balconies of a hotel did not materially affect the external appearance of the building. The floodlights were unnoticeable and virtually invisible during daylight hours, hence their impact was minimal. Although they altered the appearance of the building at night, the use of electricity was not an operation within the definition of development.

Material change of use

Whether a change of use is material is a matter of fact and degree in the circumstances for the planning authority to determine. Character and intensity of use are relevant factors in assessing whether there has been a material change.

The planning unit

The planning authority must, however, establish which unit of land is the relevant one to assess the change against. This unit is known as the planning unit. Once the planning unit has been determined then the planning authority may assess the materiality of any change. Normally, if it is possible to recognize a single main purpose of the occupier's use of the land, the planning unit will be presumed to be the whole unit of occupation. That presumption would hold good even if the occupier carried on several diverse activities on the property, none of which could be clearly identified as a primary use. But where a single property can be separated and each part has as its purpose something different from the others, then each such part would be regarded as a separate planning unit. A good example of this was *Williams* v *Minister of Housing and Local Government* (1967) 18 P & CR 419 which concerned a nursery garden the produce from which the owner sold out of a wooden shed. Business was so good that he began to import produce from the market to supplement what he could not grow himself. The question was whether the appropriate unit was the wooden shed or the garden and the shed taken together. If it was the shed, then there was no change as it had all along been used for retail purpose. But if it was the whole unit of occupancy then there was a material change because the primary use was no longer the garden but the retail business. It was the latter view which prevailed.

Character of use

It is the character of the use of land which must be considered not the particular purpose of occupier. So when the use of land was changed from storing coal for transport by rail to storing motor vehicles for transport by rail, it was held that the character of the use remained the same (*East Barnet UDC* v *British Transport Commission* [1962] 2 QB 484).

The character of use is determined by the *primary* use of the land. A piece of land may have different uses, one of which is the primary use and the other ancillary. An example of an ancillary use would be a pharmacy in a doctor's surgery (*Hounslow London Borough Council* v *Gossain* (1989) 4 PAD 216) or a gift shop in a hotel lobby. If the ancillary use changes there will not be a material change of use unless the ancillary use comes to be the primary use. For example, land used as a quarry subject to a condition that waste material would be backfilled into the quarry workings, was now proposed to be used for the deposit of waste. The owners claimed that they had planning permission for such use by virtue of the condition, but it was held that the primary use was the quarrying and to use the land now only for waste deposit represented a material change (*Alexandra Transport* v *Secretary of State for Scotland* 1974 SLT 81). However, where a hotel proprietor wished to expand a hotel to provide a non-residents' bar in addition to a residents' bar this was held not to be a material change of use since the opening of the bar to the public was merely incidental to the existing use of the premises as a hotel (*Emma Hotels* v *Secretary of State for the Environment* (1980) 41 P & CR 255).

Change in intensity of use

Intensification of an existing use may amount to a material change if there is a significant alteration from a planning point of view although the Use Classes Order (UCO – discussed below) limits the application of this principle (*Brooks & Burton* v

Secretary of State for the Environment [1978] 1 All ER 733). In certain cases intensification of use can result in a change of class, as for example, when a house becomes a hotel even though its use is still residential.

The Use Classes Order

This piece of delegated legislation assists in determining whether a particular change of use is material or not. Its full title is the Town and Country Planning (Use Classes) Order 1987 (as amended) (UCO). The UCO divides uses of premises into various classes. Where a change takes place within the same class it is not taken to involve development and so is exempt from requirement for planning permission. A change from one class to another will normally be regarded as a material change of use and hence require planning permission. Furthermore, a change of use from or to a use not specified in the UCO will also require planning permission. The classes in the UCO are as follows:

A1   Shops
A2   Financial and professional services
A3   Food and drink
B1   Business
B2   General industrial
[B3–B7 Special industrial groups A-E (repealed)]
B8   Storage or distribution
C1   Hotels
C2   Residential institutions
C3   Dwellinghouses
D1   Non-residential institutions
D2   Assembly and leisure

The following uses are expressly stated to be outwith the classes specified in the Order:

1. as a theatre;
2. as an amusement arcade or centre, or a funfair;
3. as a launderette;
4. for the sale of fuel for motor vehicles;
5. for the sale or display for sale of motor vehicles;
6. for a taxi business or business for the hire of motor vehicles;
7. as a scrapyard or a yard for the storage or distribution of minerals or the breaking of motor vehicles;
8. for any work registrable under the Alkali etc. Works Regulation Act 1906 (now repealed in England and Wales);
9. as a hostel.

A change to or from one of these uses will always be regarded as a material change of use.

    The Scottish equivalent is called the Town and Country Planning (Use Classes) (Scotland) Order 1997. You should note that it is not identical to the English and Welsh UCO although its principles are the same.

Demolition, abandonment and temporary discontinuation of use

Where a building is demolished the right to use the land in the way it was used before demolition ceases and resumption of that use after demolition would require planning permission.

However, where a use is temporarily discontinued this does not necessarily lead to a loss of existing use rights. No planning permission is therefore required to resume the existing use. However, if the use is discontinued for a substantial period and then the owner resumes the former use, that might be a material change since the former use might be considered to have been abandoned. This would not be so in the case of seasonal or occasional use, such as a racecourse which is only in use for a few days each year; it would be illogical to require the operators to apply for permission each time there was a race meeting scheduled just because it had not been used for that purpose for a long time. However, where a use has been abandoned, then planning permission would be required for any resumption of that type of use. How can temporary discontinuation of use and abandonment be distinguished?

In order to distinguish temporary discontinuation of use from abandonment the courts have suggested that a number of factors such as the physical condition of the land or building, the length of period of non-use, whether there has been any other use and evidence of the owner's intention should be considered (*Trustees of Castel-y-Mynach* v *Secretary of State for Wales* [1985] JPL 40).

Development which does not require submission of a planning application

Development which does not require planning permission

There are a few circumstances that according to statute do not require planning permission even though they do actually constitute development. The main area where development can be carried out without the need to apply for permission is where the land concerned is owned or occupied by the Crown which, in general, is not subject to planning legislation.

Permission deemed to be granted

Again in limited circumstances, permission may be deemed to have been granted thus saving the developer the need to apply for it. It is important to appreciate the distinction that is being made here between activities which do not amount to development and those covered by this provision which do constitute development. Deemed permission is thus a concession.

The most commonplace example of this is the use of the outside of a building for the display of advertisements. Although this is specifically stated to be development in the legislation and therefore permission for it is required, under the relevant regulations, permission is deemed to have been granted provided the advertisement complies with the terms of the regulations.

A planning authority which is proposing to carry out development in its own area also obtains the benefit of permission having been deemed to be granted provided it has followed procedural requirements.

The General Permitted Development Order

If every form of development had to receive specific approval, local authority planning departments would soon seize up. The Town and Country Planning (General Permitted Development) Order 1995 (as amended) (GPDO) (in Scotland, the Town and Country Planning (General Permitted Development) (Scotland) Order 1992 (as amended)) is the means by which such a log-jam is avoided. It achieves this by providing that a broad range of what might be described as routine or minor developments are given automatic approval, often subject to conditions set out in the GPDO, thus saving the time and trouble of making an application.

This does not mean the activities concerned are not development – they are. The GPDO is simply a means of freeing the system of large numbers of proposals which are normally non-contentious. This is important because it is open to a planning authority to withdraw the automatic permission and demand a specific application. This may be done by means of what is known as an Article 4 Direction. This is often used in Conservation Areas (areas which are subject to enhanced planning controls because of their outstanding character) to ensure that the character of the area is not affected by the appearance of satellite TV dishes etc.

The GPDO defines certain types of development which it is designed to cover. The most important are developments associated with the improvement or extension to a dwelling house or within the attached garden ground; various minor operations; certain changes of use; and temporary buildings and uses.

Applications for planning permission

Outline planning permission

When a person is proposing a development involving erection of a building which will entail an elaborate detailed application, for example, a retail park, and there is some doubt as to how the planning authority will react, it makes sense to ascertain the local authority's views on the principle of the development by submitting an outline application. There is nothing to restrict an application to the owner or occupier of a particular property, so a would-be developer may well use this procedure to establish whether it is worthwhile acquiring the land for a project from the owner.

If the outline application is refused, then the developer knows where he/she stands and has saved the trouble and expense of a full-blown application which would involve a variety of professional fees, for example architect's fees for detailed plans. If on the other hand, there is a favourable reaction, then the developer can proceed with all the details of the actual development.

A positive response from the planning authority represents a commitment by them to permit some sort of development along the lines indicated, but reserving their position on important matters such as design, siting and access.

Outline planning permission lasts for three years during which an application for matters of detail not covered by the outline application, known as a reserved matters application, must be submitted and the actual development begun within a further two years from the granting of permission on the reserved matters application.

Full/detailed planning permission

This is appropriate for smaller scale developments and for larger scale developments where the applicant is aware that the planning authority is in favour of the principle of the development.

Application procedure

Application for planning permission must be made in accordance with procedures laid down by the Town and Country Planning (General Development Procedure) Order 1995 (as amended) (in Scotland, the Town and Country Planning (General Development Procedure) (Scotland) Order 1992 (as amended). The planning authority must ensure that the application is accompanied by all requisite plans and notification certificates before acknowledging it and entering it in the register of applications (see below).

The application should be submitted to the planning authority for the area in which the development is proposed on a form issued by the planning authority. Various information must be supplied together with the appropriate application fee, notification certificates and a plan.

The description of the development in the application is very important as it governs the extent of permission sought. The description is also important because it is served on those who are entitled to notification. It must be accurate and must convey the substance of what has been applied for and give full and fair notice to potential objectors. For example, in the Scottish case *Cumming* v *Secretary of State for Scotland* 1993 SLT 228, Cumming, the owner of an inn near the application site, did not object to the proposal since it was described as a roadside petrol station and service area. However, in reality the proposed development consisted of petrol stations on each side of the road together with a 40 bed lodge, a restaurant and car parks. Cumming successfully challenged the granting of outline permission since the description was defective.

Various parties are entitled to notification including the owner, agricultural tenants and specified neighbours. The owner must be notified (since the applicant need not be the owner) so that the applicant does not obtain planning permission without the owner's knowledge and enter into an agreement with the owner to purchase the property at a price well below its value in the light of the granting of planning permission. The notice to the owner includes a statement that the granting of planning permission in no way affects the owner's right to retain or sell the property so that the owner does not feel pressurized into selling up. Owners and agricultural tenants have 21 days to make representations to the planning authority which cannot make its decision until following the expiry of this period. There are rules to determine who is a neighbour for neighbour notification purposes. Neighbours may make written representations within 14 days from the date of the notice. The applicant must submit certificates with the application indicating that he/she has complied with notification requirements. Advertisements in newspapers are only required in certain circumstances. These include bad neighbour developments, cases where the development is likely to affect the character or appearance of a conservation area or setting of a listed building, where the proposed development is contrary to development plan, and where an environmental assessment is required.

The legislation requires planning authorities to keep a register of applications which must be available for inspection by members of the public at all reasonable hours (TCPA, s.69; TCPSA, s.36).

Determination of planning applications

Time limits

The planning authority has two months from the date of the registration of the application to determine it. Failure to determine an application within two months counts as a deemed refusal entitling the applicant to appeal to the Secretary of State (TCPA, s.78; TCPSA, s.47).

Each application must be considered on its merits

A planning authority is not allowed to fetter its discretion by, for example, deciding in advance how it will determine certain types of applications. Each application must be considered on its own merits. A good example of this arose in *Stringer* v *Minister of Housing & Local Government* [1970] 1 WLR 1281, in which a planning authority gave an undertaking to Manchester University that it would refuse permission for developments which might interfere with the operation of the University's Jodrell Bank radio telescope. This undertaking was held to be unlawful as the planning authority was therefore not considering each application on its merits.

'Call-in' powers

A number of planning applications submitted to a planning authority will have implications which take it beyond the limitations of a purely local issue. Given that planning strategy is in the hands of the Secretary of State, it is entirely logical that he/she should have some powers of intervention in appropriate cases. The Secretary of State has the power to direct that an application for consent must be referred to him/her instead of being considered by the planning authority (TCPA, s.77; TCPSA, s.46).

If either the authority or the applicant require it, the Secretary of State must give them the chance to 'state their case' usually in the form of a public local inquiry. That in itself gives the flavour of the type of circumstance in which this power is exercised – something fairly sensitive is involved.

In practice, these powers are rarely used. However, where national issues are at stake, the Secretary of State may well call in the application as, for example, has happened in the case of the application by Redland Aggregates to develop a superquarry on the island of Harris in the Western Isles.

Presumption in favour of development in accordance with the development plan

There has been a presumption in favour of development for several years (PPG 1, para. 5; NPPG 1, para. 44). However, the presumption was recently modified by the Planning and Compensation Act 1991 to a presumption in favour of development in accordance with the development plan (TCPA, s.54A; TCPSA, s.25). Thus the legislation now requires that, in determining any application, the planning authority must determine the application in accordance with the plan unless material considerations indicate otherwise.

This presumption gives enhanced status to the development plan which formerly had the same status as any other material consideration. This new presumption also provides greater certainty for developers that if they make an application which adheres to the policies in the development plan, it is more likely that it will be granted. The presumption is at its strongest when the development plan is up to date. Where the development plan is out of date the presumption is much easier to displace.

However, you should remember that it is only a presumption and it appears that it will not be difficult to displace if the planning authority attaches importance to a material consideration which indicates that permission should not be granted (*St Albans District Council* v *Secretary of State for the Environment* [1993] JPL 374).

Material considerations

There is no statutory definition of 'material considerations' although several can be identified indirectly from the statute and government guidance. These include any representations by persons with a notifiable interest (see above) and by statutory consultees.

Essentially the courts have held that material considerations must be (1) planning considerations (i.e. have some link to land use planning); and (2) relevant to the application in question. All material considerations must be taken into account. It is ultimately a question of law for the courts to decide whether a particular matter is a material consideration. Therefore, where the court decides that a planning authority has not taken into account a material consideration, it may quash the decision of the planning authority and require them to re-determine the application taking into account the consideration in question. For example, in *Envirocor Waste Holdings Ltd* v *Secretary of State for the Environment* [1996] JPL 489, an application to develop a waste transfer station adjacent to a food processing plant, the risk posed by the development, in particular in relation to its proximity to the food processing plant, was not given adequate consideration when it was clearly a material consideration which should have been taken into account.

However, the weight or importance to be attached to a material consideration is entirely a matter for the planning authority and the courts will not interfere with such a decision unless it is manifestly unreasonable. So, for example, in the Scottish case *London & Midland Developments* v *Secretary of State for Scotland and Dawn Construction Ltd* [1996] 8 ELM 167, the court took the view that the Secretary of State was perfectly entitled to attach more weight to environmental impact than to considerations of economic regeneration in relation to two competing retail development proposals.

Many matters have been identified as material considerations in particular circumstances by the courts. These include:

1. the existence of other legal controls which may be relevant to the application, such as environmental protection controls (*Gateshead MBC* v *Secretary of State for the Environment* [1995] JPL 432);

2. compatibility with existing uses such as the impact of an out of town retail development proposal on the vitality and viability of existing town centres (*R* v *Doncaster Metropolitan District, ex p. British Railways Board* [1987] JPL 444);
3. government guidance on the particular type of development (*J A Pye (Oxford) Estates Ltd* v *Wychavon District Council* [1982] JPL 575).

Many other factors may also be material considerations.

Essentially, determining a planning application is a matter of balancing competing considerations. This is very clearly illustrated by the Scottish case *M-I Great Britain Ltd* v *Secretary of State for Scotland* 1996 SLT 1025, which concerned an application to develop a barytes (a mineral used in the North Sea Oil industry) mine in an area of outstanding beauty and conservation value in Perthshire. The Secretary of State essentially had to balance the economic considerations against the environmental impact. He attached more weight to the environmental impact and the Court of Session refused to interfere with his decision.

Environmental assessment

Development usually has an impact on the environment. For example, a new hotel will produce sewage and solid waste which has to be disposed of, it may cause noise especially if it incorporates a disco and it may well affect visual amenity by spoiling an attractive view. All these are adverse environmental impacts.

Environmental assessment is a procedure whereby development projects which may have an adverse impact on the environment can be identified at an early stage. This may result in their impacts being satisfactorily mitigated. This is because it is a key feature of EC environmental policy that pollution should be prevented rather than subsequently trying to clean it up, or to put it simply: prevention is better than cure.

To ensure that this approach was adopted throughout the EC, the Directive on the Assessment of the Effects of Certain Private and Public Projects on the Environment (85/337/EEC) was adopted. This Directive has been principally implemented in England and Wales by the Town and Country Planning (Assessment of Environmental Effects) Regulations 1988 (as amended) and in Scotland by the Environmental Assessment (Scotland) Regulations 1988 (as amended). Directive 85/337/EEC is being amended by Directive 97/11/EC. The amendments must be brought into force by member states by 14 March 1999. The amendments extend the range of projects where an environmental assessment (EA) may be necessary, establish clearer criteria for determining when an assessment is required and clarify consultation requirements.

The legislation provides that for certain major projects an environmental assessment is mandatory. These are listed in Annex I and are referred to as Annex I projects. They include industrial facilities such as power stations, major chemical works, motorways, ports and canals. For certain other projects listed in Annex II ('Annex II projects') an environmental assessment may be required if the planning authority considers that the project is likely to give rise to significant environmental effects. 'Significant effects' are assessed with reference to (1) the physical scale of the project including whether or not the project is of more than local importance; (2) whether it is intended for a particularly sensitive location, for example, an area designated for nature conservation purposes; and (3) whether the project is thought likely to give rise to particularly complex or adverse effects, such as in terms of discharge of pollutants. Annex II as amended by Directive 97/11/EC now contains a tourism and leisure category which includes ski-runs, ski-lifts, cable cars, marinas, holiday villages and hotel complexes outside urban areas, permanent camp sites and caravan sites and theme parks. Directive 97/11/EC introduces a set of selection criteria which member states must take into account when deciding whether an Annex II project should be subject to an EA. These include issues such as the size of the project, its use of natural resources and waste production, the absorption capacity of the natural environment in the area (with special attention being paid to highly sensitive areas, especially those protected by EC nature conservation legislation) and the characteristics of the project's potential environmental impact. This is to ensure greater consistency in the application of EA than has been the case to date. For example, a proposal to develop a large hotel complex and marina (both Annex II projects) on the banks of Loch Lomond is likely to require an EA because of the beauty and sensitivity of the area and the likelihood of adverse impacts such as sewage and noise pollution from power boats.

A developer may decide that an EA is required. However, if a developer is unsure he may request a determination from the planning authority whether or not an EA is required. If the developer does not, the planning authority may decide that an EA is required once a planning application has been submitted by the developer. The planning authority must make public its determination as to whether an EA is required for an Annex II project.

If a developer is unhappy with the decision of a planning authority that an EA is required, an appeal may be made to the appropriate Secretary of State. The courts will only interfere with a decision that an EA is or is not required when the decision is irrational or unreasonable (see Chapter One, p. 34).

Where an EA is required planning permission cannot be granted unless and until the environmental statement has been considered along with any representations made.

Where an EA is required, the developer must prepare and submit an environmental statement with the planning application. The aim of an environmental statement is to provide a full and systematic account of a development's likely effects on the environment, including those which are subject to pollution controls, and the measures which are envisaged to avoid, reduce or remedy significant adverse effects. Possible impacts on human beings, flora, fauna, soil, water, air, climate, landscape, interaction between the foregoing, material assets and the cultural heritage will be considered. Directive 97/11/EC now also requires the developer to provide an outline of the main alternative sites and indications of the reasons for the site selected. A non-technical summary must be provided for the public. The applicant must consult with certain statutory consultees such as the Environment Agency, English Nature (in England) or the Scottish Environment Protection Agency and Scottish Natural Heritage (in Scotland) and may consult with others before preparing the environmental statement. After its submission to the planning authority it must be made available to the statutory consultees and the public who may make representations concerning it to the planning authority. It is only after the statement and representations made about it have been considered that the planning authority may determine the planning application.

The decision

The planning authority may approve the application unconditionally or subject to conditions or it may refuse the application (TCPA s.70(1); TCPSA s.37(1)(a)). Where the authority refuses the application or a conditional application is granted, reasons must be given. Equally, where the application is refused or a conditional application granted, the applicant may appeal to the Secretary of State if he/she so chooses (TCPA, s.78(1); TCPSA, s.47(1)). As we noted above, if the planning authority fails to determine the application within two months, this is deemed to be a refusal which entitles the applicant to appeal to the Secretary of State (TCPA, s.78(2); TCPSA, s.47(2)).

A refusal does not entitle the applicant to any kind of compensation although there are very limited cases where that might happen. The use of land is perceived to carry with it certain limitations vaguely considered to be in the public interest and there may just be circumstances in which freedom to do what one likes with one's own land is so heavily compromised by restrictions imposed for the community interest that a case for compensation may be made.

It may also happen that refusal of permission renders the land incapable of any beneficial use and in that case, a purchase notice may be served on the planning authority (TCPA, ss 137–148; TCPSA, ss 88–99). This is the obverse of compulsory purchase and is designed to force the planning authority to buy the land which their refusal decision has effectively 'sterilized'. If the notice is accepted, the owner is able to obtain from the planning authority the value of the land as it would be if it were capable of some use of value.

This mechanism is parallel to the blight notice procedure available to the owner of land which is adversely affected by a proposal within the development plan which reduces its market value (TCPA, ss 149–171; TCPSA, ss 100–122). For instance, if the plan were to show that one's land would be required for the route of a proposed new road, it could not be expected to fetch anything like the price attainable without this blight. Again, the effect is to offload the blighted property on to the planning authority at unblighted market value.

Conditions

Introduction

Planning authorities have a power under the legislation to grant planning permission subject to such conditions as they think fit (TCPA, s.70(1); TCPSA, s.37(1)(a)). One condition which is contained in every planning permission (it is implied if it is not actually made express) is that the development must be started within five years. The permission lapses if the development is not commenced within this period. The imposition of conditions enables the planning authority to exercise a greater degree of control and indeed ongoing control over the development.

Although the above power appears to be very wide this provision has been interpreted fairly narrowly by the courts. They have held that conditions must:

1. have a planning purpose;
2. fairly and reasonably relate to the development;
3. be reasonable (*Newbury District Council* v *Secretary of State for the Environment* [1981] AC 578).

Planning purpose

The *Newbury* case illustrates the first of these tests well. The court held that a condition requiring the removal of former aircraft hangers which were being used as warehouses had been imposed for a planning purpose since they were an intrusion in the landscape. The condition was, however, held to be unlawful on other grounds.

Fairly and reasonably relate to the development

The Scottish case *British Airports Authority and Others* v *Secretary of State for Scotland* 1979 SC 200 illustrates the application of the second test. In that case conditions requiring no night flying and restricting the direction of take off and landing were imposed in three permissions, two of which concerned the expansion of terminal facilities and aircraft aprons at Aberdeen airport. It was held that the conditions fairly and reasonably related to these developments. However, the third development concerned the building of a headquarters for a helicopter business and the court held that these conditions did not fairly and reasonably relate to that development since it did not involve any flying activities but was simply an office development.

Reasonable

The third test, reasonableness, encompasses such matters as uncertainty and enforceability. For example, in *Hall & Co. Ltd* v *Shoreham-By-Sea Urban District Council* [1964] 1 WLR 240 the planning authority imposed a condition requiring the developer to build a public road to relieve traffic congestion which would result from the development and which would provide access to several existing sites. This was held to be unlawful since it essentially required the developer to take over the function of the highways authority and took away the developer's property without compensation. The condition was clearly unenforceable because it required the developer to do something which only the highways authority could in fact do. This case also illustrates to an extent that authorities cannot impose a condition requiring the payment of a financial contribution, for example towards infrastructure costs by the applicant or requiring the applicant to give up land for public use. The *British Airports Authority* case (see above) also illustrates the point about unenforceable conditions. The only body which can secure the direction of take off and landing of aircraft is the Civil Aviation Authority. The developers could not themselves secure this and so the court held that that condition was unlawful. However, the court held that it was wrong because it was unnecessary, but this judgment is thought to be incorrect since it seems to involve the courts in consideration of the planning merits of the condition rather than its strict legality. It is probably correct to view the condition as being unreasonable because it was unenforceable.

Grampian conditions

While conditions requiring the applicant to do something outwith his/her control are not enforceable and hence unlawful (see above), negative or suspensive conditions have been held to be legal since they are enforceable. Such conditions are often known as 'Grampian' conditions after the Scottish case *Grampian Regional Council v City of Aberdeen District Council* 1984 SLT 197 in which the House of Lords held that it would have been possible to impose a condition requiring a road to be closed prior to the development commencing. This was enforceable since the planning authority can take enforcement action against the developer if the development does commence. However, it leaves it up to the developer to arrange for the road closure with the highways (in Scotland, roads) authority.

It was thought until recently that it would be unreasonable and unlawful to impose a negative condition on a grant of planning permission unless there was a reasonable prospect of the condition being fulfilled. However, in *British Railways Board* v *Secretary of State for the Environment* [1994] JPL 32 the House of Lords held that such a condition is lawful even where there appears to be no reasonable prospect of its fulfilment. This case concerned a condition imposed requiring access to be secured over a piece of land prior to the commencement of a residential development scheme on a former marshalling yard. The owner of the land in question refused to permit access and it did not seem that there was any reasonable prospect of the condition being fulfilled. However, that did not mean that it was unlawful. Furthermore, the British Railways Board had five years from the granting of planning permission to secure access over the land before the planning permission expired. It was up to them to make best use of this time to negotiate access. Grampian conditions can be used to control separate stages of a development, for example, by forbidding the commencement of a development until the infrastructure is in place.

Where an applicant is unhappy with the conditions which are imposed he/she can appeal to the Secretary of State on the grounds that they are unlawful by reference to one of the tests discussed above (TCPA, s.78; TCPSA, s.47).

Planning agreements

Introduction

Planning authorities also have the power under the planning legislation to enter into agreements with developers (and others) for the purpose of restricting or regulating the development or use of land. Such agreements are contracts and are often known as Section 106 Agreements after the section of the TCPA which currently provides for them. In Scotland they were known as 'Section 50 Agreements' after s.50 of the TCPSA 1972 although this section has recently been replaced by s.75 of the TCPSA.

The merits of planning agreements

There are considerable advantages, especially to the planning authority, in entering into such agreements. First, since the agreements may be registered in the appropriate land register they impose burdens which run with the land and are enforceable against all future owners of the land. Secondly, they may lawfully be used to require the applicant to make a financial contribution towards, for example, infrastructure costs of a development, unlike conditions. Thirdly, they are enforceable by means of contractual remedies in the courts and so provide an alternative means of enforcement of planning controls. Fourthly, unlike conditions, agreements cannot be appealed to the Secretary of State and so they may provide a means of getting around government policy. Finally, authorities may be able to use such agreements to obtain 'planning gain' from a developer, such as provision of infrastructure required for a development; for example, the upgrading of a road in return for the granting of planning permission. For developers, the principal advantage is that entering into an agreement may actually enable them to get planning permission for a lucrative development.

Considerable controversy surrounds the use of planning agreements particularly because they are negotiated in secret and are not subject to the same degree of transparency as the rest of the planning system. There is also concern that some planning authorities effectively hold developers to ransom by requiring 'planning gain' in return for granting planning permission although there is not much evidence to support this. However, in *R v Plymouth CC ex p. Plymouth and South Devon Cooperative Society Ltd* (1994) 67 P&CR 78, a 'beauty contest' between competing supermarket developers resulted in two developers who offered considerable planning gain, including contributions towards a park and ride scheme, art works and a nature reserve, getting planning permission, whereas the Co-op, which offered nothing, did not get permission. This was still held to be lawful although whether the decision is correct is doubtful since the wrong test for the legality of the agreements was applied and there seemed to be little connection between what the two developers were offering and their actual developments (see below for the correct test). The Government is also unhappy with planning agreements since there is no appeal to the Secretary of State. Its guidance urges planning authorities to use conditions to control development where possible, and to use agreements as a last resort where the development would otherwise be unacceptable.

Planning agreements as material considerations

Use of planning agreements is not a substitute for planning permission. That is still required but the existence of an agreement or the offer by the developer to enter into an agreement is a material consideration which must be considered when the planning authority determines the application. *Tesco Stores Ltd v Secretary of State for the Environment and Others* [1995] JPL 581, concerned an offer by Tesco to build a relief road in a town where they were proposing to develop a superstore. This was held to be a material consideration but the House of Lords held that the weight or importance to be attached to it was entirely a matter for the Secretary of State. He was entitled to consider it to be of little importance and hence to prefer a competing application.

Test for legality of planning agreements

The courts have held that agreements must serve a planning purpose and must be reasonable. Their provisions must also have some relationship to the proposed development although it seems that this may be fairly tenuous (*Tesco*, see above).

Uses of planning agreements

Agreements are often used to require contributions to infrastructure improvements which the development would require such as the provision of sewers, roads and schools. For example, in *R v South Northamptonshire DC, ex p. Crest Homes plc*

[1995] JPL 200 it was held that an agreement which required housing developers to make a contribution towards upgrading the road infrastructure to cope with the impact of the development was lawful. However, perhaps a more acceptable alternative for obtaining infrastructure improvements which would be open to public scrutiny is the use of Grampian conditions (see p. 202).

Enforcement of planning control

Introduction

A breach of planning control occurs when development is carried out without the required planning permission or where there is a failure to comply with any condition or restriction imposed as part of the permission (TCPA, s.171A(1); TCPA, s.123(1)). A breach of planning control is not in itself a criminal offence but failure to comply with enforcement action taken by a planning authority to secure compliance with planning control is normally a criminal offence and may result in fines being imposed. There are a number of enforcement mechanisms available to a planning authority. In practice it is often the case that formal enforcement measures are not used but matters are resolved by persuasion, for example, by planning officers requesting that a person applies retrospectively for planning permission. There are many reasons for this including a lack of resources to investigate and follow up all breaches of planning control, and the fact that the criminal justice system does not regard planning offences as being serious and so cases are not prosecuted and, even if they are, low penalties tend to be imposed. Enforcement action may also not always be appropriate in the circumstances.

Planning contravention notices

If planning officers decide to use their formal powers they may initially serve a planning contravention notice (TCPA, ss 171C-D; TCPSA, ss 125–126), to ascertain whether a breach of planning control has taken place.

Inspection powers

Inspection of the site is possible (TCPA, ss 196A–C; TCPSA, ss 156–158). An inspection may be required to ascertain whether a breach of planning control has actually occurred. However, a formal inspection can often result in steps being taken to remedy the breach.

Enforcement notices

The most common form of enforcement mechanism is the enforcement notice which the planning authority may serve stating the matters which the authority considers to constitute the breach, specifying what steps are to be taken in order to remedy the alleged breach and specifying the date by which these steps are to be carried out (TCPA, ss 172–182; TCPSA, ss 127–139). The scope of the notice is all embracing as it can demand the alteration or removal of building or works, the carrying out of any building or other operations, the demolition of a building or the cessation of specified activities on the land to which it relates. Failure to comply with the notice is a criminal offence. The maximum penalties are a fine of up to £20,000 on summary conviction or an unlimited fine on conviction on indictment. An appeal against the notice lies to the Secretary of State. Appeals suspend the operation of the notice and there is evidence from research that recipients of enforcement notices normally do appeal against them. This obviously delays enforcement action. Where an enforcement notice stipulates that work is to be carried out in order to secure compliance and such steps are not carried out, the planning authority may carry out the work itself, and recover the costs from the owner or occupier (TCPA, s.178; TCPSA, s.135).

Breach of condition notices

Where the breach of planning control involves a failure to comply with a condition imposed as part of the permission, a Breach of Condition Notice is appropriate (TCPA s.187A; TCPSA, s.145). This notice is similar to an enforcement notice but there is no right of appeal available which is clearly an advantage to the planning authority but the maximum penalty is only a fine of £1,000.

Injunctions and stop notices

The Planning and Compensation Act 1991 also gave planning authorities the power to apply to the courts for an injunction (TCPA, s.187B) (in Scotland, an interdict (TCPSA, s.146)), which would have the effect of forcing someone engaged in unauthorized operations to stop immediately. An alternative to an injunction is the stop notice which is designed to prevent misuse of the appeal procedures to allow unauthorized development to continue pending the outcome of the appeal with possible prejudice in favour of the developer (TCPA, ss 183–187; TCPSA, ss 140–144)). Contravention of stop notices may give rise to the same penalties as for contravention of an enforcement notice. In practice both these mechanisms are used sparingly as the planning authority would be liable for compensation if it were subsequently established that there was in fact no breach.

Immunity from enforcement action

You should note that operational development becomes immune from enforcement action in four years from the date of substantial completion of the operations. A change of use of any building to a dwellinghouse will also become lawful after four years. However, where there is a change in use of a dwellinghouse from a family home to a house in multiple occupation with occupants sharing facilities, immunity from enforcement action only comes about ten years after the change. All other material changes of use and breach of conditions only become immune from enforcement action ten years from the date of the change of use or breach of condition as the case may be. Where enforcement action is anticipated a person can apply for a Certificate of Lawful Use or Development as a means of preventing enforcement proceedings (TCPA, ss 191–196; TCPSA, ss 150–155). The procedure is similar to, although simpler than, obtaining planning permission and there are rights of appeal to the Secretary of State. It is also possible for a developer who is unsure about whether a particular proposed development or change of use requires planning permission to apply to the planning authority for a Certificate of Lawfulness of Proposed Use or Development (TCPA, s.192; TCPSA, s.151).

ENVIRONMENTAL LAW

Introduction

First of all, what is environmental law and how is it relevant to the hospitality and tourism industries? Environmental law is largely statutory law which is designed to try to prevent damage to the environment caused by pollution, to punish those who are responsible for such damage, to allocate liabilities for cleaning up environmental damage and to protect sensitive flora, fauna and their habitats. However, you should be aware that the common law is also relevant in the environmental sphere and the torts of negligence and nuisance which we discussed in detail in Chapter Two may well be applicable to nuisances or personal injury or property damage caused by pollution. Indeed several of the examples which we give in Chapter Two are of cases involving various types of pollution.

Environmental law is relevant to the hospitality and tourism industries because the environment itself is important for tourism. Tourists hope to find an attractive environment with clean drinking and bathing water, fresh air and as little rubbish as possible at their destinations. Governments and the operators of tourist facilities who fail to recognize this, risk losing millions of pounds worth of holiday business. There are also potential criminal and civil liabilities for tourism and hospitality businesses which ignore environmental law.

In this section we consider, first, international and EC developments in environmental law which are of particular significance to the tourism and hospitality industries. Secondly, we outline how the current system of environmental law has developed in Great Britain. Thirdly, we explain the administrative structure of environmental law in Great Britain. Fourthly, we outline the principal environmental legislation which is relevant to the tourism and hospitality industries. Fifthly we consider the enforcement of the law. Finally, liability for injury, damage or loss caused by environmental problems overseas may arise under the common law or the Package Travel, Package Holidays and Package Tours Regulations 1992.

International and EC environmental measures

International developments

We provide a general introduction to treaties as a source of law for the tourism and hospitality industries in Chapter One (pp. 4–6) and you may wish to refer back to that section before you read on.

You have probably heard of the United Nations Rio Earth Summit that took place in 1992 and the Framework Convention on Climate Change, one of the international treaties that resulted from it, which is designed to reduce greenhouse gas emissions and so reduce the degree of climate change. Clearly whether this treaty is successful or not will have a considerable impact on all our lives. There are many other international treaties which impact indirectly on tourism. These include the Vienna Convention for the Protection of the Ozone Layer 26 ILM 1529 (1987) and its Montreal Protocol 26 ILM 1550 (1987) which are designed to combat ozone depletion which has been caused by the emission of chlorofluorocarbons (CFCs) from aerosols, air conditioning equipment and refrigerators. Ozone depletion allows more ultra violet radiation from the sun on to the surface of the earth and has impacted considerably on our awareness of the risks of developing skin cancer as a result of sunbathing. In addition, there are regional treaties on water quality, always an important tourist resource. For example, the Barcelona Convention for the Protection of the Mediterranean Sea Against Pollution 1976 15 ILM (1976) 290 has endeavoured to reduce the amount of rubbish being dumped in the Mediterranean and to encourage better sewage treatment.

A key feature of international environmental law is sustainable development. We provided a definition of this in the section on planning law above (p. 186) which you may wish to refer back to. The importance of sustainable development as an aim of environmental law is demonstrated by the fact that it was the key element in the Declaration that resulted from the Rio Conference as principle 4 illustrates:

> In order to achieve sustainable development, environmental protection shall constitute an integral part of the development process and cannot be considered in isolation from it.

The concept now permeates both EC and domestic environmental law and one of the principal aims of environmental law is to contribute to achieving sustainable development. Implementation of sustainable development at a national level involves more careful management of natural resources, for example, in terms of energy use, waste minimization so that our land is not spoiled with countless waste tips and less reliance on polluting forms of transport such as the car.

EC developments

For a discussion of the basic principles of EC law and enforcement of the law by the EC Commission and individuals you should consult Chapter One (pp. 6–9). Here we concern ourselves with policy and legal developments which are of particular relevance to the tourism and hospitality industries.

Environmental protection is now an express goal of the European Community. EC environmental law rests on a number of basic principles including the principle that environmental damage should be prevented at source, and the 'polluter pays' principle. The most recent objectives of environmental protection policy are contained in the Fifth Action Programme on the Environment, *Towards Sustainability* (1993 COM(92) 23/II final). This places much emphasis on tourism, stressing that tourism is an important element in the social and economic life of the EC. It states that tourism

> represents a good example of the fundamental link which exists between economic development and environment, with all the attendant benefits, tensions and potential conflicts. (Executive Summary, para. 28)

The Action Programme explains that the EC supports tourism particularly through its investments in necessary infrastructure. The integration of environmental protection considerations into such investment decisions, for example on transport infrastructure, by means of an environmental assessment (see pp. 199–200) can ensure that the environment is adequately protected when development proceeds.

The Action Programme proposes three main lines of action in relation to tourism. These are

- diversification of tourism activities, including better management of the phenomenon of mass tourism, and encouragement of different types of tourism;
- quality of tourist services, including information and awareness-building and visitor management and facilities;
- tourist behaviour, including media campaigns, codes of behaviour and choice of transport. (Executive Summary, para. 30)

The Action Programme recognizes that to a large degree these lines of action can only be achieved by promoting greater environmental awareness and better environmental behaviour amongst tourists and that this is something which can really only be achieved through education over time rather than by legislation. However, legislation does have a role to play as we hope to demonstrate.

There are around 300 pieces of EC legislation relating to the environment. Several of these are of particular relevance to tourism. We consider measures relating to bathing water quality and eco-management and audit below. In addition measures relating to drinking water are obviously important for tourist resorts as are measures ensuring the proper management of waste.

Water quality is under considerable pressure in many parts of the EC, such as the Mediterranean, as a result of tourist-related development. In such cases the very environment, including bathing water, which the tourist is coming to enjoy, is being harmed by the number of visitors using the resorts. The EC has been active in promoting legislation to improve water quality for bathing, in particular Directive 76/160/EEC on bathing water quality and Directive 92/271 on urban waste water treatment. The former Directive sets standards for bathing waters while the latter tackles the issue from the point of view of ensuring better treatment of sewage.

There has been considerable controversy surrounding the implementation of Directive 76/160/EEC on bathing water in Great Britain. The Directive requires member states to identify bathing waters to which the standards set out in the Directive will apply, notify these to the EC and then ensure that they meet the requisite standards. The Directive defines bathing waters as waters where bathing is either expressly permitted or where it is traditionally practised by large numbers. There are no beaches in the UK where bathing is expressly authorized and so the UK relies on the second definition in its implementation of the Directive. In applying this definition the UK originally adopted one criterion, whether the waters were used by a particular high number of bathers. Having applied this test only 27 waters were initially identified in the UK and these did not include waters at Blackpool or Southport! By way of contrast Belgium, which has a much shorter coastline (roughly the distance along the coast from Glasgow to Ayr in Scotland), had notified far more beaches! The EC Commission took the view that the UK had not properly implemented the Directive and brought enforcement proceedings against the UK in the European Court of Justice (ECJ) (*EC Commission* v *UK*, C-56/90 [1994] 1 CMLR 769). One of the UK's principal arguments in its defence was that the definition of bathing water was too vague to give effect to. However, the ECJ took the view that whether bathing was practised by large numbers in particular waters was objectively identifiable. A range of objective factors could be looked at, for example, the provision of changing facilities, toilets, lifeguards, kiosks and deck chairs rather than simply looking at the numbers actually bathing on a particular day to establish whether bathing was traditionally practised by large numbers in the waters. It was wrong to look simply to numbers because people might be deterred from bathing by the poor quality of the water and that approach would defeat the whole purpose of the Directive which was to improve water quality in such locations. The ECJ had no doubt that bathing was traditionally practised by large numbers at Blackpool and Southport! This has meant that the UK has had to spend large sums on sewage treatment facilities at these and other locations to try to bring the waters up to the standard required by the Directive. There are now well over 350 bathing waters identified in the UK following the adoption of the criteria suggested by the ECJ.

The Eco Management and Audit Scheme (EMAS) Regulation (1836/93/EEC) came into force in April 1995. Its aim is to promote improvements in the environmental performance of business by the establishment and implementation of environmental management systems by companies, and the systematic, objective and periodic evaluation of the environmental performance of these systems. Indeed information on performance must be made public. This is done by means of an environmental statement which must contain a summary of the relevant figures on pollution emissions, waste generation, raw material usage and energy and water consumption which must be published every year. The statement has to be validated by an independent, accredited verifier who will also verify the company's policy, objectives and audit programme for conformity with the Regulation. The Regulation is voluntary in the sense that no business is obliged to sign up to its requirements, but once a business has decided to seek accreditation under the Regulation, it must then meet the requirements set out. There are also similar but not identical environmental managements systems provided for at an international level, ISO 14001, and at a domestic level, BS7750. Neither is quite as demanding as the EMAS Regulation.

These eco-management systems can bring about considerable savings in terms of energy usage and waste minimization. They can also be used as a marketing tool to attract environmentally sensitive tourists. There is certainly some customer pressure for 'greener' tourist facilities and it may become a tourist board requirement that hotels and other tourist facilities are subjected to an environmental appraisal. A pilot EMAS was promoted by Fife Council in St Andrews in Scotland. It was applied to certain hotels, guest houses and bed and breakfast establishments. Considerable areas for potential savings were identified aside from attracting environmentally conscious tourists. Savings on energy bills have been made with the installation of low energy light bulbs, ensuring that TVs are not left on standby, improving control of boilers and heating and enhancing pipe insulation. Savings in waste disposal costs and new purchases were made by reusing plastic bathroom containers. Water consumption and sewage effluent discharge were reduced with accompanying cost savings by the installation of short flush toilets. Considerable guidance on environmental benefits and associated cost savings which can be made may be found in the International Hotels Environmental Initiative Action Pack.

Development of current system of environmental regulation in Great Britain

Weaknesses of common law

The common law was originally the principal legal mechanism for dealing with pollution in the early part of the industrial revolution. Indeed, today its importance is considerable where an individual has suffered injury or property damage as a result of pollution (see Chapter Two pp. 57–73). However, the common law is beset with weaknesses. For a start there needs to be someone who has suffered some kind of harm and who is willing and able to undertake litigation. Given that litigation is stressful and may involve considerable delay, risk and expense many people are simply not prepared to take court action. Furthermore, the common law is principally reactive, that is, a person can get compensation for harm which has occurred but it is not easy to prevent harm from occurring. The common law also works on a case by case basis and does not necessarily result in uniform environmental protection across the country.

Development of statutory controls

For this reason, statutory controls were developed from the mid-nineteenth century onwards, for example the Alkali Act 1863. Public regulatory agencies were empowered to act in the public interest and so no injured party was required. The statutory systems of control were proactive rather than reactive. Control was exercised in advance by the requirement for a licence. The licence would contain conditions requiring adherence to standards. The statutes also often empowered regulatory agencies to clean up pollution and recover the costs from the polluter.

Today's environmental statutes such as the Environmental Protection Act 1990 (EPA 1990) and the Water Resources Act 1991 (WRA 1991) share many features with the early statutes. Most environmental statutes share a variety of common features. These include criminalization of a particular act, such as discharge of material into water or air, without a licence obtained from a regulatory body. The regulatory body has discretion to grant the licence or not and may impose conditions in it to ensure that standards are adhered to. Extensive enforcement powers are available to the regulators and clean up powers are also normally available. There is the possibility of heavy fines and imprisonment of corporate officers if no licence is obtained or licence conditions are breached. For example, in *National Rivers Authority* v *Shell (UK) Ltd* [1990] Water Law 40, Shell was fined £1 million for polluting the River Mersey and was landed with a £1.2 million clean-up bill. The system is also relatively transparent since licence applications, the licences themselves and details of enforcement action must all be included on registers which are open to public inspection. In addition, in some cases members of the public may object to licence applications and their objections must be considered by the regulatory body deciding the application.

Weaknesses of the statutory system and developments addressing those weaknesses

However, the statutory system is not without its problems. A very fragmentary system developed over time with different legal regimes applying to pollution of different environmental media and many regulatory agencies were involved in the enforcement of the law. To an extent enactment of the EPA 1990 and the Environment Act 1995 (EA 1995) have gone some way to addressing these problems. First, the EPA 1990 introduced a new concept called integrated pollution control (IPC) which regulates the emissions of industrial processes to air, water and land in an integrated way so that instead of requiring separate licences for discharges to each, only a single authorization is required. An integrated approach also ensures that reducing pollution of one medium does not simply lead to its displacement to another medium. However, the system only applies to the most polluting industries and it does not cover matters such as noise and energy efficiency. Improvements are on the way, however, with the forthcoming implementation of the EC Directive on integrated pollution prevention and control (96/61/EC) (IPPC) from 1999 onwards (see below) which will extend IPC to more processes and will require controls to be exercised over matters such as raw material use, energy efficiency and noise.

Secondly, the EA 1995 established the Environment Agency ('the Agency') for England and Wales and the Scottish Environment Protection Agency ('SEPA') for Scotland from 1 April 1996 which have largely solved the problem of having a fragmentary system of administration of the statutory controls. The establishment of these bodies will also encourage an integrated approach to environmental protection. However, central government, local authorities and certain other bodies are also involved in the administration of environmental law as we explain below.

Other problems exist in the administration of environmental law however. The Agencies are not well funded and have small staffs. This means that their enforcement of the law is not always as vigorous as it might be and they tend to use persuasion rather than prosecution where possible.

Environmental law is very much focused on sustainable development today (see above p. 208). The law also seeks to prevent harm occurring through the licensing system. Indeed where the risks of an activity are very great, precautionary action may be taken even in the absence of scientific evidence that harm will definitely result from the activity. The law is also based where possible on the polluter pays principle which is designed to ensure that the polluter pays for the clean up of pollution caused, pays for the cost of regulation and internalizes the environmental costs of the activities being carried out.

Administration of environmental law in Great Britain

Secretary of State

As in the planning system the Secretary of State has considerable functions. These include the development of policy guidance, the exercise of reserve powers if the other bodies involved in environmental regulation fail to act or act improperly, and hearing appeals against decisions of the other environmental regulators.

Environment Agency/Scottish Environment Protection Agency

The principal environmental regulator in England and Wales is the Environment Agency. It is the body responsible for enforcing integrated pollution control (EPA 1990, Part I), waste controls (EPA 1990, Part II), contaminated land provisions in relation to special sites (EPA 1990, Part IIA), water pollution and abstraction controls

(WRA 1991) and controls over the use of radioactive substances and the disposal of radioactive waste (Radioactive Substances Act 1993). North of the border SEPA has similar although not identical functions. While SEPA lacks comprehensive controls over water abstraction, nevertheless it is responsible for enforcing local air pollution control (LAPC) which is administered by local authorities in England and Wales (EPA 1990, Part I).

Local authorities

Local authorities are responsible for enforcing statutory nuisance provisions (EPA 1990, Part III), clean air provisions (Clean Air Act 1993), contaminated land provisions in relation to all sites except special sites which are the responsibility of the Agency or SEPA (EPA 1990, Part IIA – not in force at the time of writing) and new air quality provisions (EA 1995, Part IV). In addition, in England and Wales, local authorities are responsible for enforcing LAPC which is enforced by SEPA in Scotland (EPA, Part I).

Water and sewerage undertakers

In England and Wales, private sector water and sewerage undertakers are responsible for the provision of water supplies and sewerage services (WIA 1991). In relation to the former, regulation is provided by the Secretary of State and the Director General of Water Services. However, these private companies actually regulate discharges into their sewers under the Water Industry Act 1991. However, in Scotland, water and sewerage services are provided by three public sector water and sewerage authorities (East, North and West of Scotland Water) established by the Local Government etc. (Scotland) Act 1994 (Sewerage (Scotland) Act 1968; Water (Scotland) Act 1980). Like their counterparts in England and Wales, the Scottish water authorities regulate discharges into their sewers (Sewerage (Scotland) Act 1968).

Relationship of planning law and environmental law

We need to explain briefly how planning law and environmental law relate to each other. Planning law is designed to regulate land use (see pp. 185–186). So a decision whether a development is suitable for a particular site is a matter for planning law. Environmental law on the other hand seeks to control emissions from the development, not the site of the development. It seeks to establish whether emissions can be controlled satisfactorily. The two systems are not meant to overlap but rather to be complementary (Department of the Environment, Planning Policy Guidance 23 *Planning and Pollution Control* (1994); Scottish Office, National Planning Policy Guideline 10, *Planning and Waste Management* (1996).

Principal environmental legislation in Great Britain

Introduction

In this section we explain some of the principal environmental legislation and try to illustrate its relevance to the tourism and hospitality industries. Some legislation, such as the Radioactive Substances Act 1993, which controls the keeping and use of radioactive material and the disposal of radioactive waste, is not directly relevant at all, and so is not discussed, although its operation may indirectly affect tourism in an area, for example, if the radioactive waste is not being disposed of safely and this is posing a health threat. The discovery of radioactive particles on beaches near the Dounreay nuclear facility on the north coast of Scotland has certainly affected tourism in the area.

Environmental Protection Act 1990 (EPA 1990)

Part I: Integrated Pollution Control/Local Air Pollution Control

Part I of the EPA 1990 provides for the systems of Integrated Pollution Control (IPC) and Local Air Pollution Control (LAPC). IPC is regulated in England and Wales by the Agency and, in Scotland, by SEPA while LAPC is regulated in England and Wales by local authorities and in Scotland by SEPA. To ascertain whether a process is subject to IPC or LAPC the Environmental Protection (Prescribed Processes and Substances) Regulations 1991 (as amended) should be consulted. IPC is unlikely to be relevant to the hospitality and tourism industries since it is designed to regulate emissions to air, water and land from the largest, most harmful industrial processes. LAPC, however, which regulates emissions to air from smaller industrial plants such as boilers with a net rated thermal input of between 20 and 50 megawatts and small incinerators, may be of relevance to the hospitality and tourism sectors since large holiday complexes may operate their own boilers for heating and waste incinerators. If a process is subject to IPC or LAPC, the operator of the process must obtain an authorization from the appropriate regulator. This will contain conditions regulating the process. There are criminal penalties (discussed further below) for operating a process without an authorization and for breaching authorization conditions. There are also a variety of other enforcement mechanisms available to the regulators (see below). EC Directive 96/61 on integrated pollution prevention and control will require more LAPC processes to be re-prescribed for IPC and will also require the imposition of conditions relating to matters such as energy efficiency, noise and post closure provision. The implementation of this Directive may have considerable cost implications for business generally.

Part II: Waste

Part II of the EPA 1990 contains the legal framework for waste management together with the Waste Management Licensing Regulations 1994 (as amended) (the 1994 Regulations) and the Special Waste Regulations 1996 (as amended). Part II and the 1994 Regulations criminalize the treatment, keeping or disposal of waste without a waste management licence (WML). Such licences must be obtained from the Agency in England and Wales and from SEPA in Scotland. A number of exemptions from this requirement are provided for in the 1994 Regulations including, importantly:

1. an exemption for the storing of waste pending its transport or disposal elsewhere providing the amount does not exceed 50 cubic metres and it is not stored for longer than three months (Sch. 3, para. 41);
2. an exemption for the baling, compacting, crushing, shredding or pulverizing of waste at the place where it is produced and the storage of waste treated in such a way at the place where it is produced (Sch. 3, para. 27);

3. an exemption for the sorting, crushing, compacting, baling, washing etc. of waste plastic, textiles, paper or cardboard, glass, steel cans, aluminium cans or foil and waste food or drinks cartons if the operation is carried out with a view to recovery (i.e. recycling) or re-use and stipulated weekly limits in tonnes are not exceeded.

So for example, if a hotel washed up to 100 tonnes of waste plastic (e.g. bathroom toiletry containers) with a view to their re-use or sorted up to 1000 tonnes of waste glass bottles per week with a view to their re-use or recycling no WML would be required. It is likely that in many cases a hotel or tourist facility will be able to take advantage of one of these exemptions although this may not always be the case. Where an exemption applies, the 1994 Regulations provide that it must be registered with the Agency/SEPA although Department of the Environment Circular 11/94 indicates that registration of the exemption for storing waste temporarily pending its transport elsewhere for final disposal is not in fact required. Given that it is clearly a legal requirement under the 1994 Regulations to register and government guidance is not binding, the hotel or tourist facility should seek advice from the Agency or SEPA as to what its attitude to registration is in such a case. There are a variety of enforcement mechanisms available to the Agency and SEPA under Part II including criminal penalties.

Part II also provides for the duty of care for waste (discussed in greater detail below). This duty applies to every person in the waste chain from producers to carriers to those who operate disposal facilities regardless of whether they need a WML or fall within the scope of an exemption. As hotels and tourist facilities produce waste they will be subject to its requirements, which are designed to ensure that waste is safely handled from cradle to grave (see below). Contravention of the requirements of the duty of care for waste is a criminal offence.

The Special Waste Regulations 1996 provide for additional controls in relation to hazardous waste (known as special waste). These controls principally involve provisions for detailed consignment notes and record-keeping in order that consignments of special waste may be tracked. It should be noted that these regulations introduce a new definition of special waste to reflect the new definition of hazardous waste in EC Directive 91/689 (as amended) which has replaced the definition in the old Control of Pollution (Special Waste) Regulations 1980 which have been repealed. Contravention of the requirements of the Special Waste Regulations is a criminal offence.

Part IIA: Contaminated land

Part IIA of the EPA 1990 (which was added by the Environment Act 1995) establishes a new regime to deal with the clean-up of contaminated land. At the time of writing this was not yet in force. In general, buying land for development can be a risky business. Buyers may face potentially large environmental liabilities when they purchase land which is contaminated in some way. A hotel or tourist facility developer needs to ensure that a site is not contaminated or at least that contamination has been cleaned up. Essentially the buyer must beware. The dangers are clear: legal liability for cleaning up the contamination may fall upon the purchaser of the site at common law under the principles of nuisance or negligence discussed in Chapter Two or under a variety of statutory provisions. For example, in the Scottish Sheriff Court case *Clydebank District Council* v *Monaville Estates Ltd* 1982 SLT (Sh.Ct.) 2, statutory nuisance powers were used to enforce the clean up of a site contaminated by asbestos deposits. These were removed and the site is now a private hospital! You should, however, note that statutory nuisance provisions will no longer be able to be used in respect of contaminated land when Part IIA of the EPA 1990 comes into force.

Part IIA imposes a duty on local authorities to inspect their areas for contaminated land. If they identify contaminated sites, they must serve 'remediation notices' on 'appropriate persons' who are to bear the liability for clean-up in proportion to their contributions to the contamination. Appropriate persons are, firstly, the polluter(s) and, secondly, the owner and/or occupier. Liability will therefore principally fall upon the polluter(s) if they can be found. If they cannot liability will fall upon the current owner and/or occupier which could be an hotel or tourist facility. Given that the regime is designed to deal with historic pollution, it is likely that there will be many cases in which the polluter(s) cannot be found. You should note that there is a three month period before a local authority can serve a remediation notice requiring the site to be cleaned up. The purpose of this period appears to be to encourage all the parties involved to come to an agreement on crucial issues about who should fund the clean up, what the standard of clean up should be, and who should carry out the clean up etc. It is only after this period has expired that further action may be taken under the statute by the local authority. The remediation notice stipulates not only what must be done in terms of cleaning up the site but also investigating and looking after it in the long term. There are criminal penalties for failing to comply with a remediation notice. The maximum penalty is £20,000 together with a £2,000 maximum fine for each day the failure to comply continues. In certain circumstances the local authority may carry out the clean up itself and recover the costs from the appropriate person. Responsibility for serving remediation notices in the case of the most highly contaminated sites which are known in the legislation as 'special sites' falls upon the Agency/SEPA. Finally, however, it should be noted that these provisions are not yet in force and that the new Government is reviewing the regime. Although therefore the timescale for the implementation of Part IIA remains unclear hotels and tourist facilities, especially those established on or developing 'brownfield' sites, must be aware of potential future liabilities.

It should be clear that these provisions could have a major impact on property development generally. There are, however, ways in which developers can seek to protect themselves when buying property. They can instruct environmental consultants to carry out an investigation of the target property. In their contracts with the sellers they can seek what are known as environmental warranties and indemnities. Environmental warranties are representations by the seller to the effect that, for example, the land is not contaminated or at least not contaminated beyond an agreed level. Indemnities are financial provisions whereby if one of the warranties is breached, for example, because the land is contaminated beyond a certain level, the seller will indemnify the purchaser up to an agreed sum. Such clauses are of course worthless in situations where the seller is insolvent.

Part III: Statutory nuisance

We discussed this regime briefly in Chapter Two (pp. 72–73). You should, however, note that the same legislation now applies both south and north of the border with Part III finally replacing the old Scottish statutory nuisance provisions in the Public Health

(Scotland) Act 1897 and the Control of Pollution Act 1974 from 1 April 1996. In the tourism and hospitality sector statutory nuisances could arise, for example from smell or fumes from kitchens and noise from premises such as discos within hotels.

Clean Air Act 1993

If a furnace is not regulated under the EPA 1990's LAPC system because it falls below the prescribed threshold, it will be regulated by the relevant local authority under the Clean Air Act 1993. New furnaces require advance permission from the local authority which may also regulate the chimney height. Furthermore the 1993 Act prevents the emission of dark smoke from trade or industrial premises whether or not the smoke is emitted from a chimney. Hotels and tourist facilities are likely to be regarded as trade premises.

Water Industry Act 1991 (England and Wales); Sewerage (Scotland) Act 1968; and Water (Scotland) Act 1980 (Scotland)

These Acts govern the provision of wholesome drinking water and also the disposal of effluent to sewers. The Water Industry Act 1991 (WIA 1991) contains all the English and Welsh provisions whilst the 1968 and 1980 Acts contain the sewerage and drinking water legislation respectively for Scotland. This legislation is principally relevant for the hospitality and tourism sector in terms of trade effluent discharges to sewers. A person who wished to discharge trade effluent, namely effluent which does not consist of domestic sewage (i.e. lavatory waste) to a sewer requires a discharge consent. This must be obtained from the relevant water company which acts as sewerage undertaker in England and Wales or from the relevant public water authority in Scotland. The consent may contain conditions relating to the matters including the composition, volume, temperature, rate and timing of the discharge. Charges are levied by the consenting body for the discharge of such effluent to sewers. The charge is normally calculated according to a formula based upon the volume and strength of the discharge. Criminal penalties may apply for discharge without a consent or breach of consent conditions.

Water Resources Act 1991 (England and Wales); Control of Pollution Act 1974 (Scotland)

The Water Resources Act 1991 (WRA 1991) and the Control of Pollution Act (COPA) contain the principal water pollution controls which make it an offence for a person to cause or knowingly permit poisonous, noxious or polluting matter or any solid waste matter to enter any controlled waters or to cause or knowingly permit any trade or sewage effluent to be discharged into such waters unless the discharge is made under a consent. Controlled waters include coastal, inland and ground waters. If a hotel or tourist facility wishes to make a discharge to such waters a consent is required from the Agency in England and Wales and from SEPA in Scotland. Discharge without a consent is a criminal offence as the recent Scottish case *O'Donnell* v *Costley & Costley Hoteliers* [1997] 9 ELM 214 illustrates. An unconsented discharge of sewage effluent from a hotel in Troon resulted in a £500 fine being imposed by the Sheriff Court. The consent may contain conditions on matters such as the composition, volume and temperature of the discharge. If such a consent is refused the applicant may appeal to the Secretary of State. A variety of enforcement mechanisms including criminal sanctions are available to the Agency and SEPA to deal with contraventions of consents or unconsented discharges. The WRA 1991 also provides that a person seeking to abstract water from rivers or groundwater, for example for a water leisure complex, must obtain a licence to do so from the Agency.

Environment Act 1995

The Environment Act 1995 (EA 1995) established the Agency for England and Wales (EA 1995, s.1) which took over the IPC and radioactive substances functions of Her Majesty's Inspectorate of Pollution (HMIP), the water pollution control and water resources management functions of the National Rivers Authority (NRA) and the waste regulation functions of local authorities (EA 1995, s.2). It also established the SEPA for Scotland (EA 1995, s.20) which took over the IPC and radioactive substances functions of Her Majesty's Industrial Pollution Inspectorate (HMIPI), the IPC and water pollution control functions of river purification authorities and the LAPC and waste regulation functions of local authorities (EA 1995, s.21).

The 1995 Act also brought about significant changes to other statutes, for example by attempting to harmonize the enforcement mechanisms available in the various statutes.

Furthermore, the 1995 Act also inserted the new Part IIA dealing with contaminated land into the EPA 1990 (discussed above) (EA 1995, s.57), new provision on local air quality management (ss 80–91) and, perhaps most significantly, producer responsibility for waste (EA 1995, ss 93–95). The producer responsibility provisions aim to ensure that persons within particular waste chains achieve recycling and recovery targets. The provisions have initially been applied to the packaging and packaging waste stream in line with the requirements of EC Directive 94/62 on packaging and packaging waste. However, it is likely that they will be extended to other waste streams such as tyres, batteries, end of life vehicles, clinical waste and electrical and electronic goods. Where a business has a turnover of over £5 million (reducing to £1 million from the year 2000) and handles over 50 tonnes of packaging it is caught by the provisions and must attain various recycling and recovery targets. There are two routes by which a person may comply with producer responsibility: (1) by registering with the Agency or SEPA and seeking to comply individually with the required targets or (2) by joining a registered compliance scheme which will secure the achievement of the targets on that person's behalf. There are criminal penalties for failing to register, providing false information and indeed failing to meet the requisite targets. The principal penalty in relation to compliance schemes is de-registration.

Enforcement and liabilities

General introduction

Although the Agency and SEPA in general tend to work by means of persuasion and education there is no doubt that they are prepared to use the wide battery of enforcement powers at their disposal including prosecution when criminal sanctions are deemed appropriate, for example in the case of a serious and deliberate or repeated violation of the law. The establishment of the Agency and SEPA has resulted in certain benefits in relation to enforcement including the fact that uniform practices and policies have been adopted by each agency replacing the wide variety of practices and policies used by their predecessors. Both agencies have interim enforcement policies. These policies stress the need for transparency, consistency and fairness in the enforcement process. If the Agency/SEPA proposes taking enforcement action and the situation is not an emergency the person against whom such action is proposed is entitled to an explanation of why such action is considered necessary and to an opportunity to make representations to the appropriate agency. Appeal rights should also be explained by the Agency/SEPA.

Administrative notices

The two agencies have a variety of administrative notices which they may serve to secure compliance with particular legislative requirements. For example, they may serve enforcement notices to secure compliance with LAPC authorization conditions (EPA 1990, s.13) and discharge consents under the WRA 1991 and COPA (WRA 1991, ss 90B and 91; COPA ss 49A-B) (although the COPA enforcement notice provisions have not yet been brought into force). Such notices require a particular breach of a licence condition to be rectified by the taking of specified steps within a stipulated timescale. Prohibition notices are available in emergencies in several cases and in most environmental law areas there are provisions enabling a licence to be revoked.

Criminal sanctions

Many activities will give rise to criminal liability in environmental law. For example, where a licence is required for a particular activity such as the disposal of waste, performance of that activity without such a licence is criminalized. Furthermore, breach of the conditions set out in a licence is normally a criminal offence as is contravention of the requirements of an administrative notice such as an enforcement notice. It is also a criminal offence to obstruct an officer from the Agency/SEPA and indeed to impersonate such an officer!

Penalties

The penalties available are generally fairly severe. For example, in the case of disposal of waste without a WML or the discharge of polluting matter to controlled waters without a discharge consent, the maximum fine on summary conviction (i.e. after a trial without a jury) is £20,000, with an unlimited fine on conviction on indictment (i.e. after a trial with a jury). Breach of the conditions in a licence or the requirements of an administrative notice usually attracts penalties of the same level. In other cases the maximum fine is often £5,000 on summary conviction.

There is also the possibility of imprisonment both for individuals who commit offences and in certain circumstances for officers of bodies corporate which could obviously include companies involved in the hospitality or tourism industries. In some serious cases such as operating a process prescribed for LAPC under the EPA

1990 without an authorization a prison sentence of up to three months is available on summary conviction. On conviction on indictment prison terms of up to two years (five in case of special waste or radioactive substances offences) are normally available. Despite their traditional reluctance to imprison individuals for what is perceived as white collar crime, the courts have shown an increasing willingness to imprison individuals for environmental offences with a number of company directors being imprisoned for the disposal of waste without a WML for periods of up to 18 months.

Criminal liability of officers of bodies corporate

There are provisions in each environmental statute which extend criminal liability to certain officers of bodies corporate in certain circumstances if the body corporate is convicted of an offence (see also Chapter Five p. 114). The officers encompassed are directors, managers, company secretaries, and other similar officers. In the case of companies, directors and company secretaries are easily identified. It is the terms 'manager' or 'other similar officer' which pose difficulties. Case law has consistently indicated that these provisions are designed to catch those who are in a position to determine corporate policy and strategy, that is high ranking officers and not those the courts have somewhat patronizingly described as 'underlings'. The title of the officer in question does not matter: it is the actual scope of his or her authority which matters. 'Underlings' who have escaped liability have included the Assistant General Manager of Foyles bookshop in London in connection with a fire certificate offence (in reality he was the chief book buyer with no management or health and safety training: *R* v *Boal* [1992] QB 591) and a General Manager of a landfill site (he reported to a Director on the company's board and had no authority to determine overall corporate policy or strategy: *Woodhouse* v *Walsall MBC* [1994] Env LR 30). However, the director of a Scottish local authority roads department has been held liable for a health and safety offence (involving the death of a roads department employee) since the council had delegated to him the task of preparing and implementing a department-specific health and safety policy in accordance with a general policy produced by the council (*Armour* v *Skeen* [1976] IRLR 310). It is essentially a question of fact whether a person has sufficient authority to fall within the scope of the personal liability provisions and so the question of which persons may be liable may be answered differently in different hospitality and tourism businesses.

However, even if an officer is encompassed by these provisions, it must be proved that he or she either consented to the commission of the offence, that is expressly agreed to it, or connived at its commission, that is knew that the offence was being committed but acquiesced in its commission or that the commission of the offence was attributable to his or her neglect. The Scottish case *Armour* v *Skeen* (above) provides a good (or perhaps bad!) example of neglect. As explained above he failed to prepare and implement a departmental health and safety policy despite having a duty to do so. Neglect will therefore normally arise where an officer does have a duty to act but fails to discharge that duty.

Duty of care for waste

Introduction

One legislative provision which is of considerable relevance to all hospitality and tourism businesses since they all produce waste is the duty of care for waste (EPA 1990, s.34). For this reason we have included a more detailed discussion of its requirements.

The rationale for the introduction of the duty was that producers of waste should not escape liability for escape of waste and damage caused thereby simply by passing on the waste to someone else. The duty is designed to ensure that persons in the waste chain (from production to disposal) take care that the waste is properly handled. The idea is that all waste holders can only satisfy their own obligations under the duty of care by checking up on others in the waste chain, for example the carrier or disposer to whom they transfer the waste. The duty of care was introduced by the EPA 1990 and came into force on 1 April 1992.

Who is subject to the duty?

Any person who imports, produces, carries, keeps, treats or disposes of controlled waste or, as a broker, has control of such waste. Hospitality and tourism businesses will normally be waste producers in the waste chain.

What are the requirements of the duty of care and how can compliance be achieved?

Each person in the waste chain must take all such measures as are applicable in their capacity as are reasonable in the circumstances to discharge four obligations. The responsibilities of parties therefore vary depending on their position in the waste chain.

The four obligations are:

1. to prevent any contravention by any other person of s.33 of the EPA 1990 (this is the section which prevents people from disposing of waste without a licence or managing it in such a way as to cause harm to human health or pollution of the environment);
2. to prevent the escape of waste from their control or that of any other person;
3. to transfer waste only to an *authorized person* or *to a person for authorized transport purposes;* and
4. to ensure that when waste is transferred it is accompanied by a written description which will enable other persons to avoid a contravention of s.33 and to comply with the duty as respects the escape of waste.

The Secretary of State has produced good practical guidance on how to discharge the requirements of the duty of care: *Waste Management – The Duty of Care: A Code of Practice,* Department of the Environment 1996. This Code of Practice replaces the original Code which was issued in 1991.

The Code of Practice is admissible in court proceedings and if any provision of the Code appears to be relevant to any question arising in the proceedings it must be taken into account in determining the issue. It should also be noted that compliance with the guidance in the Code will not necessarily mean that the requirements of duty of care have been satisfied. This is because in particular circumstances the requirements of the duty of care may be more onerous than general advice given by the Code suggests, for example, because of the hazardous nature of a particular type of waste and its specific handling requirements. Likewise, failure to adhere to the provisions of the Code will not necessarily indicate a breach of the duty of care.

Obligation (1) requires a producer of waste to ensure that every other person in the waste chain complies with s.33 of the EPA 1990 and prevents waste escaping. This may be achieved by checking that the person to whom the waste is transferred for transport is an authorized person (see further below) and by visiting the disposal or treatment facility which is the final destination of the waste. There is extensive guidance in the Code on the checks which are necessary. For example, where waste is being transferred to another person for transport, the producer of the waste needs to check that the carrier is registered under the Control of Pollution (Amendment) Act 1989. It is not enough to accept an assurance by the carrier that he is registered: the carrier's certificate of registration needs to be checked. Furthermore, the Code provides that it is not sufficient to see a photocopy: the original or a copy certified by the Agency or SEPA must be seen. The Code also suggests that it is worthwhile also checking with the Agency or SEPA to ensure that the registration is still valid. Furthermore, the waste producer must also establish that a carrier is actually capable of transporting the waste in question as the certificate of registration is no guarantee that the carrier can actually transport a particular type of waste.

The disposal or treatment site should also be visited. It is not sufficient for a producer simply to obtain a licence number for the facility and there have been prosecutions of producers who consigned waste to unlicensed facilities having been satisfied by being given a false licence number (*Cleveland County Council* v *Earth Mover Tyres Ltd* [1993] 218 ENDS Report 44). The producer should check the facility's WML to ensure that it is current and that it permits the disposal of the type of waste which the producer wishes to consign to the facility. A tour of the site to check its security etc. is also advisable. However, where there are regular consignments of the same type of waste, the need for such checks is reduced although good practice would suggest six monthly or annual checks at minimum.

Where the business is a large one it would appear to be more cost effective to organize waste disposal centrally and to use one contractor with an appropriate disposal or treatment facility where possible. This would minimize the costs involved in auditing waste management facilities and reduce the likelihood of a contravention of the duty of care occurring. Centralization of waste management within a business would also appear to offer advantages in terms of record keeping (see further below).

Obligation (2) essentially involves ensuring that the waste is packed securely for transport and not, for example, leaving food waste from a hotel in open bins where it would be accessible to scavenging animals. Primary responsibility for this falls upon the producer of the waste, who is in the best position to ensure adequate packaging.

Obligation (3) makes it a requirement that waste is transferred only to *authorized persons* or *to a person for authorized transport purposes*. Authorized persons are waste collection authorities (in England, the district council or the metropolitan borough council; and in Wales and Scotland the unitary local authority), holders of waste management licences, waste carriers registered under the Control of Pollution (Amendment) Act 1989, or persons exempt from registration under the Control of

Pollution (Amendment) Act 1989 and, in Scotland, a Waste Disposal Authority (i.e. a unitary local authority). Exempt persons include wholly owned subsidiaries of British Rail when carrying waste by rail (there are none left – all have now been privatized and the exemption does not apply to private rail freight companies); charities and voluntary organizations; waste collection authorities (local authorities) collecting any waste themselves (though an authority's contractors are not exempt) and ship operators where waste is to be disposed of at sea under the authority of the Food and Environment Protection Act 1985. Authorized transport purposes are:

1. the transport of waste within the same premises between different places in those premises;
2. the import of waste to its first landing in Great Britain;
3. export of waste from Great Britain.

There have been several prosecutions of producers of waste for failing to transfer waste to an authorized person, usually as a result of inadequate checks being made by the producer to establish whether the person is an authorized person. Indeed the very first prosecution brought under the duty of care was in the context of the tourism and hospitality industries. It involved a restaurant owner being found guilty at Birkenhead Magistrates' Court on 23 September 1992 and fined £200 with costs of £100 because he failed to ensure that waste was transferred to an authorized person for transport or to an authorized person for disposal (Croner's Environment Briefing, Issue 9, 28/9/92, p. 3).

Obligation (4) provides that a written description must accompany the waste. This should be entered on the transfer note. In the case of special, i.e. hazardous, waste, a more onerous transfer note system, known as the consignment note system, applies although it has recently been simplified by the Special Waste Regulations 1996 (as amended). Once again the primary obligation to produce an adequate description falls upon the producer of the waste who is clearly in the best position to fulfil this requirement. The more complex the waste being consigned, the more detailed the description required. Where there are regular consignments of the same type of waste, there are 'season ticket' provisions whereby a single transfer note may suffice for the consignments for up to a year. In practice, failure to provide an adequate description is the most frequent breach of the duty of care. Several prosecutions of large companies including ICI (*Greater Manchester Waste Regulation Authority* v *ICI* [1993] 223 ENDS Report 42) and DuPont Chemicals (*West Yorkshire County Council* v *DuPont* [1996] 252 ENDS Report 45) have resulted from a failure to provide an adequate description. In the prosecution of ICI, the failure to provide an adequate description of the waste resulted in its mishandling at the treatment facility which led to an explosion and fire. Copies of transfer/consignment notes must be kept for two years. It would seem sensible to ensure that these are kept in a central facility rather than within individual departments of a business. A single set of administrative practices for record keeping would appear to offer advantages over a variety of departmental practices which might not all be satisfactory and might lead to an increased risk of a breach of the duty of care.

Penalties

Breach of the duty is a *criminal* offence. The maximum penalties are a £5,000 fine on summary conviction and an unlimited fine on conviction on indictment. However, it is common to prosecute duty of care offences along with other offences such as a charge under s.33 for disposing of waste without a WML. The penalties available for such a charge are heavier and may involve imprisonment.

Although sentencing obviously depends on all the circumstances of the case, it did appear initially that the courts were not taking breaches of the duty of care very seriously. Recent case law indicates that although the penalties imposed for duty of care offences remain relatively low, they are increasing and fines of £1,000 or over are becoming fairly common. Where the prosecutions for duty of care offences are linked to disposal of waste without a WML, penalties of up to £30,000 have been imposed and convicted individuals have on occasion been jailed for up to 18 months for associated waste offences.

Liability of tour operators for environmental problems at tourist facilities

Introduction

We discuss the law relating to holidays, particularly package holidays, in Chapter Twelve. However, we have provided a brief discussion of the potential liability of tour operators for environmental problems at resorts here. This is now an area which is almost exclusively covered by the Package Travel, Package Holidays and Package Tours Regulations 1992 ('the Package Holiday Regulations'). However, the common law remains relevant in cases where the Package Holiday Regulations are inapplicable, for example, where no package was booked but only accommodation, and for that reason we begin by noting the common law position.

Common law position

Tour operators are primarily liable for any defects in holidays at common law. Services provided must actually correspond to those offered. Operators may escape liability if they can show that they have used reasonable care and skill in their selection of hotels and carriers. Operators can recover damages from carriers or hoteliers if the problem was their fault.

By an implied term in the holiday contract and by virtue of a common duty of care, tour operators are under a duty to take such steps as are reasonable, taking all the circumstances into account, to avoid exposing their clients to any significant risk of danger or injury to their health including risks arising out of environmental hazards at resorts. The case *Davey* v *Cosmos Air Holidays* 1989 CLY 2561 illustrates this admirably. The Davey family had booked a two week holiday at a Portuguese holiday resort. The resort had severe sewage problems with raw sewage being pumped into the sea a short distance from the beach. This problem had featured in the Portuguese and English press and Cosmos had a representative at the resort. After swimming off the beach at this resort the Davey family all became ill to varying degrees. Some members of the family contracted dysentery; clothes were soiled and the family had a miserable time. Mr Davey sued Cosmos and won. Cosmos were in a position to know about the problems at the resort and should have warned the Daveys about them. The court held that Cosmos were under a duty to take such steps as were reasonable, taking all the circumstances into account, to avoid exposing their clients to any significant risk of danger or injury to their health.

The position under the Package Holiday Regulations

Today, whenever the holiday concerned involves a package, the position will be governed by the Package Holiday Regulations. Briefly the Regulations imply terms into packages that where a significant proportion of the services contracted for are not provided, for example, water sports are not available because of sewage problems at a resort, the tour operator (known as the 'organizer' in the Regulations) must make suitable arrangements at no extra cost to the holidaymaker (known as the 'consumer' in the Regulations) and, where appropriate, compensate the consumer for the difference between the services offered and those actually provided (reg.14). The organizer is made liable to the consumer for the proper performance of the contract even though the obligations are being performed by another person, for example an overseas hotelier (reg.15). There is a defence available that it was due to the fault of a third party unconnected with the provision of the services and was unforeseeable and unavoidable although in cases such as *Davey* the problem certainly was foreseeable (it had been in the Press) and it was avoidable (they could have been offered a holiday at another resort).

HEALTH AND SAFETY LAW

Introduction

This is a vast topic which we cannot hope to do justice to in a work such as this. However, we provide a very brief outline of the law here. As we discussed in Chapter Two (pp. 61–62), originally the common law set out what an employer's duty towards his/her employees was in terms of their health and safety:

> To take reasonable care, and to use reasonable skill, first to provide and maintain proper machinery, plant, appliances and works; secondly, to select properly skilled persons to manage and superintend the business; and thirdly, to provide a proper system of working (*English* v *Wilsons & Clyde Coal Co* 1937 SC(HL) 46).

However, providing workers with a right to compensation was not a great enough incentive to employers to improve health and safety. Therefore Parliament began to intervene in the field with statutes such as the Factories Act 1961 and the Offices, Shops and Railway Premises Act 1963 which set out minimum standards in relation to health, safety and welfare in the workplace. Breach of these Acts gave rise to strict civil liability. The principal legislation is now contained in Regulations made under the Health and Safety at Work etc. Act 1974 (HASAW), which aims to minimize risks to health and safety.

The Health and Safety at Work etc. Act 1974

The HASAW is very much a framework statute. It imposes a general duty on employers to ensure, so far as is reasonably practicable, the health, safety and welfare of their employees (HASAW, s.2) and to carry on their business in such as way that persons who are not employed by them but who might be affected by the carrying on of their business such as visitors and passers-by are not exposed to risks to their health and safety (HASAW, s.3). Employees are also placed under a duty to take reasonable care for their own health and safety and the health and safety of other persons who might be affected by their acts or omissions at work (HASAW, s.7). Since the HASAW is a framework statute it enables Regulations to be made fleshing out the general duties above by imposing particular requirements to minimize risks to health and safety. As we mentioned above the purpose of the HASAW is principally to prevent accidents. This is achieved by making breach of its requirements and of requirements in Regulations made under it a criminal offence. Enforcement of its provisions is carried out by the Health and Safety Executive who tend to avoid prosecution where possible and instead work by persuasion to bring about improvements in health and safety practices at work. Breach of the HASAW itself does not give rise to civil liability (HASAW, s.47(1)(a)). However, as we explain below, breach of Regulations made under the HASAW may give rise to civil liability (HASAW, s.47(2)).

The health and safety revolution

Recently, health and safety legislation has undergone a virtual revolution with the EC passing a number of Directives in the field. These have been implemented in Great Britain by delegated legislation in the form of Regulations made under the HASAW. Safety in the workplace is now regulated under the Management of Health and Safety at Work Regulations 1992, the Workplace (Health, Safety and Welfare) Regulations 1992, the Personal Protective Equipment at Work Regulations 1992, the Health and Safety (Display Screen Equipment) Regulations 1992 and the Manual Handling Operations Regulations 1992. These various regulations came into force in relation to all new workplaces and equipment from 1 January 1993 but did not come into force in relation to existing workplaces and work equipment until 1 January 1997 until which time the Factories Act 1961 and the Offices, Shops and Railway Premises Act 1963 continued to apply. The Regulations seek to impose standards higher than those imposed under the HASAW. Once again, their purpose is preventive, with breach of their provisions giving rise to criminal liability and enforcement being in the hands of the Health and Safety Executive. Breach of the Regulations may also give rise to civil liability by virtue of s.47(2) HASAW.

Inns, innkeepers and their duties, liabilities and rights

9

INTRODUCTION

In this chapter we examine the legal duties, liabilities and rights of persons known in law as innkeepers. A special regime of duties, liabilities and rights has applied to innkeepers since Roman times. The reason for this is that innkeepers were often in league with highwaymen and would often rob guests of their belongings. To improve this situation Roman law imposed strict liability on innkeepers under a provision known as the Praetorian Edict. The law relating to liabilities and rights of innkeepers derives in Scotland from this Roman provision although in England and Wales it derives from custom but has the same effect.

Parliament has now enacted the Hotel Proprietors Act 1956 (HPA) in relation to innkeepers' duties, liabilities and rights. However, the HPA expressly preserved the pre-existing duties, liabilities and rights of the innkeeper deriving as mentioned above from Roman law in Scotland and custom in England and Wales subject to certain modifications which the HPA and certain other legislative provisions have brought about (HPA, s.1(1)).

INNS AND HOTELS

Statutory definition

A hotel within the meaning of the HPA is deemed to be an inn (HPA, s.1(1)). No other establishment is deemed to be an inn. What then is the definition of hotel in the HPA? Section 1(3) of the HPA defines 'hotel' as

> an establishment held out by the proprietor as offering food, drink and, if so required, sleeping accommodation, without special contract, to any traveller presenting himself who appears able and willing to pay a reasonable sum for the services and facilities and who is in a fit state to be received.

Innkeeper

Who then is an innkeeper? The HPA does not define innkeeper but the term is used in relation to the proprietor of a hotel (HPA, s.1(2)). If the proprietor is a company, the innkeeper is the company and not the hotel manager even though the licence for the sale of intoxicating liquor is in the name of the manager (*Dixon* v *Birch* (1873) LR 8 Exch 135). We discuss the licensing system in Chapter Eleven.

Distinguishing inns from other establishments

Establishments which do not fall within the definition of hotel in the HPA are accordingly not hotels and their proprietors are not innkeepers. Clearly, certain types of facilities will not be regarded as inns and hence as hotels in terms of the HPA. These include restaurants, cafes and public houses. In determining whether an establishment is an inn, its name is not conclusive (*Pidgeon* v *Legge* (1857) 21 JP 743). Although the HPA's definition of hotel requires that the establishment offers drink, which is generally understood to be alcoholic drink (*Armstrong* v *Clark* [1957] 2 QB 391), a temperance hotel may be a hotel for the purposes of the HPA (*Cunningham* v *Philp* (1896) 12 TLR 352).

Proprietors of accommodation may seek to deny that they are innkeepers by calling their establishments 'private hotel', 'guest house', 'boarding house' or 'bed and breakfast'. Since the law looks objectively at the actions of a person, it may be that a person seeking to deny that he/she is an innkeeper by using one of these designations would not succeed. However, many such establishments are undoubtedly not inns. For example, a public house may be a hotel but the law assumes it not to be since it normally holds a licence for the sale of intoxicating liquor but does not offer sleeping accommodation for travellers who wished to stay there (*Collis* v *Selden* (1868) 37 LJCP 233). The proprietor of a boarding or lodging house is likewise not regarded as an innkeeper since he/she does not hold herself out to receive all persons but normally makes a specific contract for a set period such as a week or a month (*Thompson* v *Lacy* (1820) 3 B & Ald 283). The fact that an establishment keeps a register is not conclusive evidence that it is an hotel in terms of the HPA since the Immigration (Hotel Records) Order 1972 applies both to inns and other establishments.

If a person is not an innkeeper in law, their duties, rights and liabilities differ from those of the innkeeper. We discuss the duties, liabilities and rights of proprietors of establishments which are not inns at the end of this chapter (see pp. 237–238). You should also note that certain laws such as health and safety, consumer protection, occupier's liability apply to both innkeepers and proprietors of establishments such as guest houses which are not inns.

INNKEEPERS' DUTIES

To whom are an innkeeper's duties owed?

You will recall that the HPA states that a hotel is

an establishment held out by the proprietor as offering food, drink and, if so required, sleeping accommodation, without special contract, to any traveller presenting himself . . . (HPA, s.1(1)).

An innkeeper's duties are therefore owed only to travellers. Who then is a traveller? Whether a person is a traveller is essentially a question of fact (*Lamond* v *Richard* [1897] 1 QB 541, CA). Length of stay is not conclusive but is one factor to be taken into consideration. Length of journey is also not conclusive as a very short journey will be sufficient as was the case in *Williams* v *Linnitt* [1951] 1 KB 565. In that case a farmer who was a local resident called at an inn for refreshment but not accommodation. He was held to be a traveller by the court even though he was only at the inn for temporary refreshment. If a person stays at a hotel for a lengthy period they may cease to be a traveller and the innkeeper may refuse to provide accommodation and refreshment any longer and may ask them to leave after giving reasonable notice (*Lamond* v *Richard* above). In that case Mrs Lamond stayed at a hotel from November 1895 to August 1896. In August she was given notice to quit but did not do so and while she was out her luggage was packed and she was refused access to her room on her return. Although she claimed she had a right to stay at the hotel since other rooms were free the court held the hotel's action to be lawful since she had ceased to be a traveller.

A friend of the innkeeper staying at the hotel is not a traveller (*Cayle's Case* (1584) 8 Co Rep 32a) but a person staying with a traveller by arrangement with the innkeeper is also regarded as a traveller (*Cryan* v *Hotel Rembrandt Ltd* (1925) 133 LT 395).

Duty to receive

Introduction

In contrast to a shopkeeper who by placing goods in a window with or without their prices only makes an invitation to treat and does not make an offer (see Chapter Two, pp. 39–40), a person who is an innkeeper makes a continuous offer of accommodation. The duty is to receive and lodge in the inn all travellers and to entertain them at reasonable prices without any special or previous contract unless there is some reasonable ground for refusing to do so (see pp. 230–231). An innkeeper cannot fulfil the duty by offering accommodation at another hotel as was done in *Constantine* v *Imperial Hotels Ltd* [1944] KB 693 where the famous West Indian cricketer, Sir Learie Constantine, was refused accommodation at the Imperial Hotel because he was black but instead offered accommodation at the Bedford Hotel. The court held that an innkeeper owes separate duties to travellers at each inn which he/she controls.

Scope of the duty

Although the innkeeper must provide accommodation if requested, subject to the reasonable grounds for refusal discussed below, a traveller does not have the right to insist on accommodation in a particular room (*Fell* v *Knight* (1841) 8 M & W 269, a case in which a traveller wished to sit up all night in a room upstairs, but was offered a room downstairs). Furthermore, the innkeeper is only bound to provide such reasonable and proper accommodation for the traveller and any luggage and goods as they in fact possess. This is illustrated by *Winkworth* v *Raven* [1931] 1 KB 652 where a court held that an innkeeper was not bound to provide a frost-proof garage for a guest's car. What amounts to reasonable accommodation is a question of fact in each case. There is no duty to receive a traveller's goods alone where he/she does not come to the inn for refreshment or accommodation although the court held in the old case *York* v *Grindstone (Grenhaugh)* (1703) Salk (6th Edn) 388 that an innkeeper was obliged to look after a traveller's horse in such circumstances but not any trunk or dead thing.

The duty extends to receiving all the goods with which the traveller normally travels (*Broadwood* v *Granara* (1854) 10 Exch 417) or their luggage (*Robins & Co* v *Gray* [1895] 2 QB 501). This is the case even if the luggage does not belong to the traveller. Only if the luggage or goods are of an exceptional character would that enable an innkeeper to refuse to receive them. An innkeeper has historically been bound to receive a traveller's horse (*Stanyon* v *Davis* (1704) 6 Mod Rep 223) in the inn's stables and to feed it. Where no stables are available or the stables are full, this would be a reasonable excuse for refusing to receive a traveller's horse (*Thompson* v *Lacy* (1820) 3 B & Ald 283). This duty is obviously not of great significance today but it has been held that an innkeeper is now under a duty to receive a traveller's motor car where facilities are available (*Gresham* v *Lyon* [1954] 2 All ER 786). However, there is no need to provide special garaging for a car as we saw in the case *Winkworth* v *Raven* (above).

When can an innkeeper refuse to receive a guest?

An innkeeper is not under a duty to receive a traveller when all the bedrooms of the inn are full (*Medawar* v *Grand Hotel Co.* [1891] 2 QB 11). An innkeeper is also within his/her rights to refuse to allow a traveller to sleep in one of the public rooms of the inn when all the bedrooms are full. This was held to be the case in *Browne* v *Brandt* [1902] 1 KB 696 where a motorist whose car had broken down came to an inn in the early hours of the morning and was refused permission to sleep in a public room since all the bedrooms were full. Furthermore, an innkeeper may refuse to provide accommodation where the traveller is not in a fit state to be received, for example, because he/she is drunk (*Thompson* v *McKenzie* [1908] 1 KB 905), or where the traveller is not suitably dressed, as in *Pidgeon* v *Legge* (1857) 21 JP 743 which involved a chimney sweep in his working clothes, or where the traveller behaves inappropriately (*Rothfield* v *North British Railway Railway Co.*1920 SC 805). The Scottish case *Rothfield* v *North British Railway Railway Co.* involved a moneylender of German origin staying in what was then the North British Hotel in Edinburgh during and after the First World War. He was removed from the hotel because his behaviour in seeking business at the hotel was offending guests. Furthermore, British Army officers staying at the hotel objected to his presence. Although it is undoubtedly the case that inappropriate behaviour is a ground either for not receiving a traveller or for removing him/her from the hotel, there are special circumstances present in the *Rothfield* case which make it a somewhat unreliable authority. These circumstances were that the case displays considerable anti-German sentiment as a result of the war and indeed some anti-Semitism as Rothfield was a German Jew.

An innkeeper, however, cannot refuse to receive a traveller simply because he/she arrives very late (*R* v *Ivens* (1835) 7 C & P 213) or because the traveller wants to sit up all night (*Fell* v *Knight* (1841) 8 M & W 269). *R* v *Ivens* (above) also indicates that an innkeeper cannot refuse to receive a traveller because he/she refuses to supply his/her name and address although this rule has now been modified by legislation. The Immigration (Hotel Records) Order 1972, SI 1972/1689 requires innkeepers providing accommodation for payment to require that any person staying at the premises must sign a statement as to their nationality and, in the case of an alien, must provide their name, nationality, date of arrival, passport number and last address although it is not required that the person's passport be produced for inspection. These records must be kept for a period of 12 months. Interestingly it is not an offence to provide a false name!

Although the old case *R* v *Luellin* (1701) 12 Mod Rep 445 suggests that illness of a traveller is not a sufficient ground for refusing to receive them, the position has once again been modified by legislation. In the case of a notifiable disease (cholera, plague, relapsing fever, smallpox or typhus) a justice of the peace may order a person suffering from such a disease to be removed by a local authority officer to a hospital (Public Health (Control of Disease) Act 1984, ss 10 and 37). Section 17 of this statute makes it an offence for a person who knows they are suffering from a notifiable disease to expose other persons to the risk of infection by their presence or conduct and for a person to have such a person in their care.

Before the advent of anti-discrimination legislation it had been held unlawful to turn away a person on the basis of skin colour as we saw in *Constantine* v *Imperial Hotels Ltd* (above). However, statute now provides that the duty to receive travellers applies regardless of their sex or race (Sex Discrimination Act 1975, ss 2(1), 29(1), (2)(b),(e); Race Relations Act 1976, s.20(1),(2)(b),(e)) and so would form the basis of such an action today. We discuss the issue of discrimination more fully in Chapter Seven.

Duty to provide refreshment

An innkeeper is under a duty to provide refreshment at common law to travellers. The duty is to provide reasonable refreshment at any time of the day or night. The use of the word reasonable suggests the flexible nature of the duty. It does not require an innkeeper to lay on three course meals at all times of the day and night. As long as an innkeeper provides reasonable refreshments such as sandwiches at other times, it would be perfectly acceptable to offer such meals at certain times of the day only. Hence it is our view that a traveller calling at a hotel in the early hours of the morning cannot expect to be provided with a three course dinner but will be entitled to something which is reasonable at that hour such as sandwiches. Furthermore a traveller stopping for temporary refreshment would only be entitled to alcoholic drinks during licensing hours.

The duty to provide reasonable refreshment also means that there is no duty on innkeepers to provide refreshment which they do not have available in the inn. So they need not send out for further supplies. They may also place the needs of guests, that is those travellers staying at the inn, above those of travellers simply stopping for refreshment only. The case *R* v *Higgins* [1948] 1 KB 165, CA illustrates this point. A family arrived at an inn on a Sunday lunchtime and asked for a meal. Although tables were available in the restaurant the innkeeper refused to provide them with a meal. Instead he offered them sandwiches on the grounds that he had a limited supply of food which was needed for existing guests' Sunday evening meal and Monday breakfast. The court held that there was a duty to provide refreshment but that the innkeeper could refuse if there was a reasonable excuse. They held that it could be a reasonable excuse if limited supplies of food were available, and there was no requirement to send out for additional supplies to satisfy the demands of travellers. The court also took the view that the supplies which were available could be reserved for existing guests. On the facts, the innkeeper had a reasonable excuse for refusing to serve the travellers. This decision does not appear to encourage good management since it suggests that an incompetent innkeeper who has allowed food stocks to run down will have a reasonable excuse for not providing travellers with a meal. One judge in the case also observed that there was no reason why an innkeeper could not operate a system of prior booking for meals and that it did not breach the requirement to provide refreshment without prior contract. However, we think it likely that if a hotel operated a prior booking system for meals and refused to provide a traveller who had not booked with any refreshment, the duty would be breached. In order to avoid this, light meal or snack menus are commonly available in bars or lounges in the hotel.

An innkeeper might also refuse service if the traveller is not in a fit state to be received or if they appear unwilling to pay a reasonable sum. This is used by innkeepers to regulate standards of clientele. However, it cannot be used to enforce a discriminatory approach to travellers on the grounds of gender or race as this would breach the requirements of the Sex Discrimination Act 1975 (s.29) and the Race Relations Act 1976 (s.20). If a traveller insists upon bringing a dog (or other animal) into the inn the innkeeper may reasonably refuse to serve the traveller. For example, in *R* v *Rymer* [1877] 2 QBD 136 a traveller wanted to bring a muzzled mastiff into the inn but the innkeeper was held to be justified in refusing to serve the traveller as the dog was unhygienic and a potential source of alarm and annoyance to other guests.

Liability for guests' safety

The innkeeper is under a duty to take reasonable care of travellers who are guests so that they are not harmed by anything happening to them through the innkeeper's or his/her employees' negligence while they are guests. The duty, formerly a matter of common law (*Sandys* v *Florence* (1878) 47 LJQB 598) is now governed by the occupiers' liability legislation (Occupiers' Liability Act 1957; Occupiers' Liability Act 1984; Occupiers' Liability (Scotland) Act 1960). We discuss the occupiers' liability legislation in some detail in Chapter Two (see pp. 63–65). The duty is not absolute and certainly does not extend to every part of the hotel. It would only extend to where the guest might reasonably be expected to go. In *Campbell* v *Shelbourne Hotel Ltd* [1939] 2 KB 534, a guest who fell and injured himself in an unlit passage at a reasonable hour recovered damages. The passage was one which a guest might reasonably be expected to use. Likewise, a guest who was injured during a fire alarm recovered damages as he had not been shown the layout of the hotel (*MacLenan* v *Segar* [1917] 2 KB 325). However, where a guest sought out a toilet, ignoring one which was clearly marked for guests' use, and was killed after falling down a lift shaft, the court held that the hotel had not been negligent (*Walker* v *Midland Railway Co.* (1886) 55 LT 489). Similarly in *Bell* v *Travco Hotels Ltd* [1953] 1 QB 473, a guest who fell on a slippery driveway leading to a hotel and injured her ankle was unable to recover damages as the court held that the hotel had taken reasonable care in relation to the driveway. *Ward* v *Ritz Hotel*, The Independent, 21 May, 1992 provides a more recent example of such a case brought under the Occupiers' Liability Act 1957. The case involved a guest at a lunch party at the Ritz Hotel being injured after falling over 25 feet on to an iron staircase and concrete floor. He had been leaning against a balustrade, the height of which had been reduced after alterations were made to the adjacent floor. The Court of Appeal found in favour of the injured guest by a majority. They attached considerable weight to the fact that the balustrade was below the level recommended by British Safety Standards. The duty is owed to guests but not to personal guests of the innkeeper or employees (*Indermaur* v *Dames* (1866) 35 LJCP 184). We discuss employers' duty towards their employees in Chapter Two (see pp. 61–62). For example, in *Southcote* v *Stanley* (1856) 1 H & N 247 an innkeeper's personal guest was injured as he opened a door which was in a dangerous condition. He was unable to recover damages in his capacity as the innkeeper's guest.

Liability for guests' property

Introduction

The liability of an innkeeper for loss or damage to travellers' property is very old although today it is contained in the HPA. The origin of innkeepers' liability differs in England and Scotland. In England it is said to depend on custom (*Cayle's Case* (1584) 8 Co Rep 32a whereas in Scotland it depends on Roman law in the Praetorian Edict: Dig. IV,9,1 '*Nautae, caupones, stabularii, quod cuiusque salvum fore receperint, nisi restituant, in eos judicium dabo*'. (I will give judgment against those . . . innkeepers . . . who receive a guest's property safe if they do not restore it to the guest). The innkeeper is strictly liable for loss or damage to guests' property. Strict liability means that there is no need to demonstrate negligence on the part of the innkeeper or his/her employees. The liability attaches only to innkeepers and not to owners of other establishments such as guest houses or restaurants (*Ultzen* v *Nicols* [1894] 1 QB 92). For liability of proprietors of other establishments see pp. 237–238.

When does the duty arise?

Without prejudice to any other ground of liability, the innkeeper is only liable to make good loss or damage to the property of a traveller for whom at the time of the loss or damage sleeping accommodation had been engaged, and where the loss or damage occurred during the period commencing with the midnight immediately preceding, and ending with the midnight immediately following, a period for which the traveller was a guest at the hotel and entitled to use such accommodation (HPA, s.2(1)). Thus the rule applies only in the case of those who have engaged accommodation, not simply travellers stopping for temporary refreshment.

Scope of the innkeeper's duty

The innkeeper's liability extends to the making good to any guest of any damage to property brought to the hotel, as well as loss of such property (HPA, s.1(2)). It is irrelevant if the goods are stolen by burglars or by the innkeeper's employees or by another guest. However, if the goods are lost by the guest herself, the innkeeper is not liable (*Robins & Co.* v *Gray* [1895] 2 QB 501, CA). Furthermore, if the goods are stolen by a guest's companion or employee, the innkeeper is not liable as the very old *Cayle's Case* (1584) 8 Co Rep 32a illustrates.

We now need to define more clearly what is actually encompassed by the term 'inn'. Does it, for example, include adjoining car parks or is it simply the buildings of the inn? The innkeeper's liability applies for any loss or theft of goods or damage to them within what is known as the hospitium of the inn. The hospitium of an inn consists of all the buildings of the inn and those precincts which are so closely related to them that they are to be treated as forming part of the inn, such as a hotel car park (*Williams* v *Linnit* [1951] 1 KB 565). In *Williams* v *Linnit* stable buildings and garages annexed to an inn, inner courts enclosed by its walls and car parks were held to be within the hospitium of an inn. The case indicated that the test to be applied to determine whether an area was within the hospitium of an inn is whether the place is a part of the inn premises and suitable for use in connection with the innkeeper's business.

However, the scope of the innkeeper's liability has been restricted by the HPA. The innkeeper's liability no longer extends to the loss of or damage to any vehicle or property left inside it or any horse or other live animal or its harness or equipment within the hospitium of the inn (HPA, s.2(2)). However, this does not mean that an innkeeper will not be liable for such loss at all: it simply means that he/she cannot be liable under innkeeper's strict liability. The innkeeper may well be liable if the loss or damage was caused by his/her negligence or the negligence of one of his/her employees.

Defences

Although liability is strict, it is not absolute as the innkeeper may rely on one of three defences. These are: where the loss or damage was caused by either:

1. an act of God, which would include severe weather such as a gale blowing off the hotel's roof,
2. an act of the Queen's enemies, which would encompass war damage, although probably not terrorist damage, or:
3. negligent behaviour by the guest. There has been a considerable number of cases on loss or damage caused by the guest's negligence.

For example, where a guest left money lying around in a place where others could not fail to see it, that was evidence of negligence (*Armistead* v *Wilde* (1851) 17 QB 261). However, where a guest left a diamond ring in an unlocked jewel case in her bedroom but locked the bedroom door and the ring and jewel case were subsequently stolen, there was no negligence as she had taken reasonable care (*Carpenter* v *Haymarket Hotel Ltd* [1931] 1 KB 364). Leaving a bedroom door unlocked is not necessarily evidence of negligence especially where the hotel itself wishes rooms to be left open for cleaning. Thus, in *Shacklock* v *Ethorpe Ltd* [1939] 3 All ER 372, HL, where a woman left jewellery and money in a locked jewel box inside a locked case but left the room open as she knew the hotel wished the doors left open for room cleaning and the case was stolen by another guest, the hotel was held to be liable.

Limitation of liability

The proprietor may also limit his/her liability as an innkeeper to £50 for any one article or £100 in the aggregate, provided that at the time when the property in question was brought to the hotel a notice in statutory form (see HPA, Sched.) was conspicuously displayed in a place where it could conveniently be read by the guests at or near the reception desk or, if there was no reception desk, at or near the main entrance. In *Shacklock* v *Ethorpe Ltd* [1937] 4 All ER 672, which reached the House of Lords on another issue, the court held (in relation to earlier innkeepers' legislation) that the requirements of the legislation had been met by the display of the notice in a corridor above a glass case about six feet from the ground. If the notice is somehow misprinted, this will mean that the innkeeper's liability is not limited, even if the misprint is unintentional (*Spice* v *Bacon* (1877) 2 ExD 643, CA).

The limits have not been raised since the passing of the HPA and are clearly somewhat unrealistic today. Given that they are laid down in statute and given that innkeeper's liability for the loss or damage to guests' property does not depend on contract, we do not consider that the Unfair Contract Terms Act 1977 would apply (see Chapter Two, pp. 45–47). Parliament would need to legislate if the limits are to be revised upwards.

The limits do not apply where:

1. the loss or damage was caused by the default, neglect or wilful act of the proprietor or an employee (*Kott and Kott* v *Gordon Hotels* [1968] 2 Ll.Rep.228);
2. the property was deposited expressly for safe custody; or
3. if not so deposited, it had been offered for deposit and refused, or if not so offered, where the guest wishing to offer it for deposit was unable to do so through the default of the proprietor or his/her servant (HPA, s.2(3)).

In the Scottish House of Lords case, *Whitehouse* v *Pickett* [1908] AC 357, HL; 1908 SC (HL) 31, the court held under the Innkeepers' Liability Act 1863 that in order to satisfy the condition that the property has been 'deposited expressly' the fact of the deposit must be definitely brought to the innkeeper's notice, and that where there is no such express deposit the onus of proof of fault or neglect on the part of the innkeeper lies on the guest. In *Whitehouse* the court held that it was not enough for a guest to place a bag containing valuables (which he did not disclose as such) in the hotel office even though he had done this on many previous occasions.

Enforcement of liabilities

Civil law

If an innkeeper refuses without lawful excuse to receive a traveller he/she will be liable to a civil action. The claim should be made against the defendant as a common innkeeper. The action is not based on a breach of contract but the innkeeper will be civilly liable in damages. Additional civil remedies are provided where the refusal is based on grounds of sex or race (Sex Discrimination Act 1975, ss 66–71; Race Relations Act 1976, ss 57–62; see Chapter Seven, p. 176).

Where a traveller has sustained harm while staying at the inn as a guest or while partaking of refreshment in the inn, a civil action in negligence will lie against the innkeeper.

Where a guest wishes to sue in relation to loss or damage to property, an action should be brought against the innkeeper and the plaintiff should plead that the defendant is the proprietor of what was at all material times an inn.

Criminal law

Refusal to receive a guest without lawful excuse will also render an innkeeper criminally liable on indictment at common law in England and Wales (*R* v *Ivens* (1835) 7 C & P 213; *R* v *Higgins* [1948] 1 KB 165).

INNKEEPERS' RIGHTS

Contractual rights

Although innkeepers' contractual rights are modified to the extent that they must receive travellers and provide accommodation and refreshment for them unless they have a lawful excuse (see above), their contractual rights to payment are otherwise similar to those of proprietors of other establishments except that they have a right to demand payment in advance (*Mulliner* v *Florence* (1878) 3 QBD 484). This is because they are only under a duty to receive travellers who 'appear able and willing to pay a reasonable sum for the services and facilities provided' (HPA, s.1(3)). If a traveller insists upon their right to stay at an inn, they must tender a reasonable sum in advance. We discuss the law of contract in Chapter Two (see pp. 37–54).

Lien for unpaid bills

If a guest fails to pay the bill for accommodation or for food and drink, an innkeeper has what is known as a lien over the guest's luggage or property. A lien is a right to retain property to the value of the unpaid bill and is a way of exerting pressure on a guest to pay the bill. The Scottish case *Ferguson* v *Peterkin* 1953 SLT (Sh Ct) 91 suggests that the right of lien is not available to cover the value of damage caused by a guest during their stay.

The right only extends to property brought by the guest within the hospitium of the inn (on the meaning of hospitium, see p. 234 above) and does not extend to detaining the guest or the clothes which they are wearing (*Sunbolf* v *Alford* (1838) 3 M & W 248). Certain property of the guest is also excluded from the innkeeper's right of lien by statute. Section 2(2) of the HPA states that lien does not extend to 'any vehicle or any property left therein, or any horse or other live animal or its harness or other equipment'. This reflects the fact that an innkeeper's liability no longer extends to cover vehicles and their contents and horses etc. (see p. 234). *Mulliner* v *Florence* (above) indicates that where a married couple go to an inn, a wife's luggage may be subject to the innkeeper's lien even though the unpaid bill is in the husband's name. The right of lien also extends to goods which have been hired by a guest and are brought with her at the time she is received by the innkeeper, as *Threfall* v *Borwick* (1875) LR 10 QB 210, Ex Ch, which involved a hired piano, illustrates. However, *Broadwood* v *Granara* (1854) 10 Ex. 417, which also involved a hired piano, indicates that the right of lien does not cover goods hired with the knowledge of the innkeeper during a guest's stay at the inn as this would be contrary to good faith. Furthermore, property owned by a third party which is brought to the inn for a guest, may be subject to the right of lien even if it was stolen by the guest (*Marsh* v *Police Commissioner* [1945] KB 43).

The lien continues only so long as the innkeeper actually has control over the goods (*Jones* v *Pearle* (1723) 1 Stra 557). The innkeeper has a duty to take reasonable care of the property retained under the right of lien.

Right of sale of goods

In order to realize the value of the property retained under the right of lien, innkeepers have a right of sale under the Innkeepers Act 1878. Under s.1 of this statute an innkeeper is entitled, after advertisement, to sell by auction goods brought to or left in the inn, provided that a debt for board and lodging, or for the keep of any horse, shall have been outstanding for six weeks. The innkeeper is entitled to recoup the expenses of the auction. The innkeeper must account to the guest for any surplus raised by the auction.

DUTIES, LIABILITIES AND RIGHTS OF PROPRIETORS OF HOTELS ETC. WHICH ARE NOT INNS

Receiving guests

Whereas an innkeeper has a duty to receive all travellers, the proprietor of a private hotel, guest house, boarding house or similar establishment may choose between travellers, subject obviously to the law on discrimination. This means that the proprietor could, for example, put up notices indicating that children or coach parties are not accepted.

Liability for guests' personal safety

The position of proprietors of establishments which do not qualify as inns is in fact the same as for innkeepers and depends on occupiers' liability legislation (see above, pp. 232–233).

Liability for loss or damage to guests' property

Whereas an innkeeper incurs liability for loss or damage to a traveller's property, although only where that person has engaged accommodation, the proprietor of an establishment which is not an inn incurs no liability unless he/she or the staff are negligent or unless he/she has accepted liability under the terms of the contract with the guest (*Scarborough* v *Cosgrove* [1905] 2 KB 805; *Olley* v *Marlborough Court Ltd* [1949] 1 KB 532). It is unlikely that such a proprietor could exclude liability by means of an exemption clause in the contract because of the Unfair Contract Terms Act 1977 but he/she could certainly seek to limit liability (see Chapter Two, pp. 42–47).

Rights over guests' property

Finally, whereas the innkeeper has a right of lien over the goods of guests, the proprietor of an establishment which is not an inn has none, subject in England and Wales to the provisions of the Torts (Interference with Goods) Act 1977 whereby a bailee may sell goods bailed with him/her in order to secure payment of the bill.

Food safety 10

INTRODUCTION

History and development of food safety law

In the UK there has been a long history of legislation on food safety and quality remarkably illustrated by the Assize of Bread and Ale which was passed for the protection of the public in 1266 – only two hundred years after the Norman Conquest! Further legislation followed down through the ages and the law has essentially developed around five main elements of protection:

- protection of the consumer – health;
- protection of the consumer – quality;
- protection of the honest trader;
- encouraging freedom of choice; and
- promoting fair competition.

However, the emphasis given to each of these has varied according to the ethos of the era.

During the nineteenth century a wider selection of foods became available, production techniques were developed and improving scientific knowledge enabled elementary chemical analysis of the content of food to be developed. In addition, there was at this time considerable adulteration of food, often with drastic consequences. One Scottish writer, Francis McManus, in an article entitled *'Unfit Food'* (1996 JLSS 105), mentions various alarming additives used in food production, such as strychnine in rum, lead chromate in mustard, lead in wine and cider and red lead to enhance the colour of cheese. As you will appreciate the cumulative effect of these substances was often fatal. Consequently, new legislation was passed controlling the content of foodstuffs with the general aim of protecting the public.

The Sale of Food and Drugs Act 1875 is generally considered to be the forerunner of modern food protection legislation. During the twentieth century there has been considerable legislative activity seeking to keep pace with advances in food production and consumer expectation. This led to piecemeal development of the law and difficulty in identifying the law as it was contained in various statutes. Attempts to consolidate the law into one statute were made in 1928, 1938 and again in 1956 but were rapidly overtaken as the need for further legislation was identified covering such matters as composition and labelling of food and legal controls on its preparation, advertisement and sale.

A further attempt at consolidation was made in the Food Act 1984, but again this legislation did not fully address the need for a modern application of the law to take account of the rapid advances being made in technology of food production. Even as the 1984 Act was being passed, the Government announced a review of food legislation. Extensive consultations were held with the food industry and Environmental Health Departments who were responsible for enforcement of the law. The Government recognized that any new law would require to take account of two recent developments: (1) the increasing influence of the laws of the European Community on national law and (2) increasing consumer expectation of protection from all risks. We shall mention the EC influence later. First of all we focus on consumer protection, the increasing importance of which was reflected in the title of the Government White Paper published in 1989: *Food Safety – Protecting the Consumer.*

The result of the 1989 White Paper was the Food Safety Act 1990 (FSA) which received Royal Assent on 29 June 1990. Instead of simply consolidating earlier laws as its predecessors had, the Act established a new regime for the implementation and enforcement of all aspects of the law relating to food production and sale. In doing so, it avoided the earlier practice of having separate legislation for Scotland and so the Act applies to England, Wales and Scotland. To enable the law to keep pace with future developments, including requirements arising under the law of the European Community, it delegates to Ministers powers to pass supplementary legislation on specified topics.

Scope of the chapter

In this chapter, we examine the FSA in some detail. First, we discuss the scope of, and definitions contained in, the FSA and explain which authorities are responsible for its enforcement. Then we consider the requirement for the registration of food premises and outline the various enforcement powers available to the enforcement authorities. In the context of emergency provisions we also outline powers which are available under the Food and Environment Protection Act 1985. We then discuss various offences which are created by the FSA, both in relation to food safety and consumer protection. After that we look at the defences which are available to a person charged with these offences, before outlining the penalties imposed by the legislation. The chapter concludes with a look at the current and future developments in food safety law, discussing topics such as the recent E-coli and BSE/CJD outbreaks.

THE FOOD SAFETY ACT 1990 (FSA): SCOPE, DEFINITIONS AND ENFORCEMENT BODIES

General introduction

The FSA establishes a system of administrative regulation whereby local authorities are made responsible for ensuring that food businesses comply with the requirements of the Act. Food businesses are required to register with local authorities. Local authority officers are given extensive enforcement powers to inspect premises and deal with contraventions of the FSA. Compliance is mainly achieved by means of four principal offences which carry severe penalties. Part II of the FSA creates four main offences under the headings 'Food Safety' and 'Consumer Protection'. There are two food safety offences which involve (1) rendering food injurious to health (FSA, s.7); and (2) the sale of food which does not meet food safety requirements by being unfit for human consumption (FSA, s.8). The consumer protection offences are (1) sale of food not of the nature, substance or quality demanded by the purchaser (FSA, s.14); and (2) falsely advertising, describing or presenting food (FSA, s.15). This last provision is designed in part to implement the EC Food Labelling Directive (79/112/EEC). The consumer protection provisions are intended to offer general protection to the public against unscrupulous traders. All these offences are based mainly upon the offences in earlier legislation but have been tightened up in the light of experience and in particular case law. Breach of any of the provisions is a criminal offence potentially carrying substantial penalties as we shall see later. We discuss these four offences in more detail on pp. 247–252.

As part of the overall scheme of protection envisaged under the FSA, ss 16–19 give the Secretary of State wide ranging powers to make regulations regarding all aspects of food production. These may in particular relate to (under s.16): the composition of food; the fitness of food for human consumption; the processing and treatment of food; the marking, presenting and advertising of food; and inspection of food related premises.

Special provision is made in s.17 for ministers to make regulations to ensure compliance with EC provisions.

Section 18 provides for the control of 'novel' foods. This has been of particular interest in relation to two matters of recent controversy: genetically engineered food production, and the promotion of novelty foods as supposed slimming aids. Provision for regulation of the production of milk is also made in s.18 (2).

Many regulations have been made by ministers in terms of the FSA and provision was also made for regulations made under pre-existing legislation to remain in force.

Scope of the FSA

The whole thrust of the FSA is to cover (1) all types of food, whatever the source, (2) all premises connected with food preparation, production or sale and (3) all persons, including bodies corporate involved in the food business in any way. This is highlighted in s.2 where the FSA is stated to cover food which is given away or offered as a prize or reward, provided it is in the course of a trade or a business. The key provision is that the food or food source must be from a trade or a business. Thus, for example, food purchased at a church fete would not be covered by the FSA.

Definitions

Introduction

Having reached this point in the chapter you may already be asking yourself a number of questions: What counts as food? What is a food business? The FSA contains answers to these questions in certain important definitions. The key ones are contained in s.1.

Food

The definition of 'food' encompasses drink, including bottled water, but not tap water which is covered by the Water Industry Act 1991 in England and Wales and the Water (Scotland) Act 1980 in Scotland. It also includes articles and substances of no nutritional value which are used for human consumption, chewing gum, and all articles and substances of 'food' (FSA, s.1(1)). Specifically it does not include live animals, birds, or fish which are not used for human consumption while they are alive; feeding stuffs for animals, birds or fish; controlled drugs and medicines (FSA, s.1(2)).

Food source

'Food source' means any growing crop or live animal, bird or fish from which food is intended to be derived (whether by harvesting, slaughtering, milking, collecting eggs or otherwise) (FSA, s.1(3)).

Food business

'Food business' is defined as any business in the course of which commercial operations with respect to food or food sources are carried out. The terms 'business and commercial operation' suggest a profit making element but the FSA specifically includes potential non profit-making operations such as canteens, clubs, schools, hospitals or institutions (FSA, s.1(3)).

Food premises

'Food premises' are any premises used for the purpose of a food business, 'premises' includes any vehicle, stall or movable structure and any ship or aircraft (FSA, s.1(3)).

Contact material

'Contact material' is any article or substance which is intended to come into contact with food (FSA, s.1(3)).

Commercial operation

Finally, 'commercial operation' in relation to any food or contact material, means any of the following, namely:

1. selling, possessing for sale and offering, exposing or advertising for sale;
2. consigning, delivering or serving by way of sale;
3. preparing for sale or presenting, labelling or wrapping for the purpose of sale;
4. storing or transporting for the purpose of sale;
5. importing and exporting;

and in relation to any food source, means deriving food from it for the purpose of sale or for purposes connected with sale (FSA, s.1(3)).

Bodies responsible for supervision and enforcement of the FSA

We have already briefly mentioned that local authorities are responsible for ensuring compliance with the requirements of the FSA. Section 5 of the FSA gives enforcement powers to the food authority for each area. In England and Wales, this will be the appropriate district, unitary or metropolitan borough council for the area. In Scotland the local authority will be one of the new 'unitary' authorities which were created by the Local Government etc. (Scotland) Act 1994, with effect from 1 April 1996.

The supervision of the FSA is carried out by authorized local authority officers (FSA, s.5(6)). In practice these are primarily environmental health officers and trading standards officers.

We discuss the various enforcement powers which local authorities may exercise under the FSA below at pp. 244–246.

REQUIREMENT FOR REGISTRATION OF FOOD PREMISES

Importantly s.19 of the FSA provides for the licensing of all food premises. The Secretary of State is given the power, under this section, to make regulations for the registration and licensing of food premises. Regulations can be made to allow local authorities to register premises which are currently used, or are proposed to be used, for the purposes of a food business and for prohibiting the use for those purposes of any premises which are not registered under the regulations (FSA, s.19(1)(a)). The Secretary of State can also make regulations which allow the authorities to issue licences for premises which are used as food businesses and again to prohibit the use for these purposes of any premises except in accordance with a licence issued under the regulations (FSA, s.19(1)(b)). Regulations in respect of such licences may only be made, however, if the Secretary of State is satisfied that they are necessary or expedient, either to ensure that food complies with food safety requirements or in the interests of the public health, or for the purpose of protecting or promoting the interests of consumers (FSA, s.19(2)).

The Food Premises (Registration) Regulations 1991 were made under s.19 of the FSA and require both existing and proposed food businesses to be registered with the local food authority. New businesses must register at least 28 days before they begin trading. Registration is a simple procedure, involving one form and no fee. There is no need to renew registration. A fine may, however, be imposed on any food business which does not comply with the registration process.

Not every food business needs to be registered. Exceptions to the registration requirement include retail sales by vending machine and businesses which operate for less than five days in any five week period. The Food Premises (Registration) Amendment Regulations 1997 exempt domestic premises used for a food business where the proprietor resides at those premises and the only commercial food operation is preparing food to be sold from a market stall run by WI County Markets Limited. Existing records need only be altered at the request of such a food business proprietor.

Codes of Practice (a form of soft law discussed in Chapter One, pp. 10–11) can be issued under s.40 of the FSA. These give guidance on the enforcement of the registration regulations. These Codes have, however, been criticized for giving powers which are too weak to enforce the FSA provisions effectively.

Although s.19 of the FSA allows regulations to be made requiring licences for food premises, no such regulations have been made. It is not therefore possible to refuse or withdraw permission to operate a food business on a licence-based system, such as that maintained for businesses selling alcoholic liquor (see Chapter Eleven). The system has been criticized as hopelessly ineffective. We would argue that a licence-based system which requires applicants to be fit and proper persons as is the case with applicants for liquor licences (see Chapter Eleven) or waste management licences (see Chapter Eight) would provide a more effective means of regulating food safety. Under the existing system there is not even a requirement to intimate the closure or transfer of a business with the result that it is impossible to have an accurate record of food premises in operation.

ENFORCEMENT POWERS

Introduction

Although the system of registration of food premises is somewhat ineffective, a considerable range of enforcement powers is available to the local authority officers charged with responsibility for enforcing the FSA. These include powers to inspect and seize suspect food, powers to serve improvement or prohibition notices, powers to take emergency action and ultimately a battery of criminal sanctions. Given the importance of the latter we discuss them in detail at pp. 247–252.

Inspection and seizure of suspect food

An authorized officer may at all reasonable times inspect any food which is intended for human consumption and if the officer believes the food to be unsafe, he/she is empowered either to serve a notice preventing its sale for human consumption and its removal, or to take the food immediately before a justice of the peace to request an order for its destruction (FSA, s.9). The reference to a justice of the peace includes a reference to a magistrate and, in Scotland, a sheriff.

The notice may be given if the officer reasonably believes the food not to comply with food safety requirements (FSA, s.9(1)). This is therefore a preliminary stage before any definite judgment is made. Thereafter, the officer is required to establish whether or not the food does in fact comply with the food safety requirements and to do so, as soon as is reasonably practicable, and in any event within 21 days (FSA, s.9(4)(a)). If it has transpired that the food is in fact safe the notice must be withdrawn at once (FSA, s.9(4)(a)). If it is established that the food is unsafe the officer must seize it and remove it to enable it to be dealt with by a justice of the peace (FSA, s.9(4)(b)).

Once the food is seized, the person who was in charge of it must be notified of the officer's intention to place the matter before a justice of the peace (FSA, s.9(5)). Having considered the appropriate evidence presented by the officer and the defendant (if they so wish) the magistrate decides whether or not the food contravenes the food safety requirements. If the magistrate finds that it does not, he/she will refuse to condemn the food and the food authority will require to compensate the owner of the food for any depreciation in its value resulting from the officer's actions. Compensation is also payable if the officer withdraws the notice mentioned above (FSA, s.9(7)). Any dispute regarding the right to or the amount of any compensation payable shall be determined by arbitration (FSA, s.9(8)). Another consideration in these circumstances is that the authority may require to reimburse the owner the cost of defending the proceedings as Clydesdale District Council found to its significant cost in the celebrated Lanark Blue cheese case: *Clydesdale District Council* v *Errington,* Lanark Sheriff Court, 5 December 1995, unreported, the appeal: *Errington (t/a Errington & Co)* v *Wilson* 1995 SCLR 875, IH and the reprise on referral back to the sheriff. In this case, a food authority officer, under s.9 of the FSA, seized batches of Mr Errington's 'Lanark Blue' cheese on the grounds that it was contaminated with *listeria monocytogenes* and so was unfit for human consumption. The case was heard before a justice of the peace, who refused to allow cross examination of witnesses and decided the cheese was in fact unfit for human consumption. The Court of Session decided, however, that the justice had not complied with the rules of natural justice by refusing to allow the cross-examination of witnesses. Clydesdale District Council then sought a condemnation order in the Sheriff Court, where the case turned on the question of whether the cheese was or was likely to be injurious to consumers' health, in terms of s.8 of the FSA. The condemnation order was refused on the grounds of lack of evidence.

If the magistrate finds that the food does fail to comply with the food safety requirements he/she must condemn the food, order it to be destroyed or otherwise disposed of and find the owner responsible for the cost of such destruction or disposal.

Improvement notices

An authorized officer who has reasonable grounds for believing that the proprietor of a food business is failing to comply with any food safety regulation may serve on the proprietor an 'improvement notice' (FSA, s.10). The notice must state the officer's grounds for believing that the proprietor is failing to comply with the regulations and specify the matter which he believes constitutes the failure to comply. The notice should specify the measures which the officer believes should be taken to remedy the contravention and require the owner to complete these measures within a specified time, which must not be less than 14 days (FSA, s.10(1)).

Prohibition orders

Section 11 of the FSA enables the court to make a prohibition order where the proprietor of a food business has been convicted of an offence under the FSA and the court is satisfied that there is a continuing public health risk. The court's concern may relate to the operation of a process or treatment or the use of the premises or of particular equipment and the prohibition contained in the court order may relate to the specific aspect of concern. This is a new power included in the FSA specifically in response to concerns for public safety.

Emergency provisions

Where an urgent risk to public health is perceived, ss 12 and 13 permit immediate action in the form of emergency prohibition notices to be taken to protect public health.

Under s.12 the action may be taken by an authorized officer immediately by serving an emergency prohibition notice on the proprietor of the food business (FSA, s.12(1)). This notice may require the proprietor to stop any process or treatment being carried out, stop the use of the premises or stop the use of particular equipment. As soon as possible the officer must affix a copy of the notice to the premises and proceed to obtain an emergency prohibition order, confirming the notice, from the court (FSA, s.12(5)). Application to the court must be made within three days of service of the notice and the proprietor must be given at lease one day's notice of the officer's intention to apply to the court (FSA, s.12(7)). In *East Kilbride District Council* v *King* 1996 SLT 30 an emergency prohibition notice was served upon the owners of a dairy farm, prohibiting the use of certain equipment which was said to constitute a health hazard. By the time the subsequent application for an emergency prohibition order was brought before the sheriff two days later he was satisfied that the health hazard had been removed and refused the order. However, he was satisfied that a health hazard had existed when the officer served the emergency prohibition notice and accordingly refused an award of compensation to the farm owners.

Under s.13 where there is a perceived widespread and immediate risk to health the Minister may take immediate emergency action by way of an 'emergency control order' (FSA, s.13(1)). This may apply to a particular range or class of businesses operating in the sector which is the cause of concern.

The order may relate to the food itself, sources of the food or contact materials in relation to the food. The Minister may make an order preventing particular food operations. Failure to comply with an order is an offence (FSA, s.13(2)).

The Minister also has powers under a separate statute, the Food and Environment Protection Act 1985 (FEPA), to make an emergency order if he/she is of the opinion that circumstances exist or may exist which are likely to create a hazard to human health through consumption of food (FEPA, s.1(1)). Such an order may prohibit activities in the designated area to which the order applies including agricultural activities, the slaughtering of animals, fishing and food processing and preparation. The order may also prohibit the movement of food into, within and out of the area and furthermore may prohibit activities throughout the United Kingdom such as the landing of fish from the designated area. The Minister has made a number of such orders including orders to prevent human consumption of food contaminated by radioactive substances which escaped from the Chernobyl Nuclear Power Station in the former USSR as a result of the accident there in April 1986. Several of these orders remain in force at the time of writing.

Consumer protection offences

Sale of food not of the nature etc. demanded by the purchaser

Section 14(1) of the FSA makes it an offence to sell to the purchaser's prejudice food which is not of the nature, substance or quality demanded by the purchaser. Sale is to be construed as a sale for human consumption (FSA, s.14(2)). In order that enforcement of these provisions by local authority officers is not hampered the FSA provides that it is not a defence that the purchaser was not prejudiced because he/she bought for analysis or examination.

The offence is based upon a similar provision in earlier legislation. It is possible that the same incident may lead to offences under both ss 8 and 14 but you should bear in mind that for there to be an offence under s.14 there must be a 'sale' of the food. It will be seen that there are three possible elements of consideration – 'nature', 'substance' and 'quality'. 'Nature' would cover the situation where the product differed completely from that anticipated. For example, in *Meah* v *Roberts* [1977] 1 WLR 1187 caustic soda was mistakenly sold as lemonade. This therefore covers the situation where what is sold is not food at all but has been mistakenly supplanted for what was intended to be food.

The use of the term 'substance' has commonly arisen when extraneous matter has been found in the food and will commonly, though not always, give rise to an offence under s.14 (*J Miller Ltd* v *Battersea Borough Council* and *Chibnall's Bakeries* v *Brown Cope*; see p. 249) In *Smedley's Ltd* v *Breed* [1973] QB 977 where the charge concerned a caterpillar contained in a tin of peas which was almost indistinguishable from the peas, the House of Lords was critical of the local authority for bringing proceedings against Smedley's. Consideration was given to the term 'sells to the purchaser's prejudice' and the court suggested that any prosecution should be taken only if it was for the benefit of consumers.

In *Barber* v *CWS Ltd* [1983] Crim LR 476 QBD the prosecution concerned a sealed bottle of milk which contained a plastic straw. There was no evidence to show that the straw had any effect on the milk and the magistrate dismissed the charge. On appeal it was found that an offence had been committed, since it was only necessary for the prosecution to show that the presence of the object could lead to the purchaser reasonably objecting to its presence in the food.

In 1996 a dairy pleaded guilty to a charge under s.14 of the FSA after supplying a customer with milk containing an earwig despite having some of the most modern equipment available (Colchester Magistrates' Court, 15 April 1996).

Consequently, it would seem that the presence of extraneous matter in food may render it to be not of the quality or substance demanded only if a reasonable purchaser would object to its presence. The measure is the quality of the food which the purchaser demands. The term 'quality' is a subjective matter and has led to several interesting cases.

In *McDonald's Hamburgers Ltd* v *Windle* [1987] Crim LR 200 QBD the case concerned McDonald's Cola sold as Diet McDonald's Cola to a sampling officer who had requested the 'Diet' Cola on two occasions. A nutrition guide displayed by McDonald's in their restaurants had stated that the 'ordinary Cola' contained between 96 and 187 kilocalories per serving (depending on size) whereas the 'Diet Cola' contained less than 1 kilocalorie per serving. McDonald's were convicted of a supply 'not of the quality demanded by the purchaser' and this was upheld on appeal.

THE PRINCIPAL OFFENCES UNDER THE FSA

Food safety offences

Rendering food injurious to health

Section 7(1) of the FSA provides that it is an offence for any person to render any food injurious to health by:

1. adding any article or substance to it;
2. using any article or substance as an ingredient in its preparation;
3. abstracting any constituent from it; or
4. subjecting it to any other process or treatment, with the intention that it is sold for human consumption.

The term 'person' includes the proprietor of a business and any employee, as well as a corporate body. In determining whether any food is injurious to health, s.7(2) provides that not only the probable effect of that food on the health of a person consuming it but also the cumulative effect of a person consuming such food in ordinary quantities must be considered.

Section 7 is essentially a restatement of the offence first introduced in the Adulteration of Food and Drink Act 1860. Parliament has amended the old offence to address modern day concerns about the effects on food of the various treatments and processes which may form part of the food production process.

You can see that the rendering of food injurious to health is the essential element of the offence under this section. Section 7(2) also makes it clear that the offence includes consideration of any 'probable cumulative effect of (the) food' when consumed over a period. Thus, a food which may not cause immediate injury to health would be caught by the provision if it were shown that reasonable regular consumption could become injurious to health. In other words the probable cumulative effect of regular ingestion may be considered. This may be of particular importance when considering any of the additives, preservatives, colourings etc. which it is now common to add to food during the production process.

You should note that the mere sale of the food which is injurious to health is not an offence under this section (although that would be caught by s.8, see below). It is the 'rendering of food' injurious to health which is the offence under s.7. The offence is therefore concerned principally with those involved in the production or processing of food, but would also cover those who for illegal purposes add articles or substances such as glass to food on a supermarket shelf.

The rendering of food injurious to health involves a positive act so that a failure to do something, such as a failure to pasteurize milk properly or thaw frozen poultry, is not an offence under s.7 but may be an offence under s.8 (see below). A statement, for example on a label, disclosing the presence of an injurious ingredient has been held not to constitute a defence (*Haigh* v *Aerated Bread Co. Ltd* (1916) 1 KB 878).

Parliament has also broadened the meaning to include temporary impairment, for example, temporary sickness as well as conditions causing permanent injury, illness and impairment or injury which becomes apparent only after the passage of time (FSA, s.7(3)).

You should bear in mind that the offence contemplated in s.7(1) is an offence of 'strict liability' in that it may be committed without any intention or recklessness on the part of the person responsible (see Chapter Five, pp. 110–111). It is the fact that the food is injurious to health which creates the offence rather that the intention of the person responsible. However, in the absence of intent, the person responsible may be able to rely on the due diligence defence permitted in s.21 to escape conviction (see pp. 252–253). To constitute an offence the prosecution must establish as a fact that the food product has been rendered injurious to health. It has been held in *Cullen* v *McNair* (1908) 72 JP 376 that food is not injurious only because of its effect on the health of people suffering exceptional conditions and that to be considered injurious to health it must potentially affect a substantial proportion of the community likely to use it. However, given the substantial increase in consumer expectation and consumer protection since 1908 it must be doubtful that such reasoning would be upheld today.

Sale etc. of food which does not comply with food safety requirements

Section 8 introduced a new offence of selling food which does not comply with food safety requirements. Specifically, it is an offence for any person to sell, offer to sell, expose for sale or advertise for sale, or to possess for the purpose of sale or of preparation for such sale, or to deposit with or consign to any other person for the purpose of sale or of preparation for sale for human consumption any food which fails to comply with food safety requirements. In earlier legislation, the comparable provision related only to the 'sale' of food. You can see that this has been expanded to include the possession of food for the purposes of preparation for sale and depositing food with or consigning food to another person.

Food fails to comply with food safety requirements if it has been rendered injurious to health in terms of s.7(1) or is unfit for human consumption or is so contaminated that it would not be reasonable to expect it to be used for human consumption in that state (FSA, s.8(2)).

It is possible for food to be considered unfit for human consumption without it being necessarily injurious to health. Mould on food is a common occurrence, which may render the food unedifying without being injurious to health.

The question whether or not food is unfit for human consumption is essentially a question of fact to be decided on the facts of the particular case. However, the issue of 'unfitness' has often troubled judges, who have struggled in several cases to adequately resolve just what the law means by the term 'unfit' particularly where mouldy food is at issue. This is illustrated by the following cases.

In *David Grieg Ltd* v *Goldfinch* [1961] 59 LGR 304 (QBD) a customer purchased a pie from the defendants. When he cut into it later on the day of purchase he found mould under the pie crust. It transpired that the pie had been baked by the defendants four days previously. The court held that the word 'unfit' meant something more than unsuitable for consumption, that it should be considered in a broad sense and so it was a question of degree in each case whether the food was 'unfit'. However, the court confirmed that 'unfit' should not be restricted to the situation where the food would cause injury to health and that in this case although the mould involved would not normally be injurious to health the court found that the pie was unfit for human consumption.

In *Guild* v *Gateway Foodmarkets Ltd* 1990 SCCR 179, 1990 JC 277, the court had to consider whether a pizza which was mouldy was unfit for human consumption. The court held that whether the pizza was unfit for human consumption was a question of circumstances and degree. In other words the mere presence of mould was not conclusive proof of unfitness. This point was dramatically highlighted in the lengthy saga of the Lanark Blue cheese case, referred to above at p. 245.

Other cases on the point have proved equally troublesome to the courts. A study of cases preceding the FSA shows they have not always been decided in a predictable way by the courts. Thus a loaf containing a dirty bandage was held to be 'unfit': *Chibnalls Bakeries* v *Cope Brown* [1956] Crim LR 263 (DC) but a cream bun containing a piece of metal (*J Miller Ltd* v *Battersea Borough Council* [1956] 1 QB 43) and a slice of bread containing a piece of string (*Turner & Son* v *Owen* [1956] 1 QB 48) were found not to be unfit for human consumption. You should, however, bear in mind that in the latter two cases, had the cases been brought today, the defendants might have been convicted of an offence under s.14 (which deals with food not of the nature, substance or quality demanded by the purchaser; see pp. 250–251) and were in fact convicted of an equivalent offence under the legislation of the time.

However, you ought to approach consideration of the older cases with care as consumer expectation of protection has changed considerably and courts now may be more likely to convict a producer. For example, we do not think that it is likely that a court now would be impressed by the comment of Lord Goddard CJ in *Turner & Son*:

> Because by some pure accident a little foreign body gets into a perfectly good loaf is no reason for saying the food is unfit for human consumption.

A nasty shock and injury awaited the woman eating a sweet in the case of *R* v *F & M Dobson, The Times*, 8 March 1995, CA. She cut her mouth because the sweet she was eating had the blade of a Stanley knife inside it! The manufacturers were found guilty of selling food which did not comply with food safety standards. The Court of Appeal said that there was a very high duty on the company in this case to ensure that no foreign bodies, particularly dangerous ones, got into their products.

The Kellogg Company of Great Britain was recently fined (Bromley Magistrates' Court, 30 October 1996) after pleading guilty to the offence of selling 'for human consumption food which failed to comply with Food Safety Requirements in that it was so contaminated that it would not be reasonable to expect it to be used for human consumption in that state' under s.8 of the FSA. The customer discovered a sharp piece of metal in a packet of Frosties breakfast cereal. This turned out to be a metal turning or drilling with sharp edges and ragged sides. The court considered the presence of this metal in the breakfast cereal to be dangerous.

There is a rebuttable presumption that where the food which fails to comply with food safety requirements is part of a batch, lot or consignment of food of the same class or description, all of the food in that batch, lot or consignment fails to comply with those requirements (FSA, s.8(3)).

Meat and other products derived from an animal slaughtered otherwise than in a knacker's yard or slaughterhouse are deemed to be unfit for human consumption, since such meat is not subject to statutory inspections, (FSA, s.8(4)). An exception to this is permitted, in relation to Scotland only, where the animal is slaughtered outwith a slaughterhouse due to some 'accident, illness or emergency affecting the animal' (FSA, s.8(5)).

Two cases from the early 1980s concerned the quality of minced beef sold by butchers: *Goldup* v *Manson* [1982] QB 161 and *Lawrence* v *Burleigh* (1981) 146 JP 134. In *Goldup* the shop in question offered mince of two different standards. A notice in the shop declared that mince sold there contained up to 30 per cent fat. A sample purchased by a sampling officer was found to have a 33 per cent fat content. Evidence was led by the prosecution to the effect that minced beef in general should not contain more than 25 per cent fat and this was the basis of the charge. The court was, however, influenced by the facts that the shop offered two grades of mince, had a notice declaring up to 30 per cent fat content and accordingly a purchaser of the cheaper grade should expect a fat content of around 30 per cent. The court regarded the extra 3 per cent as not being significant. This was upheld on appeal.

In *Lawrence* the case concerned mince sold and found to have a fat content of 30.8 per cent. On appeal it was stated that it was for the court to decide as a question of fact whether food was of the quality demanded. The question was whether the purchaser was prejudiced. In this case the court was impressed by the evidence of the purchaser herself. She had regularly bought mince at the shop in question and stated that when she first saw the mince she immediately considered it to be of inferior quality to that which she expected. Evidence of an experienced analyst had confirmed that the fat content was high. Since there was no fixed standard for the fat content of mince, the magistrates had been correct to evaluate the evidence and conclude that a reasonable standard had not been met.

False advertising, description or labelling of food

Section 15 of the FSA, which is based on a provision in earlier legislation dealing with the false description or advertisement of food but also includes an additional offence of false presentation of food, creates a number of important offences. Under s.15 an actual sale is not necessary: it is sufficient that the food is in the person's possession for the purposes of sale or is offered or exposed for sale.

Section 15(1) makes it an offence for any person to provide a label with food, whether or not attached to or printed on the wrapper or container, which falsely describes the food with which it is sold or displayed; or is likely to mislead as to the nature or substance or quality of any food.

Two recent prosecutions of Tesco illustrate the offence of falsely labelling products. In the first case Tesco were fined following the discovery that a hot chocolate drink which was labelled as 'low calorie, low-fat' with a fat content of 3 per cent actually had a fat content of 7.3 per cent and that Tesco's Chicken Tikka Samosas which were labelled as having a meat content of 10 per cent had a meat content of only 6 per cent (Colchester Magistrates' Court, 17 June 1996). The court found that the food had been falsely labelled in such a way that was likely to mislead as to its nature or substance or quality. In the second prosecution, Tesco were fined when they labelled mince as 'Tesco's Healthy Eating Lean Beef Mince', indicating that it had a fat content of between 7 and 9 per cent. A sample taken of the food showed a fat content of 19 per cent. Tesco were unable to show that they had checked the end product to ensure that it was properly labelled. The company was found guilty of the offence of falsely labelling food under s.15(1)(a) of the FSA.

Section 15(2) makes it an offence for any person to publish, or be a party to the publication of, an advertisement (not being such a label given or displayed by him as mentioned in s.15(1) which falsely describes the food; or is likely to mislead as to the nature or substance or quality of the food.

Where there is a prosecution for an offence under s.15(1) or (2), the fact that a label or advertisement in respect of which the offence is alleged to have been committed contained an accurate statement of the composition of the food shall not prevent the court from finding that the offence was committed (FSA, s.15(4)).

Section 15(3) makes it an offence for any person to sell, or offer or expose for sale, or have in their possession for the purpose of sale, any food the presentation of which is likely to mislead as to the nature or substance or quality of the food.

All references to sale in s.15 of the FSA are to be construed as references to sale for human consumption (FSA, s.15(5)).

The offence is similar to that under s.3 of the Trades Description Act 1968, which stated that a false trades description is one which is false to a material degree. In *Kirshenboim* v *Salmon and Gluckstein Ltd* [1898] 2 QB 19 the case concerned cigarettes which were described as 'hand made' but were in fact machine made. Although the cigarettes were made of the same quality paper, starch and tobacco as found in hand-made cigarettes and so it would appear that a customer would not be significantly prejudiced, it was held that the description had been intended to deceive and an offence had been committed.

You should also be aware that s.15 is designed in part to implement EC law requirements. The EC has been concerned with consumer protection since 1975 when an EC Council Resolution was passed ([1975] OJ C92/1) and has made a wide range of subsequent Decisions, Directives, Regulations and Recommendations on the topic (see Chapter One, pp. 6–9). The EC Commission has indicated that key areas for future legislation will be the consumers' information needs and protection in relation to foodstuffs.

In 1978, the EC Council issued a Directive on labelling, presentation and advertising foodstuffs for sale to the ultimate consumer (79/112/EEC), which was amended in 1989 to include foodstuffs which are intended for supply to restaurants, hospitals, canteens and other similar mass caterers (89/395/EEC).

The Directive states that labelling on foodstuffs must not mislead purchasers as to its character. It also provides a list of the details which must, subject to some exceptions, be included on food labels. These include the ingredients, the name and address of the manufacturer or packager, the 'use by' date and any special storage conditions or conditions of use.

The Directive also gives detailed provisions on the definition of 'ingredients', specifically excluding certain additives. The order and manner in which ingredients are to be listed on packaging is also given in the Directive.

DEFENCES

There are three possible defences to charges under the FSA. Put simply, these are: (1) that the offence was due to the fault of someone else not under the control of the accused (FSA, s.20); (2) that due diligence was exercised by the accused (FSA, s.21); and (3) that in relation to advertising that the publication was in the course of business (FSA, s.22). The due diligence defence is likely to prove the most important and it is a new statutory defence. Essentially this defence can be made out if the person charged can demonstrate that he/she took all steps which are reasonably practical to ensure that an offence could not be committed. For example, he/she would probably have to show that staff were properly trained and instructed in the cleaning, inspection and preparation of food, that all reasonable checks were carried out to make sure that the proper procedures were being adhered to and that the process for production or treatment of food had been considered in detail and set up in such a way as to minimize the possibility of contamination.

In practice this will not be an easy defence to sustain as there will frequently be some ground for suggesting that the producer could have improved the system and the interests of consumer protection will prevail. However, a producer who can clearly establish that their system is well considered and well run should invoke some sympathy from the court.

PENALTIES

Substantial penalties for offences are laid down in the FSA. Technically, serious offences can be prosecuted on indictment with up to two years imprisonment and an unlimited fine or both possible (FSA, s.35(2)). In practice, most offences will be dealt with by summary prosecution in the Magistrates' Court in England and Wales and the Sheriff Court in Scotland. There the maximum penalty for offences under ss 7, 8 or 14 is six months imprisonment and a fine of up to £20,000 or both (FSA, s.35(3)). For all other offences on summary conviction under the FSA the maximum penalties are six months imprisonment and a fine of up to the statutory maximum which, at the time of writing, was £5,000. If a licence for the premises is held, such as for a knackers yard or slaughterhouse, the licence may also be revoked by the court (FSA, s.35(4)).

You should also bear in mind that where the body responsible for the offence is a corporate body, certain corporate officers including directors, company secretaries and managers may also be liable to prosecution in certain circumstances (FSA, s.36). We discuss which corporate officers may be caught by such provisions and the circumstances in which they may be liable in Chapter Five (p. 114).

CURRENT AND FUTURE DEVELOPMENTS

Food safety scares

At this time there is unprecedented interest in food safety regulation. Several major food scares during the past few years, some resulting in deaths, have led to considerable public concern. These have included scares involving Salmonella in eggs and poultry, Listeria in unpasturized cheese, BSE in beef and beef products and E-coli in beef and cooked meat. The most serious outbreak of E-coli ever in the UK resulting in 20 deaths in Scotland occurred in November 1996. As well as the understandable public concern which reached a peak with the E-coli outbreak the alleged connection between BSE and its human counterpart, Creuzfeld Jacob Disease (CJD) has resulted in an EC ban on British beef. The problems have sparked further inquiry into food production with a view to increasing food safety. In Britain the

Pennington Group was established by the Government to report on the major Scottish E-coli outbreak. In Europe, the European Commission has recently issued a Green Paper on food safety.

Accordingly, further changes in food safety law are likely. In the UK it is likely that the Pennington Report will form the basis for developments in food safety law in the near future. We shall therefore consider the principal points of the Report.

The Pennington Report

Following the serious outbreak of infection of the bacterium E-coli 0157 in Central Scotland in November 1996 which led to 20 deaths, and the subsequent outbreaks at the beginning of 1997, the Government set up the Pennington Group to establish the circumstances which led to the outbreak and to advise on the future of food safety. It is anticipated that the law will be changed to take account of many of the recommendations of the Pennington Group. It is therefore helpful to consider the main points of the Report which may be reflected in new legislation.

Human infection from E-coli 0157 can occur from direct contact with animals carrying the organism or through consumption of contaminated food or water. Although the bacterium is killed by heating, it can survive if food is not properly cooked. There can also be cross-contamination between raw meat carrying the organism and cooked or ready to eat foods.

EC food law, with the aid of the Hazard Analysis and Critical Control Point (HACCP) System, places the responsibility for ensuring consumer safety and protection with individual food businesses. HACCP, a structured approach to identifying and analysing the potential hazards in an operation and deciding the critical points to control to ensure consumer safety is not presently legally binding. The Pennington Group were overwhelmingly in favour of such a system in the food handling and production area.

HACCP is based on seven principles which were defined as follows in the Pennington Report:

1. Conduct a hazard analysis, identifying the potential hazards in food production and identifying the preventive measures necessary for their control;
2. Determine the critical control points (CCPs). Identify the procedures and operational steps that can be controlled to eliminate or minimize the hazards;
3. Establish critical limit(s). Set targets to ensure that CCP is under control;
4. Establish a system to monitor, control the CCPs;
5. Establish corrective actions when a particular CCP is not under control;
6. Establish procedures to confirm that HACCP system is working effectively; and
7. Establish documentation on all procedures and records appropriate to these principles and their application.

The Pennington Group focused on the importance of food safety in each stage in the food production process, 'from farm to fork'. The Group recommended more research into the spread of infection of E-coli 0157 within farms, together with an educational awareness programme for farm workers on issues such as personal hygiene. At the slaughterhouse stage in the food production process, HACCP is recommended and the importance of high hygiene standards both within slaughterhouses and in transporting carcasses and meat is highlighted. HACCP was again recommended for butchers' premises, the next stage in the food production process. The Meat Products (Hygiene) Regulations 1994, made under the FSA apply to certain categories of premises producing meat products and require premises to be approved in relation to layout, facilities, hygiene and separation of raw and cooked products.

However, these Regulations do not apply to certain premises supplying the 'final consumer'. The application of these Regulations is complex and confusing. Many businesses are exempt from the 1994 Regulations. Those that are exempt are covered by the Food Safety (General Food Hygiene) Regulations 1995. These Regulations do not require premises to be approved, imposing only general requirements on structural matters, transport, equipment and food handling and storage. The Pennington Group were critical of the differentiation between premises covered by the 1994 Regulations and those covered only by the 1995 Regulations and recommended tighter food safety requirements for premises covered only by the 1995 Regulations. The recommendations included requirements for the separation of raw and cooked meat products and the introduction of selective licensing arrangements for butchers and producers who are handling raw and cooked meats.

At the final stage, the point of consumption, the Group recommended raising awareness of potential food contamination among everyone who handles food, whether they are people preparing food at home or those who cater for large groups at other venues. Awareness should be raised by education and ongoing methods promoting safe food preparation as well as additional enforcement methods to ensure food safety measures are properly implemented, such as accelerated implementation of HACCP for high risk premises, risk assessments and designated local authority and environmental health officers with the training, experience and expertise to head food safety within the authority. The Group also set down detailed guidelines for the surveillance and control of any future outbreaks.

Proposed Food Standards Agency

In April 1997, Professor Philip James put forward proposals for a Food Standards Agency to operate in the UK. The proposed Agency was to restore public confidence in the country's food handling procedures and improve the standards of food safety generally. The Agency is to have a wide remit, covering almost all aspects of food safety law throughout the whole of the UK.

Professor James recommended that the new Agency encourage public involvement. It is to be a non-departmental public body with executive powers to be made up of a commission with around ten members, to be appointed by the Prime Minister. The Agency is also to be staffed by administrative and scientific civil servants.

The Agency is to deal with all UK food policy matters, including genetically modified foods, food standards and labelling. It was also to be responsible for proposing and drafting new legislation on food matters and also for providing public education and information.

Professor James recommended that the Food Standards Agency be given the task of enforcing food law. It is to set the appropriate standards and monitor the enforcement procedure, ensuring compliance by the appropriate bodies.

The proposed Agency aims to bring together the activities of a number of public bodies, including the Public Health Laboratory Service, local authorities, the

Ministry of Agriculture, Fisheries and Food and its Scottish Office counterpart, the Department of Health and the Health Education Authority. The cost of this reorganization was said to be advantageous to the significant costs involved in dealing with food related diseases such as those currently arising.

The Food Standards Agency will require to be established by statute. Professor James estimated that the new legislation would probably not appear before 1998–99 due to pressures on Parliamentary time. In the meantime, however, he suggested that the Government establish the commission element of the Agency, which he suggested be called 'The Food and Health Commission'.

Professor James's proposals were welcomed in May 1997 by the Prime Minister who indicated that a new ministerial group on food safety would be set up. The current legislative programme includes a commitment from the Government to achieving high standards of food safety and ensuring consultation on the recommendations for a Food Standards Agency.

The licensing system 11

INTRODUCTION

In this chapter we examine how the sale of intoxicating liquor is regulated by means of the licensing system. We consider the law in England and Wales first and then look at licensing in Scotland. Although Scots licensing law is broadly similar to the English and Welsh law, it is governed by separate legislation and there are certain differences which require comment. In both sections we look at the different types of licence available and how they are obtained, whether as a new licence, by way of renewal, transfer or removal. In this regard you should note that licensing provisions in England, Wales and Scotland do not apply to aircraft, vessels and trains provided, in the case of trains, that food is also available for passengers. Theatres which are licensed under the Theatres Act 1968 are also exempt from these licensing controls except that they may not sell alcohol outside permitted hours (for permitted hours, see pp. 268–271 and pp. 281–283). We then consider the types of customers who may and may not be served on licensed premises.

The law regulates the hours during which licensed premises may operate and we shall consider these Regulations and the various ways in which the hours may be extended or restricted.

The special provisions which apply to children in licensed premises will be considered, before a discussion of some of the peculiar provisions which apply to the supply of intoxicating liquor in private clubs.

LICENSING IN ENGLAND AND WALES

Introduction

The licensing system in England and Wales is governed by the Licensing Act 1964 as amended principally by the Licensing Act 1988 (LA 1964). Anyone who sells or exposes for retail sale, intoxicating liquor must generally hold a justices' licence, or they will commit a criminal offence. Intoxicating liquor includes spirits, wine, beer, cider and any fermented, distilled or spiritous liquor.

The licensing justices

In order to acquire a justices' licence, an applicant must apply to the licensing justices who issue and regulate the licences. The justices convene as a committee, holding meetings which are known as transfer sessions. The committee must meet in the first 14 days of February for their general annual licensing meeting, known as the brewster sessions, and hold at least four transfer sessions throughout the rest of the year (LA 1964, s.2(3)). The transfer sessions do not operate as a court, and there is no requirement that lawyers be used. Most committees publish a policy statement containing their particular policies. There must be a minimum of three licensing justices on each committee and the LA 1964 contains restrictions on who may be a committee member (LA 1964, Sch. 1, para. 2A). A justice must not, for example, be or be in partnership with, a brewer, distiller, maker of malt or of any intoxicating liquor (LA 1964, s.193).

Who may hold a licence?

Licensing justices may grant a justices' licence to any person who is not disqualified from holding one and whom they consider to be a fit and proper person (LA 1964, s.3(1)). The following are disqualified persons:

- a sheriff's officer or any court officer or official;
- a person convicted of forging a justices' licence or knowingly using a forged licence; and
- a person convicted of allowing licensed premises to be a brothel (LA 1964, s.9(1)).

Where a disqualified person purports to hold a justices' licence, the licence is void (LA 1964, s.9(6)).

THE LICENCES

On-licences/off licences

There are two basic types of licence which licensing justices may grant. These are on-licences and off-licences (LA 1964, s.2(2)). According to Home Office figures for the period from July 1994 to June 1995, the number of on-licensed premises in England and Wales was around 110 000, while the number of off-licensed premises was around 46 000. On-licences allow the sale of intoxicating liquor for consumption both on and off the licensed premises (LA 1964, s.2(2)(a)). They can cover:

- intoxicating liquor of all descriptions (a full on-licence);
- beer, cider and wine only;
- beer and cider only;
- cider only; or
- wine only.

Off-licences allow consumption off the premises only (LA 1964, s.2(2)(b)). There are only two possible types of off-licence, covering:

- intoxicating liquor of all descriptions; or
- beer, cider and wine.

Premises are not defined but certainly include a building or part of a building. *Frost* v *Caslon, Frost* v *Wilkins* [1929] 2 KB 138 indicates that a room occupied separately but within the structure of a larger building may constitute 'premises'.

A licence may be granted as a new licence (LA 1964, s.4; see below), or by way of renewal (LA 1964, s.7; see p. 262), transfer (LA 1964, s.8; see pp. 262–264) or removal (LA 1964, s.5; see pp. 264–265).

New licences

General

New licences are generally granted for premises which have not previously been licensed, but will only be granted if the licensing justices consider the premises structurally suitable for the type of licence required (LA 1964, s.4(2)).

Where the premises are either being or are about to be constructed, altered or extended, a provisional grant of a new licence may be made (LA 1964, s.6). The applicant must then complete the necessary works and request the justices to declare the provisional grant final (LA 1964, s.6(4)). This must be confirmed within 12 months (LA 1964, s.6(5)(b)) and only if the justices are satisfied that the premises comply with the plans submitted or that the premises are likely to comply with them before the date of the next licensing session.

Applying for a new on-licence

A person who wishes to hold a new justices' on-licence must apply to the licensing justices and meet the application requirements. These are set out in Schedule 2 to the LA 1964.

The first step towards obtaining a justices' on-licence is the submission of a notice of application to various authorities, including the Chief of Police, the local authority, the fire authority and the clerk to the licensing justices at least 21 days before the relevant transfer sessions (LA, Sch. 2, para. 1(a)). These bodies must appear at the head of the licensing notice. Whether the application is for a grant or a provisional grant of a licence, and whether the applicant is seeking a special or ordinary removal should also be indicated in the notice. The category of licence requested should also be stated (LA 1964, Sch. 2, para. 4(d)). The notice must also identify the applicant's own name, address, and occupation (LA 1964, Sch. 2, para. 4(b)), as well as the name and location of the premises (LA 1964, Sch. 2, para. 4(c)). It should be signed either by the applicant or their authorized agent (LA 1964, Sch. 2, para. 4(a)).

Notice of the application is advertised in a newspaper circulating in the area of the premises to be licensed not more than 28 days or less than 14 days before the hearing (LA 1964, Sch. 2, para. 1(c)(ii)). It must also be displayed on or near the premises, or near the proposed site of those premises in the case of an application for a provisional grant for seven days, where it can conveniently be seen and read by the public (LA 1964, Sch. 2, para. 1(c)(i)).

Evidence required

An important part of an application for a justices' licence is the plan of the premises (LA 1964, Sch. 2, para. 3). This should be deposited with the notice of application if the application is for the grant or ordinary removal of an on-licence, or the provisional grant or ordinary removal of an off-licence. The plan should contain as much useful information as possible, while excluding irrelevant information. Useful information includes all points of access, the bar counter, toilet accommodation, kitchens, liquor storage areas and seating areas.

Radius maps are often required by licensing committees to show that there is a need or a demand for a new licence to be granted in a particular area. These indicate the location of, and distance to, other licensed premises within the area. The applicant should also consider other evidence he/she may wish to use at the hearing, such as photographs, product lists, menus, petitions and market research.

Preparation of the case for hearing

In preparing the case for the hearing by the licensing justices the applicant should consider various issues, including their own experience, training and qualifications in the licensed trade. He/she must be considered to be 'a fit and proper person' (LA 1964, s.3(1)). The premises themselves must be, as mentioned above, structurally adapted for the class of licence which is sought (LA 1964, s.4(2)) and should not be disqualified, for example, by virtue of being used primarily as a garage or motorway service area (LA 1964, s.9(3), (4A), (4B)). At this stage, the applicant should check that the authorities are happy with the plans and planning permission. Finally, even though the applicant may comply with all the procedural requirements and may be a fit and proper person and the premises are adapted for their intended use, it must be considered what practical benefit the outlet will bring, if any, to the area in which it is located, before an application will be granted.

The hearing and the decision

At the hearing itself, the applicant's case is stated before the licensing justices and any objectors are given a chance to be heard; any person may object in writing or orally. The committee may ask the applicant questions and any of the authorities may make representations to the licensing committee before the case is finally summed up.

A new licence may be granted subject to conditions and may restrict the sale of intoxicating liquor as appropriate to, for example, the area or the premises in question (LA 1964, s.4(1)). The conditions must not, however, completely change the character of the licence.

On-licences may be granted as seasonal licences where there are no permitted hours in the premises during a particular part or parts of the year (LA 1964, s.64), as six-day licences where there are no permitted hours on a Sunday (LA 1964, s.65) and as early-closing licences where the permitted hours end one hour earlier in the evening than the general licensing hours (LA 1964, s.65).

Restaurant and residential licences (known as Part IV Licences) are on-licences granted for premises which provide meals, subject only to conditions imposed by the licensing justices, as well as possible conditions as to permitted hours, six-day, early-closing or seasonal licences or conditions restricting sales in registered clubs to non-members.

Generally, the only way to vary conditions is to apply for a new licence.

It is not possible to attach conditions to the grant of an off-licence (LA 1964, s.4(1)). However, as conditions are sometimes better than no licence at all, the practice of undertakings has developed. Here, licensing committees are offered, and accept undertakings or assurances from the applicant for a licence (*R* v *Beesly, ex p. Hodson* [1912] 3 KB 583, DC). It is not a criminal offence to breach these, but could be a ground for refusing to renew the licence.

The committee are not obliged to give reasons for whatever decision they reach, though they often do so. Written reasons are needed where the application for a Part IV licence has been refused (LA 1964, s. 98(6)).

If an application for a new justices' on-licence has been refused, an applicant may choose to immediately request a restaurant and/or residential licence instead (LA 1964, s.99).

Costs

The justices may make such an order as they consider just and reasonable for the payment of costs by any person opposing an application to the applicant or by the applicant to such a person (LA 1964, s.193B). This is to deter frivolous or vexatious objections.

After the hearing

If anyone objected to the granting of the licence, the licence only becomes operative after 21 days (LA 1964, s.27). If there is an appeal against the decision to grant a licence, the licence only becomes effective after the appeal is either withdrawn or is determined in the applicant's favour.

If a provisional licence is granted, a final order must be sought, as indicated above, within 12 months (LA 1964, s.6(5)(b)).

Re-applications and appeals

Any person aggrieved by a decision of the committee, which would include the applicant where a licence had been refused (LA 1964, s.22(2)), has three possible options available to them (LA 1964, s.21(1)). These are re-application, appeal to the Crown Court and appeal to the High Court. Re-applications are quicker and cheaper than appeal and may be made if there are grounds for believing that the justices may have arrived at a different conclusion if certain aspects of the application had been modified. An applicant can appeal to the Crown Court within 21 days against a refusal to grant a licence (LA 1964, s.22(1)). The applicant may appeal to the High Court if he/she believes the licensing committee has made an error of law which is likely to be repeated in the Crown Court.

Renewal of licences

General

The second method of obtaining a justices' licence is through renewal (LA 1964, s.7). An existing licence-holder may apply to renew a licence when it is due to expire. Licensing justices have a wide discretion to refuse the renewal of licences, though in practice most are in fact granted. Special provisions, however, apply in relation to old on-licences (LA 1964, s.12). Justices cannot refuse the renewal of an old on-licence (that is, an on-licence which has been in force continuously since 15 August 1904) other than an old beer-house licence (one which has been maintained continuously without removal since 1 May 1869), except if the applicant is not a fit and proper person and/or the licensed premises have been ill-conducted (e.g. licence-holder persistently and unreasonably refused to supply non-alcoholic drinks), or are structurally deficient or unsuitable (LA 1964, s.12(2)–(4)). Written reasons must be given to an applicant for any refusal to renew an old on-licence (LA 1964, s.12(6)). There is a right of appeal against a refusal, though not a grant, of any renewal of a justices' licence (LA 1964, s.21(4)).

The application for renewal

No notice is generally required for a renewal (LA 1964, Sch. 2), but anyone who wants to oppose a renewal must give the applicant and the clerk notice in writing of this intention, along with the general grounds of the opposition, at least seven days before the relevant licensing sessions (LA 1964, s.7(2)). The licensing justices may only consider grounds of opposition which are set out in the notice (*R* v *Walley* [1916] BTRLR 44).

The LA 1964 now allows the clerk, subject to certain exceptions, to exercise the licensing justices' powers of renewing a licence if the application is unopposed or is not opposed on a ground which allows refusal of the application (LA 1964, s.193A). Even if the licensing committee deals with the renewal, the applicant need not attend unless there is an objection to the application (LA 1964, Sch. 2, para. 8).

On renewing a licence, the licensing justices may require a plan of the premises (LA 1964, s.19(1)). They may then impose an order for structural alterations to be made in the part of the premises where intoxicating liquor is sold or consumed as they think reasonably necessary to secure the proper conduct of the business (LA 1964, s.19(1)). They can only impose such an order every five years (LA 1964, s.19(3)).

The terms of a renewed licence are not limited to those in the original licence but the renewal cannot vary the premises (*Stringer* v *Huddersfield JJ* (1875) 33 LT 568).

Transfer of licences

General

A transfer of a justices' licence becomes necessary when intoxicating liquor begins to be sold at premises without the authority of the person named on the licence. This situation often arises when managers of licensed premises decide to move their business to new premises. A transfer of a licence is, like a renewal or a removal, technically the grant of a new licence.

Transfers may only be granted in particular circumstances, generally to the new tenant or occupier of the licensed premises or to a representative of the licence-holder (LA 1964, s.8). The circumstances include where the licence-holder has died, become incapable of carrying on the business through illness or has given up or is about to give up carrying on the business (LA 1964, s.8(1)(a),(b),(d)). A transfer may also occur if the occupier of the premises, being about to leave them, has deliberately failed to apply for the renewal of the licence or where the owner or someone acting for the owner has been granted a protection order because the licence has been forfeited or the licensee disqualified (LA 1964, s.8(1)(e),(f)). Where a tenant who has had an application for renewal refused leaves the premises, the licensing justices must hear the application of a new tenant for a transfer (*R* v *Osgoldcross* (1889) 53 JP 823).

The applicant

Training and experience of new licensees is becoming increasingly important, and many licensing justices now insist that they attend training courses. The person to whom the licence is transferred must be a fit and proper person and not be disqualified (LA 1964, s.3(1)). It will be a question of circumstances in each case whether a person who has convictions will be granted a transfer. Although there is technically no minimum (or maximum) age for a licensee, in practice they must be over 18, and in many cases, over 21. Breweries or other multiple operators of on- and off-licence premises often have their premises held in joint names. This affords some protection against the problems created when a sole licensee suddenly leaves or is dismissed.

Licensing justices have the power to decide the minimum period that should elapse between transfer applications, though the rule may be dispensed with in appropriate cases (LA 1964, s.8(4)).

The application

The application procedure is set out in Schedule 2 to the LA 1964. At least 21 days' notice must be given to the relevant authorities, which are: the clerk to the licensing justices, the chief officer of police, the local authority, the town/parish/community council and existing licensees. Transfers are often dealt with in the absence of the applicant if there is no objection to the application. If justices refuse the transfer of an old on-licence or an old beerhouse licence, they must state the grounds for refusal in writing. Any person aggrieved by a refusal to transfer a licence can appeal to the Crown Court.

Protection orders

Anyone who proposes to apply for the transfer of a justices' licence may apply for a 'protection order' (LA 1964, s.10(1)). This gives a person the same authority to sell intoxicating liquor on premises as given by the existing or last in force justices' licence, when the licensee becomes no longer involved with the premises or the liquor sales (LA 1964, s.10(2)). A protection order is not a temporary transfer, as the licensee retains the authority to sell intoxicating liquor at the premises should he/she return.

The same categories of people may apply for protection orders, and in the same situations, as for transfers. In addition, the owner or someone acting on his/her behalf may apply for a protection order if the licensee has become disqualified from holding a licence or has had the licence forfeited. An applicant must generally give the chief officer of police seven days' notice of the application.

A protection order lasts until the end of the second licensing sessions after its grant (LA 1964, s.10(4)). It becomes invalid if a further protection order, transfer or removal is granted for the premises (LA 1964, s.10(4)). A further protection order will only be granted if the holder of the existing protection order allows it to be superseded or if he/she no longer proposes to apply for a transfer of the licence. It may also be granted if the existing holder becomes disqualified from applying for the transfer or becomes unable to carry on the business.

The law deems a protection order to be granted if the licensee dies, is adjudicated bankrupt, has a voluntary arrangement approved (under the Insolvency Act 1986) or executes a deed of arrangement (LA 1964, s.10(5)).

Removal of licences

General

The fourth and final method of obtaining a justices' licence is by way of removal. A licence may be 'removed' from the premises for which it was granted and be granted for other premises (LA 1964, s.3(3)(b)). It is not possible, however, to have a licence granted by way of removal of a Part IV licence (LA 1964, s.93(4)). Licensing committees have generally the same power to grant or refuse a removal of a justices' licence as they have for a new licence (LA 1964, s.5(1)). This fact has led some to be critical of the need for removals which have additional problems to new licences.

Ordinary and special removals

A removal may be either ordinary or special. An 'ordinary removal' is a removal which is not a special removal, a planning removal or a temporary premises removal (LA 1964, s.5(6)). An ordinary removal can only be granted if there is no objection by the owner of the premises, the holder of the licence or any other person whom the justices consider have a right to object to the removal, where the licence is a justices' on-licence (LA 1964, s.5(5)). However, the objection of an owner is not a complete bar to the re-establishment of the licensed premises: the old licence could be surrendered and an application for a new licence made (*Laceby* v *Lacon* [1899] AC 222). If the licence is an off-licence, there must be no objection from either the holder of the licence or any other person considered to have a right to object (LA 1964, s.5(5)).

A 'special removal' may only be granted for an old on-licence and only then if the premises are or are about to be pulled down or occupied under any Act for the improvement of highways, or for any other public purpose or are unfit due to fire, tempest or other unforeseen and unavoidable calamity (LA 1964, s.15). A special removal of an old on-licence may only be refused if the new premises are not structurally suitable or if the applicant is not a fit and proper person (*R* v *Weymouth JJ, ex p. Sleep* [1942] 1 KB 465).

Applications

Application for both ordinary and special removals have generally the same notice and procedure requirements as new licences, though no conditions may be attached to ordinary removals (LA 1964, Sch. 2). A provisional grant of an ordinary removal of an on-licence may be made to premises being or about to be constructed (LA 1964, s.6). For special removals, there is an obligation to adjourn the hearing and give notice to the owner on the justices requesting the applicant to give an undertaking and a restriction on the power to refuse the application (LA 1964, ss 12(5), 15(1)).

Revocation of justices' licences

Licensing justices may revoke a justices' licence either by themselves or on the application of any person (LA 1964, s.20A(1)). Licences may be revoked on any ground that can be used to refuse to renew a licence of that description, for example because the premises are unsatisfactory, the licensee is guilty of some misconduct or there is evidence of disturbance or annoyance in the neighbourhood (LA 1964, s.20A(2)). Written notice must be given to the licence holder of an intention to revoke a licence at least 21 days before the beginning of the sessions (LA 1964, s.20A(3)). A decision to revoke a licence does not take effect until the time limit for appealing against it has expired or, in cases where an appeal proceeds, until the appeal is disposed of (LA 1964, s.20A(5)). Old on-licences and beerhouse licences are protected in a similar way to their limitations on refusals of transfers or renewals.

Occasional licences and occasional permissions

Occasional licences and occasional permissions give temporary authority to sell or supply intoxicating liquor where no authority otherwise exists.

Occasional permissions

Occasional permissions allow organizations which are not carried on for private gain to hold a limited number of functions each year where intoxicating liquor may be sold. They are governed by the Licensing (Occasional Permissions) Act 1983. The applicant must be a fit and proper person to sell intoxicating liquor and the premises must be a suitable place for intoxicating liquor to be sold. The applicant must reside, and the premises must be situated, in the relevant licensing district. A further condition to the grant of an occasional licence is that the sale of intoxicating liquor at the function must not be likely to cause disturbance or annoyance to residents in the neighbourhood, or any disorderly conduct. One month's notice must be given for this application. The licensing justices may impose any condition they consider proper.

Occasional licences

Occasional licences allow an existing on-licence holder to sell intoxicating liquor at premises other than those to which his/her on-licence extends (LA 1964, s.180). They can be granted for periods of up to three weeks and may be granted on one occasion for consecutive weeks. Occasional licences can be used where a club registration certificate, a justices' on- or off-licence or a special hours certificate has lapsed. Only 24 hours' notice need be given.

Duration of licences

Licences which were granted after 4 April 1989, apply from the date they were granted until the end of the current licensing period (i.e. three years beginning with 5 April 1989 or any triennial of that date) (LA 1964, s.26(1)). Licences granted in the last three months of that period apply until the end of the next licensing period. Licences are superseded when a licence is granted by way of renewal, transfer or removal of it. Licences can be forfeited, surrendered or become void.

THE PREMISES

Intoxicating liquor can only be sold on premises authorized by a justices' licence. If there are reasonable grounds to believe that intoxicating liquor is being sold or exposed for sale in unlicensed premises, a search warrant allowing search, seizure and forfeiture of any such intoxicating liquor may be issued (LA 1964, s.187(1)).

The holder of an off-licence may be fined if a customer drinks intoxicating liquor bought from him on or near the premises with the licence-holder's privity or consent (LA 1964, s.164).

With the exception of certain club premises and residential licensed premises, licensed premises must have a sign stating the word 'licensed', the licence-holder's name, the type of business the licence applies to and the type of licence in force (LA 1964, s.183).

A licence which has been granted for premises which are in fact disqualified, is void (LA 1964, s.9(6)). Disqualified premises include premises used as a garage (LA 1964, s.9(4A)–(4B)) and premises where within two years, two persons severally holding a justices' licence for any premises forfeit their licences (LA 1964, s.9(2)) and premises which are on land acquired by a special road authority, in other words, motorway service areas (LA, s.9(4)).

On-licensed premises cannot be altered in such a way as to increase the drinking facilities in a public part of the premises, conceal any part of the premises used for drinking or affect the communication between the part of the premises where intoxicating liquor is sold and the rest of the premises or any street, unless the licensing justices allow it, or it is a requirement by order of some lawful authority (LA 1964, s.20(1)). If this is not complied with, the works may be destroyed, the licence forfeited and the individual no longer seen as a fit and proper person (LA 1964, s.20(3)). As discussed above, structural alterations may be imposed upon on-licensed premises upon renewal, every five years (LA 1964, s.19(1), (3)). Licensing justices cannot interfere with off-licensed premises without proper cause.

CUSTOMERS

A licence-holder will be guilty of an offence if he/she knowingly sells or supplies intoxicating liquor to persons he/she is not allowed to under the conditions of the licence (LA 1964, s.161). Intoxicating liquor may not be sold to persons under the age of 18 (LA 1964, s.169(1)), although anyone who has attained the age of 16 may drink beer, porter, cider or perry with a meal (LA 1964, s.169(4) (see p. 271). A licence-holder is also prohibited from selling intoxicating liquor to a drunken person (LA 1964, s.172(3)). No knowledge that the person is drunk is necessary for this offence to be committed (*Cundy* v *Le Cocq* (1884) 13 QBD 207). The licensee will be vicariously liable for his/her manager or employee selling alcohol to a drunk person even where there are express instructions that such persons are not to be served (*Commissioners of Police* v *Cartman* [1896] 1 QB 655). The licensee will also be liable where intoxicating liquor is sold to a sober person who then supplies it to a drunken person (*Scatchard* v *Johnson* (1888) 52 JP 389). Anyone who, in licensed premises, procures or attempts to procure intoxicating liquor for a drunken person, or who aids a drunken person in obtaining or consuming intoxicating liquor in licensed premises, is guilty of an offence (LA 1964, s.173). A constable on duty must not be supplied intoxicating liquor, except by the authority of his/her superior officer (LA 1964, s.178). The licence-holder will not, however, be liable for this if he/she is unaware that the constable was on duty (*Sherras* v *De Rutzen* [1895] 1 QB 918).

Any person who is drunken, violent, quarrelsome or disorderly, may be refused entry or may be expelled from the premises by the licence-holder (LA 1964, s.174). The courts can now exclude certain categories of convicted persons from licensed premises.

Anyone who provides intoxicating liquor must not discriminate against customers on the grounds of race or sex by refusing or deliberately omitting to provide liquor or refusing or deliberately omitting to provide liquor of the like quality or in the like manner and on the like terms as they would for other members of the public in the case of racial discrimination, or for male members of the public for sex discrimination (Race Relations Act 1976, s.20; Sex Discrimination Act 1975, s.29. See also Chapter Seven). For example, in *Gill* v *El Vino Co. Ltd* [1983] QB 425 the refusal to serve women in a wine bar unless they were seated at a table, when men were also served at the bar, was held to amount to unlawful discrimination under the Sex Discrimination Act 1975, s.29.

PERMITTED HOURS

Offence of selling outside permitted hours

It is an offence for any person or his/her servant or agent to sell or supply intoxicating liquor in licensed premises, or to consume it in, or take it from, such premises, except within permitted hours (LA 1964, s.59(1)–(2)). The offence is one of absolute liability, that is, one for which there are no defences (*Cundy* v *Le Cocq* (1884) 13 QBD 207). For example, a mistake as to time is not an excuse (*Hopkins* v *Ellis* (1924) 88 JPJ 446). To establish the offence it is not necessary to prove that money changed hands or that alcohol was in fact consumed (LA 1964, ss 196(1)–(2); *Thompson* v *Greig* (1869) 34 JP 214) and it was held in *Jefferson* v *Richardson* (1871) 35 JP 470 that the departure of a number of men in a drunken state from a public house at 1.00am was sufficient evidence that the offence was committed. The provisions as to hours do not apply to occasional licences (LA 1964, s.59(3)). Subject to certain exceptions, licence holders can generally close their premises at any time; the permitted hours provisions only restrict the times of selling intoxicating liquor on those premises.

Standard permitted hours for on-licensed premises

On-licensed premises have different permitted hours from off-licensed premises. For on-licensed premises the hours are, from Monday to Saturday, 11.00 am to 11.00 pm, unless the licensing justices believe it would be desirable in the district to allow them to begin as early as 10.00 am (LA 1964, s.60(1)(a), (4)). On Good Friday and Sunday, the permitted hours are 12 noon to 10.30 pm and on Christmas Day, 12 noon to 3.00 pm and 7.00 pm to 10.30 pm.

Permitted hours for off-licensed premises

The permitted hours for off-sales are, from Monday to Saturday: 8.00 am to 11.00 pm (LA 1964, s.60(6)), Good Friday: 8.00 am to 10.30 pm, Christmas Day: 12 noon to 3.00 pm and 7.00 pm to 10.30pm and for Sunday: 10.00 am to 10.30 pm.

Extension of permitted hours

Supper hour/restaurant certificate

A restaurant's permitted hours can be extended by what is known as a section 68 certificate to add a further hour to the general licensing hours or to cover the gap between 3.00 pm and 7.00 pm on Christmas Day (LA 1964, s.68). This certificate will only be granted if the premises are structurally adapted and are used, or intended to be used, for providing substantial refreshment, to which the sale and supply of intoxicating liquor is ancillary (LA 1964, s.68(3)). If these requirements are met, the certificate must be granted. The terms of any extension granted must be displayed on the premises.

Extended hours order

An extended hours order allows restaurants providing live entertainment to have their permitted hours extended to 1.00 am (LA 1964, s.70). Customers must consume intoxicating liquor ancillary to substantial refreshment and that entertainment and there must be a section 68 certificate already in force for the premises (LA 1964, s.70(1)).

An extended hours order will be refused or have its hours limited, even though these requirements are satisfied, if the licensing justices believe this would be reasonable in all the circumstances, and in particular to the comfort and convenience of those living near the premises.

If an order is granted, notice of the effect of the order must be displayed on the premises.

Intoxicating liquor must not be supplied after the entertainment and the substantial refreshment have stopped (LA 1964, s.70(2)). No sale or supply may be made to a person admitted to the premises either after midnight or less than half an hour before the entertainment ends (LA 1964, s.70(2)).

The applicant must tell the chief officer of police within 14 days of the order being granted (LA 1964, s.71), who may apply for the revocation of the order. It will be revoked if the use allowed by the order has not been made of the premises or there has been disorderly or indecent conduct or the premises have been ill-conducted.

Special hours certificates

A special hours certificate can extend the permitted hours on weekdays until 2.00 am, or 3.00 am in parts of the London metropolis (LA 1964, s.76(2)–(3)). It may only be granted if the premises are structurally adapted and the sale of alcohol will be ancillary to music and dancing and substantial refreshment, combined (LA 1964, s.77). In addition, there must be a public entertainments licence in force for the premises (LA 1964, s.77).

Premises to be used for public dancing or music and any other similar public entertainment in a London borough or the City of London need a public entertainments licence, granted under the London Government Act 1963. Outside Greater London, local authorities issue licences for any public entertainments.

Anyone who applies for a special hours certificate must give the clerk to the licensing justices and the chief officer of police at least 21 days written notice and advertise in the local press no more than 28 days, or less than 14 days, before the hearing. They must also display, for 7 days, a copy of the notice where it can conveniently be read by the public on or near the application premises, not more than 28 days or less than 14 days before the hearing.

The application proceeds in a similar way to an application for a new justices' licence. Anyone wishing to oppose the application must give the applicant and clerk at least 7 days written notice, stating the general grounds of opposition. The certificate may be granted with limitations as to particular times and dates (LA 1964, s.78A). It has been possible since May 1996 to obtain provisional special hours certificates.

A special hours certificate will be revoked if the public entertainments licence for the premises in question has not been renewed (LA 1964, s.81(1)). It may also be revoked on application of the chief officer of police if the premises have not been used for providing 'music and dancing and substantial refreshment to which the sale of intoxicating liquor is ancillary', a person has been convicted for the sale, supply or consumption of intoxicating liquor at those premises outside permitted hours, or customers are there during the additional hours to obtain intoxicating liquor rather than primarily to dance or take food (LA 1964, s.81(2)). The certificate must be revoked if this would prevent disorderly or indecent conduct in the premises (LA 1964, s.81(4)). Any person aggrieved by a decision to grant or revoke a special hours certificate or attach limitations or not has a right of appeal against that decision (LA 1964, ss 21, 50).

General orders of exemption

A general order of exemption to add to the permitted hours will be granted if it would accommodate a considerable number of people attending a public market or following a lawful trade or calling in the immediate neighbourhood of licensed premises (LA 1964, s.74(1)–(2). General orders of exemption can be varied or revoked (LA 1964, s.74(3)).

Special orders of exemption

Special orders of exemption allow the permitted hours to be extended on special occasions (LA 1964, s.74(4)). It is for the justices to determine what is a special occasion, but as a general guide, public holidays such as Christmas Eve and New Year's Eve (*Devine* v *Keeling* (1886) 50 JP 551), special birthdays and anniversaries and weddings may well be considered special occasions, while events organized primarily for the licensee's benefit and Christmas shopping week will not be special occasions.

Restriction of permitted hours

Licence conditions

Permitted hours of on-licensed premises can be restricted by conditions attached to the licence. Conditions may specify that the licence is to be a seasonal licence, where there are no permitted hours at certain times of the year, a six-day licence where there are no permitted hours on a Sunday or an early closing licence where the permitted hours end one hour earlier than the general licensing hours.

Restriction orders

It is also possible to restrict the permitted hours of on-licensed premises by means of a restriction order (LA 1964, s.67A). Such an order can specify any time between 2.30 pm and 5.30 pm on weekdays or 3.00 to 7.00 pm on Sunday and Good Friday for the permitted hours of on-licensed premises. They may apply to particular days of the week and particular periods of the year. Restriction orders do not apply to premises licensed for the sale of intoxicating liquor to be consumed off the premises, registered clubs or premises where there is an occasional licence (LA 1964, s.67A(1)). They can be made to prevent or reduce disturbance of or annoyance to persons living or working in the neighbourhood or disorderly conduct in or around the premises (LA 1964, s.67A(7)). There is a right of appeal to the Crown Court against the granting of a restriction order (LA 1964, s.67B).

Exceptions from the prohibition of sale or consumption outside permitted hours

Drinking up time or taking away

Intoxicating liquor which has been supplied during the permitted hours may be consumed on the premises 20 minutes after the end of the permitted hours, unless it was supplied or taken away in an open vessel (LA 1964, s.63(1)(a)). There are 30 minutes 'drinking up time' if the liquor is supplied to be consumed with a meal (LA 1964, s.63(1)(b)).

Residents, their private friends and employees

Residents of licensed premises can buy or be supplied with and drink intoxicating liquor outside the permitted hours (LA 1964, s.63(2)). A resident, for these purposes, also includes anyone carrying on or in charge of the business on licensed premises even though they are not residing there (LA 1964, s.63(4)). Residents may also supply intoxicating liquor outside permitted hours at the licensed premises to their private friends, provided they are entertaining them at their own expense (LA 1964, s.63(3)(b)). It is up to the defendant to prove that the persons are genuinely 'private friends' (*Atkins* v *Agar* [1914] 1 KB 26). Employees may be supplied with intoxicating liquor outwith permitted hours if supplied at the employer's expense or at the expense of the person conducting or owning the business (LA 1964, s.63(3)(c)).

Orders or deliveries

Intoxicating liquor may be ordered outside the permitted hours if the liquor is to be consumed off the premises (LA 1964, s.63(2)(b)).

Traders and clubs

A trader or a registered club may be sold intoxicating liquor outside permitted hours if it is to be used for the purposes of the trade or of the club (LA 1964, s.63(2)(c)).

International airports

Certain international airports approved by the Secretary of State are exempt from the provision prohibiting the sale of intoxicating liquor outside permitted hours (LA 1964, s.87). Similar provisions now apply to international ports.

Sports grounds

Permitted hours generally do not apply to licensed premises or registered clubs within the area of a sports ground designated by the Secretary of State for any designated sporting event and a general prohibition is imposed on the sale or supply of intoxicating liquor from such premises for such a period (Sporting Events (Control of Alcohol) Act 1985, s.3(1)).

CHILDREN AND YOUNG PERSONS

Persons under 18 years of age

A licence-holder or his/her servant, that is employee, must not sell intoxicating liquor to a person under the age of 18 or allow them to consume such liquor in a bar (LA 1964, s.169(1)). A bar includes the area used exclusively or mainly for the sale or consumption of intoxicating liquor (LA 1964, s.201(1)). A licensee must also not knowingly allow any person to sell intoxicating liquor to an under 18 year old (LA 1964, s.169(1)). No one under 18 is allowed to buy or attempt to buy intoxicating liquor from licensed premises or consume it in a bar (LA 1964, s.169(2)), and no person can buy or attempt to buy intoxicating liquor there for consumption in a bar by an under-18 (LA 1964, s.169(3)). However, a person of 16 or over may buy beer, porter, cider or perry to drink with a meal in a part of the premises usually set aside for meals which is not a bar (LA 1964, s.169(4)).

Someone charged with selling intoxicating liquor to an under-18 has a defence if they can prove that they exercised all due diligence to avoid the offence being committed or that they had no reason to suspect that the person was under 18 (LA 1964, s.169(4)).

Persons under 14 years of age

Generally, persons under 14 years of age are not allowed in the bar of licensed premises during permitted hours (LA 1964, s.168(1)). However, since 3 January 1995, it has been possible for licensing justices to grant a 'children's certificate' to anyone who holds or is applying for a justices' licence (LA 1964, ss 168(3A) and 168A as inserted by the Deregulation and Contracting Out Act 1994, s.19). From July to December 1995 there were 2326 applications for children's certificates and 81 per cent of those dealt with were granted ('Liquor Licensing – Facts and Figures' 1996 JP 160(6) 91–92). If there is such a certificate in force on the premises in question, and it is operational, no offence will be committed when a person under 14 enters the bar of licensed premises during permitted hours with a person who is over 18 years of age (LA 1964, s.168 and Sch. 2A – as inserted by Deregulation and Contracting Out Act 1994, s.19 and Sch. 7).

A children's certificate may be granted if the area applied for constitutes a suitable environment for under-14s, and meals and non-alcoholic drinks will be available in that area (LA 1964, s.168A(2)). In *Solomon* v *Green* (1955) 119 JP 289 sandwiches and sausages on sticks were held to constitute a meal and in *Timmis* v *Millman* (1965) SJ 31 a substantial sandwich eaten with beetroot and pickles was said to be sufficient to constitute a meal. Even if these requirements are satisfied, however, it is still at the justices' discretion to refuse the application. They may consider such issues as whether there is a safe play area for children in the premises, whether there are children's menus and soft drinks available and the character of the premises (Deregulation and Contracting Out Act 1994, s.4(2)).

All children's certificates are granted subject to at least the condition that meals and non-alcoholic drinks are available in the area in question (LA 1964, s.168A(2)). Other conditions may also be imposed including, for example, conditions restricting the hours and/or days on which the certificate is operational. The holder of a children's certificate must display it and its conditions in some obvious place in the area to which it relates (LA 1964, s.168A(3)). Anyone who is unhappy with a decision in relation to children's certificates may appeal to the Crown Court within 21 days (LA 1964, Sch. 12A, para. 10).

A certificate may be revoked, on application by the licensing justices or the police if the area does not constitute a suitable environment for under-14s or if there has been a serious or persistent failure to comply with any conditions attached to the certificate.

Under-14s may lawfully enter and remain in premises where alcohol is sold or consumed, but which do not hold a children's certificate if they are outside the bar, in unlicensed premises, residing on the premises or using them as an access to elsewhere where there is no alternative route (LA 1964, s.168(4)). Children are allowed in the bar of a registered club, unless the club's own rules state otherwise. Children under 14 may also enter a bar at any time when it is usual for it to be and is set apart for table meals, and intoxicating liquor is sold only as an ancillary to meals.

If none of the exemptions described above apply, and a licence-holder allows a child under 14 years of age into the bar of licensed premises during permitted hours, he/she must establish either that all due diligence was exercised to prevent the offence or that the person under 14 had apparently attained that age (LA 1964, s.168(3)).

Other offences in relation to young persons

A licence holder will be liable to a fine if he/she employs any person under 18 years of age in any bar of licensed premises when the bar is open for the sale or consumption of intoxicating liquor (LA 1964, s.170(1)).

A person who gives, or causes to be given, to a child under five any intoxicating liquor, except on medical grounds, is liable to a fine (Children and Young Persons Act 1933, s.5; Criminal Justice Act 1967, s.96(1), Sch. 3, Part I).

REGISTERED CLUBS

Introduction

Private clubs can only supply intoxicating liquor to their members if they are registered under the LA 1964, or hold a justices' licence (LA 1964, s.39(1)). Several requirements must be met before a club registration certificate will be granted by a Magistrates' Court, including that the club must already be established with at least 25 members and be a non-profit-making body (LA 1964, s.41). The statute also requires the club rules to contain certain provisions on membership and general meetings (LA 1964, s.41).

Application for a registration certificate

On an application for a club registration certificate, the police, fire and local authority may inspect the premises (LA 1964, ss 45–46). These bodies are then entitled to object to the application, along with anyone who is affected because of their occupation of or interest in other premises (LA 1964, s.44(1)). There are several grounds for objection, including:

1. that the application does not comply with the legislation's requirements;
2. that the premises are not suitable for that club;
3. that the club rules do not satisfy the Act's requirements on membership application or the club does not comply with the restrictions on the supply of intoxicating liquor in the statute. An objection may also be made if the premises are disqualified under s.47 of the LA 1964, or if anyone involved in managing the club is not a fit and proper person;
4. that the club is conducted in a disorderly manner or for an unlawful purpose; or
5. that the premises are being used for an unlawful purpose or there have been illegal sales of intoxicating liquor (LA 1964, s.44(1)).

Registration certificates last for 12 months, but can be renewed once this term has expired (LA 1964, s.40(2)). Similar provisions apply to renewals as for grants of club registration certificates. The certificate can be renewed for a year initially, and then for up to ten years on second or subsequent applications (LA 1964, s.40(3)).

Permitted hours

Registered clubs have the same permitted hours as licensed premises, with the exception of Christmas Day where the hours are as fixed by the club rules, though not before 12 noon or after 10.30 pm and for not more than six and a half hours. There must also be a minimum afternoon break between 3.00 pm and 5.00 pm and there must be no more than three and a half hours after 5.00 pm.

Extension of permitted hours

As for licensed premises, registered club premises may have a section 68 (supper hour) certificate although the notice provision for club applications differs from those for licensed premises, a section 70 (extended hours) order or a special order of exemption granted. They may also have a section 77 (special hours) certificate granted, but in the case of registered clubs, a certificate of suitability must be obtained from the local authority, rather than a public entertainments licence.

A single registration certificate may relate to a number of premises of the same club. Intoxicating liquor can only be supplied by or on behalf of a registered club at the premises where the club is registered, except when the club uses other premises on a special occasion, when only the members and guests may be allowed access to the premises. There are no restrictions on the hours of supply here and the club's other premises may also remain open during this 'special occasion'.

The police or local authority can apply to have the registration certificate cancelled on grounds similar to those for objecting to a new grant (LA 1964, s.44(2)). If a cancellation is granted, the premises can be disqualified, initially for up to 12 months and then for up to 5 years (LA 1964, s.47(1)–(2)).

LICENSING LAW IN SCOTLAND

Introduction

Licensing law in Scotland is regulated by the Licensing (Scotland) Act 1976, as amended (LSA). As in England and Wales, it is an offence to sell by retail intoxicating liquor without a licence. Alcoholic liquor in Scotland includes spirits, wine, porter, ale, beer, cider, perry and made-wine (LSA, s.139(1)). The distribution and control of licences in Scotland is effected by licensing boards which, like the English licensing committees, operate within specified districts (LSA, s.1). Licensing boards must meet at least four times in a year (LSA, s.4(1)(a)).

Who may hold a licence?

Anyone may make application for a liquor licence provided they have not been disqualified and are regarded as fit and proper persons. Applicants can be either an individual or a non-natural person, such as a company, club or association. In these cases an employee or agent who will be responsible for the running of the premises must be nominated.

The licences

Public house licence

A public house licence allows alcoholic liquor to be sold for consumption either on or off the premises (LSA, s.119(2)). It is required not only for the traditional 'pub', but also for restaurants which sell alcoholic liquor as a refreshment or with food not amounting to a 'meal'.

Off-sale licence

An off-sale licence allows alcoholic liquor to be sold for consumption off the licensed premises only (LSA, Sch. 1). If alcohol is consumed on off-licensed premises the licence-holder, his/her employee or agent will commit an offence unless the customer gave no prior indication of his/her intention to do so or the alcohol was supplied free of charge (LSA, s.97(1)).

Hotel licence

A hotel licence allows the licence holder to sell alcoholic liquor for consumption either on or off the premises of a hotel. A hotel is defined as a house with a minimum of four apartments to be used for travellers' sleeping accommodation when it is in a town or a suburban area, or with at least two such apartments when it is in an area with a population of under 1000 people (LSA, s.139(1)).

Restricted hotel licence

This licence is the Scottish equivalent to the English Part IV 'residential and restaurant licence'. A restricted hotel licence may be granted for a hotel which is structurally adapted and used, or intended to be used, to provide lunch or dinner or both for those using the hotel, whether they are resident there or not and which does not contain a bar counter (LSA, Sch. 1).

This licence authorizes alcoholic liquor to be sold or supplied, as an ancillary to a table meal or to a resident of the hotel for their own consumption on the premises or that of a 'private friend' who is being entertained at their expense (LSA, Sch. 1). It also allows alcohol to be sold or supplied at the premises as an ancillary to a meal to residents or to private friends entertained at their expense but to be consumed elsewhere (LSA, s.54(3)(e)).

Restaurant licence

A restaurant licence may be granted for similar premises to those of a restricted hotel licence, but here alcoholic liquor can only be sold or supplied as an ancillary to table meals taken in the premises (LSA, Sch. 1).

Refreshment licence

A refreshment licence allows alcoholic liquor to be sold or supplied on premises which are structurally adapted and *bona fide* used or intended to be used to provide refreshments including food, which need not amount to a 'meal', and non-alcoholic drinks to be consumed on the premises (LSA, Sch. 1). Again, there must be no bar counter.

Entertainment licence

An entertainment licence may be granted for places of public entertainment such as cinemas, theatres, dance halls and proprietory clubs (LSA, Sch. 1). It authorizes the sale or supply of alcoholic liquor on those premises as an ancillary to the entertainment, subject to conditions the licensing board may impose (LSA, Sch. 1).

Provisional licence

A provisional licence may be granted to any licence-holder whose premises are being reconstructed to allow business to be carried on in temporary premises (LSA, s.27).

Occasional licences

In Scotland, an occasional licence may be granted to any licence-holder other than one who holds a refreshment or an entertainment licence (LSA, s.33(10)). It allows alcoholic liquor to be sold for up to 14 days while catering for an event which is taking place outwith the licensed premises (LSA, s.33(1)).

An occasional licence may be granted subject to such conditions as the board thinks fit, but one granted to the holder of a restricted hotel or a restaurant licence must be subject to a condition that the sale of alcoholic liquor shall be ancillary to the provision of 'substantial refreshment' (LSA, s.33(3)). 'Substantial refreshment' must merely be available rather than actually provided. The occasional licence is not subject to any conditions that may be attached to the 'parent' licence (LSA, s.139).

Occasional permissions

Voluntary organizations may be granted an occasional permission, allowing the sale of alcoholic liquor for a maximum of 14 days at an event outwith licensed premises, which is related to or arises from activities of the organization (LSA, s.34(1)).

A maximum of four occasional permissions may be granted in any one year to the same voluntary organization (LSA, s.34(2)). Such conditions as the board thinks fit may be attached to the grant, contravention of which is an offence (LSA, s.34(3),(6)).

As with English liquor licences, Scottish licences may be granted as a new licence, by way of transfer or by renewal.

New licences

A new licence is generally granted for premises which were previously unlicensed or licensed under a different form of licence (LSA, s.139(1)). There are three main types of application.

Grant of a new licence

A new licence can only be granted for premises which are completed (LSA, s.23(1)). The application must be accompanied by detailed plans of the premises and certificates of suitability as to planning, building control and food hygiene (LSA, s.23(1)).

Full provisional grant of a new licence

Where premises are about to be or are being constructed a provisional grant of a new licence may be applied for (LSA, s.26). Similar plans and certificates of suitability to new licence applications are required. A grant may be made if the board are satisfied that the premises will be fit and convenient for their purpose and that it would have granted a licence to premises completed in accordance with the plans (LSA, s.26(1)). Once the premises do comply with the plans submitted, it becomes a 'full provisional grant' after an application for 'finalization' (LSA, s.26(4)).

Outline provisional grant of a new licence

An 'outline provisional grant' may be made with only a location plan and a brief description. Once granted, it must be 'affirmed' within 12 months by an application made to the board, together with more detailed plans of the premises which must not materially differ from the original plan and description submitted. Affirmation will be granted if the premises are completed in accordance with the plan. Affirmation is followed by finalization when the premises have been completed.

Application for a grant or provisional grant of a new licence

A notice intimating the application must be displayed at the premises to be easily read by the public and given to neighbouring occupiers at least 21 days before the quarterly meeting begins (LSA, s.10(2)(b), (3)(b)). If the application is for a public house it should state whether the Sunday permitted hours are intended to be used (LSA, s.10(3A)). Applications must also be published at least three weeks before the quarterly meeting in at least one newspaper circulating in the board's area (LSA, s.12(1)).

At least seven days before the board meeting, objections to applications can be made by the people listed in s.16(1) of the LSA, which include:

1. persons 'owning or occupying property' in the neighbourhood;
2. the local community council;
3. the chief constable;
4. the fire authority;
5. the local authority.

Persons 'owning or occupying property' in the neighbourhood include proprietors of rival licensed premises in the neighbourhood (*Loosefoot Entertainments Ltd* v *Glasgow District Licensing Board* 1990 SCLR 584) but not the daughter of a neighbouring proprietor who merely resided with him (*McDonald* v *Finlay* 1957 SLT 81). The grounds of objection must be specified in the notice by the objector (LSA, s.16(2)(a)). It is not sufficient simply to repeat the grounds of objections set out in the statute (*Chief Constable of Grampian* v *Aberdeen District Licensing Board* 1979 SLT (Sh Ct) 2). However, objections may only be entertained by the licensing board if they are relevant to one or more of the grounds set out in s.17 of the LSA. Where the objection is that the applicant is not a fit and proper person by reason of previous convictions of certain of its directors, it is not sufficient to staple the previous conviction schedules of the individuals concerned to a letter stating that the applicant is not a fit and proper person without at least identifying the individuals as directors of the applicant (*Fereneze Leisure Ltd* v *Renfrew District Licensing Board* 1990 SCLR 436).

Grounds of refusal

A new licence can be refused on four main grounds (LSA, s.17(1)). The first is on the suitability of the applicant. The applicant, the person the applicant will manage the premises for or anyone named in the application must be a fit and proper person to hold a licence. Criminal convictions, including convictions for offences under planning legislation (*Sutherland* v *Edinburgh District Licensing Board* 1984 SLT (Sh Ct) 241), may be considered in this respect, as may experience in the licensed trade. The second ground relates to the suitability of the premises. If the premises are not suitable or convenient for selling liquor, taking account of their location, character and condition, the nature and extent of their proposed use and the persons likely to use the premises, such as children, the application must be refused. A further ground of refusal exists where selling alcoholic liquor from premises is likely to cause undue public nuisance, or be a threat to public order or safety (e.g. *Freeland* v *Glasgow District Licensing Board* 1980 SLT (Sh Ct) 125). Finally, an application will be refused if granting it would cause over-provision of licensed premises in the locality in question. If an application for a new licence is refused, a subsequent application may not be made within two years unless otherwise stated or a section 14 direction is requested by the applicant at the time of refusal. Failure to request such a direction therefore has very serious consequences (LSA, s.14). An unsuccessful applicant or objector should also request a statement of reason for the Board's decision (LSA, s.18). An appeal against the decision may be made to the Sheriff Court (LSA, s.17).

Transfer of licences

Transfer to new tenant or to new or existing occupant

A licence transferred in these circumstances is subject to the conditions on which it was originally granted. There are two types of transfer possible:

1. the two-step system (temporary and permanent); or
2. the one-step permanent transfer (LSA, s.25(7)).

Under the former system, a temporary transfer is granted which remains effective until the next appropriate quarterly meeting of the board when the board decides on the licence's permanent transfer. Although anyone can object at this stage, the only ground of refusal is the suitability of the applicant to hold a licence. The transfer may not be granted subject to conditions. This first system involves risks and uncertainties, making the second one-step system frequently more attractive.

Under the latter system, an application for permanent transfer is made simply to a quarterly meeting. Objections can be made but again the only ground of refusal is the suitability of the applicant. *Fereneze Leisure Ltd* v *Renfrew District Licensing Board* 1990 SCLR 436 suggests that a transfer in favour of a shelf company with no possible unfavourable record and the existing manager, provided his record remains unblemished, is not open to refusal. Where the application is refused, the licence simply remains with the transferor.

The provisional grant of a licence may not be transferred.

In the case of death, bankruptcy or incapacity

A licence may be transfered to:

1. the executors, representatives or disponees of anyone who died before their licence expired or
2. the trustee, judicial factor or curator bonis of a licence-holder who has become bankrupt, insolvent or incapable before the licence expires,

provided the applicant is in possession of the premises (LSA, s.25).

Substitution of employee or agent

Where a licence is held by a non-natural person and an employee or agent, an application to substitute a new nominee must take place within 8 weeks of the employee or agent ceasing to be responsible for the day to day running of the premises or the licence will cease to have effect (LSA, s.11(4)). However, this provision does not mean that after the licence has ceased to have effect, an application cannot be made for its transfer to another employee or agent (*Argyll Arms (McManus) Ltd* v *Lorne, etc. Divisional Licensing Board* 1988 SLT 290).

Matters not affected by transfer

Any existing occasional and regular extensions of permitted hours, Sunday permitted hours and children's certificates remain unaffected by permanent transfers, transfers on death, bankruptcy and incapacity and substitutions of employees or agents.

Renewal of licences

A licence-holder may apply to the board to renew a licence which is about to expire (LSA, s.10). Objections may be made by the various bodies on the grounds of suitability of the applicant, suitability of the premises and public nuisance (LSA, s.16(1)). The relevant date for consideration of the suitability of the applicant or premises is the date of the hearing of the application for renewal and former deficiencies in the premises which have been rectified cannot be used to justify refusal of a renewal (*Bantop Ltd* v *Glasgow District Licensing Board* 1989 SCLR 731). Defects in the premises may be used as grounds for refusal of a licence renewal on the basis that they provide evidence that the applicant is not a fit and proper person (*Coppola* v *Midlothian District Licensing Board* 1983 SLT (Sh Ct) 95).

An application for renewing a public house or refreshment licence must state whether Sunday permitted hours are intended to be used (LSA, s.10(3A)). Similarly, any intention to apply for a children's certificate must be stated in a renewal application for a public house or hotel licence (Law Reform (Miscellaneous Provisions) (Scotland) Act 1990, Sch. 5, para. 6).

Suspension of licences

Suspension following a complaint

Where anyone listed in s.16(1) LSA makes a complaint, a licence may be suspended for up to one year if it would be in the public interest to do so, on the grounds that:

1. the licence-holder is no longer a fit and proper person to hold a licence; or
2. the use of the premises has caused undue public nuisance or a threat to public order or safety (LSA, s.31(1)-(2),(7)).

The board may take account of any misconduct by the licence-holder or by those frequenting the licensed premises (LSA, s.31(3)). It has been held that the cumulative effect of 33 incidents of under-age drinking and disorderly conduct over a two-year period was sufficient to prove both grounds for suspending a licence (*McKay* v *Banff and Buchan Western District Licensing Board* 1991 SLT 20).

Closure orders

If licensed premises are no longer suitable to sell alcoholic liquor, having regard to their character and condition, the nature and extent of the use of the premises, a closure order may be made (LSA, s.32(1)). Where a closure order is made the licence ceases to have effect and the closure order will remain in force until the matters have been 'satisfactorily remedied' (LSA, s.32(1),(4)).

The premises

Premises built on land acquired or appropriated by a special road authority, in other words, motorway service areas, may not be granted a new licence (LSA, s.28). However, although the English and Welsh legislation disqualifies garages from holding liquor licences, the Scottish legislation does not, despite the connection between drinking and driving.

In general, licensed premises cannot be reconstructed, extended or altered so as to affect a public part of the premises or communication with it, without the licensing board's consent, unless the change is required by order of some lawful authority (LSA, s.35(1)). Off-licensed premises do not need such consent.

Duration

All licences are valid until the quarterly meeting of the licensing board three years after the meeting at which the licence was granted or renewed (LSA, s.30(3)).

Permitted hours

Basic permitted hours

Generally, alcoholic liquor can only be sold or supplied in licensed premises within the permitted hours. All licensed premises (except off-sale premises) and registered clubs in Scotland have the following permitted hours:

Monday to Saturday: 11.00 am to 11.00 pm
Sunday: 12.30 pm to 2.30 pm and 6.30 pm to 11.00 pm
(LSA, s.53(1)).

Public houses and refreshment-licensed premises may only enjoy Sunday permitted hours if this intention was stated in the application for the grant, provisional grant or renewal of the licence (Law Reform (Miscellaneous Provisions) (Scotland) Act 1990, s.46(1)(a)). Sunday permitted hours may be refused for the grant or provisional grant of a new public house or refreshment licence if they would cause undue disturbance or public nuisance in the locality (LSA, s.17(2A)).

Off-licensed premises and separate off-sale departments of public houses and hotels which are subject to conditions under s.119(2) of the LSA have the following 'trading hours':

Monday to Saturday: 8.00 am to 10.00 pm
Sunday: No permitted hours (LSA, s.119(3)).

Extensions of the permitted hours

A licence-holder, other than one who holds an off-sale licence, may apply to the licensing board for a regular or an occasional extension of permitted hours, either of which may be granted unless they would be likely to cause 'undue public nuisance' or 'be a threat to public order or safety' (LSA, s.64). The permitted hours may also be extended in premises which provide table meals (LSA, ss 57–60).

Regular extensions

These may be granted if the board considers it desirable to do so, having regard to the social circumstances or activities in the area of the particular premises (LSA, s.64(3)). Objections may be made by any person mentioned in s.16(1). Conditions may also be attached (LSA, s.64(6)).

Occasional extensions

Occasional licences are granted for any occasion the board considers appropriate, such as weddings or birthday parties, and allow the sale or supply of alcoholic liquor in the appropriate premises for up to one month between such hours and on such day as the grant specifies (LSA, s.64(2)). Like regular extensions, they can also be made subject to conditions, breach of which is an offence.

Extensions for table meals

Permitted hours may be extended for the sale, supply or consumption of alcoholic liquor as an ancillary to table meals (LSA, ss 57–60). The alcoholic liquor must be sold or supplied in a part of the premises usually set apart for the service of such persons (LSA, ss 57(3), 58(3), 59(3), 60).

Sections 57 and 58 make an extra one and a half hours available at the end of the Sunday afternoon permitted hours and an additional two hours at the end of the evening permitted hours each day of the week for licensed premises, other than off-licensed premises.

Restaurant, restricted hotel, entertainment and refreshment licence-holders only need to serve notice of their intention to use these additional hours (LSA, ss 57(6), 58(6), 59(6), 60). Otherwise, the licensing board must be satisfied that the premises are structurally adapted and used or intended to be used to provide lunch or substantial refreshment, to which the sale and supply of alcoholic liquor is ancillary (LSA, ss 57(1), 58(1), 59(1)(b)(i)).

Section 59 allows a public house licence-holder with no Sunday permitted hours to sell or supply alcoholic liquor on Sundays between 12.30 pm and 2.30 pm and 6.30 pm and 11.00 pm as an ancillary to table meals.

The board must be satisfied that the premises are structurally adapted and *bona fide* used or intended to be used to provide lunch, dinner or both in a part of the premises 'usually set apart' for this and which does not contain a bar counter.

Seasonal licences

An applicant may request that permitted hours during part of the year, up to a maximum of 180 days be removed (LSA, s.62).

Exceptions to the permitted hours

There are various exceptions to the basic permitted hours:

1. There are 15 minutes drinking up time for alcoholic liquor supplied during the permitted hours or 30 minutes if the alcoholic liquor is consumed with a meal (LSA, s.54(3)(a),(h));
2. Alcoholic liquor may be taken from any premises 15 minutes after the permitted hours if it was supplied during the permitted hours, but not supplied or taken away in an open vessel (LSA, s.54(3)(b));
3. Permitted hours do not apply to any person residing on licensed premises, or to their 'private friends' entertained at their expense (LSA, s.54(3)(c)–(e));
4. The 'private friends' of a licence-holder who are entertained at his expense may be supplied with and consume alcoholic liquor outwith permitted hours (LSA, s.54(3)(g)); and
5. A trader or registered club may be sold alcoholic liquor outwith permitted hours for the purposes of the trade or club (LSA, s.54(3)(i)).

Restriction of the permitted hours

Restriction orders

Any licensed premises or registered club may have a restriction order placed on it. There are different kinds: afternoon, evening and Sunday restriction orders.

An afternoon restriction order reduces the permitted hours between 2.30 pm and 5.00 pm (LSA, s.65(1A)). An evening restriction order reduces the permitted hours in the evening, though not before 10.00 pm (LSA, s.65(1B)). They may be made where the board are satisfied that the sale or supply of alcoholic liquor in the afternoon or evening is causing 'undue public nuisance' or 'constitutes a threat to public order or safety' (LSA, s.65(1)(a)).

A Sunday restriction order provides either that there shall be no permitted hours on a Sunday or that Sunday permitted hours shall be reduced for a period as specified in the order (LSA, s.65(1C)). A board may make this order, if the use of licensed premises is causing 'undue disturbance or public nuisance having regard to the way of life in the locality on a Sunday' (LSA, s.65(1)(b)).

Temporary restriction orders

Premises, either individually or as a group in a particular area, may be closed for up to three hours if it would be in the interests of public order or safety (LSA, s.66). The purpose of this section has been held to be very narrow: to enable a senior police officer and no one else to close the premises 'on specific days in respect of particular events likely to cause trouble' (*Grainger* v *Edinburgh District Licensing Board* 1989 SLT 633).

Children and young persons

Children under 14

Generally, children under 14 may not enter the bar of licensed premises during the permitted hours (LSA, s.69(1)). A 'bar' has the same definition in Scots law as it does in English law. Any licence-holder, employee or agent who allows a person under 14 in a bar will be guilty of an offence unless he/she used all 'due diligence' to prevent it or had no reason to suspect the person was under age (LSA, ss 70(1), 71). However, under-14s may be allowed in a bar in limited circumstances:

1. outside the permitted hours;
2. where they are the children of the licence-holder, are resident in the premises or are passing through the premises where there is no other route (LSA, s.69(3)(a));
3. when the bar area is set apart for table meals and alcoholic liquor is sold as an ancillary to these meals;
4. to eat a meal in premises which hold a children's certificate, if they are accompanied by a person who is at least 18 (Law Reform (Miscellaneous Provisions) (Scotland) Act 1990, s.49(1),(3)).

Children's certificates in Scotland were introduced by the LSA and are very similar to the recently introduced English children's certificates. Children's certificates may be applied for in Scotland by anyone holding or applying for a public house or hotel licence (Law Reform (Miscellaneous Provisions) (Scotland) Act 1990, s.49(1); Sch. 5, para. 2). The premises must be a suitable environment for children to be in and meals and non-alcoholic drinks must be available. They are operational from 11.00 am to 8.00 pm. Conditions, including those restricting the time children are allowed, may be imposed (LSA, s.49(4)).

Under-14s are also allowed in premises which hold a refreshment licence during permitted hours, until 8.00 pm if they are accompanied by an over-18 (LSA, s.70(1)).

Children under 18

It is an offence to sell alcoholic liquor to under-18s in licensed premises (LSA, s.68(1)). It is also an offence for an under-18 to buy or attempt to buy alcoholic liquor in licensed premises (LSA, s.68(2)) or for someone to 'knowingly' buy or attempt to buy alcoholic liquor for an under-18 to consume in a bar (LSA, s.68(3)).

It is only an offence for an under-18 to consume alcoholic liquor *in a bar* (LSA, s.68(2)). It is therefore possible for an under-18 to consume alcoholic liquor bought by an adult in any part of the licensed premises which is not a bar.

A person aged 16 or over may be sold beer, wine, made-wine, porter, cider or perry as an ancillary to a meal in a restaurant in a part which is set apart for serving meals (LSA, s.68(4)).

As in England and Wales, a person under 18 may not be employed 'in any bar of licensed premises' when the bar is open 'for the sale or consumption of alcoholic liquor' (LSA, s.72(1)).

Registered clubs

Alcoholic liquor must not be sold or supplied in a club which does not hold a club certificate of registration, as granted by a sheriff. The club rules must contain certain provisions and comply with the LSA (LSA, s.107).

Holidays $\boxed{12}$

The travel agent

We begin with the travel agent because for many people that is where a holiday now starts. The travel agent is usually a high street shop – brightly lit and friendly. There is no obligation to buy and there are many very interesting brochures to examine. Even if a holiday is beyond a person's means the brochures are usually free and provide the food of dreams.

It was not always so. Obviously at one time people would simply make their own arrangements. Eventually people would set up in business to facilitate these arrangements. One of the pioneers was Thomas Cook. In fact he had two different good ideas. The first was the idea of the package. He arranged for a railway company to run a special train for a temperance meeting. Eventually the company promised to make the arrangement permanent if Cook would provide the passengers. This earliest of examples shows the economic balance moving from the monopoly or powerful provider to the person who can provide users or as might be said now – consumers. This beginning later brought about much more expensive tours including a Grand Tour of Europe. Sir Arnold Lunn did much the same for winter holidays, arranging for railways and hotels to remain open in the winter. Indeed his Public Schools Ski Club Annual was in effect a precursor of the ski brochure being published before the year it bears in its cover and carrying extensive details on hotel accommodation.

Later Cook began instead to sell tickets for overseas travel. It is here that the idea of 'agency' in its purer legal sense can be seen. It is appropriate for us to begin with the answer to the question – what, in law, is an agent?

We set out the general law of agency in Chapter Two (pp. 54–56). However, we need to examine it in the context of travel agency. You should also be aware that many legal precedents were decided in the days when travel agency was a lot less complex than today. Now it may well be the case that the high street travel agent is a wholly owned subsidiary of the tour operator company which may itself own or be owned by a hotel chain or an airline. There are, however, many independent local travel agents who are independent of these corporate structures.

The basic position is that the agent brings the customer and the principal into a contractual relationship and the agent has no part in the contract. In practice most Association of British Travel Agents (ABTA) agents have a detailed formal agency agreement with all of the companies with whom they deal. This will deal with the stocking of brochures, the use of booking forms, the dealings with money, a prohibition against the making of warranties and rights of indemnity.

One of the important issues to be determined is: who in law is the travel agent an agent of? Many consumers will think the agent is their agent. The uniformed employee is so helpful in trying to meet their needs and to help them get what they want. But as we have already pointed out, that friendly uniformed employee works for an organization which has a written formal contract with client organizations. So at first sight you probably think that the travel agent is the agent of organizations he/she represents when meeting the public. It is they who pay the wages of the uniformed employee indirectly. The tour operator pays a commission to the agent. The most interesting feature of all of this is that the agency issue arises because what is being sold is contracts – expectancies. Economically the analysis would be to see the traveller as consumer, the agent as retailer and the tour operator as producer. Legally, we must still ask, who is the principal and who the agent? The practical relevance becomes clear when the travel agent makes a representation about the holiday. If the travel agent is the agent of the principal, the principal should be bound. If not, the consumer. So the point is a practical one. The issue has come before the courts, although in *Kemp* v *Intasun Ltd* 1987 2 FTLR 234 the court refused to decide the matter. We may obtain some assistance, however, from insurance cases regarding the position of the insurance broker who is in some ways in a similar position to the travel agent. In the field of insurance the courts have held that the insurance broker is the agent of the insured and not of the insurance company – even though the insurance company pays the commission (*Anglo-African Merchants Ltd* v *Bayley* [1970] 1 QB 311).

So the answer is that there is no final answer! All the paper work has to be read through. With ABTA agents it is clear from the ABTA Travel Agents Code of Conduct that they are the operators' agents. But the member of the public does not know this. However, in cases where the Package Travel, Package Holidays and Package Tours Regulations 1992 ('the Package Holiday Regulations') apply the consumer has rights anyway and all this old common law does not matter.

Naturally, tour operators have many common interests and as a result of this concentration there was a reference to the Monopolies and Mergers Commission (MMC) by the Director General of Fair Trading as a result of steps which Thomson, Horizon and Intasun had taken to prevent a travel agent from supplying their holidays at a lower price than that set by those operators in their brochures. The MMC concluded that the public interest was not being served since competition between travel agents was being stifled because of the way in which the operators were interfering with the way an agent induced customers to make bookings through it rather than through another agent.

Accordingly delegated legislation in the form of the Restriction on Agreements and Conduct (Tour Operators) Order 1987 was passed to ensure that these agreements are controlled. The Order provides that

> a travel agent is free to offer inducements to customers to buy foreign package holidays through him, rather than through another agent, provided that the inducement is made expressly on his own behalf.

If the EC Directive on package travel, package holidays and package tours (Directive 90/314/EEC) ('the Package Travel Directive') succeeds in fostering a trans-European market then similar conduct will be restrained by EC competition law preventing among other things the abuse of a dominant position, certain concentrations and mergers.

The representative

The representative features in many of the provisions of the Package Holiday Regulations and, for example, under regulation 8 the consumer must be given the name, address and telephone number of the representative. There is no definition of a representative. There is no specification of what degree of authority the representative must have. Clearly though the representative will have to be able to do something when contacted by the consumer.

The new personnel

The Package Holiday Regulations – discussed below – have introduced a whole new cast of characters. Thus the law now focuses on the following persons:

Organizers

An organizer is the person who otherwise than occasionally organizes packages and sells or offers them for sale, whether directly or through a retailer.

Retailers

A retailer is a person who sells or offers for sale a package put together by the organizer.

Other party

Perhaps the most curious character is 'the other party to the contract' who is the party other than the consumer being the organizer or retailer or both of them. Thus even though the retailer might well describe the person he/she sold a holiday to as the other party to a contract they are not so far as the law is concerned!

Enforcement authority

For the purposes of the Regulations, every local weights and measures authority – which we more commonly know as Trading Standards Departments – in Great Britain is an enforcement authority and they are duty bound to enforce regulations 5, 7, 8, 16 and 22. Local authorities are the local weights and measures authorities. In Northern Ireland the duty falls on the Department of Economic Development (Sch. 3 para. 1(1)–(2)).

Director General of Fair Trading

The Director General is consulted before prosecutions proceed in name of the enforcement authority (Sch. 3, para. 2; but not in Scotland Sch. 3, para. 2(2)).

Authorized institution

An authorized institution is a person authorized under the law of a member state of the European Economic Area to carry on the business of entering into bonds of the kind envisaged by the Regulations (regs 17–18) in relation to the provision of sufficient evidence of security for the refund of money prepaid by consumers and for the repatriation of consumers in the event of the organizer and/or retailer becoming insolvent (reg. 16; see pp. 299–301). In practice such persons in the UK are banks and insurance companies.

A bond is a guarantee, which cannot be revoked, provided by such an institution which will be paid to an approved body (see below) to provide a fund to be paid out to consumers who have prepaid their holidays and to enable consumers on holiday to be repatriated in the event that the organizer and/or retailer becomes insolvent. The Package Holiday Regulations were recently amended to provide that such institutions included those authorized in the Channel Islands or the Isle of Man to carry on the business of entering into bonds: Package Travel, Package Holidays and Package Tours (Amendment) Regulations 1995.

Approved bodies

In terms of the bonding regulations (regs 17–18) the other party to a contract must pay money to an authorized institution (see above) to provide for payment to such a body to provide for insolvency (see pp. 299–301). Such a body is one which is, for the time being, approved by the Secretary of State. Bodies including ABTA, the Federation of Tour Operators (FTO) and the Association of Independent Tour Operators (AITO) have been approved by the Secretary of State. Approved bodies may now have insurance cover with an insurer authorized in the Channel Islands or Isle of Man: Package Travel, Package Holidays and Package Tours (Amendment) Regulations 1995.

Consumer

The definition in the Package Travel Regulations means not only the person who takes or agrees to take the package (who is known as the 'principal contractor') but also, where the context requires, any person on whose behalf the principal contractor agrees to purchase the package (who are known as the other beneficiaries) or any person to whom the principal contractor or any of the other beneficiaries transfers the package (who is known as the transferee). This is a very interesting definition because it provides that even though the persons who benefit from the holiday are not necessarily parties to the contract, they are still to be regarded as consumers and thus benefit from the protection which the Package Travel Regulations affords. This is a significant exception to the rule about privity of contract (see Chapter Two, pp. 52–53).

THE HOLIDAY

Travel only

It is possible that a traveller purchases only travel. In these cases the matter is regulated by the contract which, if it is for international travel, may well be covered by conditions (for a discussion of the law relating to conditions in contracts, see Chapter Two pp. 42–47).

Accommodation only

Travellers may drive themselves to a destination and be seeking accommodation only. Much of this is supplied by the agent and ordinary principles of contract apply. For a discussion of the law relating to innkeepers and their liabilities, see Chapter Nine.

Package travel

Following the Package Travel Directive, 'package' in the Regulations means

the pre-arranged combination of at least two of the following components when sold or offered for sale at an inclusive price and when the service covers a period of more than twenty-four hours or includes overnight accommodation:

(a) transport;

(b) accommodation;

(c) other tourist services not ancillary to transport or accommodation and accounting for a significant proportion of the package, and

(i) the submission of separate accounts for different components shall not cause the arrangements to be other than a package;

(ii) the fact that a combination is arranged at the request of the consumer and in accordance with his specific instructions (whether modified or not) shall not of itself cause it to be treated as other than pre-arranged (reg. 2(1)).

The Department of Trade and Industry (DTI) has provided unofficial guidance on this definition. If a group of people share the cost of a package they have put together themselves then this is not sold or offered for sale and may fall outside the definition. The DTI also suggests that a geology field trip would not fall within the scope of the Regulations. Although it is clear that separate billing cannot 'unpackage' a holiday the DTI point out correctly that if a person buys a plane ticket one day and goes back a day later to buy accommodation this does not make a package.

More subtly if the traveller pays the agent for the travel but pays the hotel direct at the end of the stay this too is not a package. The DTI go even further and indicate that if a traveller asks a travel agent to book the specific travel and a hotel not already on the books then the package was not pre-arranged and not within the scope of the rules even if the customer pays for both at the same time. Helpfully the DTI indicate that a *de minimis* approach is to be taken and that free transport to take hotel guests from the airport to the hotel would not constitute a transport element and in the same way a berth on a cross-channel ferry would not create a package. A cabin on a cruise ship is considered to be different because the purpose of the cabin is not just travel. More difficult would be travel by the Orient Express. The DTI properly consider many factual situations that test the Package Travel Directive and the Package Travel Regulations and perhaps gloss the Package Travel Directive when making a distinction between services and facilities:

Access to fishing rights on a local river would normally be a service. Provision of a swimming pool at a hotel would be a facility. Provision of facilities does not create a package. The department does not regard evening entertainment at an hotel as a tourist service. For a tourist service to be significant its presence would have to be a significant part of the reason for the package. For example if, as part of a week long stay during the Salzburg Festival, an hotel offered opera tickets at an inclusive price together with accommodation it would be likely to be a package. But an hotel in London offering a theatre ticket during a week long stay may not be, though an overnight stay plus theatre tickets would be.

It is clear then that there will be difficulties of interpretation and there may be differences across national boundaries. The best idea for the practically minded is always to bear in mind what it is the Package Travel Directive is seeking to do and assume it has done so. Educational conferences gave the DTI cause for much thought and these are unlikely to be packages because they are not of a tourist nature but organizers will have to be careful just how many excursions there are 'on the side'.

One final point to note regarding the 'packages' referred to in the Package Travel Regulations. The packages are not simply those for holidays within the UK or EC: they are packages for any destination whatsoever sold within the UK which could, for example, be for Himalayan trekking expeditions or seabird spotting holidays in the Galapagos islands.

THE OBLIGATIONS

Civil liability

Common law

The leading case is *Jarvis* v *Swans Tours Ltd* [1973] 1 All ER 71. The brochure advertised a houseparty in Morlialp. There was to be a welcome party. There was to be a yodler. The plaintiff, a local authority solicitor, booked a holiday. For the second week he was the only party in the houseparty. The yodler was a local man in his working clothes who sang a few songs very quickly and left. The bar was an unoccupied annexe open on only one evening. The skis supplied were the wrong size. The skiing piste was some distance away. There was no welcome party and 'not much fun at night'. The Court of Appeal awarded the plaintiff damages on the basis of his disappointment at the holiday. The court said that this was consonant with general principles in that the reason damages were awarded in this case was that the contract itself contemplated pleasure and enjoyment. This case opened the door to claims for poor holidays based on contract.

However, in a subsequent case an interesting point was raised as to the scope of liability under the contract. In *Jackson* v *Horizon Holidays* [1975] 3 All ER 92 a man sued for the poor holiday he had but also sued for the poor holiday his family had. The legal point of interest was that while Mr Jarvis could recover, the members of his family were not direct contracting parties. Mr Jackson wrote a letter which is a model of what should be done by a consumer when booking. It was clear he wanted a luxury holiday – everything of the highest standard. However, there was a catalogue of defects. These included the fact that there was no bath, the children's room was full of fungus, the toilet was stained and there was no swimming pool. The court held that there was no need to resort to the fiction that the father was the agent of the family. Only the father had a claim but his damages could reflect the loss of enjoyment of the other members of the family. This is a partial exception to the general rule regarding privity of contract (see Chapter Two, pp. 52–53).

There has since been a catalogue of cases where holiday makers have recovered for inadequate accommodation. Thus, where a holidaymaker was first put in a room with fungus and slime on the wall and then moved into another room from which beetles later emerged, damages were recovered for breach of contract (*Bragg* v *Yugotours* [1982] CLY 777). In another case, this time in Malta, the apartment had not been cleaned, the toilet had broken away from the wall, the mattress was stained with blood and urine and green mould was found in the fridge. A witness described the place as 'grotty, grimy and horrible'. The court awarded damages for breach of contract for the cost of the holiday which was completely wasted and for discomfort and distress (*Rhodes* v *Sunspot Tours* [1983] CLY 984).

Scott and Scott v *Blue Sky Holidays* [1985] CLY 943 is especially interesting. The plaintiffs booked a four star hotel in Tenerife. They were put into a cramped room without twin beds. Their meals were greasy and cold. Because the holiday was supposed to be luxurious the court would have awarded substantial damages but as the plaintiffs had not mitigated their loss by complaining on site their award was less.

In another case the holiday was in an exclusive villa, but a plumber was still working on it. It was damp inside and the family had to sleep with their clothes on. The children could not play because there was a vicious dog nearby. The court awarded damages (*Carter* v *Thomson Travel* [1986] CLY 976). You will not be surprised to find that a man who booked a luxury villa in St Jean Cap Ferrat and was given a cramped apartment instead was entitled to damages (*McLeod* v *Hunter* [1987] CLY 1162). Where all the facilities advertised were not available because of a dispute the court awarded damages *(Jones and Jones* v *Villa Ramos (Algarve)* [1988] CLY 1061).

Duthie v *Thomson Holidays* [1988] CLY 1058 is laden with irony. The plaintiff made a claim because she had booked a fortnight in Greece with hostel accommodation and when she got there she was told there was no accommodation. She sued and was successful. However, the background to this is that at the time Greek law required charter passengers to have accommodation. Thus informal arrangements grew up whereby travel companies and travellers pretended there was accommodation to get the cheap flights. In 1989 awards as high as £100 and awards of £50 per day were made to plaintiffs who got a reasonable bungalow instead of an excellent one. Although this seems a lot, a look at any brochure shows how the seller often charges more for each little extra. Clients who booked class A accommodation which was filthy and had bad electrics were transferred to category E accommodation which was infested with cockroaches. The court awarded damages (*Booth and Ingram* v *Best Travel* [1990] CLY 1542).

It is quite clear that the common law quickly developed solutions to protect expectations and control wrongdoing. Nonetheless, the common law has to work from case to case and it may well be that the complex relationships involved in package travel required statutory reorganization any way.

The Package Travel Regulations

Introduction

As the Package Travel Directive is now implemented by UK Regulations, this section sets out the nature of the legislation and its purposes as well. The authority for these following statements is the preamble of the Directive itself. Differences between the Regulations and the Directive will be noted where the particular point arises. Directive 90/314/EEC on package travel, package holidays and package tours proceeded on the basis of the harmonization needed for completion of the internal market in 1992. The EC considered the tourist sector to be an essential part of the internal market. It had been accepted that the national laws of member states showed many disparities and that practices were different giving rise to obstacles to the freedom to provide services and thus distorting competition. The EC accepted that tourism played an increasingly important part in the economies of member states and that the package system was 'fundamental' to tourism. It considered that common rules would stimulate growth in the sector and not just among member states but would attract tourists from outside the EC. The Package Travel Directive also appeared against the general background of consumer protection. Thus the intention was that the consumer should be protected regardless of the vagaries of national legal systems. The concepts which can be seen in the Package Travel Regulations are envisaged in principle as well as in the letter of the Package Travel Directive.

The Package Travel Regulations are now the main source of law in the UK in relation to most disputes that will arise and the legal environment of the business for the foreseeable future. The discussion of the Package Travel Directive above fully explains what the Package Travel Regulations are about but so far as disputes between parties are concerned the social and economic considerations are deeply subordinated to the particular and detailed rules now laid down in this delegated legislation.

The Package Travel Regulations came into force on 23 December 1992 having been made on 22 December 1992. They apply to packages sold or offered for sale in the territory of the United Kingdom.

Certain ordinary words of the English language are given very technical meanings and many of these result from the Package Travel Directive. Indeed they are so technical that a lawyer unfamiliar with the Regulations might find the meaning elusive. A good example of this is the definition of the word 'offer'. In the Regulations it 'includes an invitation to treat whether by means of advertising or otherwise and cognate expressions shall be construed accordingly'. Thus the important legal distinctions discussed in Chapter Two between an 'offer' and an 'invitation to treat' (pp. 39–40) are of much less relevance.

Misleading descriptive matter

There is a right to compensation if descriptive matter is misleading to the extent of any loss suffered in consequence (reg. 4). The most significant feature is that the particulars of the brochure constitute implied warranties in England and implied terms in Scotland (reg. 6; see also Chapter Two, pp. 42–47). This rule does not apply to the statement of arrangements for security for money paid over and for the repatriation of the consumer in the event of insolvency. The parties may agree after contract that some of the terms should not be terms of the contract. Although the regulation says nothing about it, the fact that the brochure becomes a contractual document means that it should be possible to sue for breach of contract much more easily.

It is also an implied condition in England and Wales and an implied term in Scotland that reg. 9(1) has been complied with. That regulation requires that the contract contains the Schedule 2 matters noted at the end of this paragraph and that all the terms of the contract are set out in writing or another form that is comprehensible and accessible to the consumer and communicated to the consumer before the contract is made. This is subject to exemption where there is a very short period of time involved. Regulation 9(1) requires a written copy of the terms to be supplied to the consumer once the contract is made. The Schedule 2 matters are as follows:

1. The travel destinations and, where periods of stay are involved, the relevant periods, with dates.
2. The means, characteristics and categories of transport to be used and the dates, times and points of departure and return.
3. Where the package includes accommodation, its location, its tourist category or degree of comfort, its main features and, where the accommodation is to be provided in a member state, its compliance with the rules of that member state.
4. The meals which are included in the package.
5. Whether a minimum number of persons is required for the package to take place and, if so, the deadline for informing the consumer in the event of cancellation.
6. The itinerary.
7. Visits, excursions or other services which are included in the total price agreed for the package.
8. The name and address of the organizer, the retailer and, where appropriate, the insurer.
9. The price of the package, if the price may be revised in accordance with the term which may be included in the contract under regulation 11, an indication of the possibility of such price revisions, and an indication of any dues, taxes or fees chargeable for certain services (landing, embarkation or disembarkation fees at ports and airports and tourist taxes) where such costs are not included in the package.
10. The payment schedule and method of payment.
11. Special requirements which the consumer has communicated to the organizer or retailer when making the booking and which both have accepted.
12. The periods within which the consumer must make any complaint about the failure to perform or the inadequate performance of the contract.

Transfer of package when consumer prevented from proceeding with package
There is an implied term that where the consumer is prevented from proceeding with the package the consumer can transfer his/her booking to another acceptable person providing notice is given (reg. 10). Both parties are jointly and severally liable to the operator. This is a difficult provision. The regulation reflects the Package Travel Directive's use of the word 'prevented'. The DTI guidance says it is not intended to cover a change of mind. Thus it might be said that it certainly would not allow a person to sell on for a premium. Failure to allow the transfer would constitute a breach of contract. Examples suggested by the DTI are illness, death of a close

relative, jury service or the requirements of an employer. The DTI point out that the choice of the other party must be the consumer's and there should not be a requirement that it should be transferred to a person at the top of a waiting list.

Price revisions

Price revision clauses are – on the face of it – void (reg. 11). However, they may be allowed if the following conditions are met:

1. the contract states precisely how the revised price is to be calculated;
2. the contract provides that price revisions are to be made solely to allow for variations in:
   (a) transportation costs, including the cost of fuel;
   (b) dues, taxes or fees chargeable for services such as landing taxes or embarkation or disembarkation fees at ports and airports (and this in the view of the DTI includes VAT);
   (c) exchange rate variation.

In any event no increase can be made within 30 days of the departure (or a longer period if specified). A price rise even if justified cannot exceed 20 per cent of the cost.

Significant alterations to package before departure

It is an implied term that where the operator does have to alter an essential term of the contract the operator must notify the consumer as quickly as possible to allow the consumer to withdraw without penalty or accept a rider to the contract subject to any impact on the price (reg. 12). The consumer is bound by an implied condition to inform the organizer or retailer as soon as possible if he/she wishes to withdraw or accept the alteration.

Withdrawal by consumer and cancellation by organizer

There are a series of implied terms where there is a legal cancellation (reg. 13). The consumer is entitled to do any one of three things:

1. to take a substitute package of equivalent or superior quality if the other party to the contract is able to offer such a substitute;
2. to take a substitute package of lower quality if the other party to the contract is able to offer one and to recover the difference in price;
3. to have repaid as soon as possible all the monies paid under the contract.

The consumer is to be compensated for non-performance unless the package was cancelled because the numbers who have agreed to take the package are less than the required minimum or unless there are unusual and unforeseeable circumstances beyond the party's control, the consequences of which could not have been avoided by all due care (reg. 13(3)) although overbooking is expressly excluded from this exemption (reg. 13(4)).

Implied terms where apparent that significant proportion of services will not be provided post-departure

Terms are implied to cover cases where after departure it becomes apparent some services will not be available (reg. 14). The organizer must make suitable alternative arrangements at no extra cost for the continuation of the package and compensate the consumer for the difference in the services. The DTI guidance suggests that disappointment and inconvenience ought to be included within the compensation. If the organizer cannot continue the package then at no cost the consumer should be returned to the point of departure and compensated.

Other party to contract liable for proper performance of obligations under contract

The core provision is probably reg. 15 which makes the other party to the contract liable to the consumer for the proper performance of obligations under the contract irrespective of whether such obligations are to be performed by that other party or by another supplier. This is achieved without affecting any right to proceed against other suppliers of services direct. This is clearly a consumer protection measure since it is easier for the consumer to take action against the retailer or organizer than against suppliers such as hoteliers in other countries. So the organizer and/or retailer are made primarily responsible for the performance of the contract even where the services are provided by other persons (as will often be the case). However, if the retailer and/or organizer is sued by a consumer then the retailer and/or organizer may have a right of action against the other suppliers.

Under the common law there was a duty on tour operators to use reasonable care in the selection of suppliers and the strict liability imposed by the Package Travel Regulations certainly requires a similar approach to be adopted by retailers and/or organizers. The regulation imposes *prima facie* strict liability subject to exemptions set out in the regulation. The other party is liable for any damage caused by the failure to perform or improper performance unless the failure is not due to the other party's fault or other supplier because:

1. the failures are attributable to the consumer;
2. the failures are attributable to an unconnected third party and are unforeseeable or unavoidable;
3. the failures are due to unusual and unforeseeable circumstances beyond the other party's control or which could not with all due care be foreseen or forestalled.

An example of the consumer causing the loss or damage which would probably have satisfied the first defence, although it arose prior to the introduction of the Package Travel Regulations, is *Spencer* v *Cosmos Air Holidays* [1990] CLY 635. In this case the plaintiff and her friends were excluded from their hotel because of their objectionable behaviour. After spending two nights on the beach they were given inferior alternative accommodation 15 miles away by the defendants' representative. They argued that they had been wrongly identified as troublemakers and were entitled to damages. The Court of Appeal held that their claim would fail if it was found that they had misbehaved themselves. It was an implied term of the contract that they would not conduct themselves in a manner which was objectionable to other guests and staff.

The DTI consider that the third defence covers air traffic control delays, bad weather not reasonably to be expected and industrial action outside the organizer's control. It is also an implied term that in the event of the last two reasons for failure the operator will give prompt assistance to a consumer in difficulty. Limitations to liability based on international conventions may be adopted, for example Warsaw Convention on Carriage of Passengers by Air 1929. In cases not involving personal injuries a reasonable limitation may be placed on damages.

It is an implied term that if a consumer complains about a defect in performance, the other party or his/her local representative will make prompt efforts to find appropriate solutions.

The contract must oblige the consumer to communicate their complaints at the earliest opportunity in writing or any other appropriate form, to the supplier and to the other party. So far as the DTI are concerned, a failure to do this will not result in the loss of the right of action but could lead to an abatement of damages.

These provisions cannot be contracted out of.

Criminal law liability

Introduction

The principal cases of liability are now likely to be those set out below under the Package Travel Regulations. In particular, attention is drawn to the extensive new offences and powers of the enforcement authority to exercise various powers. Prior to the new Regulations the most important provisions were those under the Trade Descriptions Act 1968 (TDA) and the Consumer Protection Act 1987 (CPA). These are still applicable albeit it might be expected that prosecutions may in future come under the Package Travel Regulations.

Liability under Trades Description Act 1968 (TDA)

The TDA makes it an offence to make a statement known to be false, or recklessly (made regardless of whether it is true or false) to make a statement which is false (that is, false to a material degree). The TDA applies only to certain false statements – essentially those relating to the service to be provided, including the location or amenities of any accommodation provided. Anything which might be taken to be a statement can be deemed to be a statement.

It is still a *prima facie* offence if a brochure falls into the hands of a purchaser and has within it a false statement, even if the company had tried to recall the brochure and did not know that the statement was false when they published the brochure (*Wings Ltd* v *Ellis* [1984] 1 All ER 1046). There is no liability for a statement to the future so long as it does not imply a present statement (*R* v *Sunair Holidays Ltd* [1973] 2 All ER 1233. However, in the overbooking case, *British Airways Board* v *Taylor* [1976] 1 All ER 65, where a traveller received written confirmation regarding his return reservation to Bermuda and subsequently found at the airport that no seat was available, it was held that the statement in the letter was known to be false rather than a false statement which had been recklessly made.

There is a defence if the tour operator can show that the offence was due to a mistake or reliance on another person or an accident and the operator took all reasonable care to avoid commission of the offence. It is possible to infer recklessness from the facts. In a case where a schooner used on the holiday was not as per the brochure picture, the reason being that the boat booked was not available, the court held the company liable (*Yugotours* v *Wadsley* [1988] *The Guardian*, 3 June).

Liability under the Consumer Protection Act 1987 (CPA)

The CPA governs misleading price indications, including price indications which become misleading if all reasonable steps are not taken to prevent consumers relying on them. There is a code of practice promulgated under the CPA which may be used as evidence of an offence (see also Chapter One, pp. 10–11). Under the code, tour operators have to make the correct price known before the contract is made; if the indication becomes misleading all travel agents must be advised and bookings made should be allowed to be cancelled; travel agents must pass on the information to customers. There are various defences.

Liability under the Package Travel Regulations

Introduction

The extent of liability under the Package Travel Regulations is considerable. The particular offences specify the principal parties liable but reg. 25 provides a general framework of liability which extends the *prima facie* liability expressed in the particular offences.

Where commission of an offence is due to an act or default committed by some other person in the course of any business he/she has, the other person is guilty of the offence regardless of whether the principal offender is proceeded against (reg. 25(1)). This extended liability is subject to a general defence that a person may prove that he/she is a person whose business it is to publish or arrange to publish brochures and that he/she received the brochure for publication in the ordinary course of business and did not know and had no reason to suspect that its publication would amount to an offence (reg. 25(5)).

Where a body corporate, such as a limited company (see Chapter Three, pp. 85–87) is guilty of an offence then in respect of any act or default which is shown to have been committed with the consent or connivance of, or to be attributable to any neglect on the part of any director, manager, secretary or other similar officer of the body corporate or any person who was purporting to act in any such capacity, that person is guilty as well as the body corporate and can be punished accordingly (reg. 25(2), see also Chapter Five, p. 114). The provisions extend even further: where a body corporate is managed by its members (i.e. its shareholders), a member will be liable in respect of their functions of management as if a director of the body corporate.

In Scotland a partnership is a kind of separate legal person (see Chapter Three, p. 78) and the Regulations provide that the partners as well as the partnership shall be liable (reg. 25(4)).

Proceedings must be taken within three years from the date of commission of the offence or the end of a year from the date of discovery of the offence whichever is the earlier (reg. 26(1)).

Brochure requirements

Regulation 5 provides, subject to a transitional provision for brochures first made available before December 1992 (reg. 5(4)), that no organizer can make available a brochure to a possible consumer unless it indicates in a legible, comprehensible and accurate manner the price and adequate information about the matters specified in Schedule 1 to the extent relevant (reg. 5(1)). A similar obligation is put upon a retailer where he or she knows or has reasonable cause to believe that a brochure does not comply with the rules. The information required is as follows:

1. the destination and the means, characteristics and categories of transport used;
2. the type of accommodation, its location, category or degree of comfort and its main features and, where the accommodation is to be provided in a member state;
3. the meals which are included in the package;
4. the itinerary;
5. general information about passport and visa requirements which apply for British citizens and health formalities required for the journey and the stay;
6. either the monetary amount or the percentage of the price which is to be paid on account and the timetable for payment of the balance;
7. whether a minimum number of persons is required for the package to take place and, if so, the deadline for informing the consumer in the event of cancellation;
8. the arrangements (if any) which apply if consumers are delayed at the outward or homeward points of departure; and
9. the arrangements for security of money paid over for the repatriation of the consumer in the event of insolvency (Schedule 1).

The consequences of breach are that the organizer or retailer is guilty of an offence and liable to a maximum fine of £5,000 on summary conviction and an unlimited fine on conviction on indictment.

Information to be provided prior to conclusion of contract

Moving on to the next stage, information is to be provided before a contract is concluded. The information must be in writing or in some other appropriate form. The potential criminal in this situation is the other party to the contract defined above (see p. 287). The information required to avoid falling foul of the criminal law in these circumstances is:

1. general information about passport and visa requirements which apply to British citizens who purchase the package including information about the length of time it is likely to take to obtain the appropriate passports and visas;
2. information about health formalities required for the journey and the stay; and
3. the arrangements for security for the money paid over and where applicable for the repatriation of the consumer in the event of insolvency (reg. 7(2)).

Again the maximum penalty is a fine of £5,000 on summary conviction or an unlimited fine on conviction on indictment (reg. 7(3)).

Pre-departure information

As the consumer comes ever closer to their Brigadoon more information must come their way. The other party to the contract must, in good time before the start of the journey, provide the consumer with the following information in writing or in some other appropriate form:

1. the times and places of intermediate stops and transport connections and particulars of the place to be occupied by the traveller. Here the regulation eschews legalese and offers some examples and they are whether the accommodation is a berth on a ship or a sleeper compartment on a train;

2. the name, address and telephone number of the representative in the locality or if there is no representative an agency on whose assistance the consumer could call or failing both of these a number to contact the other party to the contract;
3. in the case of a journey abroad by a child under 16 on the day when the journey is due to start information must be provided enabling direct contact to be made with the child at the place where he/she stays; and
4. details of an insurance contract available for cancellation charges if this is not already a mandatory term of the contract (reg. 8(1)).

If this information is not provided an offence is committed and the maximum fine is £5,000 on summary conviction or an unlimited fine on conviction on indictment.

Due diligence defence
It is a defence to all of the principal offences for a person to show that they took all reasonable steps and exercised all due diligence to avoid committing the offence. If the offence is based upon the conduct of another person or on reliance upon information given by another then the defence cannot be used unless notice is given of the identity of that person (or assisting in the identification of the person) not less than seven clear days before the hearing or, in Scotland, the trial diet.

Provision of sufficient evidence of security by organizers and/or retailers in the event of insolvency

Introduction

One of the most important consumer protection measures in the Package Travel Directive is Article 7 which requires the organizer and/or retailer to provide sufficient evidence of security for the refund of money paid by the consumer and for the consumer's repatriation in the event of the organizer and/or retailer's insolvency. The failure by Germany to enact legislation implementing Article 7 by the due date, 31 December 1992, which resulted in a number of consumers being unable to go on holiday, or having to pay to travel home at their own expense, as a result of two tour operators becoming insolvent, gave those consumers a right to compensation from the German Government (*Dillenkofer and others* v *Germany*, Joined cases C-178, 179, 189 and 190/94 [1996] All ER (EC) 917; see also Chapter One, p. 9).

Prior to the regime instituted by the Package Travel Regulations which implement the Package Travel Directive, a variety of statutory and voluntary mechanisms had grown up to provide security for holidaymakers in the event of a tour operator becoming insolvent.

The statutory mechanism is the Air Travel Organizers Licence (ATOL) scheme administered by the Civil Aviation Authority (CAA) under the Civil Aviation Act 1982 and the Civil Aviation (Air Travel Organizers' Licensing) Regulations 1995. This licensing scheme requires air travel organizers to have a valid financial bond in place to guarantee the availability of funds to meet payments to consumers in the event of insolvency of such an organizer. A bond is a guarantee which cannot be revoked and is provided by an insurance company or bank. Without such a bond, an air travel organizer cannot obtain a licence to operate. This scheme applies to any holiday package arrangements which include a flight as part of the package. The CAA imposes standard terms on licence holders to ensure the licence holder's fitness in relation to a variety of factors. This scheme is unaffected by the Package Travel Regulations and provides sufficient evidence of financial security required by those Regulations (reg. 16(2)(b)).

The principal voluntary mechanism for providing security in the event of insolvency of a tour operator was provided by ABTA's bonding scheme. Similar schemes are operated by the FTO, the AITO, the Passenger Shipping Association (PSA) and the Bus and Coach Council (BCC). Like the CAA's ATOL scheme ABTA applies stringent quality control measures to members through its Tour Operators' and Travel Agents' Codes of Conduct.

In return for ABTA bonding, ABTA members came under the stabilizer arrangement whereby no ABTA member could sell its packages through any retailer other than an ABTA travel agency although direct sales were permitted and no ABTA travel agency could sell packages put together by any organizer other than an ABTA member. This was a restrictive trade practice and was referred to the Restrictive Trade Practices Court in 1982: *Re Association of British Travel Agents Ltd's Agreement* [1984] ICR 12. The court held that the stabilizer was not against the public interest as it was designed to provide financial protection for the public and allowed it to continue. However, since the Package Travel Regulations require all package organizers to provide financial security, the ABTA restrictive practice is no longer required in the public interest. For this reason ABTA voluntarily repealed its stabilizer arrangement in 1993. ABTA members may now sell their packages through any outlet.

Prior to the coming into force of the Package Travel Regulations operators who did not provide an air element in the package (and hence were not subject to the ATOL scheme) or who were not members of a voluntary bonding scheme such as the ABTA scheme discussed above could collapse leaving holidaymakers stranded abroad and consumers who had prepaid their holidays with no means of recovering the money which they had paid out. Although the provisions of the Package Travel Regulations in theory mean that this should not happen again in the case of packages at least, it is very doubtful whether this will in fact be the case.

Requirement in the Package Travel Regulations to provide evidence of security in event of insolvency

The Package Travel Regulations require that the other party to the contract must at all times be able to provide sufficient evidence of security for the refund of money paid over and for the repatriation of the consumer in the event of insolvency (reg. 16(1)). It is a criminal offence to contravene this requirement (reg. 16(3)). Although this suggests that the enforcement authority, the local Trading Standards Department, has the power to demand such evidence at any time, the Regulations also state that Trading Standards Officers only have powers to demand evidence when they have reasonable grounds for suspecting that an offence has been committed (Sch. 3, para. 3).

Acceptable evidence of security under the Package Travel Regulations

There are several methods by which such security may be provided. Firstly, where the package is covered by the ATOL scheme under the Civil Aviation (Air Travel Organisers' Licensing) Regulations 1972, no further evidence of security is required (reg. 16(2)(b)).

In other cases, evidence of security may be provided either by bonding (reg. 17); bonding where the approved body has a reserve fund or insurance (reg. 18); insurance (reg. 19); money placed in trust (reg. 20); or monies placed in trust where the other party to the contract is acting otherwise than in the course of business (reg. 21(1)).

In the case of bonding, the other party to the contract is required to obtain a bond from an authorized institution (see p. 288), in practice a bank or insurance company whereby that institution obliges itself to pay a sum to an approved body (see p. 288) of which the other party is a member. The bond must not be less than 25 per cent of the other party's annual turnover. An approved body is one approved for the time being by the Secretary of State. Various travel industry bodies such as ABTA, AITO, PSA, BCC and the new Association of Bonded Travel Organizations have been approved. It is the approved body which is responsible for calling in the bond and distributing funds to consumers in the event of insolvency.

Bonding where the approved body has a reserve fund or insurance under reg. 18 is similar to bonding under reg. 17 except that the bond need only be for not less than 10 per cent of the other party's annual turnover. This is for the obvious reason that the approved body's reserve fund or insurance will meet the other financial requirements. The Package Travel Regulations do not deal with the creation of reserve funds. That is a matter left to approved bodies which may create such a fund by means of membership fees or other methods.

Evidence of security may also be provided by insurance and persons providing such insurance must be authorized by the DTI (reg. 19).

Money may alternatively be held in trust by someone acting as a trustee until the contract has been fully performed. The Package Travel Regulations do not prescribe the persons who may act as trustees although they should be independent since otherwise there could be a conflict of interest. Solicitors, accountants or bankers could certainly act as trustees.

Conclusions

Bonding is very expensive and realistically only the larger tour operators can afford bonding. Although insurance appeared to be a better route for smaller operators, there has been a dearth of suitable insurance products available, and where they are available they too are usually expensive. Since it is particularly difficult to police, the trust account route was thought to be highly inappropriate. However, it has proved to be very popular with smaller businesses largely because of the expenses associated with bonding and insurances. This is also in spite of the fact that trust accounts adversely affect the cash flow of smaller businesses by tying up funds in trust accounts until packages have been completed. The Travel Trust Association has been formed with the aim of enhancing the credibility of this method of providing security and hence giving consumers some comfort. The Association itself does not act as a trustee but insists that members use as a trustee a chartered accountant, banker or solicitor who has been in business for at least three years, is not a sole practitioner and who is independent of the organizer.

If the Government had insisted on bonding as the sole method of providing insurance it is likely that competition within the travel business would have been severely affected since only the larger companies can afford bonding. By establishing these various means of compliance, the Government has enabled smaller businesses to remain in competition with the larger companies.

However, the weakness of the system is enforcement. It is far from clear that Trading Standards Departments have sufficient resources to police the provisions of the Package Travel Regulations. Training in understanding accounts will also need to be provided if the officers are to be able to enforce the provisions relating to security in the event of insolvency. It seems inevitable that rogue companies operating without such security will escape the attention of hard pressed trading standards officers (TSOs) especially given that they are only to exercise their enforcement powers when they have reasonable grounds for suspecting that an offence is being committed. In time it is likely therefore that pressure will grow for a move towards a licensing system along the lines of the ATOL model to give consumers a higher level of protection, although the price of such protection may be a reduction in competition through a narrower choice of tour operators. It seems that it is very difficult in practice to attain the Package Travel Directive's aim of promoting competition in the package holiday industry while at the same time seeking to enhance consumer protection by requiring organizers and/or retailers to demonstrate evidence of adequate security in the event of insolvency. The Package Travel Regulations have adopted an approach which favours the aim of enhanced competition and could also ensure better consumer protection if resources devoted to enforcement were increased and TSOs were permitted to adopt a more proactive approach to enforcement.

DISPUTE RESOLUTION

The courts

If the consumer believes they have a claim in relation to their holiday, they may obviously go to court to seek compensation under the provisions of the Package Travel Regulations or the common law if the holiday was not a package. Usually such a claim would be made in the County Court's Small Claims Arbitration procedure in England and Wales which handles claims of up to £3,000. It should be noted that this is not a form of arbitration but is an informal court procedure and should not be confused with the ABTA Arbitration Scheme discussed below. In Scotland claims are likely to be brought in the Sheriff Court. Depending on their value they could be brought under the Small Claims (up to £750), Summary Cause (over £750 and up to £1,500) or Ordinary Cause (over £1,500) procedures. A discussion of these courts and going to law in the courts may be found in Chapter One (see pp. 15–17).

Alternatives to court

Introduction

Rather than going to court, which may take time, be expensive and be stressful, the consumer has considerable scope for alternatives to court action in relation to holidays. In Chapter One we considered some of these alternative forms of dispute resolution. Clearly, one option is simply to reach an amicable settlement. For example, in relation to ABTA members, the ABTA Travel Agents' Code of Conduct encourages travel agents 'to reach an amicable and speedy solution' in the event of a dispute (para. 2.10). The ABTA Tour Operators' Code of Conduct includes a similar provision (para. 4.9). However, in addition, ABTA also offers a Conciliation Service and an Arbitration Scheme and these are considered in more detail below.

ABTA Conciliation Service

ABTA offers a Conciliation Service which consumers may use where attempts at amicable dispute resolution have failed. If the consumer chooses to make use of this service he or she is not precluded from going to court or using ABTA's Arbitration Scheme.

ABTA Arbitration Scheme

ABTA has made it a requirement that a condition is included in every booking form which entitles the consumer to refer any dispute which has not been settled amicably or through the ABTA Conciliation Service to the ABTA Arbitration Scheme. The Scheme was devised by the Chartered Institute of Arbitrators and a member of the Institute acts as the arbitrator. Use of the Scheme is entirely voluntary but if a consumer opts to use the Scheme then he/she must agree to be bound by the arbitrator's decision. If the consumer opts for arbitration, the tour operator must agree to arbitration.

The Scheme may be used for claims of up to £1,500 per person or £7,500 per booking form. However, no personal injury or illness claims may be referred to arbitration. Use of the Scheme has considerable advantages for the consumer. It is inexpensive: there is only a small registration fee to pay. Also, the consumer's liability for the expenses of the arbitration is limited to twice the amount of the registration fee. By way of contrast the tour operator must pay a substantial fee. The Scheme operates on the basis of written representations alone: there is no hearing. This has the advantage to the consumer of avoiding the stress of a court appearance but on the other hand both the consumer and the tour operator are to an extent disadvantaged by not being able to make their case in person which may have a greater impact on the judge than written documents have on the arbitrator. There is also the problem that consumers may not be able to express themselves effectively on paper.

The consumer must set out the claim in full on a prescribed form. This must be submitted to the arbitrator within nine months following return from the holiday in question together with copies of all relevant supporting documents. The tour operator then has the opportunity of submitting a defence to the arbitrator together with any supporting documents. The consumer is given an opportunity to respond to the tour company's defence. The arbitrator then considers all the representations and supporting documents and issues a written decision. If necessary, this decision can be enforced through the courts.

Interestingly, research by the consumer magazine '*Which*?' suggests that awards made by arbitrators in favour of consumers under the Scheme tend to be lower than awards made by the courts. This perhaps suggests that the fact the consumer cannot present his/her case in person does affect the amount of compensation awarded.

Select bibliography

CHAPTER ONE: THE LEGAL SYSTEM

Bailey, S.H. and Gunn, M.J., *The Modern English Legal System* (3rd edition, Sweet & Maxwell, London, 1996)

Paterson, A.A. and Bates, T.St.J., *The Legal System of Scotland* (3rd edition, W Green, Edinburgh, 1993)

Steiner, J. and Woods, L., *Textbook on EC Law* (5th edition, Blackstone Press, London, 1996)

CHAPTER TWO: PRINCIPLES OF PRIVATE LAW

Downes, J. and Paton, T., *Travel Agency Law* (Pitman Publishing, London, 1993)

Fleming, J.G. *The Law of Torts* (8th edition, The Law Book Co Ltd, Sydney, 1997)

Furmston, M.P., *Cheshire Fifoot & Furmston's The Law of Contract* (12th edition, Butterworths, London, 1994)

Stewart, W.J., *Delict* (2nd edition, W Green, Edinburgh, 1993)

Woolman, S., *Contract* (2nd edition, W Green, Edinburgh, 1994)

CHAPTER THREE: FORMS OF BUSINESS ORGANISATION

MacMillan, M. and Lambie, S., *Scottish Business Law* (3rd edition, Pitman Publishing, London, 1997)

Mayson, S.W., French, D. and Ryan, C.L., *Company Law* (14th edition, Blackstone Press, London, 1997)

CHAPTER FOUR: PRODUCT LIABILITY

Clark, A., *Product Liability* (Sweet & Maxwell, London, 1989)

DTI, *Guide to the Consumer Protection Act 1987*

Howells, G.G. and Weatherill, S., *Consumer Protection Law* (Dartmouth, Aldershot, 1995)

CHAPTER FIVE: CRIMINAL RESPONSIBILITY

Clarkson, C.M.V., *Understanding Criminal Law* (2nd edition, Fontana Press, London, 1995)

McCall Smith, R.A.A. and Sheldon, D., *Scots Criminal Law* (2nd edition, Butterworths, Edinburgh, 1997)

Rowan-Robinson, J., Watchman, P.Q., and Barker, C., *Crime and Regulation* (T & T Clark, Edinburgh, 1991)

Wells, C., *Corporations and Criminal Responsibility* (Clarendon Press, Oxford, 1993)

CHAPTER SIX: EMPLOYMENT IN THE HOSPITALITY AND TOURISM INDUSTRIES

Craig, V. and Miller, K., *Employment Law in Scotland* (2nd edition, T & T Clark, Edinburgh, 1997)

Selwyn, N.M., *Selwyn's Law of Employment* (9th edition, Butterworths, London, 1996)

Smith, I.T. and Thomas, G.H. *Smith & Wood's Industrial Law* (6th edition, Butterworths, London, 1996)

CHAPTER SEVEN: DISCRIMINATION

Bourn, C.J. and Whitmore, J., *Anti-Discrimination Law in Britain* (3rd edition, Sweet & Maxwell, London 1996)

Doyle, B.J., *Disability Discrimination: Law and Practice* (Jordan Publishing, Bristol, 1996)

Palmer, C., Moon, G. and Cox, S., *Discrimination at Work: The Law on Sex, Race and Disability Discrimination* (3rd edition, Legal Action Group, London, 1997)

CHAPTER EIGHT: PLANNING, ENVIRONMENTAL AND HEALTH AND SAFETY LAW

Bell, S., *Ball & Bell's Environmental Law* (4th edition, Blackstone Press, London, 1997)

Collar, N., *Planning Law* (W Green, Edinburgh, 1994)

Craig, V. and Miller, K., *Health and Safety at Work in Scotland* (W Green, Edinburgh, 1995)

Moore, V, *A Practical Approach to Planning Law* (5th edition, Blackstone Press, London, 1995)

Smith, C., Collar, N. and Poustie, M. *Pollution Control: The Law in Scotland* (T & T Clark, Edinburgh, 1997)

Smith, I., Goddard, C. and Randall, N., *Health and Safety: The New Legal Framework* (Butterworths, London, 1993)

CHAPTER NINE: INNS, INNKEEPERS AND THEIR DUTIES, LIABILITIES AND RIGHTS

Lord Hailsham of St Marylebone (ed.), *Halsbury's Laws of England, vol 24* (4th edition, Butterworths, London, 1979 and supplement, 1995)
Pannett, A., *Principles of Hotel and Catering Law* (4th edition, Cassell, London, 1997)

CHAPTER TEN: FOOD SAFETY

Hitchcock, T., *Food Safety – A Practical Guide to the 1990 Act* (Fourmat Publishing, London, 1990)
Jukes, D.J., *Food Legislation of the UK – A Concise Guide* (3rd edition, Butterworths/Heinemann, Oxford/Boston, 1993)
Lister, C. *Regulation of Food Products by the European Community* (Butterworths, London, 1992)
Painter, A.A., *Butterworths Food Law* (Butterworths, London, 1992)

CHAPTER ELEVEN: THE LICENSING SYSTEM

Cummins, J.C., *Licensing Law in Scotland* (Butterworths/Law Society of Scotland, Edinburgh, 1993)
Lord Hailsham of St Marylebone (ed.) *Halsbury's Laws of England, vol 26* (4th edition, Butterworths, London, 1979 and supplement 1995)
Jameson, J.N. St. C., *A Practical Guide to Licensing in Scotland* (2nd edition, Jameson Publishing, Edinburgh, 1991)

CHAPTER TWELVE: HOLIDAYS

Corke, J., *Tourism Law* (2nd edition, ELM Publications, Huntingdon, 1993)
Downes, J. and Paton, T., *Travel Agency Law* (Pitman Publishing, London, 1993)
Grant, D. and Mason, S., *Holiday Law* (Sweet & Maxwell, London, 1995)

Some of these books will provide further reading on more than one issue. For example, Pannett, *Principles of Hotel and Catering Management* (see Chapter 9) includes material on contract, forms of business organization and employment as well as innkeepers' liability.

Readers who are interested in property issues should consult Cheshire and Burns' *Modern Law of Real Property* (15th edition, Butterworths, London, 1994) for the position in England and Wales and Robson and Miller, *Property Law* (W Green, Edinburgh, 1991) for the position in Scotland.

Index